THE AGING PROCESS OF POPULATION

3

AGING PROCESS
OF POPULATION

by
EDWARD ROSSET

Translated from the Polish by
I. DOBOSZ, R. JANIKOWSKA,
K. KOZŁOWSKA, W. SKIBICKI

Translation edited by
H. INFELD

PERGAMON PRESS
OXFORD · LONDON · EDINBURGH
NEW YORK · PARIS · FRANKFURT
1964

PERGAMON PRESS LTD.

Headington Hill Hall, Oxford

4 & 5 Fitzroy Square, London W.1

PERGAMON PRESS (SCOTLAND) LTD.

2 & 3 Teviot Place, Edinburgh 1

PERGAMON PRESS INC.

122 East 55th Street, New York 22, N.Y.

GAUTHIER-VILLARS ED.

55 Quai des Grands-Augustins, Paris 6

PERGAMON PRESS G.m.b.H.

Kaiserstrasse, 75 Frankfurt am Main

Distributed in the Western Hemisphere by

THE MACMILLAN COMPANY · NEW YORK

pursuant to a special arrangement with

Pergamon Press Limited

Library of Congress Catalog Card Number 63-19956

Printed in Poland

Contents

PART III

POPULATION AGING TRENDS

Preface

THE present work deals with the quantitative and qualitative transformations occurring in the structure of modern societies, known as population aging.

This process can be measured by different methods. The appropriate means will be dealt with in detail, but that which is measured is the increasing proportion of the aged in society.

The society involved in the process of aging experiences transformations that are not only of a demographic nature. In such a society everything is changing: economic, social and political conditions. And the inevitable result is the altered psychological character of the aging society.

In the Swiss medical journal *Triangle* it was reported that in Great Britain most patients visited at their homes by medical practitioners are over 65 years of age; for every visit to a patient under 65 there are more than three to patients over that age. And still more revealing are the figures concerning the visits of nurses: for each such visit to a patient below 65, there are eight visits to patients over 65. It hardly requires proof that this state of affairs compels the British health service to develop its work along new lines.*

This is true not only as regards Great Britain. A similar, if not identical, phenomenon can be observed in the United States, and a striking example can be quoted from a sociological article describing the living conditions of the aged in a district of that country (Alleghany County). Thus, the article states that the nurses of the public health service, over a period of 3 years, had to treble their visits to old patients.†

The authors of the work from which this information is taken accept it without great surprise: the increase in the number of benefits

---

* Information about the program of activities, organization and progressive development of geriatric centres in Great Britain—that is health centres for old people— is contained in *Social Problems for Old Age. A Review of Social Provision for Old Age in Great Britain* by B. E. SHENFIELD (London 1957, Routledge and Kegan Paul Ltd., p. 183).

† MARGARET DECK and DALE SMITH: *Needs of People over 60 and Resources Available in Alleghany County.* A Study Made in the Area Study Research Seminar, May 1956.

to the aged is quite understandable, since the number of old people increases and the need for medical care is greater after the age of 65 than at any other period of life.

Let us quote one more example from the field of health conditions. It is well known that in a number of countries—primarily in Sweden—the infant mortality rate is on the way to complete disappearance: the Swedish figure is below 2 per cent. Thus it does not require an exuberant imagination to realize that a geriatrist will be more in demand than a pediatrician.

Let us now consider the occupational field.

Not so long ago in the United States the prevailing principle was that there is no place in the factories for workers over 40. Today this brutal principle is condemned by many and it is shown to be economic nonsense. The change in point of view is undoubtedly a product of the new demographic conditions that are characterized by a high and still increasing proportion of old people in American society.

The American sociologist Paul H. Landis (*Population Problems. A Cultural Interpretation*, 1954) states that in 1940 old people (65 and over) made up 10 per cent of the total number of voters; in 1980, according to the computation of the same author, they will increase to 15–18 per cent. These figures cannot be regarded as a revelation since the demographic forecasts predict a much higher proportion of old people among the voters. Thus the British delegates R. E. Tunbridge and E. C. Warren stated at the Gerontological Congress in Saint Louis (1954) (*Journal of Gerontology*, Vol. 6, Suppl. to No 3) that the aged (the authors refer to men over 65 and women over 60) will constitute more than one quarter of the total number of voters in Great Britain.

Let us add that at the same time (1980) the number of people of pension age in Great Britain will be one fifth of the total population.

Of course, it is not only a matter of figures. More essential are their consequences. Thus, according to the American demographer Warren S. Thompson, the aging societies should be prepared for a constant and considerable increase in the political significance of the older population groups. The author considers the problem whether the great conservatism of the French in business, family life, standard of living, and in many other fields, is due to the fact that France has a high proportion of old people in its population. Transposing this correlation to his own country's conditions, the American demographer investigates whether the economic progressiveness of the

United States and their characteristic lack of respect for traditional methods of activity are not at least partly a consequence of the high percentage of people under 40, particularly in the past. "If so," writes Thompson, "what will be the effects on our life of an aging population? Will we become more conservative in business, in government, in personal habits, etc.?"* From these considerations the author draws the conclusion that "as the average age of the nation mounts we shall find ourselves confronted by many new and puzzling problems"†.

There will be a great many such new and puzzling problems resulting from the aging of the population.

One very important problem is the constantly increasing cost of maintaining the growing numbers of old people. Gerhard Mackenroth draws the correct conclusion that this trend must considerably increase the burden on the productive part of the population and that the social policy of countries with a large number of aged must seriously take this fact into account.‡

The Austrian demographer Dr Egon Kern also writes about the uneasiness aroused in many countries by the spectre of the great cost of maintaining old people: *Jedenfalls ist es darauf in erster Linie zurückzuführen, dass die Tatsache der Überalterung heute vielerorts Beunruhigung auslöst...*§

Besides the basic and increasingly disturbing problem of the burden of maintaining the growing number of old people there is the problem of a declining birth rate and increasing mortality rate resulting from changes in the age structure of the population. Since we mention the changes which should be expected in demographic conditions as a result of the aging of the population, it should be pointed out that in some countries, for example Great Britain, it is predicted that within one generation the number of the aged will equal the number of children. In Great Britain this should take place around 1990:

---

* WARREN S. THOMPSON: *Population Problems*, McGraw-Hill Publications in Sociology, third edition, New York and London, 1942, p. 103.

† *Op. cit.*, p. 103.

‡ "...die Zahl der zu versorgenden wächst im Verhältnis zur Zahl der Erwerbsfähigen, die Erwerbsquote sinkt also und die Versorgungslasten je Kopf des Erwerbsfähigen steigen. ... Diese Tatsache muss im Aufbau der Sozialpolitik berücksichtigt werden, die Zukunft wird stärkere Belastungen des Sozialbudgets bringen, die im Verteilungsplan des Sozialprodukts Veränderungen notwendig machen" (GERHARD MACKENROTH: *Bevölkerungslehre. Theorie, Soziologie und Statistik der Bevölkerung*, Springer-Verlag, Berlin-Göttingen-Heidelberg 1953, pp. 462–463).

§ EGON KERN: *Die Frage der Überalterung*, "Allgemeines Statistisches Archiv", 41. Band, Erstes Heft, 1958, p. 33.

one British forecast predicts that at this date there will be 19·3 per cent of children below 15 and the same percentage of people of pensionable age (i.e. men of 65 and over; women 60 and over). Let us add that at present the number of children in Great Britain is 50 per cent greater than the number of people of pensionable age.*

But the consequences of the population aging process should not be discussed only in the future tense, for the problem concerns the present, in some countries at least.

The Swiss statistician, Dr Albert Koller (*Umschichtungen in der schweizerischen Bevölkerung*, 1956) points out that the extension of compulsory military service, before World War II to the age of 60 (previously 48) was a practical result of the longer duration of human life.

These few examples, though not the most characteristic, may suffice for the moment since, in our view, they will be sufficient to help formulate certain generalizations necessary for further consideration.

Thus, the above examples show that some changes—one should rather say perturbations—are to be observed in the previous conditions of population aging. It is obvious that with the development of this process the old order of things is undergoing a thorough transformation and that many a previous social standard must give way to a new standard better adapted to the altered morphology of the age of society.

The social relations and norms prevailing in a society having a greater proportion of young people must differ considerably from those in an aging society and particularly in an old society. The world in which we live is not very similar to that in which our fathers lived. The world of our children and our grandchildren will undoubtedly change, too. It will be different not only on account of technical and economic changes but also because of demographic transformations. The process of population aging involves a thorough alteration in the image of a society, of its legal, moral, and even all its standards.

It is essential, therefore to analyse this process. That this task is of prime importance in the modern study of demography was stated by the French demographer Jean Daric who, in one of his latest works on population aging (*Le Vieillissement de la Population en France et ses Conséquences Économiques et Sociales*, 1955) wrote: "Si les phéno-mènes démographiques ont une influence déterminante sur le destin des nations, il en est un parmi eux qui mérite une attention par-

---

* CARLTON WALLACE: *How to Retire Successfully*, Evans Brothers Limited. London 1956, p. 15.

ticulière, en raison de ses retentissements profonds. Il s'agit du vieillissement de la population." These words are like a scientific testament left to us by this fine scholar.

The investigation of the process of population aging cannot be confined to ascertaining its present state. The horizon of the researcher must also embrace the past and the future of the process.

The demographic past of humanity is but little known. Particularly poor is our knowledge about the age structure of societies in ancient times. Archaeological excavations and retrospective demographic computations (such as are given in the work of Josiah Cox Russell, *British Medieval Population*, 1948) lift the veil on the past a little. In our work we shall attempt to make use of these scarce and inevitably unreliable sources.

It may seem paradoxical that we can say much more about the demographic future of humanity than about its past—we mean, of course, the not-too-distant future, and the not-too-recent past. Computations from a perspective have become the common work of statisticians. It should be pointed out here that among the uncertain demographic forecasts, the least uncertain is the future number of the aged, since all who will, in 60 years time—and especially even earlier—increase the number of old people, are already alive. We shall return to these computations in our work to draw from them perspectives of the process of population aging.

A look at the history of the aging of society will enable us to understand the connection between this process and the civilization of mankind. It will also free us from the primitive idea that demographic "old age" is synonymous with the twilight of nations. What is more, the comparative analysis of relations in the "young" and "old" societies will enable us to contest the validity of this classification which I do not consider proved.

To learn the essence of the problem of population aging one must discover the genesis of this phenomenon and know its development and consequences which are diverse as we can already see and which on many levels upset the present order of things.

This whole rich complexity of problems appears to the researcher interested in this field of demography. To this the following investigations are devoted.

EDWARD ROSSET

Part I
METHODOLOGICAL PROBLEMS

Introduction

IN investigations of the process of population aging, methodological problems predominate. This is due to the following reasons:

(a) the phenomenon of a society's aging is comparatively recent;

(b) only recently has this effect attracted the demographer's interest.

For these two reasons the problem of population aging is still in a nascent state from the methodological standpoint.

Under these conditions it seems necessary to devote the first part of this work to the problem of methodology. The following points will be discussed:

(1) the methods used to measure demographic old age (or youth); we shall call them *measures of old age* (Chapter I);

(2) hypothetical and perspective computations as instruments for the analysis of changes in the structure of the population by age (Chapter II);

(3) types of age structure (Chapter III);

(4) the deficiencies and methodological non-uniformity of sources concerning the population structure by age and the difficulties resulting from comparative analysis (Chapter IV);

(5) the variety of views as to the beginning of old age (Chapter V).

In discussing these problems we should not like to restrict ourselves to a mere presentation of their present state. So far as we are able, we shall attempt to advance one step further the methodology of investigating population aging and bring some of the methodological aspects nearer to a definitive solution.

CHAPTER 1

Measures of Old Age

THE elementary requirement of precision in definitions used makes it necessary to distinguish between two related but not identical notions: *old age* and *aging*.[1]

Old age is a static notion; *aging* is dynamic. When investigating the age structure of the populations of various countries and establishing appropriate comparisons, we can immediately define the degree of the youth or age of individual societies; such comparisons lead directly to a differentiation of their demographies as "young" and "old". But when we examine the population structure of one country at different periods and compare the results we observe a process of the aging (seldom the becoming younger) of the population.

A natural consequence of this distinction is the need to distinguish between *measures of old age* and *measures of aging*. Recognizing this need, we should like to point out at once that in the practice of demographic research this principle is often ignored. This results from the fact that the measures of old age, despite their purpose, often reveal the existence and process of population aging. If in a certain country we obtain a very high old age index, it will hardly be strange to consider it as a symptom of a highly advanced process of population aging. Conversely, a very low old age index will be an infallible proof of the non-existence of such a process. Thus a theoretically correct means of distinguishing measures of old age and measures of aging is not always observed in actual demographic investigations.

Besides this undoubtedly essential reservation, one more observation should be made. Namely, for any given age of a population there exist not one but many measures of old age. Some are used more, others less frequently. Can this be considered an indication of their comparative value? Probably not. Anyone who has dealt with the theory of statistics knows that the application of statistical measures is not always determined by their value.

Thus it seems reasonable to consider not only the measures of old age commonly used, but also those less often employed.

9

1. THE COEFFICIENT OF OLD AGE

The measure of old age most frequently used is the ratio of the aged to the whole population. We shall call this measure *the coefficient of old age*.[1]

The formula for computing the coefficient of old age varies with the year of life taken as the beginning of old age. Let us assume that the ages of 60 and 65 are used alternately.

If the beginning of old age is at 60 yr the formula for computing the coefficient of old age is:

$$W_{60} = \frac{l_{60+}}{L} \times 100$$

where: l_{60+} is the number of people of 60 and over, and L is the total population.

If the beginning of old age is at 65 yr the formula is modified accordingly:

$$W_{65} = \frac{l_{65+}}{L} \times 100$$

In both cases the fraction is multiplied by 100 to obtain the percentage result. The coefficients of old age are represented either as percentage or per thousand.

In practice the coefficient of old age assumes the role of a fundamental characteristic of the age of the society. Whether this is fully justified is another question. However, it is an incontestable fact that in the hands of the demographer this coefficient is an indispensable working tool and that many researchers consider the coefficient of old age as the appropriate measure of population aging.

We begin with the French demographer Jean Daric who is one of the foremost experts on population aging and whose name will often appear in this work. Daric defines population aging as a process of continuous increase in the proportion of the aged in the total population—"l'augmentation continue de la proportion des vieillards dans la population totale"—thus it follows that population aging should be measured by changes in the proportion of the aged.[2]

The Swiss statistician Dr Albert Koller states that in the period 1941–50 the total population of Switzerland increased by 10 per cent, while the number of old persons rose by 24 per cent. The following comment is added by Koller: "Thus aging progressed twice as fast as the increase in the total population."[3] This comment shows that the author measures the process of population aging by changes in the proportion of the aged.

The Swiss economist and demographer W. Bickel introduces two measures of old age. One is the absolute number of old persons, which reflects absolute population aging—"eine absolute Überalterung." The second is the proportion of old persons—"die Greisenquote." Thus, in both cases the number of aged persons is decisive in the aging process.

Predicting that the number of inhabitants of 65 and over in Switzerland will increase to 500,000 in 1960, Bickel states: "Es bedeutet dies eine weitere starke absolute Überalterung, wurden doch 1941 erst 365 000 Personen über 65 gezählt." As to the proportion of old persons, computations predicted that it would amount to over 10 per cent in 1960 as compared to 8·5 per cent in 1941.

Bickel adds the following comment: "Sollten die Geburtenziffern wieder fallen, so würde diese Quote noch etwas steigen... Dagegen würde eine Zunahme der Fruchtbarkeit natürlich eine entsprechende Reduktion dieser Quote bedeuten."[4]

As we see, the Swiss demographer takes into account both the possibility of a further decrease in fertility and conversely, of its increase. In the latter case the increase in the proportion of old people would be slower.

Bickel's standpoint as to the methodology of investigations of population aging is thus quite clear-cut. It can be given in two points:

(1) the increasing proportion of the aged is the effect of the progressive process of population aging, independently of the trend in the birth rate and consequently of the proportion of children;

(2) in consequence, however, the increasing birth rate and the growing number of children in the society exert an influence on the composition of the whole population by age and thus on the proportion of old persons, and these factors, in turn, affect the process of population aging.

It should also be stated that Bickel's position does not differ from Daric's for when measuring population aging by the proportion of the aged, Bickel bases his theory on the definition of the French demographer cited above.

Some authors, while approving the coefficient of old age as a working tool of the demographer, show some restraint as to the value of this method.

Alfred Sauvy, one of the foremost representatives of modern French demography, points out that population aging is most often defined as and measured by the proportion of old persons (for instance sixty and over) in the total population.[5]

Following this, the author mentions some other measures of old age which will be discussed here. From the available measures Sauvy chooses the coefficient of old age as most acceptable (*"plus usuelle"*).

Thus in the comments of the French demographer, the main stress is laid, not on the perceptive value of this characteristic, but on its practical feasibility. The popularity of a statistical measure and the ease of acquiring comparative material for its use can be considered as arguments in favour of applying this measure.

2. OTHER CONCEPTIONS OF MEASURES OF OLD AGE

Another, though rather isolated, standpoint as to the methodology of measuring the society's age is advocated by the Czechoslovak demographer Vladimir Srb who recommends measuring the age (or youth) of a society not, as is generally accepted, by the number of aged persons but by the number of children.[6]

The question arises whether this method of measuring age may yield results other than those obtained by applying the traditional method based on the proportion of the aged in the total population.

Under normal conditions, where an increase in the proportion of old persons in a society is accompanied by a decrease in the proportion of children, it is unimportant whether the process of population aging is measured by the number of aged—or, as the Czechoslovak demographer suggests, by the number of children. Both measured would produce in principle, if not identical, then similar results.

However, there are situations in which the use of each of these measures leads to different results.

Let us consider French conditions.

Since 1947—as derived from the figures given below—France has witnessed simultaneously a progressive increase in the proportion of children and adolescents (0–19 years) and of old persons (60 and over).

SIMULTANEOUS INCREASE OF THE PROPORTION OF CHILDREN AND ADOLESCENTS AND OF THE AGED IN FRANCE, 1946 — 1957

Date	Per cent of population at the age of:	
	0–19 yr	60 and over
Jan. 1, 1946	29·5	16·0
Jan. 1, 1956	31·1	16·3
Jan. 1, 1957	31·3	16·4

Source: *Population*, Paris, 1956, No. 4, p. 746.

The coefficient of old age, conventionally applied, shows that the process of population aging in France in this period made further progress, since the proportion of the aged increased.

However, if we were to accept the number of children as describing the age of a society, then we would have to acknowledge that, on account of the increase of the proportion of children and adolescents since 1947, the aging of the population in France has been retarded for 10 yr.

Then we obtain two, not only different, but completely opposite evaluations of the changes occurring in the population's composition by age in France.

Alfred Sauvy is inclined to adopt a compromise position. Analysing the changes in the post-war structure of the population in France by age, he concludes that in view of the progressive increase of the proportions both old and young persons we may speak about the simultaneous of aging and rejuvenation of the society. Let us quote this unexpected conclusion exactly: "La proportion des personnes âgées a augmenté en même temps que celle des jeunes, de sorte qu'on peut parler à la fois de vieillissement et de rajeunissement."[7]

The contradictory nature of such a conclusion has been pointed out in a publication issued by the U. N. on population aging. Here is the pertinent quotation from this publication on the simultaneous aging and rejuvenation of the population: "...it was said that a population ages when the proportion of aged persons increases. It is therefore natural to say that a population grows younger when the proportion of aged persons declines, but it can also be said that it grows younger when the proportion of young persons increases. The contradiction is evident: aging and rejuvenation can take place simultaneously."[8]

In our opinion nothing better reveals the fragility of the methodological principles behind a new demographic branch of research on the aging of societies than this compromise or, as the U.N. demographer has it, this contradictory formula suggested by the prominent French demographer. It undermines not only the isolated conception of Vladimir Srb which recommends the measuring of a community's age by the proportion of children it contains but also, equally important, the traditional measure approved by most researchers, based on measuring this age by the proportion of aged persons.

In the U. N. publication quoted above we find a rather unsatisfactory attempt to overcome the difficulties resulting from the insufficiently precise definition of the expression "aging of the population". The U. N. demographer perceives the solution by distinguishing two kinds of aging: *first*, "aging at the apex", and *second*, "aging from the base". In his conclusion, quoted below, the author himself concedes that the difficulties of interpretation cannot be wholly avoided.[9] We shall endeavour to formulate our own view on this difficult question.

If we had to choose one of the above concepts there is no doubt that the one used by Daric and Bickel should be given priority, that is: *the degree of population aging should be measured by the proportion of aged persons and not of children.*

We should also mention the "dependency ratio" long used by German authors.[10]

The concept of the "dependency ratio of a population" ("der Belastungskoeffizient der Bevölkerung") was presented by Karol Ballod in his handbook of statistics (*Grundriss der Statistik*, 1913). As its name indicates, this term denotes the extent of the burden the non-productive population lays upon the society. This burden, however, falls on only that part of the society which is at the productive age.[11] And those who are productive must support both those of pre-productive age (children) and those beyond it (the aged).

From what has been said above it follows that there are three kinds of dependency ratios:

(1) the ratio denoting the burdening of the productive population because of their own children;

(2) the ratio denoting the burdening of the productive population because of the aged;

(3) a total load factor resulting from both.

The dependency ratio mentioned in point (2) is interpreted by some demographers as a general measure of old age. Let us quote the views of three experts: the Austrian, Egon Kern, the Frenchman, Louis Chevalier, and the Belgian, O. Tulippe.

Dr Egon Kern believes that the percentage of aged persons in relation to the total population is not the best indicator of the society's age: the proper measure should be the ratio of old persons to the productive population. "Vom praktischen und insbesondere vom sozialpolitischen Standpunkt aus gesehen, ist an der Überalterung aber ausschliesslich das Verhältnis der Gruppe der Nicht-mehr-Erwerbstätigen zur Gruppe der Erwerbstätigen, die auch für die

Erhaltung jener aufkommen muss, von Belang," states the Austrian statistician.[12]

A similar standpoint is represented by the French demographer Louis Chevalier. In his opinion, under the term "population aging" two effects should be distinguished, one of which is purely demographic (un phénomène purement démographique), the second, biological (un phénomène humain). As to *the demographic* effect of population aging, with which we are particularly concerned, then, according to Chevalier, it results from the increase in the number of old persons in relation to the number of adults: "Le phénomène démographique résulte de la proportion accrue du nombre des vieillards par rapport au nombre des adultes". Thus the proper demographic measure of the aging of societies is the ratio of aged persons, not to the total population, but to the number of adults. Chevalier does not reject factors of the first kind; indeed, he recommends their use—but with the provision that they should be treated as a simple and not as the best measure.[13]

Professor Tulippe, too, considers as very desirable the measure of old age based on the ratio of the number of old persons to the adult population. He stresses the undoubtedly greater practical usefulness of this measure. "The secret of the value of this measure," writes the Belgian scholar, "is based on its exposing the relation of the non-productive elements to those composing the productive class of the society."[14]

It is obvious that the dependency ratios also depend on the classification of age assumed by the researcher. Ernst Kahn based his factors on the age classification used in German statistics. He computed the number of children below 15 yr and old persons over 65 per 100 persons from 15–64.

In one of his numerous papers on population aging, Jean Daric deals with three types of measures of old age.[15] If we add to his three points [(a), (b) and (c)] our own measure [point (d)] we have the following indices of population aging:

(a) number of old persons per 100 adults;
(b) number of adults for each aged person;
(c) number of old persons per 100 young people;
(d) number of children for each aged person.

The first two measures are the dependency ratios already known to us from the works of German statisticians. The first answers the question: how many aged are maintained by 100 adults? The second defines how many adults must contribute to the upkeep of one old person.

Daric stresses the desirability of the third index. The process of population aging is most strongly reflected in the number of young people and the number of aged persons—the former decreases and the latter increases. Thus, the ratio between these two age groups is a particularly sensitive seismograph of the changes occurring in the structure of population by age.

Alfred Sauvy is also a supporter of this method of measuring population aging. His standpoint is substantiated by the following arguments: "In all the countries of Europe the proportion of adults in the population is close to 54 per cent. Essential differences are to be observed in the numbers of young people and aged persons. In countries least developed demographically there are 10 per cent aged persons (over 60) and 36 per cent young people; in the most developed countries there are 16 per cent aged persons and 30 per cent, or even less, young people. For the purpose of characterizing particular countries we can use the index of old age (*l'indice de vieillesse*) i.e. the number of aged persons per 100 young people."[16]

Especial significance is to be ascribed to the last of the four measures of old age mentioned above, i.e. the number of children for each aged person. It reflects the abundance or scarcity of grandchildren in relation to the number of grandparents, thus giving an idea of the youth or age of the society.

For illustration we present data on the number of children (0–14) per aged person (65 and over) in some countries of Latin America and Sweden.[17]

Costa Rica	1950	14·8
Honduras	1950	10·4
Chile	1952	9·3
Argentina	1947	7·5
Sweden	1950	2·3

Such measures have great informative value. The above data expressively prove the demographic youth of Latin America and, vice versa the age of Sweden.

However, the adequacy of these measures is unequal, and must be discussed further.

The cradle of the phenomenon of population aging was France. In addition France is the country in which the process of population aging has reached unusual dimensions. It seems reasonable to check the mechanism of action of different measures of old age with French data.

THE PROCESS OF POPULATION AGING IN FRANCE ON THE BASIS OF VARIOUS INDICES

Year	Number of aged persons (60 and over)			Number of adults (20–59) per aged person (60 and over)
	per 100 in general	per 100 adults (20–59)	per 100 young people (0–19)	
1851	9·9	18·6	26·7	5·4
1881	12·3	23·5	34·8	4.3
1901	12·4	23·4	35·8	4.3
1921	13·8	25·3	43·7	4·0
1936	14·7	26·7	48·7	3·7
1947	16·2	30·0	54·3	3.3
1956	16.3	31·0	52·4	3.2
1957	16·4	31·4	52·4	3·2

Sources: (1) JEAN DARIC, *Vieillissement de la population et prolongation de la vie active*, pp. 19 and 22. (2) *Population*, Paris, No. 4, p. 746.

Here we are interested in the methodological problem, namely in the usefulness of particular indices as instruments for measuring the process of population aging. Thus, it clearly follows from the above table that the *general* trend of aging of French society is reflected by all indices. On the other hand, when considering particular phases of this process, short-term tendencies, the rate of development of population aging, we should be aware that the usefulness of particular indices as measuring instruments may vary.

Some instances will support our thesis.

(1) When comparing data from 1881 with those of 1901 we see that on the basis of one index the process of aging in France has been stopped and even retarded, while the other two coefficients show it to have progressed.

(2) A similar situation may be observed in the last few years: a comparison of data from 1947 with those of 1956/7 suggests quite different conclusions depending on the index used for analysis. According to one index the process of population aging slightly receded while all others show it to have progressed.

The data on the demographic conditions in France would seem to recommend the index showing retardation of the process of population aging. Which of the indicators should be used? A new trend is best expressed by the ratio of the number of aged to that of young persons, which is why this index is particularly recommended by Daric and used in an inverted form by the author of the present work.

Before using this indicator we should state the following:

(1) in 1901, in France, the process of population aging did not stop, still less reverse, as compared with the condition in 1881;

(2) in the last ten years (1947–56) France has experienced a reversal of the process of population aging unknown for a hundred years.

We can now summarize our considerations and draw some conclusions.

There are various measures of old age. When applied to the same material they may produce different, sometimes quite opposite, results. However, it does not follow that one measure is better than another, nor does it mean that they differ in accuracy.

The differences are of another nature: each of the known measures has its own recognizable content; therefore, the results obtained by applying various measures may differ not only as to the figures obtained but also as to their meaning. For this reason we cannot distinguish better and worse measures: we can only speak of *various* measures of old age being *equally valid*.

The above conclusion naturally concerns only those measures which we have already considered. But there are other, auxiliary characteristics of the population structure by age, with recognizable values and practical uses that are, in our opinion, less important.

They should be discussed separately.

3. AUXILIARY CHARACTERISTICS OF AGE STRUCTURE

Sometimes the *median age* is used as the demographic measure of "youth" or "age".

We know from the theory of statistics that the median is the value of the middle item when the items are arranged according to size. It follows from this definition that the median has the same number of items before as after it.

If we have a set of values placed in order:

$$x_1, x_2, x_3, x_4, \ldots x_{n-2}, x_{n-1}, x_n$$

the median will be:

(a) the value of item $x_{\frac{n+1}{2}}$ if there are an odd number of items since
by definition it has the same number of items before as after it;

(b) the arithmetic mean of the values of the two middle items, which are:

$x_{\frac{n}{2}}$ and $x_{\frac{n}{2}+1}$ if there are an even number of items.

In the case of a distribution array, which is the rule in the work of a statistician, we apply the formula recommended by Wilhelm Winkler in his handbook of statistics.[18]

This is the formula:

$$Me = x_0 + i \cdot \frac{M + S - P}{2M}$$

where: x_0 is the lower value of the class interval in which the median is contained;

   i is the width of the class interval in which the median is contained;

   M is the frequency of the proper class, i.e. in which the median is contained;

   S is the total frequency of subsequent classes;

   P is the total frequency of preceding classes.

The average age of living persons computed in this way is called the *median age*. It is obvious that this age divides the population into two equal parts; one not yet reached, the other already passed.

Another type of average age is the *mean age* calculated as the arithmetic average of the ages of all living inhabitants of the country. It is calculated on the basis of the usual formula for a weighted average:

$$A = \frac{x_1 l_1 + x_2 l_2 + x_3 l_3 + \dots + x_n l_n}{l_1 + l_2 + l_3 + \dots + l_n} = \frac{\sum xl}{\sum l}$$

At one time this formula was the favourite.

French statisticians computed the average age of living persons at each population census. A paper giving the results of the French census of 1896 contained data about the evolution of the mean age of the French people during the second half of the 19th century.

The mean age was given in this publication in years and months (e.g. 31 years $10\frac{2}{3}$ months) and in this form these data were repeated by the German statistician Gottlieb Schnapper-Arndt. We reproduce these data below, using decimals in place of months.

AVERAGE AGE OF PERSONS LIVING IN FRANCE 1851–1896

Census year	Total population	Men	Women
1851	30·9	30·5	31·4
1856	31·0	30·7	31·2
1861	31·2	30·9	31·5
1866	31·9	32·2	31·7
1872	31·7	31·2	32·0
1876	31·7	31·3	31·8
1881	31·9	31·7	32·2
1886	31·8	31·6	31·9
1891	32·1	31·8	32·3
1896	32·2	31·9	32·5

Source: GOTTLIEB SCHNAPPER-ARNDT, *Sozialstatistik*, Leipzig, 1912, p. 113.

Schnapper-Arndt recalls that the median age of living persons has often been computed in America. Here are some results:

U.S.A.   1890 . . . . 21·9 yr
Cuba   1899 . . . . 20·7 yr
Puerto Rico 1899 . . . . 18·1 yr

At the same time (end of the 19th century) a similar computation for his own country and France was made by the German demographer von Fircks. The results are:

France . . . . 29 yr
Germany . . . . 24 yr

The preference for these measures has weakened with the years. The demographers and the practical statisticians have lost their concern for the median as an expression of age composition. Thus the Swiss statistician Professor Hans Schorer writes: *Die früher üblichen Anwendungen im Bereich der Bevölkerungsstatistik (Altersgliederung, wahrscheinliche Lebensdauer, Bevölkerungsstabilität [und -wanderung) sind fast ganz aufgegeben worden.*[19]

The caution expressed in the above formulation (*fast ganz*) is well founded, since such an important statistical institution as the Statistical Office of the United Nations in New York uses the median in its publications as a representative figure and for comparison of the population composition by age in the international section.

In the *U. N. Demographic Yearbook* (1949–50) we find, in Table IV, beside indices defining the proportion of the population at the ages of: 0–14, 15–44, 45–64, and 65 and over, a column under the heading *Median Age*, in which data about the median age of the population are given. The figures are repeated below.

MEDIAN AGE OF POPULATION OF SOME COUNTRIES AROUND 1945

Country	Year	Median age (in years)
Belgium	1949	35·6
England and Wales	1948	34·0
Sweden	1947	33·8
Scotland	1948	33·2
Switzerland	1945	33·1
Norway	1948	32·3
New Zealand	1945	31·4
Denmark	1948	31·4
Australia	1947	30·9
U.S.A.	1950	30·1
France	1950	30·0
Italy	1947	29·3
Finland	1948	28·7
Northern Ireland	1948	28·2
Netherlands	1949	28·0
Canada	1949	26·8
Hungary	1941	25·0
Jamaica	1947	22·2
Egypt	1937	21·7
Chile	1940	21·5
British Guiana	1946	21·4
Ceylon	1946	21·4
Japan	1948	21·2
Venezuela	1945	19·3
Peru	1940	19·2

Source: *Demographic Yearbook 1949–1950*, United Nations, Table IV.

It cannot be denied that in the table quoted above three types of population structure by age are clearly distinguishable. We can separate three groups of countries:

(1) countries with a *high* median age of the population (30 and over);

(2) countries with a *low* median age of the population (below 25);

(3) countries occupying intermediate positions (25–30).

In the first group are: Belgium, England and Wales, Sweden, Scotland, Switzerland, Norway, New Zealand (excepting, of course,

the Maoris), Denmark, Australia, the U.S.A. and France. In a demographic sense these are *old* countries. In the second group are:
Jamaica, Egypt, Chile, British Guiana, Ceylon, Japan, Venezuela
and Peru. These are considered to be *young* countries.

The intermediate group comprises: Italy, Finland, Northern
Ireland, the Netherlands, Canada, and Hungary. We could say that
these countries are becoming old. Of course, many more countries
could be thus classified than appear in the above table.

We shall not now investigate which should be placed in this group;
this is one of the basic problems to be dealt with later in this book.
We only wish to add that Poland should be included in the intermediate
group, for the computation for 1949 gives her median age as 26·2 yr.

Returning to the methodological problem which concerns us, we
would like to analyse briefly the value of the above parameters of
population age. There is no doubt that these indices result in some
differences on an international scale, expressing the diversity of the
population composition by age. The image thus obtained should
be made more *precise*.

It follows from our investigations that in the case of extreme youth
the measuring tool used is less important; whether we take a less
or more precise tool the demographic youth will be fully proved.

However, the question is not so simple if we are dealing with a less
or a more advanced process of aging: a less precise age measuring
tool—we refer to the *median*—may prove fallacious.

It is well known that among the aging societies of Western Europe,
France has been in the lead for dozens of years. When investigating
the age of the population by means of the *proportion of aged persons*
we find France in *first* place, which is consistent with the fact that
France leads in the advance of population aging. On the other hand
a quite false image is obtained by listing countries according to the
median age of the population, for here France is in *eleventh* place in
the world. Naturally, we have no doubt as to the correctness of the
computations made. We only contest the cognitive value of the median
as a measure of the age of a population. It is evidently an imperfect
measure of the demographic age of any country.

In a paper by Paul H. Landis we find data characterizing the evolution of the median age of the population of the United States in
the period 1890–1950, in which the data for the white and coloured
population are computed separately.

Let us analyse these data.

MEDIAN AGE OF THE U.S.A. POPULATION 1890–1950

Year	Median age (in years)		
	total	white	coloured
1890.	21·4	21·9	17·8
1900.	22·9	23·4	19·7
1910.	24·0	24·4	21·0
1920.	25·2	25·6	22·5
1930.	26·4	26·9	23·5
1940.	29·0	29·5	25·2
1950.	30·1	30·7	25·5

Source: PAUL H. LANDIS, *Population Problems. A Cultural Interpretation*, Second edition New York, 1954, p. 85.

Do the data contained in this table reflect the age composition of the U. S. population and the development trends of this structure?

The fact that American society is aging is clearly shown here. No less evident are the differences in the aging level of the white and coloured population. We do not want to draw any other conclusion than the one already formulated: a general picture of population aging, if it exists, is reflected in all characteristics of age, including the median, but it cannot be regarded as a precise measure of old age.

Thus far we have been using data on the median age based on the U. N. publication and the work of Landis. These are not the only sources in which these or other averages are used to characterize the age composition of populations and changes occurring in this composition.

The Argentinian demographer O. S. Ventura (*Tendencias y Estructura de la Población Argentina*, p. 52) illustrates the process of population aging in his country by the increasing mean age of the inhabitants:

1895 . . . . 23·2
1914 . . . . 23·5
1947 . . . . 27·9

Jacqueline Beaujeu-Garnier completes the above figures with data about the median age of the population of Jamaica (22·2), British Guiana (21·4) and Venezuela (19·3), according to figures taken from U. N. publications. The author took them from the *Demographic Yearbook* of the U.N. for 1951.[20]

There are many examples of a return to characterizing the age structure by the mean or median age of the inhabitants. Yet this return is not a decisive argument in favour of the wider application of these characteristics.

The essential thing is not the frequency of application of the measures but their cognitive value. And the cognitive value of both the mean and median age is limited since age is not a property which tends toward a definite average value. Therefore, the regional individuality and complexity of population aging so often encountered in research cannot be expressed exactly in averages characterizing the population age. It frequently happens that in quite different situations the mean and median age of the populations are very close if not identical.

In view of the above it follows that the parameters described should be used as no more than auxiliary means or to obtain a rough approximation and not for a statistical analysis of population aging.

In this work we shall not depend upon these measures.

REFERENCES

1. This term should not be confused with the similar-sounding *"indice de vieillesse"* (index of old age) which will be discussed later.
2. J. DARIC, "Le vieillissement de la population en France et ses conséquences économiques et sociales", in a collective work, *Précis de Gérontologie*, Masson et Cie, Edit. Paris, 1955, p. 95.
3. A. KOLLER, "Umschichtungen in der schweizerischen Bevölkerung", *Schweiz. Z. Volkswirtschaft u. Statistik*, 1956, No. 3, p. 286.
4. W. BICKEL, *Bevölkerungsgeschichte und Bevölkerungspolitik der Schweiz seit dem Ausgang des Mittelalters*, Büchergilde Gutenberg, Zurich, 1947, p. 254.
5. A. SAUVY, "Le vieillissement des populations et l'allongement de la vie", *Population*, (Revue trimestrielle de l'Institut National d'Études Démographiques), Paris 1954, No. 4, p. 675.
6. V. SRB, *Biologická situace v českých zemich*, Prague, 1947, p. 8.
7. A. SAUVY, "Vue générale et mise au point sur l'économie et la population française". *Population*, Paris, 1955, No. 2, p. 208.
8. *The Aging of Populations and its Economic and Social Implications*, United Nations, Department of Economic and Social Affairs, New York, 1956, p. 1.
9. The full statement of the U.N. demographer reads: "...if the proportion of aged persons increases, it may be described as aging at the apex. If, on the contrary, the proportion of young persons decreases, it can be described as aging from the base. Accordingly, the term 'aging of a population', qualified, if necessary, by 'from the base' or 'at the apex', always refers to changes in the age structure of the population, and has no other meaning. Many errors of interpretation will be avoided if this definition is kept constantly in mind". (*Op. cit.*, p. 1)
10. This coefficient will be more extensively used in Chapter 12.
11. This term is not to be confused with the crude ratio of dependence that denotes the share of persons in the pre-productive age (0–14) and the post-productive

age (65 and over) in the total population; see W. J. THORNE, *Your Future is Now*, London, 1956, p. 20.

12. E. KERN: "Die Frage der Überalterung", *Allgemeines Statistisches Archiv*, 41. Band, Erstes Heft, 1957, p. 41.

13. L. CHEVALIER, *Démographie Générale*, Librairie Dalloz, Paris, 1951, p. 102.

14. O. TULIPPE, *Le Vieillissement de la Population Belge*, Étude régionale, Les Cahiers d'Urbanisme, No. 10, Brussels, 1952, p. 4.

15. J. DARIC, *Vieillissement de la Population et Prolongation de la Vie active*, Presses Universitaires de France, Paris, 1948.

16. A. SAUVY, *L'Europe et sa Population*, Éditions internationales, Paris, p. 47 (no date of publication given).

17. These indices have been computed on the basis of figures contained in the report of H. ROMERO and R. MEDINA, "La America Latina como Laboratorio Demogràfico" given at the World Population Congress in 1954 in Rome.

18. W. WINKLER, *Grundriss der Statistik, Theoretische Statistik*, Berlin, 1931–1933, Enzyklopädie der Rechts- und Staatswissenschaften, Herausgegeben von A. Spiethof XLVI.

19. H. SCHORER, *Statistik, Grundlegung und Einführung in die statistische Methode*, Bern, 1946, pp. 130–131.

20. J. BEAUJEU-GARNIER, *Géographie de la Population*, Éditions Génin, Librairie de Médicis, Paris, 1956, vol. I, p. 412.

CHAPTER 2

Hypothetical and Perspective Calculations as a Tool to Analyse Changes in the Age Structure of the Population

THE measures discussed so far do not exhaust the means of analysis used by a demographer investigating the phenomenon of population aging. A very essential tool of analysis employed in investigating the action of various population aging factors is hypothetical computation and its derivative perspective computation.

The basis of hypothetical computation is usually composed of empirical data characterizing the distribution of population by age at a given time. From these data, assuming certain hypotheses concerning the future development of the population, we compute the age structure that would result if the assumptions were fulfilled. Thus we obtain not a real, but a hypothetical composition of the population.

Hypotheses may be of various kinds. For instance, we may assume that the number of births will be constant in future. A similar assumption may be made as to the number of deaths. The property of not changing may be given, not to the absolute numbers, but to the rates of birth or death. We may be concerned with the invariability of either the birth rate or the fertility rate. Instead of the invariability of the number of births or deaths we may assume a definite trend of change: increasing or decreasing.

There exists, therefore, an infinite variety of hypotheses about the development of births and deaths. What decides the choice made? In purely analytical investigations for scientific experiments we eliminate one or other population aging factor in order to learn the developmental direction and force of action. If we want to learn what would be the effect of the present trends in birth and death rates, we extrapolate them without change. We try to base the proper perspective computations—termed demographic forecasts—on the most probable future development of the birth and death rates.

The hypotheses underlying the perspective computations used to predict the future may, and should be, criticized. Criticism is necessary since faulty hypotheses lead to a distorted image of the future. It is different with hypotheses of the eliminative type used for scientific experiments; the reality of these hypotheses is not questioned.

1. PURELY HYPOTHETICAL COMPUTATIONS

Let us first analyse hypothetical computations on a fictitious structure of the population's age, such as *a stationary population*, or a *stable population*. This is a question of the pattern of the population based on a purely demographic criterion, which is the reproduction type of the population.

Methodologists ascribe to such theoretical constructions a basic role in scientific research. According to G. Myrdal: "Scientific facts do not exist *per se*, waiting for scientists to discover them. A scientific fact is a construction abstracted out of a complex and interwoven reality by means of arbitrary definitions and classifications." (*An American Dilemma*, 1944.) Professor Harvey Leibenstein completes the above thesis with the following, highly interesting remarks: "We know many of the factors that influence economic development and demographic change. Lists of such factors can be made. However, lists of factors are not theories. Such lists are only the merest beginnings of understanding the processes we are interested in. It is important to know these factors are related to each other; hence the need for constructing systems of interrelated hypotheses or models."[1]

For our part, we should like to add that in demographic investigations the use of theoretical models of stationary and stable populations is exceptionally fruitful.

What underlies the concepts of these two types of populations?

The *stationary population* is conceived as a population in which the numbers of births and of deaths remain constant from year to year and are equal, so that the number of the population remains constant (migrations of population are not considered). The unchanging order of dying means that a stationary population has a fixed, constant age composition depending on the order of dying. A picture of the age composition corresponding to a given order of dying is to be found in a life table. Hence some statisticians speak about the *table population* (in German literature "die Sterbetafelbevölkerung").

A *stable population* is of a different type. It is a population model which, unlike the stationary population, is characterized by a *constant fertility of women*, not by a constant number of births. In this case also we have to do with a closed population (lack of migrations), having a fixed, constant age composition. In a stable population the birth rate, death rate, and rate of natural increase are all constant. The number of the population is usually variable, that is, it either increases or decreases. An essential feature is that the rate of increase or decrease is constant.

Let us note in passing that one of the first theoreticians to analyse the model of a stable population was the Pole Władysław Bortkiewicz who was recently mentioned by Professor Wilhelm Winkler of Vienna.[2] The theory of the stable population has been discussed and extended by the American demographer Alfred J. Lotka and the German Robert R. Kuczynski. These fine scientists proved mathematically the existence of a number of correlations between the various characteristics of a stable population.

The theoretical character of these two constructions is all too evident But exactly therein lies their value as tools of statistical analysis.

What is supplied by investigations of population models?

Professor Stefan Szulc stresses that a stationary population is a fiction since the assumptions made never correspond to reality. But this fiction provides perfect conditions for studying the influence of changes in the death rate in the structure of a population.[3] The practical value of the notion of a stable population and its corresponding measures is that we can thus investigate the effects of the continued action of a constant death rate and fertility rate existing at a given moment. We thus obtain a characteristic of the totality of demographic conditions, unlike the method of the stationary population, which characterizes only the effect of the mortality rate. Yet, like stagnant populations, stable populations are pure fictions.[4]

We shall quote here a particularly interesting opinion of the German demographer Gerhard Mackenroth. Discussing the value of the above theoretical constructions he declares: "...Diese Modelle... sind reine Gedankenkonstruktionen, es gibt sie nicht in der Wirklichkeit, die Wirklichkeit weicht immer davon ab, sie gestatten uns aber, durch Art und Grad festgestellter Abweichungen bestimmte Vorstellungen von den Vorgängen der Wirklichkeit zu bekommen. Sie dienen dazu, die soziale Wirklichkeit an ihnen zu messen."[5]

As we see, Mackenroth stresses the deviations in demographic processes in an empirical population as compared with the model of a stationary or stable population: the kind and degree of these deviations may serve as a measure characterizing the phenomena investigated.

The question arises whether the same idea could not be transferred to demographic phenomena of a structural type, particularly to the age distribution of the population.

This idea is not strange to students of population problems. Its beginnings can be found in the paper of N. P. Levin: Economic and Sociological Aspects of Population Age (*J. Amer. Stat. Ass.* 23, 1928). The idea was perfected by the American demographers Louis L. Dublin and Alfred J. Lotka in *The Money Value of a Man* (New York, 1930). These researchers compare the age structure of the increasing population with the age structure of a stationary population and, following Mackenroth's idea, draw definite conclusions from the differences stated.

We find another kind of standardization of population age structure in the work of the Austrian statistician Dr Egon Kern, already cited. Kern's book is devoted to the problem of population aging, with which we ourselves are concerned in this work.[6]

Kern wants to know what changes would occur in the age distribution of the population if the annual number of births were *constant*. This is one of the fertile fictions mentioned above. The picture obtained, though concerning a fictitious population, when compared with the age distribution of a real population, makes possible appreciation of the role of this factor, which has been eliminated in the hypothetical calculation, i.e. the influence of changes in the number of births on the population structure by age.

The method of procedure used by the Austrian statistician is the following.

He constructs the hypothetical population to fit the task ("Modellbevölkerung"). This construction is based on two assumptions:

(1) the number of births has been constant for a long time;

(2) the changes in the mortality rate correspond exactly to the changes in the real population.

The transition from the real (variable) number of births to the hypothetical (constant) number is reached by reducing or increasing each age-class of the real population to such an extent that its basis— the number of births in the year to which a given age-class belongs— is greater or less than the arbitrarily assumed constants.

Using the symbols employed by the Austrian statistician, we construct the formula for calculating the individual age-classes (R_x) of the reduced population:

$$R_x = \frac{K \cdot E_x}{G_x}$$

where: K = the chosen constant;

E_x = the individual age-class of the real (empirical) population;

G_x = the numbers of births corresponding to these age-classes.

The value of the numbers submitted to this reduction will depend on the choice of the constant appearing in the above formula. Kern adds, quite rightly, that the proportions characterizing the age structure of the reduced population, which is the problem to be investigated, will not be affected.

The next variant investigated by Kern is the age structure formed by a constant increase in the number of births. The purpose of these investigations is to define the role that could be played by an increase in the number of births as an inhibiting factor for the population aging process. The author describes two methods of appropriate investigation.

The first consists in finding, in the near or more distant past, the moment regarded as the end point of a longer process of increase in the number of births. At such a moment the whole structure of the population was under the influence of the process mentioned. The population at this moment is then compared with the corresponding population reduced by the same numbers of births.

The second method consists in comparing two different standards, one of which is a stationary population and the second, which is a stable population.

The age structure of a stationary population can be read directly from the life table. To obtain the number of a stable (increasing) population the following calculation should be performed.

Denoting the ratio of increase of the annual number of births by k (as we know this ratio is stable), the number of persons surviving to the same age in the *stationary* population by S_x and the persons at the same age in the *increasing* population by W_x and assuming that the population increase has been going on for 100 years, we obtain a formula for calculating the number of persons at the same age in the *increasing population*:

$$W_x = S_x \cdot k^{100-x}$$

or, its equivalent

$$W_x = \frac{S_x}{k^x}$$

The comparison of the age structure of the *stationary* population with that of the *stable* population provides a basis for a number of essential conclusions concerning the influence exerted by the constant increase in births on the age distribution of the population.

The existence of differences in the assumptions as to the two patterns makes it possible to draw such conclusions. Since the stable population shows the same mortality rate as the stationary population, and is distinguished only by the stable and uniform increase in the number of births (the number of births being constant in the stationary population), then it is reasonable to conclude that the difference in age distribution of the stable population compared with the stationary population should be traced to the stable and uniform increase in the number of births.

Hypothetical calculations of very different kinds now constitute an indispensable tool of statisticians and demographers. Students of population aging also make use of them. But, so far, this has been primarily a prognostic use. The use of these calculations for diagnostic purposes is still in its infancy. For this reason we welcome every reference to hypothetical calculations in the analysis of causes and conditions affecting the formation of the age structure of the population.

A contribution of this type is the U. N. demographic study on population aging.[7] In this, some factors are immobilized to highlight the effects of the factor investigated. ("The problem to be solved may therefore be stated as follows: if two or three factors are invariable, what effect will the variations of the third have on composition by age?") The method of comparing the age distribution of the stable population with various levels of mortality and fertility is applied to good effect.

The U. N. demographer points out that the idea of utilizing the concept of a stable population to analyse causes affecting changes in the age structure of the population has not yet been methodologically elaborated: "Using stable populations we can isolate the intrinsic effect on age composition of a change in one demographic factor, but the method is not wholly satisfactory." This is in accordance with our view that the utilizing of hypothetical calculations for diagnostic purposes is still in its initial phase.

However, it should be pointed out that a good start has been made.

2. DEMOGRAPHIC FORECASTS

The researcher on population faces the problem of the perspectives for this process, i.e. the formation in the nearer and more distant future of the age composition of various societies, namely those in which the phenomenon of population aging occurs in an acute form and those which are less concerned with the effects of this process.

To answer the questions arising in this connection, demographic statistics must be consulted. We agree with the Swiss statistician Professor Walter Wegmüller when he states that population statistics should give us an image, not only of the past and present but also of the future ("Die Bevölkerungsstatistik hat nicht nur Vergangenes und Gegenwärtiges festzuhalten, sondern auch Ausblicke in die Zukunft zu gewähren").[8] Furthermore, it can be said that the answering of questions about the future development of population relationships is within the essential scope of demographic statistics.

This problem is handled by a special branch of statistics, already well developed in many countries. It is a branch of perspective calculations or demographic forecasts. A knowledge of the problems concerned will help us estimate properly the use of demographic forecasts as a tool of the statistician and demographer.

(a) The Essence and Significance of Demographic Forecasts

We should not expect more from a demographic forecast than it can provide. It would be naive to hope that this forecast would supply us with an exact picture of future population development and the evolution of its structure. The most effective statistical methods could not meet such requirements.

What is the task and at the same time the significance of demographic forecasts?

The demographic forecast can and should answer the following questions:

(1) what would be the future population status and age structure if the existing trends of population development were to remain invariable for a long period of time?

(2) what would be the future population status and its age structure if the births, deaths, and population migrations should follow different trends, assumed at the start?

(3) what is the extent of possible variations in population figures (general, and of particular age groups) in the light of the variants of demographic forecasts?

(4) what will the future population status and structure be, in view of the forecast variant considered most probable?

Information of this kind is significant not only for the country which is the object of the calculations. Friedrich Burgdörfer points out that such calculations may provide valuable hints for other countries, too, when the same or similar development trends prevail, The author had in mind the similarity of relationships in European countries affected by the "birth strike"; in the long run they were exposed, like Germany, to a decline in the population.[9]

From what has been said above it can be understood that although none of us knows and cannot know the true course of future events, especially the distant future, the demographic forecast may provide some information about it. Thus its cognitive tasks are quite significant.

Demographic forecasts have a far-reaching practical value. Consider only their indispensability for rational economic planning.[10] The great importance of demographic forecasts as a tool of planning and long-term economic policy is stressed by Alfred Sauvy. He describes how, after their being criticized for a prolonged period, they have developed considerably within the last thirty years and are necessary today either for general, economic or demographic policy.[11]

A special part is played by perspective calculations when there is an unfavourable natural development of the population. It then offers a warning to government and public opinion since it demonstrates the disastrous effects of continued unfavourable demographic conditions. Such warnings should lead the society to introduce the necessary precautions.

Is the demographic forecast really able to produce such far-reaching results?

There should be no doubt that this question can be answered in the affirmative, as is evidenced by French experiments. According to Alfred Sauvy, in 1939 France reversed a disastrous population regression largely because of demographic forecasts which alerted French society.

The example of France proves the creative role that can be played by demographic forecasts in changing socially undesirable demographic conditions.

Among experts there is no question as to the significance of perspective calculations from the scientific as well as the practical standpoints. There is, however, a difference of opinion—in fact a very essential one—as to the cognitive value of these calculations. By "demographic forecast" some researchers understand a forecast in its literal meaning, i.e. an attempt to guess the future state and structure of the population. Others require that the demographic forecast should demonstrate the direction of development of the state and structure of the population with certain assumptions as to the future trend of births and deaths, and often of population migrations.

Keeping in mind the different interpretations of demographic forecasts we may term forecasts of the first type *real*, and of the second type *conditional* or *hypothetical* forecasts. Let us add that the opponents of real forecasts ironically call them *prophecies*. We would quarrel with this attitude to the useful and necessary demographic forecasts.

It is worth while learning the opinions of outstanding contemporary demographers on the tasks and, in a wider sense, on the essence of the perspective calculations.

The demographer who devoted most attention to the problem of demographic forecasts and who declared himself an advocate of the conditional nature of perspective calculations was Friedrich Burgdörfer.

He stressed clearly that perspective calculations are not and cannot be prophecies. He wrote: "All diese Berechnungen sind selbstverständlich keine Prophezeiungen, sie sollen es nicht sein und wollen es auch nicht sein."[12]

Equally interesting is the positive portion of the statement of the German demographer. According to him, the aim of perspective calculations consists in delineating mathematical–statistical consequences of a general demographic situation existing at a given time, in order to determine the dynamics of the present and future population development. The results, according to Burgdörfer, are always conditioned by a double clause: (1) *rebus sic stantibus*, and (2) *ceteris paribus*. If the premises underlying the calculation were to change, of course the results would be different. From this it can be shown that if we want to have results different from those shown by the forecast, we must assume other premises not only in theory but also in practice.

Let us now consider the views of other representatives of the demographic school who, like Burgdörfer, want to free perspective calculations from the undesirable appellation "prophecies."

The Swiss statistician Walter Wegmüller, cited above, points out that a perspective calculation of population is by nature hypothetical. The author stresses that the meaning and significance of demographic forecasts consist in a demonstration of the fundamental trend of development of the future population, based on assumptions connected with facts. Wegmüller ends his considerations with the statement: "Nicht prophezeiend, sondern richtungsweisend sollen Bevölkerungs-vorausberechnungen sein, dessen sei man sich stets bewusst."[13]

Warren S. Thompson also represents the view that perspective calculations cannot pretend to be *real* estimates: they provide a *conditional* image of the future population status depending on fulfilment of the assumptions made. ("In presenting figures of probable future population, therefore, it should be made clear that they are not real estimates but rather are calculations showing what population will be if the assumptions used are actualized.")[14]

"The perspective calculations concerning the future population status," says Albert Koller, "cannot be attributed the significance of forecasts. They can only provide information about the presumptive population development under quite definite assumptions."[15]

Thus the statements of such prominent representatives of demography and statistics as Burgdörfer, Koller, Thompson and Wegmüller agree as to the definition of the specific role of demographic forecasts. In the light of their statements the essence of the demographic forecast is that it demonstrates the future development of population conditions under certain logically founded assumptions.

To complete the review of opinions on the value of demographic forecasts we quote the statement of Adolf Landry. The French demographer wrote: "Entreprise aventureuse? sans doute, si on ne s'y engage pas avec prudence et modestie; mais entreprise utile, en tant que l'on prétendra seulement dégager des possibilités... et des impossibilités."[16] As we see, the author is not afraid of forecasts based on common sense and moderation; he regards such forecasts as useful.

The view of the French demographer is influenced by the spirit of compromise which in this case is of special significance.

In our opinion all kinds of demographic forecasts, including hypothetical forecasts, various "conditional" forecasts, provided, as Burg-dörfer stated, with a double clause *rebus sic stantibus* and *ceteris paribus*, and finally those that deserve the appellation "real" (we include here forecasts based—as postulated by Mackenroth—on an analysis of the structure of the social process) are well founded in the needs of theory and practice. Consequently, none of them can be rejected without harm to theory or practice.

(b) King's Forecast

Demographers opposing demographic forecasts as "prophecies" are aided by historians of statistics who cite examples of such forecasts "repudiated by history". In support of this view it has been customary to quote the forecasts of the future development of the population of England made by a statistician of the 17th century, the Englishman Gregory King (1648–1712). The Soviet historian of statistics M. Ptucha regards this forecast as a classical example of demographic forecasts that did not meet the test of life.[17]

We shall also analyse this oldest "monument" of perspective calculations in demography. But our concern will not be to enhance the chorus of critics by one voice more. On the contrary, our aim is to attempt to rehabilitate King and his noteworthy forecasts.

This interesting historical relic is shown in the table below.

PREDICTED DEVELOPMENT OF THE POPULATION OF ENGLAND AS CALCULATED BY GREGORY KING (1696)

Year	England's population	Increase in 100 years
1300	2,860,000	
1400	3,300,000	440,000
1500	3,840,000	540,000
1600	4,620,000	780,000
1700	5,500,000	880,000
1800	6,420,000	920,000
1900	7,350,000	930,000
2000	8,280,000	930,000
2100	9,205,000	925,000
2200	10,115,000	910,000
2300	11,000,000	885,000

Source: GREGORY KING: *Natural and Political Observations and Conclusions Upon the State and Condition of England, 1696* (according to PTUCHA, *op. cit.*, p. 106).

Before dealing with the calculations and assumptions on which it was based, we should like to devote some words to its author.

Gregory King was a statistician and the author of an unpublished work containing rich data based on estimates (some of King's calculations are cited by Charles Davenant, his contemporary). King made an estimate of the population of England. By an estimative method he also computed the population increase. He attempted to compute by the same method the professional structure of the population, incidence of consumption and income, corn crops, and the remaining agricultural production. He is the co-inventor of the King–Davenant scale used to determine the dependence of corn prices on the crops harvested. This scale is also based on estimates.[18]

If we realize that the statistician in question is of the 17th century and thus of the earliest period of this science, we can appreciate how great was the scale of his interests and how prolific his research.

No less admiration is evoked by his courage in making estimates with an almost complete absence of fundamental statistical data. Not without reason did Lord Macaulay (*The History of England*) call King "a political arithmetician of great acuteness and judgment."

King based his calculation of the past and future development of England on the following idea.[19]

In 1260, that is about 200 years after the Norman conquest, the Kingdom counted 2,750,000 inhabitants, i.e. half the population in King's time; thus the English people have doubled in 435 years.

Probably the next doubling of the English people will take place within 600 years; thus approximately in 2300; at that time the country will have 11 million inhabitants; but then the next doubling (in all probability) will take place after another 1200 or 1300 years, or in the year 3500 or 3600. Then the Kingdom will have 22 million inhabitants, or four times as many as at present, assuming that the world still exists then.

Now the country occupies an area of 39 million acres, thus there would then be less than two acres per head and consequently a further increase of population will not be possible.

...Since the population of the country increased by 880,000 during the last 100 years, and will increase within the next 100 years by 920,000, we obtain for this period of time an annual increase of about 9000 souls. If we further assume that 1 in 32 die, or 170,000 and that 1 in 28 are born, or 190,000 which gives an annual increase of 20,000 heads, it should be added that:

(1) there is a decrease from exceptional mortality caused by pestilence, on *annually* the average, of	4000
(2) losses caused by external and internal wars, on the average are	3500
(3) the sea permanently claims 40,000 persons employed, thus accelerating the death of	2500
(4) colonies (beyond the increase of foreigners) involve	1000
total	11,000
Thus, the proper annual increase is only	9000
total	20,000

King's calculation reveals an amazing scrupulousness. All factors affecting the population status, e.g. the normal natural population development (births and deaths), exceptional mortality (at King's time this played an important role) and losses resulting from emigration (the balance of migration movement), have been taken into account. Could one require more from a statistician in the 17th century?

It is quite a different thing to look into the future. King looked with the eyes of his century. By this we mean that he was unable to imagine a population development on a different scale from the one he then witnessed. However, we must forgive such short-sightedness in a statistician of the 17th century.

Historians point out that King's forecast has been repudiated by history. This statement is undoubtedly true: the population of England amounts, not to 8 million, but to 50 million. But this is not the same thing as a general failure of the idea of perspective calculations of population status. What is more, we are ready to defend the thesis that the disagreement between the real and the predicted status does not strike at the calculations performed by King.

Like any perspective calculation, King's forecast is based on certain assumptions. We know that its foundation was the author's belief that an advanced stability of demographic conditions existed in his time. Nothing proves this better than the predicted numbers of natural increase:

18th century	920,000
19th ,, ...	930,000
20th ,, ...	930,000
21st ,, ...	925,000
22nd ,, ...	910,000
23rd ,, ...	885,000

We have every right to speak about the assumption of the stability of demographic conditions in King's forecast, and if so, any deviations of the real development of conditions from that given in the forecast should be considered an expression of the social progress which occurred and had not been anticipated by the author.

The statement is justified that if we were to eliminate the great advances in medicine and other factors favouring a decrease in mortality, England would not have 50 million but perhaps 8 million inhabitants today, as was predicted by King. Thus any basis for attacking King's forecast is removed and we see that the criticism of perspective calculations is absolutely unfounded.

The American demographer Joseph Spengler (*Population Theory*, Illinois, 1952) declares that the history of demographic forecasts is a history of errors. We believe that if this assertion were submitted to incisive analysis it would prove only half true. Even those errors in King's perspective calculations most publicized by critics do not constitute unquestionable argument for the American demographer's thesis.

(c) Assumptions of the Forecast

It clearly follows, in our opinion, that in the demographic forecast definite assumptions play an important part. They decide whether the forecast is *purely hypothetical*, or simply *conditional*, or *real*.

The assumptions take into consideration the future development of fertility and mortality rates as factors most strongly affecting the status of the population and its age structure. Less often too are factors influencing the evolution of population conditions considered; such factors include population migrations.

Usually not one but quite a number of assumptions are taken into consideration, which leads to many variants of demographic forecasts.

What influences such a procedure?

An argument for the choice, not of one, but of many different assumptions about the future course of fertility and mortality rates (and even population migrations) is the impossibility of predicting these rates with a sufficiently high degree of accuracy.

This particularly concerns the fertility rate which may, over a period of time, undergo important and unpredictable changes (plus or minus). U. N. demographers encourage the making of multi-assumption forecasts while taking into consideration various possible trends of the fertility rate.[20]

We on our part support the view that only multi-assumption perspective calculations can ensure a more comprehensive forecast of future conditions. However, we cannot disregard the fact that the needs of planning require operating with only one version of the perspective calculation. The best practice seems therefore to be to perform a demographic forecast in many variants and to choose one which may be regarded as the most probable.

The choice of this presumably most real version of the perspective calculation should follow an incisive analysis of the existing and future trends of the demographic process being investigated in its entirety. It should be kept in mind that the development trends of births and population migrations should be estimated with particular caution; the course of the mortality rate may be predicted more boldly, for it does not, as a rule, undergo serious oscillations.[21]

It is worth while to review some examples of multi-assumption perspective calculation.

An interesting example of such calculation is the forecast for the U.S.A. calculated by the American demographers Warren S. Thompson and Pascal K. Whelpton (1940–80).

In this forecast the following assumptions, either close to one another or plainly opposed, have been taken into consideration.

(A) Medium fertility and mortality and no net migration of foreign-born.

(B) Medium fertility and mortality and net immigration of 100,000 annually after 1940.

(C) Low fertility, high mortality, and no net migration of foreign-born.

(D) Low fertility, medium mortality, and no net migration of foreign-born.

(E) High fertility, low mortality, and net immigration of 200,000 annually after 1940.

(F) High fertility, low mortality and no net migration of foreign-born.

Thus the authors have considered a number of hypotheses, from the very pessimistic (C) to the very optimistic (E).

We shall not analyse the results of the calculations. We shall only quote the population status of the U.S.A. for 1980:

By hypothesis	Population status
(A)	153,628,000
(B)	158,967,000
(C)	127,947,000
(D)	134,381,000
(E)	186,713,000
(F)	175,151,000

The most striking aspect is the spread of the results: from a *minimum* of 128 million to a *maximum* of 187 million. It can thus be seen to what degree the results of the forecast depend on the assumptions made.

Another example of a still more extensive demographic forecast is to be noted: in Great Britain after the Second World War a forecast with sixteen variants was made. With regard to the number of assumptions made and in view of the large time period covered (100 yr: 1947–2047), particular attention should be paid to it.[23]

This forecast was elaborated by the Statistical Committee of the Royal Commission on the Population. As a starting point the population of Great Britain in 1947, amounting to 48,188,000, was assumed.

In computing the further development of the population, not three but four factors of this development were taken into account:

(a) mortality;
(b) fertility;
(c) net migration;
(d) marriage.

Within each of these factors many assumptions were made. Thus, as to mortality two hypotheses were assumed: "constant mortality" and "declining mortality".

For each of the three remaining factors, five hypotheses were considered, some of them assuming a stronger, others a weaker effect of the phenomenon.

Let us consider migrations. The hypotheses were the following:

(1) migrations are balanced;
(2) the annual balance amounts to minus 100,000;
(3) the annual balance amounts to plus 100,000;
(4) the annual balance amounts to minus 50,000;
(5) the annual balance amounts to plus 50,000.

As we can see, from these various assumptions *sixteen* particular hypotheses have been deduced. This is a record of the versatility of perspective calculations performed in one country concerning the development of the population and changes in its structure.

Naturally, the various calculations produced different results.

As to the number of population, the following extreme values were obtained for the year 2047:

minimum: 29,562,000
maximum: 61,382,000

It is not difficult to guess that from sixteen versions of the English demographic forecast for the period 1947–2047 the lowest final population status—about 30 million—was obtained by the version that assumed falling fertility. Conversely, the highest final population status—over 61 million—was obtained in a version of rising fertility.

Let us add that besides the various directions of the fertility development—in one case a fall, in another a rise—the two extreme versions of the English demographic forecast do not differ in the least: all other hypotheses, i.e. those which concern mortality, migration, and marriages, are identical in the two versions. The differences shown in the final population status are exclusively the outcome of the different assumptions as to fertility.

The English forecasts call for consideration of the utility of numerous variants in perspective calculation.

We have already had the opportunity to express our conviction that the secrets of the future can better be recognized by means of multi-assumption than of single-assumption forecasts. From the different possible variants of demographic forecasts the least useful are the extremes, i.e. the most optimistic and most pessimistic. This presumption is supported by the particularly small probability that these extreme forecasts will be fulfilled.

Our view is quite different: in the extreme versions of demographic calculations we see the limits of amplitude of the oscillation of the demographic values sought and this renders the extreme variants of particularly great cognitive value.

Consequently, we think it unreasonable to dispense with the extreme versions of the demographic forecast. On the contrary, we consider them necessary in any perspective calculation. One of the forecasts assuming the most favourable course of events in the future (increased fertility, decreased mortality) we would call the *optimistic* version; the second, based on the opposite assumptions (decreased fertility, increased mortality) we would call the *pessimistic* version. The *real* and necessary version will lie between the two; it can fulfil the role of a proper forecast.

There is still another problem which requires some consideration: this is the question of the degree of freedom available in the choice of assumptions for the demographic forecast. This freedom is large but not unlimited. Although the assumptions are chosen arbitrarily we cannot overstep the bounds determined by the logic of facts. We agree with the U. N. demographer who states: "In the case of mortality and fertility however, it is absurd to imagine that all variations are possible. Some, in fact, are extremely improbable."[24]

We then consider only those changes that conform to the logic of facts.

The reality of the presumptions made is of fundamental importance in calculating forecasts when their purpose is to determine as accurately as possible the future status and the future population composition. Having such a goal in view we will choose assumptions in accordance with the logic of facts. This, of course, does not anticipate the degree of their reality.

The American demographer, Warren S. Thompson, quoted above, states: "Obviously these calculations are of value insofar as the assumptions on which they are based are realized."[24]

This thesis appears to us somewhat risky. The most logical assumption may not be fulfilled owing to extraordinary and unpredictable events. Conversely, the same events may give an appearance of reasonableness to assumptions that do not fulfil this condition This postulate should not decide the value of a demographic forecast. In our opinion, the only reasonable gauge of the correctness of a perspective calculation is the degree to which its presumptions conform to the logic of facts evident in the specific demographic process.

If, as we have said, the most logical assumption may fail of fulfilment and, conversely, the less well-founded may prove true, there is no need to dwell on the well-known fact that the problem of the reality of assumed hypotheses, and of perspective calculations based on them, is extremely difficult.

Some statements, however, will be sufficiently founded and of practical use. We point out that:

(1) the reality of demographic forecasts, in general, decreases with increasing distance from the time of issue; it follows that long-term are less real than short-term forecasts;

(2) some elements of the future demographic structure may be computed many years in advance with fairly great accuracy; this concerns specifically the number of aged persons 60 or 65yr of age and over, which are important to us;

(3) if we are to estimate the value of a demographic forecast, we should examine the correctness of the assumptions.

In connection with the above statements we should like to add some final remarks that seem to be essential from the methodological point of view.

The first remark concerns the length of the period of the demographic forecast. From the fact that demographic forecasts lose reality with the extension of the period considered, we might conclude that the shorter the forecast period, the better. What is more, in this way we might come to accept the words of Napoleon: "Je ne vis que dans deux ans." However, the demographer takes a different position. Alfred

Sauvy, quoting this saying of "the god of war", points out that a demographer could not be satisfied with such modest anticipation: he must widen his horizon and this at least for the period of one generation.

In this connection a very interesting controversy between prominent German statisticians of the pre-war period, Friedrich Burgdörfer and Ludwig von Mises, should be mentioned.

In 1932 von Mises (a well-known probability theorist) published in the Berlin *Die Naturwissenschaft* a demographic forecast up to 1945. The author of the forecast explained the brevity of the forecast period by the fact that hypotheses concerning the evolution of fertility and mortality can reasonably be assumed for a period of not longer than 20–30 yr. ("unmöglich auf mehr als zwei oder drei Jahrzehnte hinaus vernünftigen Sinn behalten können").

The forecast by von Mises was criticized by Burgdörfer. He particularly raised objections to the period of the forecast as being too short and to the argument for short-term demographic predictions. In the opinion of the critic, von Mises would have been right if the demographic forecast were to be an "absolute prophecy", which Burgdörfer was unwilling to accept ("was ich aber immer abgelehnt habe und ablehne").

Thus we have reached the core of the matter: if a demographic forecast is to show long-term results of definite demographic trends (e.g. those operating at the given moment), it should itself be long-term; if, however, the purpose of the demographic forecast is limited to providing information necessary for economic planning, it should necessarily be adapted to the period of economic planning.[26]

A further problem is excessive caution in establishing hypotheses.

"Gebrannte Kinder fürchten das Feuer"—such an attitude characterized many a demographic forecaster, as the Swiss statistician Dr Albert Koller quite reasonably pointed out. From his pre-war statistical practice Koller quoted the following instructive fact:

In 1937 a forecast of the future development of the number of school-age children was made in Switzerland. The forecast predicted that the number of these children would *decrease* by 100,000 within the next 15–20 yr. However, in this period (1937–57) the number of school-age children in Switzerland increased by 200,000.

In the Swiss statistician's opinion, as in that of many other forecasters, the burnt child's fear has influenced this and many other forecasts. Of course, excessive caution can also be a source of faulty forecasts.[27]

From the standpoint of tasks assigned to this work it should be stated that the least number of objections to perspective calculations are raised in respect to the part concerning the number of aged persons.[28] This is not surprising since the individuals who in thirty, forty, or fifty years will compose the aged (60–65 and over) are now among us; and because the mortality trends at present do not promise any great surprises, over a longer period, by means of mortality tables we can determine with sufficient accuracy how many of these individuals will still be living in these age groups.

Thus we have a relatively good basis for establishing the perspective for future development of the population aging process, for many scores of years to come.

REFERENCES

1. H. LEIBENSTEIN, *A Theory of Economic-Demographic Development*, Foreword by Frank Notestein, Princeton, New Jersey, Princeton University Press 1954, p. 5.
2. W. WINKLER, *Grundprobleme der Ökonometrie*, Polish translation, Warsaw, 1957, p. 285.
3. S. SZULC, *Demografia (Demography)*, Lodz, 1947, p. 7, *Ibid.*, pp. 11–12.
4. S. SZULC, *Ibidem*, p. 11-12.
5. G. MACKENROTH, *Bevölkerungslehre. Theorie, Soziologie und Statistik der Bevölkerung*, Springer-Verlag, Berlin, 1953, p. 94.
6. E. KERN, *Die Frage der Überalterung*, *Allgemeines Statistisches Archiv*, 41 Band, Erstes Heft, 1957, p. 33.
7. *The Aging of Populations and its Economic and Social Implications*, United Nations, Department of Economic and Social Affairs, New York, 1956, p. 2.
8. W. WEGMÜLLER, "Die statistischen Grundlagen der Bevölkerungsprognose", *Schweiz. Z. Volkswirtsch. u. Stat.*, Jahrgang 92. No. 3, September 1956, p. 297.
9. In the work *Sterben die weissen Völker?* (Munich, 1934, pp. 40–41) Burgdörfer showed that if the development trends of the thirties of the 20th century had continued for a long period, the German population, which had increased very much during the 19th century, would decline rapidly within the 20th century; it would drop to 47,000,000 by the year 2000.
10. Thus the American demographer Warren S. Thompson states: "Obviously any long-time plans for national development must rest on estimates of our future population" (*Population Problems*, 3rd edition, p. 281).
11. A. SAUVY, *L'Europe et sa Population*, Les éditions internationales, Paris, (no date of publication given) p. 67.
12. F. BURGDÖRFER, *Geburtenschwund—die Kulturkrankheit Europas*, Kurt Vowinckel Verlag, Heidelberg–Berlin–Magdeburg, 1942, p. 56.
13. W. WEGMÜLLER, *Die statistischen Grundlagen der Bevölkerungsprognose*, p. 307.
14. W. S. THOMPSON, *Population Problems*, 3rd edition, p. 282.
15. A. KOLLER, Umschichtungen in der schweizerischen Bevölkerung, *Schweiz. Volkswirtsch. u. Stat.*, Jahrgang 92, No. 3, September 1956, p. 295.

16. A. LANDRY, *La Révolution Démographique, Études et essais sur les problèmes de la population*, Paris, 1934, p. 65.

17. M. PTUCHA, *Ocherki po istorii statistiki XVII—XVIII viekov* (*Sketches from the History of Statistics in the 17th and 18th centuries*), Moscow, 1945, p. 106.

18. E. ROSSET, *Historia statystyki* (The History of Statistics), Lodz, 1951, p. 30.

19. H. WRIGHT, *Bevölkerung, Deutsch herausgegeben von Dr Melchior Palyi*, Verlag von Julius Springer, Berlin, 1924, pp. 11–12.

20. In the U.N. publication, *The Aging of Populations and Its Economic and Social Implications*. New York 1956, p. 84, we read: "...it is clearly impossible to predict future trends with any accuracy. In the circumstances the best that can be done is to evaluate the effect of the fertility factor on the future age-structure in the lights of various assumptions concerning the average size of families in the future".

21. W. S. THOMPSON, the author of many American forecasts, writes: "In the very nature of the case one cannot foresee the precise course of the birth rate or the immigration policy which will be followed. Even the exact trend of the death rate is uncertain, although the error likely to arise from this source is not great" (*Population Problems*, third edition, McGraw-Hill, New York and London 1942, p. 282).

22. *Op. cit.*, p. 282 ff.

23. More detailed information about the English forecast of 1947 is to be found in LEO SILBERMAN's *Essential Concepts and Methods in Demography*, a supplement to the second edition of the work by Paul H. LANDIS, *Population Problems*.

24. From the U.N. study, *The Aging of Populations and Its Economic and Social Implications*, New York, 1956, p. 2.

25. W. S. THOMPSON, *op. cit.*, p. 283.

26. G. C. ALLEN's standpoint is against long-term forecasts: "Long-term forecasts of population can, however, be disregarded, for experience shows that they are seldom fulfilled, and it is to the changes of the recent past and of the next fifteen years that attention can be usefully directed" (*Japan's Economic Recovery*, Oxford University Press, London, 1958, p. 23).

27. Interesting observations on the qualifications a forecaster should possess are contributed by J. W. GRAUMAN, ("Population Estimates and Projections" in the collective work *The Study of Population, An Inventory and Appraisal*, edited by P. M. HAUSER and O. D. DUNCAN, The University of Chicago Press, Chicago, 1959, pp. 573–574).

28. A. SAUVY (*L'Europe et sa Population*) performed an instructive study by comparing computations for 1950 made before the war by the League of Nations with the real status of that year. It was shown that the least discrepancy of these data was in the group of aged persons (60 yr and over). The most fallacious estimates concerned the number of children and adolescents. About this account A. SAUVY wrote clearly: "Ces écarts confirment combien il est plus facile de parier sur la mort que sur la vie" (p. 71).

CHAPTER 3

Different Types of Age Structures

THE first investigations on the *types* of population composition by age are among the accomplishments of the last century. Today, these investigations, on the whole forgotten, have great importance for the history of our science and for the history of demographic conditions, as an expression of the then new interests which conditioned the process of population aging, in some places just beginning and elsewhere already developing.

The beginnings of research on the types of age structure are inseparably connected with the name of their pioneer, the then well-known Swedish demographer Gustave Sundbärg.

Sundbärg, "the great Swedish social demographer", as he was called years afterwards by Dorothy Swaine Thomas,[1] stirred the scientific circles of his time with his concept of three basic *types* of population structure by age and a pertinent thesis, according to which the age structure is characterized by either *constant* or *variable* factors.

As basic types of age structure of the population Sundbärg mentions the following:

(1) the progressive type;
(2) the stationary type;
(3) the regressive type.

By formulating rules concerning age structure based on these types, the Swedish scientist enriched demography with a complex of problems which were to play an important role in the development of this field. Sundbärg became one of the founders of a new and important branch of demography investigating the phenomenon of population aging.

The regressive population considered by the Swedish demographer is undoubtedly a population extremely advanced in the aging process. Consequently, the differences between types of demographic structures are nothing more than the peculiarities caused by the different degrees of advancement in population aging.

It is obvious that this 19th century demographer could not embrace the future scope and significance of problems which were then *in*

47

statu nascendi, although he was fully aware of the great cognitive value of numbers characterizing the structure of population by age.

This penetrating Swedish scholar established, in principle, an accurate diagnosis of the future development. However, he did not perceive and anticipate the far-reaching consequences of an economic, political and social nature that must accompany the advancing process of population aging.

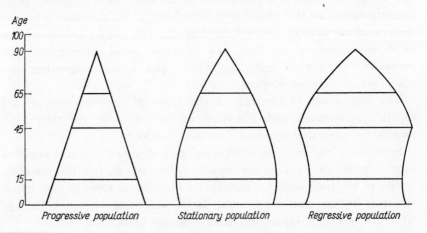

FIG. 1. Types of population structure.

Sundbärg presented his concept of definite types of population structure by age for the first time in his work *Grundlage af Befolknings-läran*, published in Stockholm in 1894. Five years later, in 1899, Sundbärg reported his idea at the International Statistical Congress in Christiania (now Oslo). His report "Sur la répartition de la population par âge et sur les taux de la mortalité" was published in the *Bulletin de l'Institut International de Statistique* (1900), vol. XII. He repeated his ideas in the work *Bevölkerungsstatistik Schwedens 1750–1900*, published in 1907 in German.

In his study the Swedish demographer considered three classes of population: "the class of children" 0–14 yr, "the class of parents" 15–49 yr, and "the class of grandparents" 50 yr and over. Using these divisions, Sundbärg characterized the particular types of age structure.

The *progressive* structure is characterized, according to Sundbärg, by the following proportions:

proportion of children 40%
proportion of parents. 50%
proportion of grandparents 10%

As the author pointed out, this is a type of population with a strongly dynamic development.

To the *stationary* type the Swedish demographer assigned the proportions:

proportion of children 27%
proportion of parents. 50%
proportion of grandparents 23%

Finally, the *regressive type* should be characterized as follows:

proportion of children 20%
proportion of parents. 50%
proportion of grandparents 30%

In Sundbärg's time the regressive type of population was in general unknown. The author mentioned that examples of this type of age structure could be found in some regions of France.

Comparing these types of populations we see that they differ in the number of children and grandparents, but not of parents: the proportion of parents is always 50 per cent. Sundbärg believed that he had succeeded in discovering the *law of age structure balance* consisting in the constancy of the percentage of adults in the general population.

When he presented his thesis to the International Congress of Statistics (1899) the Swedish demographer quoted statistical data from sixteen countries, including the U.S.A. and Japan.

From the sixteen countries covered by the Sundbärg statistics, he was able to show that twelve had the proportion of persons in the fertility age (15–49 years of age) within the limits of 49·5–50·5 per cent. Outside the limits lay the indices of four countries, namely:

Extremely low		*Extremely high*	
Norway	.48·4%	Hungary	50·6%
Netherlands	.49·2%	France	50·8%

The preponderance of indices approximating 50 per cent is evident; however, it is not without significance that one quarter of the countries show a proportion of adults which does not confirm Sundbärg's thesis. It remains to mention that the extreme values in the Swedish demo-

4

grapher's statement were 48·4% (minimum) and 50·8 per cent (maximum).

In his Congress report Sundbärg referred to the following facts also:

(1) in France the proportion of the population in the fertility age (15–49 yr) was 50·4 per cent in the 18th century and 50·8 per cent at the end of the 19th century which shows that the "law of balance" applies not only to space but also to time;

(2) in the Netherlands at a time of large emigration, the proportion of the population within the fertility age amounted to 48·6 per cent; thus even a mass exodus of adult population did not annul the "law of balance";

(3) in the U.S.A., despite great immigration, the proportion of the population within the fertility age at the end of the 19th century was 50·1 per cent, which agrees with the "law of balance". This was true because the children of the immigrants restored the equilibrium.

We should like to state that we are not at all convinced of the validity of the Sundbärg thesis, with its pretentious name.

It only requires the examination of Swedish statistics which should have been well known to the author of the thesis for the realization that the range of values of structure indices of adults (15–49 yr) in the total population is larger than would be inferred from the data used by Sundbärg.

Here are the Swedish figures:

PERCENTAGE OF PERSONS 15–49 IN THE TOTAL POPULATION OF SWEDEN IN THE PERIOD 1750—1935

Year	Percentage	Year	Percentage
1750	49·21	1850	51·04
1760	49·14	1860	50·87
1770	50·67	1870	49·23
1780	51·09	1880	48·60
1790	50·45	1890	46·35
1800	50·21	1900	47·68
1810	50·80	1910	47·55
1820	50·50	1920	49·84
1830	48·39	1930	52·78
1840	50·79	1935	52·42

Source: WILHELM WINKLER, *Grundfragen der Ökonometrie*, Springer-Verlag, Vienna, 1951 p. 158.

It cannot be denied that over a period of years the proportion of persons 15–49 yr did indeed amount to about 50 per cent. Especially close to that norm were the proportions for the years 1800 (50·21 per cent) and 1920 (48·84 per cent).

But some deviations from that norm did occur. We state below those exceeding the range appearing in Sundbärg's data:

Extremely high (%)		Extremely low (%)	
1780	51·09	1890	46·35
1850	51·04	1900	47·68
1860	50·87	1910	47·55
1930	52·78		
1935	52·42		

The span of indices ranges this time from 46·35 per cent (minimum) to 52·78 per cent (maximum).

If we were to consider the data for 1933 (omitted by Winkler) when the census for Sweden showed 54·1 per cent men and 53·3 per cent women, 15–49 yr, the highest proportion of 1930 would be exceeded (ca. 53·7 per cent).

The facts cited above contradict the thesis that the proportion of persons in the fertility age remains constant. The proportion of "parents" is affected by smaller variations than the proportion of "grandchildren" and "grandparents", but the thesis that this proportion is constant is unacceptable.

Naturally, this does not lessen the great merit of Sundbärg as the pioneer in the new branch of demographic research on the aging of societies.

Sundbärg's idea of differentiating the age structures has became an important achievement of demography. All demographers recognize today not only the need but the necessity for research on the profile of the àge of communities and the isolation of definite age structure patterns.

Such researches are suggested by the American demographer T. Lynn Smith: "It is of primary importance to the student of demography to know the nature of the age profile for each of the principal elements in a population and to understand the factors that have operated to produce the distinctive configurations that are found".[2]

Smith's assumptions about the "nature" of the age profile are being investigated by demographers in various ways. Some of them design age pyramids, others construct scales of demographic age.

The age pyramid is the preferred means of *representing* population composition in terms of age. A new method is a triangle diagram by Guilbaud, which we find in demographic analyses of recent years.

Professor Tulippe approves this new method of demonstrating population structure in order of age; he stresses its suggestivity and convenience.

Returning to the traditional means of presenting the age structure in the age pyramid, let us stress that in the hands of the demographer it becomes a tool for analysing the population age profile as well. By superimposing pyramids originating at different times and places we obtain further demonstrative and analytical effects.

The role of the age pyramid as a means of graphical demonstration and as a tool for analysing past, present and future demographic conditions has been well characterized by the French researcher Marcel R. Reinhard: "Peu de portraits sont aussi révélateurs que cet instantané: il évoque le passé, dépeint le présent, annonce l'avenir et permet des comparaisons instructives. L'histoire est inscrite dans la limite d'un siècle, ou presque".[3]

The analysis of specific age profiles has led many researchers to the same results that Sundbärg obtained by analysing appropriate tabular presentations.

The Bavarian statistician Georg von Mayr, and afterwards Gottlieb Schnapper-Arndt used four main types (Haupttypen) of the population structure by age:

(1) a pyramid or a plane triangle: an age structure type proper to societies developing due to an increasing number of births;

(2) a bell-like structure, i.e. a structure distinguished by a relatively narrow base, a small age group of young people, and a strong representation of adults and aged persons; this structure is met with in societies having a small increase in births and a favourable state of mortality;

(3) and (4) abnormal structures, e.g. onion or spindleshaped, conditioned by internal population migrations. These include populations of large cities having very large medium age groups, and, on the other hand, village populations which are losing their adults to the cities.[4]

The German demographer F. Burgdörfer distinguishes three types of population structure by age:

(1) in a young, increasing society the age structure has the shape of a pyramid ("in einem jungen, wachsenden Volk hat der Altersaufbau die Form einer ebenmässig gebauten Pyramide"); such an age structure prevailed in Germany around 1910;

(2) in an older, stationary society, which neither increases nor decreases and in which the number of births is constant, the age

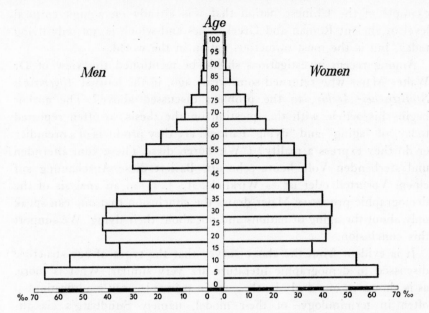

FIG. 2. Age pyramid of the Polish population as of December 31, 1955.

structure sometimes takes the form of a bell ("ein gealtertes Volk, ein stationäres Volk, das weder zu-noch abnimmt, und in dem die Geburtenzahl gleichbleibt, bildet mit der Zeit die Form einer Glocke heraus")—such, approximately, was the French type of age structure;

(3) in the last stage of population aging ("das Endstadium des überalterten und schrumpfenden Volkes") the base of the age pyramid becomes narrower than the middle and upper age layers and the top levels are abnormally broad—such a structure suggested to Burgdörfer a symbolic comparison with an urn ("ich möchte diesen Altersaufbau des schrumpfenden Volkes symbolisch mit einer Urne vergleichen...").[5]

Some authors see in an urn-shaped model of age structure a presage of the biological death of a population.

In his time Burgdörfer strongly opposed this view. The population need not perish, he asserted, and a theory that states the contrary is wrong. According to his statement, "Die Lehre vom Naturgesetz des Absterbens der Völker ist eine Irrelehre. Biologisch ist sie jedenfalls nicht begründet".[6] He stresses further that the individual must die but nations can live eternally if they want to. The author quotes the example of the Chinese nation that was already on a high cultural level in ancient Roman and Greek times and which is not only living today, but is the most numerous nation in the world.

Among recent investigations should be mentioned the view of Dr Walter Maier who returned some years ago, in the journal *Allgemeines Statistisches Archiv*, to the problem discussed above.[7] The author begins his article with the question on the thesis so often repeated today, of "aging" and "dying" nations: are they products of a prejudice or do they express a reality? ("Wir hören diese These vom alternden und sterbenden Volk heute sehr oft. Basiert diese Anschauung auf einem Vorurteil oder ist es Wirklichkeit?"). From an analysis of the demographic processes Maier draws the conclusion that one can speak only about the aging of nations and not about their dying. We support this conclusion.

It is evident from the above survey that the types of age structure discussed in demographic literature are very similar. What is more, as is shown in our analysis, they are in principle only modifications— often in terminology—of their model, namely Sundbärg's classification.

On the subject of the pyramids of age, the French author Louis Chevalier, in his handbook of demography states that there are different types of pyramids ("on distingue différents types de pyramides").

He mentions specifically three types:

(1) a pyramid corresponding to a population of a stationary type;

(2) a pyramid corresponding to a population of the progressive type;

(3) a pyramid corresponding to a population of the regressive type.[8]

It need not be stressed that the above division is the truest reflection of Sundbärg's classification.

As has already been stated, the concept of the Swedish demographer included a demographic regularity consisting of the same number of adults in societies of different types. It is interesting that this thesis, too, is again treated in articles by modern demographers. Primarily it is advocated by the French demographer Alfred Sauvy.

In one of his many works (*L'Europe et sa Population*) he makes an analytical review of the population structure of European states by age. Applying the traditional French scheme of age classification the author distinguishes:

(1) young people ("jeunes")—0–19 yr;

(2) adults ("adultes")—20–59 yr;

(3) people over 60 yr ("sexagénaires").

By comparing the proportions of the various age groups, the French demographer establishes some laws which have already been discussed. Let us repeat them:

(a) in all Europe the proportion of adults is close to 54 per cent;
(b) essential differences occur in groups of young and old;
(c) in countries demographically less developed there are 10 per cent aged persons and 36 per cent young people;[9]
(d) in more developed countries there are 16 per cent aged and 30 per cent or less young people.

One might obtain the impression that one again hears Sundbärg's voice relating his concept of the constant number of middle age groups and explaining the differences between particular models of age structure by the different numbers of young and old in the population. A new contribution by Alfred Sauvy is the different classification of age groups (as we know, Sundbärg distinguished the age groups: 0–14 yr, 15–49 yr, 50 yr and over).

The other modern French demographer, Jean Daric, stresses the almost steady character ("la quasi permanence") of the proportion of adults in France. "C'est là un fait intéressant à signaler qu'on rencontre d'ailleurs dans l'évolution de beaucoup d'autres populations, et que Sundbärg avait même cru pouvoir ériger en loi."[10]

Jean Daric states the existence of a constant proportion of adults in the same society, thus transferring the old "law of balance" from the territorial to the time profile.

We cannot approve these "rules". We do not accept the old theory of Sundbärg and we cannot approve its latest French edition. The "law of balance" does not have sufficient backing, either theoretical or empirical.

Even in the French conditions referred to by Daric, this law is not verified. It is enough to point out that in France in 1778 the age group of 20–59 amounted to 50·3 per cent of the total population (according to the estimate made by Moheau) whereas in 1936 the percentage of the population at this age was 55·1. It is then difficult to speak of a permanent or quasi-permanent proportion of adults.

Differences in space are still greater. Instead of quoting detailed international statistics we shall be content to compare two indices of structure defining the number of adult population (20–59 yr):

Romania   1930. . . . . 46·8%
Switzerland 1940. . . . . 65·8%

The spread of these indices is enough to show that the "law of balance" is not confirmed by empirical statistical data.

The investigation of age structure types paved the way for the construction of certain scales which became a convenient tool for measuring the profile of population age.

In general the scales indices have proved a great success in demography. Among those used are scales of indices of birth, general mortality, infant mortality, etc. The utility of such scales is undoubted: knowing the level of one of the indices, and using a given scale, we can state to what group of societies having a definite, qualitatively determined demographic character the investigated society belongs.

Similar advantages should be expected from the scale of structure indices characterizing the profile of population age.

Even in this field Gustave Sundbärg was the pioneer. Moreover many contemporary scales of population aging are based on the same foundations as Sundbärg's earliest scales.

Take, for example, the scale established in the work of Jacqueline Beaujeu-Garnier (of the University of Lille). The author divides European countries into three groups:

(1) countries demographically old;

(2) countries demographically young;

(3) countries of an intermediate type.

The question arises: in what does this division differ from the division applied half a century ago by Sundbärg?

We have already stated that often the differences between authors are more terminological than essential in nature. This can also be said about the differences between the concepts of Beaujeu-Garnier and the old Swedish master. We also find the concept of progressive and regressive populations in the work of the French geographer although it appears in a different form.

Besides this, Beaujeu-Garnier follows Sundbärg in applying a double criterion of demographic youth or age: firstly—depending on the proportion of young people, secondly—depending on aged persons. However, the schemes of age classification differ for the two authors; the French geographer makes use of the traditional French scheme distinguishing the age groups: 0–19 yr, 20–59 yr, 60 and over.

The French author's criteria are as follows:

(1) *aged* societies consist of those having 30·5 per cent children and adolescents (0–19 yr) and over 15 per cent of aged persons (60 yr and over);

(2) *young* societies have over 35 per cent children and adolescents and less than 12 per cent aged persons;

(3) *intermediate* societies have 30·5–35 per cent adolescents and 12–15 per cent aged persons.[11]

Demographic scales, including old age scales, depend entirely on the individual views and concepts of their authors. It should not be expected that for each demographic phenomenon only one scale will be used as a tool of the qualitative estimate of quantitatively expressed conditions. However, it is reasonable to require that different scales do not produce basically contradictory results.

For the purpose of estimating demographic youth or age we have established our own scale which will be used in the present work.

An essential peculiarity of this scale is that it has more groups than the scales previously discussed and that it fits societies into these groups on the basis of only one criterion: the proportion of aged persons (60 yr and over).

The number of four groups is obtained by subdividing the intermediate stage into two: an *anterior* one which we treat as an early stage of aging and a *posterior* one which characterizes a greater advancement of the population aging process.

The reduction of the number of criteria to one is based on the premise that since the proportion of aged persons is generally recognized as the measure of age there is no need to complicate the classification by introducing another, which is not followed in practice—the proportion of young people.

According to the above our scale has four groups:

(a) a group of societies demographically young;

(b) a group of societies in the early stages of aging;

(c) a group of aging societies;

(d) a group of aged societies.

On page 58 we state the proportions of aged persons (60 yr and over) which provide criteria for classifying societies in particular age groups.

Now, another and still more important difference between the scale proposed by us and the one we stated previously is made clear. We have in mind different locations of the starting point of demographic old age: Beaujeu-Garnier qualifies as old those societies in which aged persons (60 yr and over) constitute at least 15 per cent of the total population; in our scale a proportion of 12 per cent aged persons classifies a society as old.

How is this difference to be explained?

CLASSIFICATION OF SOCIETIES CONFORMING TO THE DEGREE OF ADVANCEMENT OF THE PROCESS OF POPULATION AGING*

Group	Proportion of aged persons (60 and over)	Characteristic of the group
I	below 8%	demographic youth
II	8–10%	early stages of aging
III	10–12%	proper aging
IV	12% and over	demographic old age

*According to the concept of the author of the present work.

It seems that this difference is due to the different origin of the two scales: our French colleague has based her scale on the profile of population age of European countries existing *today*, while the basis of our scale is the *historical* development of the aging process of the same societies. Thus, the historical concept of the problem recommends the 12 per cent proportion of aged persons, as has been assumed by us, for the proper beginning of demographic age.

The strongest argument against setting too high a limit to the age is the absurdity of the consequences of such an assumption. It suffices to point out that when accepting 15 per cent of aged persons (60 yr and over) as a criterion of demographic old age we would have to acknowledge that in the period between the two world wars (1919–39) there was in Europe no society demographically old; even France— long since a country of demographic old age—would not qualify for the category of aged countries.

The need to use some comparative scale for the degree of the population aging process has been stressed by the demographer of the United Nations who elaborated the problem of population aging as to its economic and social consequences.[12]

Stressing the arbitrariness of the criteria assumed, quite properly, it seems to us that the author distinguishes:

(1) a population defined as *young*, having less than 4 per cent of persons 65 yr and over;

(2) a population defined as *mature*, having 4–7 per cent of persons 65 yr and over;

(3) a population defined as *aged*, having 7 per cent or more of persons 65 yr and over.

Without going into detail, the U.N. demographer points out that in the light of the above scale "an overwhelming proportion of world

populations may be regarded as young or mature, and only a very small proportion as aged".

This statement does not satisfy us. We regard it as unjustified that such different groups as the first and second should be combined. If it were necessary to combine particular groups, then it would be more reasonable to do this with the second and third groups. Such a combined group would comprise all the societies affected by the aging process (though to different degrees) and would provide an image of the population aging progress on a world scale, which would be more accurate. Then it would be difficult to defend the conclusion of the U.N. demographer that the problem of population aging is limited now to a small group of countries. ("It follows that the problems of aging of populations are by no means universal, but on the contrary, are at present restricted to a small group of countries".)

In the statements of different authors as well as in our own, the old terminology of Sundbärg has been modernized: we no longer speak about progressive, stationary, or regressive populations, but we use instead the terms: young, mature and aged populations. The change of terms is of no great relevance: the essence of the matter, i.e. the variety of types of age structure, has not been affected by the change. On the other hand the application today of more precise tools to measure demographic youth or age results in significant methodological progress.

The concept of the division of societies into young, mature and aged is a logical consequence of the population aging. Since the phenomenon of population aging does occur here and there, this must mean that the societies affected by this process were once younger; today they are older, and in future will be still older. Such a conclusion must follow a comparison of the populations of different countries as to the existing age structure; such a comparison would prove that some countries are demographically young, others mature, and still others aged.

Quite contrary is the reasoning of Louis Chevalier. The French demographer begins with the differentiation of young and aged societies and from this he draws a conclusion about the action of the population aging process in the contemporary world.[13] It is not difficult to observe that the difference between the two statements is a difference of a purely didactic type.

It results from our considerations that knowledge of the age structure types initiated by Sundbärg made no progress within the first half century of its existence; the frames of his knowledge and, what is more important, its methodological basis in general remained unchanged.

The Austrian statistician Professor Wilhelm Winkler predicts a future development of the knowledge of types in demography. He himself laid foundations for this development with his work: *Typenlehre der Demographie (Reine Bevölkerungstypen)* Vienna, 1952, which introduces a proper mathematical apparatus for investigating population development types. In this opinion, his work is only an introduction to an appropriate system of demographic types, the development of which will require the studies of many scientists.

"But this is only a minor task"—observes another outstanding expert in the field of demographic researches, Professor Wilhelm Bickel of Zurich. "It is more important and difficult to explain the social basis of different types of population development and the investigation of the influence of population dynamics on this social basis."[14]

We shall attempt to make a further step forward in this field; this is the aim of socio-demographic studies about the process of population aging.

REFERENCES

1. D. S. THOMAS, *Social and Economic Aspects of Swedish Population Movements 1750–1933*, The Macmillan Company, New York, 1941, p. VI.
2. T. L. SMITH *Population Analysis*, first edition, New York, Toronto, London, 1948, p. 105.
3. M. R. REINHARD, *Histoire de la Population Mondiale de 1700 à 1948*, Paris, 1949, p. 29.
4. G. SCHNAPPER—ARNDT, *Sozialstatistik, Vorlesungen über Bevölkerungslehre, Wirtschafts- und Moralstatistik*, Leipzig 1912, p. 114.
5. F. BURGDÖRFER, *Bevölkerungsentwicklung im Dritten Reich, Tatsachen und Kritik*, Heidelberg–Berlin, 1938, p. 16.
6. F. BURGDÖRFER, *Sterben die weissen Völker?* Georg D. W. Callwey Verlag, Munich, 1934, p. 83.
7. W. MAIER, Studie über die Entwicklung der Bevölkerungsstruktur. Alterndes und sterbendes Volk? *Allg. Staat Arch.*, 39 Band, Erstes Heft, 1955, pp. 38–40.
8. L. CHEVALIER, *Démographie Générale*, Dalloz, Paris, 1951, pp. 94–95.
9. A. SAUVY, *L'Europe et sa Population*, p. 47.
10. J. DARIC, *Vieillissement de la Population et Prolongation de la Vie active*, Presses Universitaires de France, Paris, 1948, p. 20.
11. J. BEAUJEU-GARNIER, *Géographie de la Population*, Éditions Génin, Librairie de Médici, Paris, 1956, pp. 178–179.

12. *The Aging of Populations and its Economic and Social Implications*, United Nations, New York, 1956, p. 7.

13. In the work already cited (*Démographie Générale*, 1951) Chevalier writes: "Il y a des populations jeunes et des populations âgées...et cela nous amène à introduire une notion essentielle et relativement récente, celle de vieillissement de la population..." (p. 102).

14. W. Bickel, "Bevölkerungsdynamik und Gesellschaftsstruktur", *Schweiz. Z. Volkswirtsch. u. Stat.*, 92. Jahrgang, No. 3, September 1956, pp. 322–323.

CHAPTER 4

Deficiencies and Lack of Methodological Uniformity of Source Materials and the Resulting Difficulties in Comparative Analysis

STATISTICAL analysis is expected to provide a good diagnosis and a correct forecast. To fulfil this task the researcher must have at his disposal adequate statistical material.

However, such material is not always available. In many a country the data concerning the age of the inhabitants, most important in the investigation of population aging, leave much to be desired. For an analysis of the state of population composition by age, and even more of its evolution, this is a serious obstacle.

These difficulties loom more important in the case of a comparative analysis on an international scale. In addition to the lack or the uncertainty of statistical data is now added the fact that the figures from different countries cannot be compared—a new and serious source of difficulty encountered by the researcher of population phenomena.

In her work on geodemography Jacqueline Beaujeu-Garnier stresses the difficulties in demonstrating population conditions on a world scale. "L'insuffisance statistique est, malheureusement, un obstacle considérable. Que ce soit dans le présent ou dans le passé, pour évaluer un accroissement, préciser une densité, calibrer un mouvement migratoire, mesurer une évolution, les chiffres sont nécessaires. Mais ils n'existent pas toujours, et, même quand ils sont publiés, leur valeur est, fort souvent, rien moins que certaine".[1]

To the list of branches mentioned by Professor Beaujeu-Garnier as needing a solid statistical foundation for investigation, the problem of the aging of society should be added. Without statistical data it cannot be interpreted, and the state of these data is unsatisfactory.

1. DEFICIENCIES IN AGE STATISTICS

The deficiencies in age statistics are only a part of a wider problem of deficiencies in general census statistics. Let us begin with considerations concerning the whole of census materials to illustrate the inadequacy of age statistics based on the census.

Population censuses have a long and rich history, but also long and rich is the history of the errors and defects in this fundamental branch of demographic statistics. We shall not go too far back but give a list of defects registered half a century ago by the Russian statistician Professor L. Chodsky when discussing census technique in his handbook of statistics.[2]

Thus the censuses made before the mid-19th century suffered from the following defects:

(1) they were performed at irregular time intervals;

(2) they were done slowly;

(3) they had purely fiscal or military aims;

(4) they did not register the whole population and then only the legal and not actual facts;

(5) the census information comprised only a few aspects;

(6) the organization of censuses was inadequate.

A turning point in the organization of censuses was the Belgian census of 1846 based on new, scientific principles. This census initiated the epoch of modern population counts. Its organizer, the Belgian statistician Adolphe Quetelet, became well known in the history of statistics as a pioneer in modern methodology and census technique.

The development of censuses and the raising of their level were much aided by the international statistical congresses, beginning with the Brussels Congress of 1853. Let us add that the initiator of this congress, the First International Statistical Congress, was the same Belgian statistician Quetelet.

Much has changed since that time, although not everywhere. European countries have already overcome the faults of the first censuses, but these faults have not vanished in those countries outside Europe which are still in the phase of "statistical youth" most often accompanied by economic and cultural under-development.

The French geographer, Professor Beaujeu-Garnier, distinguishes the following four groups of countries from the standpoint of the value of their statistical documentation:

(1) countries with satisfactory statistical documentation; the author mentions such exemplary countries as the U.S.A., Canada, New Zealand, Argentina;

(2) countries possessing an organized statistical apparatus but whose

statistics have many serious faults; this group comprises most countries of Latin America;

(3) countries possessing fragmentary and insufficient statistics or none at all; in this group are most countries of Africa and the Middle East; an idea of the paucity of statistics of the indigenous populations of British colonies is given in the four-volume fundamental work of R. R. Kuczynski (*Demographic Survey of the British Colonial Empire 1948-1953*);

(4) countries collecting statistics but not publishing the results; this group no longer exists since the figures are now disclosed.

It is interesting to note the moderation shown by the French author in appreciating the first group of countries, undoubtedly having the best organization of official statistics: Professor Beaujeu-Garnier speaks about the *satisfactory* statistical documents in these countries. This moderation is unfortunately all too justified. In the United States, to which the author assigns first place as a representative of this group, births are still not fully registered. Leo Silberman indicates that in respect to 1940, the best birth registration was noted in the following States: Connecticut, Minnesota, and New Jersey, where 99 per cent of all births were registered. But in the state of Arkansas, registered births amounted to only 75·9 per cent of the actual number of births. Thus, one quarter of the total number of births in this state remained outside the official registers. Taking the U.S.A. as whole, among the white population the non-registered births amounted to 6 per cent, and among the coloured population 18 per cent, of the actual total number of births.[3] These are serious gaps.

Let us pass on to the deficiencies in age statistics, which are of direct interest to us.

This is an attempt to list them:

(1) data are not available in all countries of the world concerning the population composition by age; this most often results from a complete lack of or irregular censuses and causes serious gaps in international reviews characterizing the profile of population age;

(2) the statistical materials of countries taking censuses are not free from errors, the cause of this being either organizational and methodological defects in the census or erroneous answers supplied;

(3) data about the population composition by age derived from statistics of various countries are not fully comparable, as a result of methodological differences and a lack of time synchronization of these data.

Our list will be more complete if we also include a series of errors and shortcomings stated by the Statistical Office of the United Nations.[4] In the *U.N. Demographic Yearbook* for 1953 there are enumerated the following deficiencies:

(1) underenumeration of infants and young children;

(2) heaping at ages ending in 0 and 5;

(3) a preference for even ages over odd ages;

(4) an unexpectedly large difference between the numbers of males and females at certain ages;

(5) unaccountably large differences between the numbers in successive or adjacent age groups.

Some means of compensating for these shortcomings have been found; they will be discussed later.

Of course, the deficiencies of age statistics do not occur everywhere to the same degree. For the present let us mention the remark of the U.N. Statistical Office that inconsistency and other anomalies affecting age statistics can be found even in the most modern population censuses.

Recognized errors are less dangerous than unrecognized ones. Therefore we shall now proceed to an analysis of all the shortcomings included in the lists of errors of age statistics.

2. RANGE AND LEVEL OF THE STATISTICAL CIVILIZATION

A "statistical civilization" is one in which the given country takes more or less regular population censuses.

The question arises: what is the range and, probing deeper, what is the level of such a civilization?

Not all the population of the world is registered by censuses. The statistical wasteland, as we shall call those parts of the globe not covered by population counts, is still vast. Naturally, the further we go back in time the greater are its dimensions.

The American demographer Walter F. Willcox, referring to the *Statistical Yearbook 1935–1936* (League of Nations publication) gave in one of his papers the following percentages of population not covered by counts:[5]

North America	0·0
Europe	—
South America	2·5
Oceania	0·6
Africa	22·4
Asia	43·3

In the total count Willcox gave 26·1 per cent for the population of the whole globe not covered by census.

Despite the respect due to the pioneer and senior American demographer, we cannot agree with his over-optimistic calculation.

When dividing the countries of the world into those covered by censuses and those not so covered, Willcox counted in the first group all countries in which a population census had ever been taken. In this manner, besides countries taking population counts more or less regularly, he included in the list of countries covered by counts those in which censuses have been in abeyance for dozens of years. And this seems the correct procedure.

Let us look into the work of another American demographer, T. Lynn Smith.[6]

Dealing with the problem of population composition by sex, the author illustrates his considerations with data from many countries. It is striking that for some of them Lynn Smith quotes outdated figures.

Here are the dates of the figures quoted by him for the three countries mentioned below:

Argentina 1914
Bolivia 1900
Uruguay 1908

Following Willcox, let us consider an international publication: the *U.N. Demographic Yearbook* for 1959 to check the dates of censuses taken in the above three countries of South America.

In Argentina the two last censuses produced the following results:[7]

June 1, 1914 7,885,237
May 10, 1947 15,893,827

We have quoted not only the dates but also the results of the two last censuses since they are also significant.

In this connection, the following facts should be stressed:

(1) in 1940, when Willcox announced his data, Argentina had not had a census for 26 yr;

(2) the break between censuses lasted in Argentina from 1914–47, or 33 yr;

(3) the country remained without a census during a violent increase in population; in the period 1914–47 the population of Argentina doubled.

Let us now consider Bolivia.

The information concerns the two last censuses in this country:[8]

September 1, 1900	1,693,400
September 5, 1950	2,704,165

As to Bolivia a more drastic problem arises:

(1) when writing his work, Willcox was able to state that Bolivia had been without a census for forty years;

(2) the break between two censuses lasted half a century in Bolivia;

(3) during this time the population of the country increased by 60 per cent.

There remains Uruguay. The census of October 12, 1908 (1,042,686 inhabitants) is still the last population count taken there.[9]

It can be assumed that Willcox could easily have stated in 1940 that no census had been taken in Bolivia for 32 yr, just as we can state today that Bolivia has not had a population count for half a century.

It should be observed that estimates made in 1958 set the population of Bolivia at over 3,300,000.[10] Even such an enormous population increase did not convince the proper authorities in this country of the need to take a new census.

These three countries—Argentina, Bolivia, and Uruguay—include about one-fifth of the total population of South America. If they were included in the list of countries not covered by censuses, as logic requires, then the percentage of population outside censuses would amount not to 2·5, as Willcox stated, but to more than 20 per cent.

A few words about Peru. The two last censuses in this country revealed:[11]

May 14, 1876	2,699,106
June 9, 1940	6,207,967

The time lapse between these two censuses—64 yr—disqualifies Peru in our eyes as a country covered by counts. Where no count is taken for two-thirds of a century, surely there is a true statistical wasteland. Together with Peru, countries actually existing outside the "statistical civilization" include about 24 per cent of the total population of South America. In point of fact, the statistical wasteland in South America is ten times as great as that stated by Willcox.

Once the American demographer's calculations are doubtful on one point they become questionable as a whole and thus give no image of the statistical wasteland in the years between the two world wars.

Let us now consider the work of the Soviet scientist, B. Urlanis. In his history of the population development in Europe, Urlanis stresses two facts:

(1) statistics of population status have been created relatively recently: regular censuses in the United States date from 1790; in Great Britain and France from 1801; in Belgium from 1846; in Italy from 1861, etc.;

(2) to this date, in many countries population counts have not been taken at all, e.g. Abyssinia, Liberia, Ecuador, Afghanistan, Arabia, etc.[12]

From the five countries cited as examples by the Soviet demographer only Ecuador can no longer serve as an example of a total statistical wasteland: in that country in 1950 a census was taken. The remaining four countries remain outside statistical civilization.

We list below countries for which, in the *U.N. Statistical Yearbook* for 1959, the column "Latest census" contains dots in place of a number:[13]

(1) *Africa*: Ethiopia, Liberia,

(2) *Asia*: Laos, Lebanon, Muscat and Oman, Qatar, Saudi Arabia, Afghanistan, Bhutan, Aden, Syria, Vietnam, Yemen, Gaza Straits.

We have mentioned fifteen countries where censuses are still unknown. Of course this does not speak well for the statistical civilization of the world.

The appraisal of the degree of the statistical civilization would be still less favourable if we were to base it, not only on the mere fact of taking population counts, but also on the quality of the statistical material obtained from censuses and other statistical investigations.

Let us take as an example the Indian statistics before Indian independence. Population counts were taken in India regularly every ten years, beginning with 1881. Until censuses were taken in China these censuses were the largest in the world. The census apparatus in India included about two million counters.

Regarding the Indian count of 1911 Gertrude Wolf wrote: "Among particular difficulties to be overcome by a census in India, first should be mentioned the low level of education of the masses: the number of illiterates amounts to 88 per cent of the population. Further difficulties arise owing to the enormous distances and tribal differences and unrest which compel the omission of some areas and a substitution of estimates... In establishing the critical moment of the census, numerous religious holidays and popular fairs which draw thousands of guests and pilgrims must be taken into account. The main difficulty, however, lies in the amazing mosaic of languages. During the census of 1911, 220 native languages including 38 dialects and excluding European languages were distinguished."[14]

It is obvious that under such difficult conditions, the results of the statistical studies will be far from perfect. Thus, we cannot be surprised by the statement of Palme Dutt that in India the most important statistics are hopelessly inaccurate. Referring to the census of 1931, Palme Dutt states that a permissible error of up to 20 per cent has been accepted.[15]

The level of statistical civilization is today undoubtedly higher than it was twenty years ago. This is indicated by the fact that in 1950 and 1951 in many countries censuses were taken, inspired by international bodies. Forrest E. Linder[16] notes remarkable progress in the development of population counts in the years 1945–54. An event of particularly great significance was the census taken on June 30, 1953 over the vast area of the Chinese People's Republic.

While greeting all these facts with great satisfaction we must point out that:

(1) the gaps in the statistical materials from previous years have not been filled, a fact of importance for our investigations of the historical changes in the population composition by age in various countries;

(2) not all countries responded to the appeal of the international bodies; there are even some great countries that did not take censuses, which reduces the possibilities for comparative analysis;

(3) here and there the censuses are not complete; thus in Australia the aborigines are omitted; in Panama and Venezuela the counts do not include Indians; in Peru the inhabitants of jungles are not counted, etc.;

(4) the quality of census materials in underdeveloped countries, though improved, leaves much to be desired, for example the census of 1954 in Martinique and Guadeloupe (French Antilles) reported in *Population*, the first census in one hundred years which is of some value ("le premier, depuis à peu près un siècle, auquel on puisse accorder quelque valeur");[17]

(5) even the most modern population censuses are not exempt from minor or major errors.[18]

Taking all this into consideration we can conclude that the population of the world is still partly unknown, and partly known to an insufficient degree.

3. VARIETY OF ORGANIZATION AND METHODOLOGY OF POPULATION CENSUSES

In ancient Rome, which had an admirable range and quality of statistical operations, the memorable Roman censuses were among the most important state acts.[19]

And now some examples showing the difficulties or even complete failure of a census caused by the indifference of the population to it. The Soviet demographers A. Boyarsky and P. Shusherin describe the following facts:

(1) in tsarist Russia, during the census of 1897 the inhabitants of whole villages fled to the woods; some groups of peasants, to avoid "stigma of anti-Christ", even collectively committed suicide by burying themselves in the earth;

(2) during the census in India in 1931 a whole town — Ahmadabad — of 400,000 inhabitants, refused to participate in the census.[20]

These facts, although varying in their content, all confirm the great importance of the organizational factor in a census: the value of the material collected depends to some extent on the level of organization.

If we were to review the organizational principles used in censuses we would find a large variety of systems used internationally. This variety often results from the different levels of civilization, not only on the part of those being counted but also on the part of the enumerators.

In Poland, census enumerators visit house after house, flat after flat, registering every one on the spot. This manner of census taking is also used in other countries, such the U.S.S.R., U.S.A. etc.

In France and in many other European countries population counts are based on the principle of self-counting. The census enumerators leave forms with families to fill out themselves. These are then collected. This method is applicable only in the complete absence of illiteracy.

Besides these two modern methods of census taking, there are in the world other methods that are sometimes amazing.

A peculiar form of population count taken in Turkey on October 28, 1927 was reported to the 17th session of the International Statistical Institute in Cairo by the director of the Central Statistical Office in Ankara, Camille Jacquart. He stated that during the census taking the inhabitants were ordered to stay at home both in villages and cities, Istanbul included. They were kept in their homes from 8 a.m.

to 5 p.m. and in Istanbul until 10 p.m., when a cannon shot gave the signal for the end of this detention. Further, he reported that the census encountered many difficulties, primarily on account of the wide-spread illiteracy (Turkey at that time reported 80–90 per cent illiterates). The other source of difficulties was the nomadic life of a part of the population.

The organization of the population census conducted in Turkey on October 20, 1940 was very similar to the first. This time, too, the people were detained at home till the end of the census taking. The German source from which we quote this information adds that the regulation was accompanied by heavy penalties.[21] The population counting began all over the country at 8 a.m. With the end of the census-taking, signals were given by trumpeters or by gun shots, indicating that the inhabitants were allowed to leave their homes. In Istanbul with a population of about 800,000 inhabitants (exactly 789,346) traffic was restored by 2 p.m. which proved good organization of the census apparatus.

In India during the census-taking a principle of declaration was applied: the interested persons (heads of families) were obliged to appear before the authorities and submit a declaration about themselves and persons living with them.

In some African countries, residents of settlements are called for a definite date to a given place where the heads of families report the required data to the census administrators.

As has been indicated, differences in the method of census-taking are conditioned by the individual relationships in various countries; the census administrations have to adapt themselves to the conditions existing in a given country. These differences have their repercussions—to a greater or lesser degree—on the quality of the census material and in many cases raise doubts as to the possibility of comparing census results.

Various organizational principles imply differences in census programmes and perhaps still more important differences in the definitions of census terms. We shall limit our considerations to one point of the census programme, namely to the age of those counted.

In contemporary censuses a question concerning the age of the inhabitants is an understandable and necessary element of the census programme. The appearance of this column in census forms is, however, a relatively new achievement. What difficulties had to be overcome before this item was included in the census is best indicated by the stages of development of the age problem in the American census:

(a) in the earliest census of the U.S.A. taken in 1790, only the age of free, white men was of interest, and the age was registered for two groups of men: below 16 yr (first group) and 16 yr and over (second group);

(b) in the census of 1800 the number of age groups was increased to five, but still only the white population was counted;

(c) an important innovation was adopted in the census of 1820, namely the coloured people were included for the first time, items concerning the age and sex of slaves and free coloured people were introduced, and four age groups distinguished; in the same census the number of age groups for the white population was increased from five to six;

(d) a further step ahead was the introduction in the census of 1830 of a division of the white population into five and ten year age groups;

(e) finally the census of 1850 initiated a set of personal questions for every person included in the census, including one on age.

In France, in the first population censuses, only sex and family status were of interest; a question concerning age was added to the French census only in 1851.

A similar situation existed in Great Britain. The first English census, conducted under the direction of Rickmann in 1801, allowed for only one question of a demographic character; it concerned sex. Other census questions concerned economic conditions (ownership of a house and main occupation in agriculture, trade, manufacture and handicrafts). With every census, the number of questions increased. Information about age was still not obligatory in 1821 and only became so in 1841, when the ages of the rural population were entered in twenty-year groups and of the urban population in five-year groups. The English census of 1851 was described by a historian of statistics as having reached a high degree of completeness.[22]

The significance of knowledge about the morphology of population age was not recognized at once. But already in the mid-19th century the awareness of the need for investigations of population age became more general. At the end of the century one of the outstanding statisticians of that time, the author of the classical work: *Statistik als Gesellschaftslehre*, Georg von Mayr, stressed the importance of population composition by age as an extremely important problem from the social standpoint—a continuity factor of progress and cultural development. When, a quarter of a century later, Edward Byron Reuter stated that "the age distribution is perhaps the most important division of a population",[23] it was a truism (unnecessarily weakened the use of the word "perhaps").

The existing differences and changes introduced in the methods of investigation and definitions of census terms make for further possibilities of error and incomparability of census data.

The German demographer Gerhard Mackenroth calls attention to the negative side of the frequent changes in the statistical methods of investigation and in definitions of terms and features, "Dadurch werden zwar meistens die neueren Zahlen immer zuverlässiger, aber auch immer unvergleichbarer mit den älteren Zahlen. ...Es geschieht leider nur zu oft, dass aus solchen Veränderungen der Zahlenangaben falsche Schlüsse gezogen werden".[24] Thus, not only are the census data not comparable but faulty conclusions also frequently result from the changes introduced into the methodology of censuses and census definitions.

From what has been said above the following conclusions can be drawn:

(1) the beginnings of age statistics based on the proper foundation of censuses fell within the years 1840–50;

(2) questions concerning age are today the basic element of the programme of censuses in the developed societies;

(3) unfortunately, the abundance of statistical material concerning the age structure of modern societies is not accompanied by uniformity of statistical methodology and definitions of terms, which makes difficult a comparative analysis of census data originating in various countries.[25]

4. THE VALUE OF CENSUS MATERIALS CONCERNING THE AGE OF THE POPULATION

Of course, it would be unreasonable if we were to close our eyes to the frequent and troublesome omissions in census materials concerning the age of the population.

Why are age statistics exposed to such a high degree to error?

This question was answered one hundred years ago by the French statistician A. Moreau de Jonnès who stated: "Il est presque impossible de relever l'âge des personnes avec quelque exactitude, parce que les unes l'ignorent, et que les autres le cachent".[26]

The opinion cited above retains its validity today. The most important source of shortcomings in the statistics of age is undoubtedly the fact that some people do not know their age and others consciously report it falsely.

In detail, we can easily state that:

(a) women have a tendency to "grow younger";

(b) conversely, aged persons are accustomed to adding on a few years;

(c) uneducated people, especially illiterates, have difficulty in stating their birth dates and, questioned about their age, give a round figure;

(d) there are here and there specific manners of age counting, some of which disturb the proper meaning and age count;

(e) at the lowest level of civilization there is a complete failure to recognize the number of years lived.

The above deficiencies occur most often and therefore may be regarded as most important. Let us analyse them.

(a) Women's Tendency to "Grow Younger"

Women's reduction of their age has interested statisticians for a long time. We quote two original examples of investigations on this subject, one from earlier, the other from more recent times.

The British census of 1841 (the first to include a question about age) showed 852,000 girls between 10 and 15 yr. If we assume that their number within the next ten years (1841–1851) suffered no loss from emigration and that the mortality rate was 7 per thousand, then at the census of 1851 there should not have been more than 792,000 women between 20 and 25. However, the census of 1851 showed 872,000 women of that age, or 80,000 above the proper number.

Where does this unexpected increase come from?

For the statistician the problem is clear: the above increase was caused by women "growing younger". By understating their age they increased the number of women in the age group of 20–25 yr.

The English statistician Rickmann who was the "superintendent" of the first English population count (1801) and who within the next forty years conducted censuses in his country, used to say of himself that he did not know one thing: the exact ages of Englishwomen. He mentioned that his own home was no exception; he could never state exactly the age of his wife or his chambermaid.

We follow this with an example from recent times.

The demographer Giorgio Mortara calls attention to the following characteristics of Brazilian statistics:

(1) there are considerably more women than men in the age group 15–19 and 20–29;

(2) conversely, in the age groups 40–49 and 50–59 yr there is a clear deficit of women.

The Brazilian demographer makes the interesting comment: "...the female age groups of 15–19 and 20–29 yr are evidently inflated and those of 40–49 and 50–59 yr strongly deflated as a result of understatement."[27]

The World Demographic Congress of 1954 in Rome dealt with the same subject and the Brazilian statistician Arruda Gomes commented on it. He pointed out that in the Brazilian census of 1950 a 7·3 per cent surplus of women appeared in the age group 15–29 yr, while at the same time the numbers of women in older groups showed a deficit.[28]

We do not wish to conceal the fact that we regard the quoted interpretation as not fully proven. There is no proof that the figures for the age groups 15–19 and 20–29 were artificially swollen. There is also no proof that the small number of women of 50–59 results from a poor estimate.

Of course, the numbers of men and women do not need to be identical in the various age groups. The American demographer, T. Lynn Smith, already quoted, quite rightly points out the inevitability of differences in numbers of men and women in individual age groups: "Because the sex ratio at birth is not equal to 100, because females of all ages have lower mortality rates than males, and since the proportions of males and females among immigrants and emigrants are unequal, any given society may contain considerable differences between the age structures of the male and female elements in its population".[29] Thus if the statistics of a country show a preponderance of men or women in some age group it cannot be assumed that this is due to understatement or overstatement.

(b) Exaggerated Age of Older Persons

Let us analyse the problem of old people overstating their age.

In scientific literature and not only demographic, the phenomenal longevity of Bulgarians was famous. The sources of this idea were Bulgarian censuses showing an unusual number of persons one hundred years of age.

The oldest of these censuses, 1887, showed 3883 persons of 100 yr and over or 123 for every hundred thousand inhabitants. In order to show how great this is, we add the information that the coefficient of 123 applied to present Polish conditions (30 million inhabitants) would give the tremendously large figure of 37,000 people of 100 yr and over.

It is no wonder that the Bulgarian figures aroused great interest all over the world. E. Mechnikov perceived therein a confirmation of his phagocythic theorie.

However, not everyone followed the delusive principle: "Les chiffres, on ne discute pas." The experienced Bavarian statistician—"der Alt-meister der Statistik" as he was called—Georg von Mayr, was scep-tical of the extraordinarily high number of aged people. He advocated a detailed control of census declarations when the age exceeded 90 yr.

The appeals of serious statisticians and even some pressure on the part of the International Institute of Statistics resulted in an analysis of census declarations in many countries. In Bulgaria special teams including physicians and statisticians thoroughly investigated persons who, in the census of 1926, had declared themselves to be one hundred years of age.

What was the result?

While the population census of 1926 showed 1756 persons one hundred years of age and over, the control revealed that only 158 cases were genuine. Thus, 91 out of 100 declarations of an age of a hundred or more were false.

"It has been shown," says Oskar Anderson, "that there exists a coquetry of old age which induces old people to overstate their age. There was a case of an individual who declared his age as 121 while he was in fact 85; another gave himself the same age when he was in fact 80 (adding on 41 yr)."[30]

Anderson states that when measures were taken in Bulgaria against illiteracy, the number of persons claiming to be a hundred years old diminished to the same degree as the number of illiterates.

It would seem then that in countries highly developed culturally, the aged do not overstate their age. However, this cannot be confirmed.

Professor K. Freudenberg of Berlin questions the exactness of the 1950 census data in the German Federal Republic concerning the number of aged persons. Though declarations of an age of over 90 were checked, the control was made only in four provinces and the errors were not corrected in general.

"There are indications," says Freudenberg, "that in Germany in recent years the inaccuracy of data resulting from overstating of age by the aged is met with not only among persons over 90 but also 10 yr younger."[31]

A new source of inaccuracy in age statistics is stated by the U.N. demographer as follows: "The growth of the Welfare State has given rise to a comparatively new source of inaccuracy, due to a tendency on the part of persons nearing the eligibility age for pensions to overstate their age."[32]

It follows from what has been said above that in aging societies, with their steadily increasing number of aged persons, the problem of accuracy of data concerning the age of old persons will become more and more acute. Thus the question should already be considered that some international convention should oblige national statistical offices to check the correctness of census declarations of ages above 80. Such a control would be useful for both "old" and "young" countries.

(c) Rounding off the Age and Resultant Heaping at Certain Ages

Let us discuss a further and somewhat more serious source of inaccuracies in age data. These are the "age concentrations" which an American demographer calls: "the most obvious of all discrepancies in census data" (Lynn Smith).

The essence of this inaccuracy is the stating of the age in round figures. Especially preferred are ages ending in 0, then even numbers. In these ages are concentrated excessively great numbers of persons, of course at the expense of other age; especially those close by.

In their handbook on the theory of statistics, the Danish statisticians H. Westergaard and H. C. Nybolle quote figures taken from Danish population censuses of 1911 and 1921 which, the authors believe, can serve as a typical example of the result of rounding off the age.[33]

Below is the number of Denmark's inhabitants aged 50 yr as compared with the two neighbouring age classes:

(a) according to the census of 1911:

49 yr	24,688
50 yr	26,616
51 yr	25,841

(b) according to the census of 1921:

$$
\begin{aligned}
&49 \text{ yr} \ldots \ldots \ldots \ldots 27{,}921 \\
&50 \text{ yr} \ldots \ldots \ldots \ldots 29{,}512 \\
&51 \text{ yr} \ldots \ldots \ldots \ldots 27{,}608
\end{aligned}
$$

What is the background of the tendency to round off the age?

Georg von Mayr, whose experience in demographic statistics has been stressed above, saw the source of age concentrations in a lack of knowledge of the person's age and in common negligence, which he defined as the two original sins of age statistics. In the opinion of the "old master", age concentrations could be used as a measure of the correctness of census data in general.

Interesting observations on this subject have been made by the American demographer T. Lynn Smith: "The existence and nature of these discrepancies are readily revealed by charting the reported ages according to single years... Elsworth Huntington has advanced the proposition that the extent of the discrepancies in the reported ages below 25 is the best measure of the *general intelligence of a population*".[34]

It should also be noted that according to A. Boyarsky and P. Shusherin, the dimensions of age heaping are also a reflection of the quality of the work of the census personnel.

The factors mentioned above: people's ignorance of their age, the negligent attitude to the population census, the need to simplify the ideas to fit lower intelligence and bad census-taking, all produce a distorted image of population composition by age.

The heaping effects are of different intensities in different countries. Long ago the American, English, Russian and Polish censuses were famous for age heaping. The American demographer Raymond Pearl refers to "age concentrations" in U.S.A. censuses at ages ending in 0 and 5.[35]

Besides, it has been stated that:

(1) age concentrations are greater in rural than in urban districts;

(2) they are greater among women than among men.

It would seem, then, that a measure is needed for measuring and quantitatively defining the degree of age concentration in various countries, in different parts of the same country and with different sections of the population.

Many such measures have been suggested.

One of them is a *coefficient of age heaping* described by Boyarsky and

Shusherin in the handbook of demographic statistics cited already. This coefficient is so constructed as to be 100 when ideal conditions exist, e.g. when there is no age concentration.

Just such an ideal coefficient of age heaping is obtained, according to the information of Boyarsky and Shusherin, in the European part of the Soviet Union for the population census of 1926, for the *literate* male urban population. For the total male population in the European part of the U.S.S.R., i.e. together with illiterates, a coefficient of 114 is obtained.

The greatest age heapings, as might be expected, come from rural women: the heaping coefficient for this group was 168. That such heapings may be even greater is indicated by the fact that in tsarist Russia in the census of 1897 there was a coefficient of 183, and in Bulgaria in one of the older censuses, even 245.[36]

In the U.S.A. the range is enormous: from a complete lack of age heaping in the states of Minnesota and North Dakota to an unusually large amount in Mississippi.

(d) Establishment of the Age of the Population in China

The establishment of age in China encounters serious difficulties.

The source of these difficulties is specifically described by S. Krotevich in his monograph on the Chinese population census of 1953.[37] We quote some of the information it contains.

According to custom, in China a child at birth is to be considered one year old. Moreover, age is counted, not from the day of birth of each individual, but for the whole population together according to calendar years. When the calendar year ends the age of all inhabitants increases by one year. This principle leads to an artificial overstatement of age. Imagine that a child is born on New Year's Eve. According to custom, the child is already one year old. The next day — with the beginning of a new year—the age of all inhabitants and thus of this infant, increases by one year. In this way an infant of one day may be treated as a two-year-old child.

These principles mean that the age in a "current" year is always greater than the real age, by either one or two years.

A further source of difficulty is the variety of calendars used.

There are two calendars in China: the "new style" (international calendar) and the "old style" (a lunar calendar). The lunar calendar denotes particular years by cyclic signs (e.g. a snake year, hare year, tiger year, horse year, bull year, etc.). These signs are well known to the Chinese and thus serve as a starting point for establishing the birth year of each individual. Also, these cyclic signs are often associated with the reigns of various Chinese Emperors. There was no uniform chronology in China. With a change of ruler the chronology was changed too; the years were counted again from the beginning. In the second half of the 19th century and in the first years of the 20th century, up to the revolution of 1911, there were four such periods in China. The first of these lasted 11 yr (1851–61) and was called the Hsien Fêng years (first Hsien-Fêng year, etc.). The second period lasted 13 yr (1862–74) and was called the Tung-Chih years. Then came two periods from 1875–1908 and from 1909–1911. Thus, if the person being counted could state the cyclic sign of the lunar year of his birth and could also state the name of the era, the census taker could define his birth date.

Krotevich believes that "although the establishing of the age under these conditions is very complicated, yet if the information includes the two or three features mentioned, the birth date can be stated relatively exactly".

(e) The Difficulty of Establishing Age in Underdeveloped Countries

It remains to discuss the difficulties encountered in establishing age in economically and culturally backward countries. Let us consider Algeria and Indonesia as examples.

In Algeria, according to Léon Tabah, the censuses still leave much to be desired, despite considerable progress. The inaccuracies mostly concern age. Moslems have difficulty determining their year of birth and those registered in vital statistics offices, which have existed since 1882, are no exception. This difficulty is particularly noticeable in rural districts.[38]

In Indonesia the last census was taken in 1930. There were then sixty million inhabitants. Today Indonesia has over eighty million (estimated in 1954 at 81,100,000).

The Dutch sociologist W. F. Wertheim states that in the 1920 census in Indonesia only young and mature people were distinguished. But the 1930 census showed an appreciable progress in age statistics, though this was limited to certain groups of inhabitants: Europeans, Chinese, Arabs and several groups of Christian Indonesians from the eastern part of the archipelago. But the figures for most of the natives were so unreliable that the authorities did not wish to publish them.

The result was that the division into children and adults was changed only insofar as the group of children was subdivided into (1) children not yet able to walk and (2) other children.[39]

These Indonesian problems are fairly typical for underdeveloped countries. Often the determination of population structure as to age and sex encounters great, often insurmountable, difficulties.

5. SOUNDINGS AND SURVEYS IN PLACE OF POPULATION CENSUSES

We do not know very much about the demographic structure of societies not recorded by censuses, and what we do know we owe to the painstaking efforts of scientists who, using investigations of special types called "soundings" and surveys try to fill in the gap in official statistical materials.

One such sounding was reported by the French demographer Henri Bunle at the International Congress on Population Research in 1931.

The object of the investigation was to find the demographic status in the territory of Togo (West Africa). It revealed the symptom characteristic of demographic primitivism—a lack of aged persons.

Let us quote the interesting observation reported by the researcher: "Le nombre des vieillards est minime. En dehors de la très forte mortalité infantile, le climat et l'insouciance causent le décès de beaucoup d'indigènes arrivés au seuil de la cinquantaine."[40]

Thus, only a few inhabitants of this country survive to old age: the beginning of the fiftieth year is for many natives the end of life.

It is not astonishing, then, that in the lists of natives of Togo which Bunle presented to the Congress, the age classification did not exceed 60 yr. Thus it appears that Togo is a country without aged persons.

We are using Togo only as an example. The conclusions we draw from the data gathered by Bunle will be general in character.

It appears that primitive societies are distinguished, first by an extremely large number of children and second by an extremely small number of the aged.

Further, we do not yet know exactly the demographic conditions of this type. The various surveys and "soundings" have proved insufficient to draw up the age pyramid of a primitive society.

It follows that our conception of a maximum proportion of children and minimum proportion of aged persons—conceptions based on the results of population censuses—are faulty. If we could make demographic studies of primitive societies it would be shown that the known maximum proportion of children is not an absolute maximum, and the minimum proportion of aged persons is not a true minimum.

In short, the lack of data about the age composition of primitive societies curtails our demographic knowledge.

In societies having a higher level of civilization but not an official statistical apparatus, the gap in statistical materials resulting from not taking censuses and not registering the natural population development is being filled—of course, only to some degree—by means of demographic surveys.

Iranian conditions may be cited as an example.

In Iran, with over twenty million inhabitants, censuses were unknown until recently. The only tool for studying demographic conditions was the unsatisfactory survey.

In recent years three such surveys have been made in Iran: the first in 1949, the second in 1950, and the third in 1954.

The survey of 1949 covered 117 villages in the central provinces of the country (Teheran and Damawand); the sample comprised one-tenth of the total number of villages in these two provinces. The heads of communities made the surveys.

The 1950 survey also covered rural areas—173 villages near Teheran—and every fifth farmhouse was included. The questions concerned the numbers of pregnancies and births, deaths of children within the last ten years, number of persons in the families classified by age and sex, etc.

The last survey, in 1954, covered the population of the city of Teheran. The sample was small and comprised not more than 0·3 per cent of the families inhabiting Teheran. The total population of the city was divided into 21 regions; from each region 10 districts, from each district 5 houses, and from each house one family was chosen by lot.

The French commentator stresses the great importance of such investigations in casting light on the sanitary and demographic conditions of territories untouched till now by statistical civilization: "Bien que fragmentaires, ces données sont précieuses par les lumières qu'elles apportent sur les conditions sanitaires et démographiques d'une région du Moyen-Orient encore dépourvue de statistique d'état civil."[41]

Surveys have made it possible to state the population composition of Iran by sex more or less exactly. However, it cannot be said that similar success has been achieved in the second task of the investigations—the statement of population composition by age. Of course, any investigation which divides the population into only two groups: persons below 15 yr of age and those over this age, must be considered a failure.

Two types of conclusions can be drawn from the above facts:

(1) despite its limited possibilities a survey is a useful means of procedure within regions still inaccessible to exact statistical analysis;

(2) a survey cannot overcome difficulties which result from a low cultural level of the population or from customs deeply rooted in the society; in these cases a survey cannot reflect the proper demographic status of the area under investigation.

We have discussed the typical shortcomings of age statistics.

The question arises to what degree these shortcomings affect the comparative analysis of population age compositions of various countries.

There is no doubt that a pyramid does not always accurately represent the age structure. One can state that there is a positive correlation between the degree of accuracy of the age statistics and the cultural level of the society.[42]

It follows that the most trustworthy statistical material we have at our disposal concerns countries of European culture and some other countries on an equally high level. Less accurate materials come from underdeveloped countries and, highly insufficient if at all available, from primitive countries.

This statement is essential since each of the mentioned groups of countries is distinguished by a different type of age structure: economically and culturally developed countries as a rule have an old population (in the demographic sense), while backward or less developed countries are characterized by demographic youth. Thus it will be relatively easy to describe demographic old age and relatively difficult to describe demographic youth.

Of course, the U.N. Statistical Office's reservations concerning the value of data about population age should be borne in mind: even the most modern population censuses do not guarantee the required accuracy of these data. There are some means of neutralizing—if not completely, then to a great extent—the described deficiencies in age statistics. This method, which will be fully employed, consists in joining the smaller age groups with the larger.

There remains still another difficulty: the diversity of age classification schemes in various countries does not allow the achievement of full comparability of data about the population age on an international scale.

To overcome these difficulties we shall have recourse to multiplication of statements containing data about the age structure. Thus, we will often have to estimate the conditions of the same period several times, by means of statements based on various principles of classification.

These methods should, of course, not be overestimated. The value of statistical materials depends mainly on their original state and not on their interpretation.

An English author put this well:

"Nobody knows with any exactness how many people there are at present in the world. One good reason for this vagueness is that several countries have no census; another, that the accuracy of some of the figures is highly suspect."[43]

It may be reasoned that the margin of error in census data pertaining to the population structure, and particularly the age structure, is incomparably greater. This conclusion should be a warning against drawing too quick inferences from figures that are not fully reliable.

REFERENCES

1. J. Beaujeu-Garnier, *Géographie de la Population*, p. 15.
2. L. Chodsky, *Osnowaniya teorii i techniki statistiki*, 2nd edition, St. Petersburg, 1907, p. 110.
3. L. Silberman, *Essential Statistical Concepts and Methods in Demography*. Supplement to the work: P. H. Landis, *Population Problems. A Cultural Interpretation*, American Book Company, New York, 1954, second edition prepared by Paul K. Hatt, pp. VIII–IX.
4. *Demographic Yearbook 1953*, United Nations, New York, 1953, p. 10.
5. W. F. Willcox, *Studies in American Demography*, Ithaca, New York, 1940, p. 24.
6. T. L. Smith, *Population Analysis*, 1st edition, New York–Toronto–London, 1948, pp. 120–121.
7. *Demographic Yearbook 1959*, United Nations, New York, 1959, p. 117.
8. *Ibid.*
9. *Ibid.*
10. *Statistical Yearbook 1959*, United Nations, New York, 1959, p. 117.
11. *Demographic Yearbook 1959*, p. 117. If persons omitted in the count and the population living in the jungle were included, the total number of inhabitants of Peru in 1940 would exceed 7 million, according to the same source (7,023,111).
12. B. Urlanis, *Rost naselenya w Europe*, 1941, p. 13.
13. *Allg. Stat. Arch.* 9. Jahrgang, 1915, p. 737.
14. *Statistical Yearbook 1959*, United Nations, New York, 1959, pp. 109–126.

15. R. PALME DUTT, *India Today.*
16. F. E. LINDER, "World demographic data", in a joint work: *The Study of Population, An Inventory and Appraisal,* edited by Philip M. Hauser and Otis Dudley Duncan, The University of Chicago Press, 1959, pp. 329–342.
17. *Population,* Paris, 1956, No. 1, p. 157.
18. A. J. COALE indicated in *J. Amer. Stat. Ass.* March, 1955 (*The Population of the United States in 1950, Classified by Sex, Age, and Color. A Revision of Census Figures*) some omissions and other shortcomings in the latest U.S.A. census and proposed corrections to the census data illustrating the distribution of the population by sex, age, and colour.
19. P. FLASKÄMPER, *Allgemeine Statistik. Grundriss der Statistik,* Teil I, 2. Aufl. Verlag von Richard Meiner, Hamburg 1953 p. 234. The author quotes this information after B. HILDEBRAND (*Die amtliche Bevölkerungsstatistik im alten Rom,* 1866).
20. A. BOYARSKY and P. SHUSHERIN, *Demograficheskaya statistika,* Moscow, 1951, p. 201.
21. *Wirtschaft und Statistik,* Berlin 1941, p. 19.
22. A. MEITZEN: *Geschichte, Theorie und Technik der Statistik,* Berlin, 1886, p. 42–43.
23. E. B. REUTER: *Population Problems,* Philadelphia etc. 1923, p. 32.
24. G. MACKENROTH, *Bevölkerungslehre. Theorie, Soziologie und Statistik der Bevölkerung,* p. 16.
25. The U.N. demographer draws attention to the variety of conditions in time and space existing in this field: "It is necessary to point out that the quality of census data on age varies from one country to another and from one census to another" (*The Aging of Populations and its Economic and Social Implications,* United Nations, New York, 1956, p. 7). The correctness of this observation will be confirmed in our further considerations.
26. A. MOREAU DE JONNÈS, *Éléments de Statistique,* édition deuxième. Paris, 1856, p. 69.
27. G. MORTARA: "The development and structure of Brazil's population,"*Population Studies,* London, 1954, No. 2, p. 125.
28. O. L. de ARRUDA GOMES, Quelques considérations sur la précision des recensements démographiques du Brésil (*A Report to the World Population Congress in Rome,* 1954).
29. T. L. SMITH, *Population Analysis,* p. 109.
30. O. ANDERSON, "Statistik über Langlebigkeit" Abdruck aus *Allg. Stat. Arch.* 30. Band, Gustav Fischer, Jena, 1942, p. 42.
31. K. FREUDENBERG, "Die Sterblichkeit in hohen Lebensaltern", *Schweiz. Z. Volkswirtsch. u. Stat.* 91. Jahrgang, No. 4, Dezember 1955.
32. *The Aging of Populations and its Economic and Social Implications,* United Nations, New York, p. 7.
33. H. WESTERGAARD und H. C. NYBOLLE, *Grundzüge der Theorie der Statistik,* Zweite Auflage, Gustav Fischer, Jena, 1928, p. 83.
34. T. L. SMITH, *Population Analysis,* p. 89.
35. R. PEARL, *Introduction to Medical Biometry and Statistics,* 3rd edition, Philadelphia and London, 1941, p. 45.
36. A. BOYARSKY, *Kurs demograficheskoy statistiki,* p. 117. The date of the Bulgarian census is not stated in the source.
37. S. KROTEVICH, Wsekitaiskaia perepis naseleniya, *Viestnik Statistiki,* Moscow, 1955, No. 5, p. 31 ff.

38. L. Tabah, "La population algérienne. Croissance, niveau de vie, investissements", *Population*, Paris, 1956, No. 3, p. 431.
39. W. F. Wertheim, "La population de l'Indonésie et le test des 40%", *Population*, Paris, 1954, No. 4, p. 656.
40. H. Bunle, "Note sur la démographie de la population indigène au Togo". *Actes du Congrès International des Études sur la Population* édités par le Prof. Corrado Gini, Vol. 6, Rome 1934, p. 252.
41. *Population*, Paris, 1954 No. 2.
42. The U.N. demographer speaks about a parallelism between the degree of accuracy of census data and the level of the economic development of the country: "On the whole the economically developed countries produce better statistics than the less developed ones. The process of economic development is usually parallel to the improvement in the reliability of statistics" (*The Aging of Populations and Its Economic and Social Implications*, United Nations, New York, 1956, p. 7) Between this and our interpretation of the case there is, of course, no discrepancy. We differ only in the point of view.
43. W. J. Thorne, *Your Future is Now*, Eyre and Spottiswoode, London, 1956, p. 16.

Part II

OLD AGE AND THE FREQUENCY OF
SURVIVING TO THIS AGE

CHAPTER 5

The Beginning of Old Age

1. INTRODUCTION

Any researcher who deals with old age, as we do in this study, faces the question at what age this period of life should be considered to begin.

This question has been asked in all epochs of man's development, from early antiquity to present times, and all the solutions proposed have proved problematic and delusive.

A whole chain of reasons condemns to failure all attempts at precise definition of when old age begins. One of them is of fundamental importance: age does not appear from one day to the next. On the contrary, it is the result of a long process within the human organism and thus it is not possible to fix the exact beginning of old age. Moreover, the process of aging proceeds differently in different groups and individuals; with some people it begins earlier, with others later, and this makes it impossible to set a general limit separating old age from middle age.[1]

Yet some, though purely conventional limits must be set for the various periods of life. Without this we would have to forego measuring changes in the population composition by age. There could then be no discussion about the process of population aging.

What is more, we must accept the fiction that some definite limit of old age is universally applicable. This will enable us to make comparisons both in time and in space.

Such is the standpoint of the International Labour Bureau investigating labour resources, giving special consideration to the economically active population. In the journal of this institution, *Revue internationale du Travail*, we read: "Étant donné les conditions très variées qui règnent dans différentes parties du monde, il est... difficile de spécifier un âge commun au-delà duquel on est en droit d'affirmer que la vieillesse commence réellement. Cependant, pour faire des comparaisons entre différents pays, il est utile de mesurer le niveau

d'activité des personnes âgées par rapport à un âge de référence identique pour tous les pays."[2]

Thus, our next task will be to determine a conventional lower limit of old age, which will make it possible to classify the available statistical material. Let us investigate different age classifications and find the lower limits of old age put forward by competent researchers: philosophers, natural scientists, physicians, demographers, and statisticians.

2. THE ANCIENT CHINESE CLASSIFICATION

The ancient culture of the East has given us an interesting and original relic in the age classification arranged by Chinese scholars. They divided the cycle of human life into the following phases:

(1) youth . . . . up to 20 yr
(2) the age for contracting marriage . . up to 30 yr
(3) the age for performing public duties up to 40 yr
(4) learning one's faults . . . . . . up to 50 yr
(5) the final period of creative life . . up to 60 yr
(6) the longed-for age . . . . up to 70 yr
(7) old age . . . . from 70 yr

Attention should be called to the last two age classes: the sixth and seventh. The first of them is the age beautifully defined by the Chinese as the longed-for age. One longs for anything rare, not easily attained. From the classification it may be inferred that in ancient China to survive to 60 was rare. Such is, in our opinion, the logic of the term "longed-for" connected with the age of 60–70 yr.

An age rarely achieved is something other than this "old age." The fact that the age of 60–70 yr was unattainable for most Chinese does not mean that it should be called old age. The gleaning of death may be enormous even at earlier phases of the life cycle, first in childhood and then in the beginnings of old age. Thus the issue was put by Chinese scholars: even though only a small part of the population survived to the "longed-for age," old age began only with 70 yr.

3. THE CLASSIFICATION OF PYTHAGORAS

Of very ancient date, though not so old as the Chinese, is the age classification as proposed by Pythagoras: it originates from the 6th century B.C.

The Greek thinker sought analogy between the course of human life and the sequence of the seasons: as after spring follows summer, after summer, autumn, and after autumn, winter, so in the life of man

there follow one another: childhood, youth, maturity, and old age. Pythagoras assigned to these periods equal lengths: each period lasted 20 yr.

The nomenclature of the particular life periods is of interest:

        (1) the period of becoming an adult . .   0–20 yr
        (2) youth . . . . 20–40 yr
        (3) full adulthood . . . . 40–60 yr
        (4) old age and retirement . . . . . 60–80 yr

It follows from the above that, according to Pythagoras, the beginning of old age, the period of dwindling vital force, is 60 yr.

Pythagoras's age list does not exceed 80 yr. On this subject, C. W. Hufeland, the inventor of macrobiotics, which preceded modern gerontology, remarks: "...nach dieser Zeit rechne er niemand mehr unter die Lebendigen, er möge auch so lange leben, als er wolle."[3]

We do not consider this remark correct. The closing of the biometric account at a definite step of the age ladder does not in any way mean that older persons are not counted among the living.

We suppose that the Greek thinker deemed it right to close his account at the normal limits of human life, and this, no doubt, did not exceed 80 yr.

4. THE CLASSIFICATION OF HIPPOCRATES

The division of human life into periods was also a subject of interest to the famous physician Hippocrates (460–377 or 359 B.C.). He combined medical and philosophical knowledge. He set store by this association as his saying shows: the physician and the philosopher are equal in the eyes of the gods.

Proceeding from the old knowledge about the climacteric years ("anni climacterici", "anni cyclici") Hippocrates divided human life into ten periods of seven years each.[4] This classification can easily be reproduced:

        first period . . . .   0–7 yr
        second period. . . . .   7–14 yr
        third period . . . . 14–21 yr
        fourth period . . . . 21–28 yr
        fifth period . . . . 28–35 yr
        sixth period . . . . 35–42 yr
        seventh period . . . . 42–49 yr
        eigth period . . . . 49–56 yr
        ninth period . . . . 56–63 yr
        tenth period . . . . 63–70 yr

In comparison with the Pythagoras's division, Hippocrates's classification shows two differences:

(1) it operates with a greater number of age classes;

(2) it terminates the account at 70 yr, while with Pythagoras it is extended to 80 yr.

The second fact indicates that Hippocrates had a less optimistic view of the normal length of human life. This interpretation is borne out by his statement: "Ars longa, vita brevis". As a physician Hippocrates probably had a better basis than most to estimate properly the normal period of human life.

From this classification it is not clear what age Hippocrates assumed as the beginning of old age: it need not be 63. From the literature dealing with this problem it may be inferred that the adherents of the seven-year cycle theory connected the beginning of old age with the ninth cycle. We should then be near the truth to state that Hippocrates and many adherents of the seven-year cycles considered old age to begin between 56 and 63 yr, in other words at about 60 years of age.

5. THE CLASSIFICATION OF FLOURENS

Let us pass over to modern times.

It might seem that in the epoch of better-founded natural science, views about the natural periods of human life would become more uniform, at least among natural scientists. Reality does not confirm this conjecture. Not only on an international scale but also within one country, there are considerable discrepancies in the views of physiologists on this problem. The example of France will undoubtedly be convincing.

In the 19th century French physiologists used to apply a classification dividing human life into four periods:

(1) l'enfance—childhood, which for boys ends at 14 or 15 yr, for girls at 11;

(2) l'adolescence—adolescence, ending for men at 23 or 25 yr, for women at 19 or 20;

(3) l'âge adulte—adulthood, which for both sexes ends with 55 or 60 yr;

(4) la vieillesse—old age, beginning at 55 or 60 yr.

Another classification was applied by M. J. P. Flourens (1794–1867), one of the eminent French physiologists of the 19th century. It is:

(1) first period of childhood	. . . . .	0–9 yr
(2) second period of childhood	. . .	10–19 yr
(3) first youth	. . . .	20–29 yr
(4) second youth	. . . .	30–39 yr
(5) first period of maturity	. . . . .	40–54 yr
(6) second period of maturity	. . . .	55–69 yr
(7) first period of old age	. . . . . .	70–85 yr
(8) second period of old age	. . . .	after 85 yr

We see, then, that the 19th century French physiologists did not quite agree as to the age from which old age should be counted: some of them referred it to 60 yr, others to 55. But all were surpassed by the extremely optimistic theory of Flourens who shifted the beginning of old age to 70 yr.

We understand that Flourens's concept may arouse some doubts. Should old age really begin only at 70? As we read in the *Anatomy of Man* of Adam Bochenek, "between 60 and 70 years of age the hair becomes white, the face wrinkled, the nose protruding, fat fades away or decays irregularly, eyes fall in somewhat, the skin tension decreases...". Are these signs of old age not sufficient?

Involuntarily a suggestion arises that the French physiologist expressed a subjective, exaggeratedly optimistic appreciation of old age which is not corroborated by the less hopeful reality. The sober Max Rubner strengthens us in this suspicion.

In the classification of Flourens there appears a new concept of dividing old age into two periods. It may be assumed that the need to divide old age into an early and into a more advanced part has been imposed on Flourens by the new and previously unknown lengthening of the active life span. Indeed, early old age is in many cases a synonym for active old age.

6. THE CLASSIFICATION OF RUBNER

We shall now deal with the already mentioned, less optimistic classification of Rubner. Max Rubner (1854–1932), a physiologist by training, became famous in the history of German medicine as one of the foremost specialists in social hygiene, particularly nutritional hygiene.

The classification of Rubner is the following:

(1) infancy—up to 7–9 months;	(5) maturity—up to 41–50 yr;
(2) early childhood—up to 7 yr;	(6) old age—from 50 yr;
(3) later childhood—up to 13–14 yr;	(7) senility—from 70 yr.
(4) adolescence—up to 19–21 yr;	

According to Rubner old age begins at 50 yr. This is the lowest limit of old age met thus far. Rubner advarces the beginning of senility by 15 yr as compared with Flourens and of old age in general, by 20 yr.

In our view Rubner's thesis should be conceived as a regression in the appraisal of the vital forces of man. As the beginning of the old age he assumed an age in which retroactive changes in the organism become effective (in the French terminology: "l'âge de décroissement") and, in fact, these changes outweigh the progressive changes at about 50 yr.

7. THE CLASSIFICATION OF ASCHOFF

The prominent anatomic pathologist, the creator of modern functional pathology, Ludwig Aschoff (1866–1942) divides human life into the following periods:

(1) the period of foetus development in the mother's womb;
(2) the class of the new-born child—up to 7 days of life;
(3) the period of infancy—up to 7 months of life;
(4) the period of childhood—up to 7 yr;
(5) adolescence—up to 14 yr;
(6) the years of ripening—up to 25 yr;
(7) maturity—up to 45 yr;
(8) the beginning old age—up to 65 yr;
(9) old age—up to 85 yr;
(10) beyond this age—senility.

In two points Aschoff differs fundamentally from the authors of the classifications already stated: firstly—he does not omit, as others do, the foetus period; secondly—he does not mark the beginning of old age by a specific year of life, but by a broad interval of age comprising a 20 yr period from 45–65 yr.

We understand Aschoff's concept concerning old age and senility as a thesis that the first symptoms of approaching old age occur about 45 yr; henceforth the process of the aging of the organism proceeds continuously and after 20 yr approaches its end; thus, beginning with 65 yr of life we can speak about old age as an accomplished fact.

8. THE CLASSIFICATION OF ENGLISH PHYSIOLOGISTS

Contemporary English physiology classifies human life into the following periods:

(1) the period of infancy ending with 7 yr;
(2) the period of childhood lasting until 14 yr;
(3) the period of youth ending with 21 yr;
(4) the period of adult life ending with 50 yr;
(5) the period of old age, beginning with 50 yr.

As we see, Rubner is not isolated in his view that old age should be counted from 50 yr; the English physiologists agree.

9. THE CLASSIFICATION OF GERMAN ANTHROPOLOGISTS

In matters concerning the aging of man, anthropology adds a useful contribution and, therefore, the classifications it employs are of great interest to us.

We quote below the classification proposed by Ilse Schwidetzky and derived from an important German textbook on anthropology (R. Martin: *Lehrbuch der Anthropologie*, 3 volumes, second edition, Jena 1928):

first group: infancy: up to 7 yr;
second group: children: from 7–14 yr;
third group: young people from 14–20 yr;
fourth group: adults: from 20–40 yr;
fifth group: mature people: from 40–60 yr;
sixth group: senile people: over 60 yr.

It is worth while noting that this age classification is in some details similar to the classifications already discussed but differs in other aspects.

An essential feature is that in the classification of German anthropologists old age is counted from 60 yr. This beginning of old age is the one introduced by Pythagoras.

10. THE CLASSIFICATION OF BOCHENEK

Polish science contributed the classification given below, elaborated by the Cracow anatomist Adam Bochenek (1875–1913). He states that the exact delineation of age periods is not feasible "on account of the great individual, racial, and constitutional variability."[5]

Bochenek's classification is as follows:

(a) childhood (infantia): from birth to the beginning of sexual maturity, i.e. for boys–up to 16 yr, for girls-up to 14 yr. This is subdivided into two periods:

(1) infancy (infantia I): from birth to 6–9 months;
(2) early childhood (infantia II): from 6–7 yr;
(3) late childhood (infantia III): up to 14 or 16 yr;

(b) adolescence (juvenilitas): the period of full sexual maturity and further growing: for men from 16–25 yr, for women from 14–20 yr.

(c) period of vitality: for men from 25–55 yr, for women from 20–40 yr. Within these years may be distinguished: adulthood (virilitas) and maturity (maturitas).

(d) old age (senium):

1st degree of aging:	. . . . . 60–70 yr
2nd degree of aging:	. . . . . 70–80 yr
3rd degree of aging:	. . . . . 80–90 yr

The author points out that the above chronology of three degrees of aging is based on European material, especially applicable to groups living in civilized conditions, not to primitive man for whom these periods occur 10–20 yr earlier. Nor can these periods be applied to prehistoric man for whom aging probably appeared much earlier.

Bochenek's classification does not precisely state the limit between maturity and adulthood and omits the years 55–60 for men and 40–60 for women.

The observations and explanations given by Bochenek as to the particular periods are remarkable. Let us summarize some of them which concern old age:

(a) adulthood lasts to the beginning of the first faint symptoms of aging (beginning with the atrophy of particular parts of the sutures of the skull) and this limit may differ by 10 yr for different people;

(b) maturity begins with the first faint signs of aging and lasts for women until the end of fertility and in both sexes to the appearing of real senile changes (loss of hair, strong wear and falling out of teeth, advanced sclerosis of skull sutures);

(c) the last period of life—old age—is characterized by increasing regressive changes;

(d) proper old age appears at about 70 yr: however, in the second degree of old age (70–80 yr), when the elasticity of the tissues has been wholly lost, there often remains an amazing elasticity and vigour of mind.

11. VIEWS OF SOVIET GERONTOLOGISTS

The eminent Soviet gerontologist, Professor Z. Frenkel of Leningrad, quotes a number of known age classifications (among others a classification by Chinese scholars and by Rubner) and on the basis of the material analysed concludes that fairly generally the age of 60 is recognized as the beginning of old age. He writes: "Most nations, in various periods of history, have employed 60 as the beginning of old age."[6]

In the same work, four or five pages later, the rather unexpected statement is made that for hundreds and thousands of years the age of 70 has been recognized by various nations as the beginning of old age.

"We see how, over hundreds and thousands of years, in various countries, the age cycle of human life constantly repeats. During hundreds and thousands of years for the nations of various countries and epochs, old age has meant an age of 70 and over."[7] One of these ages must be a misprint. According to the classifications cited by Frenkel the age of 70 years as the beginning of old age should be correct.

Like Frenkel, another Soviet gerontologist, A. Nagorny, quotes various age classifications, providing them with a general remark that all classifications are largely conventional. Nagorny gives up the attempt to state a more exact beginning of old age and assumes that old age begins between 60 and 70 yr.[8]

12. SUMMARY

Let us sum up the views related above insofar as they concern the beginning of old age.

This task will be facilitated by the following table:

BEGINNING OF OLD AGE IN THE LIGHT OF VIEWS
EXPRESSED BY VARIOUS AUTHORS

Author	Period	Beginning of old age
Pythagoras	ancient times	60
Hippocrates	ancient times	56–63
Chinese scholars	ancient times	70
Flourens	1794–1867	70
Other French physiologists	19th century	55–60
Rubner	1854–1932	50
Aschoff	1866–1942	45–65
English physiologists	20th century	50
German anthropologists	20th century	60
Bochenek	1875–1915	60–70
Frenkel	20th century	70
Nagorny	20th century	60–70

This comparison by no means confirms Frenkel's view that age classifications invariably show the same age as the beginning of old age. Quite the contrary: the classifications we have encountered represent an unusual mosaic as to the values separating various periods of human life. A particularly large span is offered in estimates of the beginning of old age: from 45 yr as a minimum to 70 as a maximum.

It is not our task to provide an explanation for such a large divergence of estimates among the representatives of the closely interrelated natural sciences (biology, physiology, gerontology). However, we wish to make several points which, in our view, do not permit us to expect identical classifications from various authors.

The following circumstances should be kept in mind:

(a) the aging of the organism is made apparent in the form of a whole chain of symptoms (called "Alterserscheinungen");

(b) these symptoms occur at different times, some of them earlier, others later;

(c) the time of their appearance and the rate of development of particular symptoms of aging vary with various individuals;

(d) the science of physiology still has no test to determine the overall degree of aging of the organism.

Thus it would be unrealistic to postulate uniformity of age classification. The step of the ladder at which old age begins depends on the author's conception, and this will be identical with various researches only by chance.

The problem of finding a general test to determine the degree of an organism's aging is of great interest to gerontologists, who are searching for an instrument to measure the physiological age, which is not always coincident with the calendar age.

The contemporary French gerontologists Léon Binet and François Bourlière write: "D'assez nombreux chercheurs ont essayé de déterminer l'âge physiologique d'un organisme entier par un test de sénescence unique. L'omniprésence de processus de sénescence au niveau de tous nos organes et de tous nos tissus rend théoriquement concevable une telle recherche, mais les résultats pratiques ont été jusqu'ici plutôt décevants".[9]

Thus, the idea is good but the results—so far—rather elusive.

Until sufficiently exact measures are found to enable an overall estimate of the degree of aging of an organism and until statistical mass investigations can be made by such measures, the beginning of old age cannot be determined. Until then the beginning of old age will still be stated as a subjective estimate by those making classifications.

Moreover, we shall have to treat the divergent opinions we have already learned as equally valid. At the present stage of gerontological knowledge there is no adequate reason for accepting some estimates as superior to others.

13. THE CLASSIFICATION OF FARR

Now let us see what physician-statisticians have to say—those who represent both the natural and the statistical–demographic sciences.

In selecting age classifications based on the medical–statistical knowledge to be presented, we had no doubt that the work of William Farr (1807–83) should be discussed. This pioneer of English demography, a doctor and statistician, distinguished the following age classes:

0–20 Infant age; the school, the apprentice ages, age of growth, of learning;

20–40 The age when growth is complete; the athletic age, the reproductive age, the soldier's age; the beautiful age;

40–60 The intellectual age, the age of masters; the legislative, the judicial age;

60–80 The Laureate age;

80–100.

It is interesting that the classification of this 19th century English demographer agrees with the Greek thinker of the 6th century B.C. Pythagoras.

But Farr gives original definitions to the various age groups. In these definitions the distinguished mind of the English demographer is reflected.

In Farr's classification the sixtieth year of age plays a significant role. It is a kind of landmark separating the period of high intellectual activity from the period where the man—as Farr so beautifully puts it—rests on the laurels of his previous activities. Thus Farr assumes the beginning of old age to be 60 yr. The last age class comprises the years from 80–100 and is the period of senility.

14. THE CLASSIFICATION OF AMERICAN PHYSICIANS

There is another age classification based on medical–statistical knowledge. It is the classification proposed in 1939 by the section of demographic statistics of the American Public Health Association. This classification is as follows:

(1) infancy: up to 1 yr;

(2) pre-school period: from 1–4 yr;

(3) school–years: from 5–14 yr;

(4) adolescence: from 15–24 yr;

(5) years of greatest activity: from 25–44 yr;

(6) middle age: from 45–64 yr;

(7) early period of old age: 65–74 yr;

(8) old age: from 75 yr.

The above classification is undoubtedly characteristic of modern occupational conditions in countries economically highly developed.

In his interesting work about longevity and active old age Frenkel points out that this very recent classification of American physicians shifts the end of adolescence and the beginning of old age five years as compared with the oldest Chinese classifications: the end of adolescence from 20 to 25, and the beginning of old age from 70 to 75.

For five thousand years, the interval dividing these age classifications, the change is not very great. The Soviet scientist perceives herein the confirmation of the thesis that the biological features of mankind are relatively stable. Among such relatively stable features Frenkel includes the maximum life expectancy, the limits of basic age groups, the age at which growth ceases, the age of reaching sexual maturity, old age, the normal end of human life.

For our part we add that here we have to do more with a hypothesis than a scientifically proven thesis and that age classifications of various epochs, despite the many values they represent, cannot support the thesis of the invariability of biological features over thousands of years.

It should not be overlooked that age classifications are more a product of definite conceptions than a reflection of existing reality.

15. CLASSIFICATIONS USED IN STATISTICAL PRACTICE AND THEIR VARIANTS

There remains a third and last group of classification schemes showing population composition by age; these are schemes used in practice by demographers and statisticians:

DIFFERENT VARIANTS OF AGE CLASSIFICATION
USED IN DEMOGRAPHIC STATISTICS

Variant	Children and adolescents	Productive age	Aged persons
A	0–14	15–49	50+
B	0–19	20–49	50+
C	0–14	15–59	60+
D	0–19	20–59	60+
E	0–14	15–64	65+
F	0–19	20–64	65+
G	0–14	15–69	70+

Here we also find a great variety of accepted solutions. At once we can demonstrate seven different classifications of age, used more

7*

and less frequently, each with its own limits of three main age groups, i.e.: (1) children and adolescents, (2) productive population, (3) aged persons. And yet the variants so far stated are far from exhausting all the solutions found. The differences occurring are self-evident. These differences result from the fact that in some the population is divided according to biological criteria and in the others, economic. In classifications of the economic type the upper limit of the middle-age group is shifted upward by 10 or even 15 yr as compared with biological classifications.

Differences also occur in the frame of age classifications we have termed economic. This is usually connected with variety in the legal retirement age, which is usually 60 or 65.

It should be added that even within one country the retirement age is not constant. It depends on the economic situation of the country. Margaret Grant Schneider mentions the pressure exerted by the Great Crisis in all capitalistic countries from 1929–33. "Recent periods of great unemployment have fostered the theory that older workers should be forced to retire from paid employement to make room for younger unemployed workers. Demands have followed in several countries to lower the pensionable age (usually from 65 to 60 yr) and thus to force or induce more old persons to make way for the young."[10] This helps explain the diversity of age classifications used in the statistical practice of various countries at various times.

16. CONCLUSIONS

We have gathered sufficiently rich material to form some picture of the various past and present views of biologists, physiologists, gerontologists, demographers and statisticians on the cycle of human life.

However, before we proceed to sum up these views and draw practical conclusions which are necessary to our work we want to stress one feature common to all the age classifications discussed above—their *arbitrariness*. Why the age classification must be arbitrary was explained at the beginning of this chapter and there is no need to repeat it. If, however, we have to draw conclusions from the material gathered we have to envisage the essential character of the available sources. Thus for want of objective criteria we cannot distinguish "good" and "bad" classifications. On the other hand, we must arbitrarily select some age classifications as good. The available material helps us.

It may generally be observed that while the naturalists connect the beginning of old age with 60 yr, demographers and economic statisticians give another in addition—65. We well know that the shifting upward of the limit of old age is to bring the age classification into harmony with existing occupational conditions.

Should we then assume a double notion of old age: the *biological* and the *economic* senses? Each would have a different arbitrary beginning: the first 60 yr; the second 65 yr.

Of course, this is a purely working proposition which would allow demographic and occupational conditions in various countries to be compared. Not only is it useful due to the divergence of views by naturalists and economists but it is also supported by the above quoted opinion of the American demographer Walter Willcox, who agrees that 60 yr might be assumed as the beginning of old age, but objects to identifying it with the beginning of the unproductive age.

These considerations lead us to the conclusion that when analysing biological effects, priority should be given to variants C and D which assume 60 as the beginning of old age while, in the analysis of occupational conditions, variants E and F which fix the beginning of old age at 65 should be preferred.

Such a *modus procedendi* is, by the way, known in demographic literature. Apparently some such reasoning suggested similar solutions to other researchers.

Of course, it should be remembered that our conclusions are purely theoretical; their practical use can only be ascertained when commonly accepted. Until then we must base our considerations on the classifications generally used. It happens that internationally those age classifications are most used which we consider most suitable to our assumptions. This settles the matter: in our further discussions, which will not deal with method but with merit, we shall consider the beginning of old age to be 60 or 65.

REFERENCES

1. The author of an English paper about the retirement problem, Carlton Wallace, calls attention to the great spread in the beginning of old age as measured individually: "If the answer to that last question is *yes* there are some who might well be considered as old at 29, and others who are still young (in the sense of not being old) at 80 and 90" (*How to Retire Successfully*, Evans Brothers Ltd., London, 1956, p. 50).
2. La population active dans le monde. Aspects démographiques, *Revue internationale du Travail*, Vol. 73, No. 2, February 1956, p. 187.

3. C. W. HUFELAND, *Makrobiotik oder die Kunst, das menschliche Leben zu verlängern*, 4th edition, p. 76.

4. The authorship of this classification is ascribed by some scholars to the Athenian legislator Solon, who lived in the 6th century B. C. Among the adherents of the 7-yr cycles was the Latin writer Macrobius of the 5th century B.C.

5. A. BOCHENEK, *Anatomia człowieka* (Anatomy of Man) Vol. I, 5th edition, edited and completed by Michal Reicher, Warsaw 1952, pp. 155–60.

6. Z. FRENKEL, *Udlinienie zhizni i aktivnaia starost'* (*The Extension of Life and Active Old Age*), Leningrad, 1945, p. 132.

7. *Ibid.*, pp. 136–7.

8. A. NAGORNY: *Starenie i prodlenie zhizni* (*Aging and the Extension of Life*), Moscow, 1950.

9. L. BINET and F. BOURLIÈRE, "Problèmes biologiques généraux posés par la sénescence de l'organisme." (Joint work.) *Précis de Gérontologie*, Paris, 1955, p. 18.

10. M. G. SCHNEIDER, *More Security for Old Age. A Report and a Program*, New York, Twentieth Century Fund, Inc., 1937, pp. 13–14.

CHAPTER 6

The Historical Development of the Number of Persons surviving to Old Age

1. INTRODUCTION

From the previous considerations it will appear that one of the most important factors determining the demographic character of a society is the proportion of those who have reached old age; this number decides demographic "youth" or "old age". If so, sources of numerical data giving information about survival to old age must be of interest to us.

A fundamental and irreplaceable tool for investigating this effect, and at the same time a source of information about the number of persons surviving to old age, are life tables. From the column of l_x, illustrating the order of dying in a generation, we learn what portion of the new-born infants survive to an agreed-upon old age (60 or 65).

Life tables are today in common use and owing to them we can, without great difficulty, describe the actual state of survival to old age. However, if we were to go back some hundred years to reconstruct the order of dying in those times we would meet great difficulties on account of the lack of appropriate statistical material. The few tables which have been preserved are fairly unreliable, if only with regard to the faulty methods used to construct them.

The use of life tables does not come into play at all as regards early historical and still more as regards prehistoric times. For those distant epochs of mankind, other, non-statistical sources of information about the order of mortality must be consulted. These sources may be found in some ancient writings and archeological excavations.

Using accessible sources, we shall try to explore the evolution of the number of persons surviving to old age during the course of mankind's history.

2. PREHISTORIC AND EARLY HISTORICAL TIMES

Despite the difficulties connected with the reconstruction of the demographic conditions prevailing at the dawn of mankind, the complete uncertainty about these conditions in places, one fact seems to be certain: during the early steps of mankind's progress in civilization the number of aged people in society was insignificant. It seems safe to say that in primitive societies there were no aged persons at all.

How could it be otherwise when aged persons were condemned to death, not only on account of their senility but also by a custom often included in religious rites which directly ordered the extermination of old people. There is no doubt that this custom had an economic basis, resulting from the difficulty in nourishing a greater number of people. What was stated by the well-known Polish anthropologist, outstanding sociologist and statistician, Ludwik Krzywicki should be recalled.

Referring to the researches of Lippert on the cultural development of mankind, this scientist illustrated the social consequences of the discovery of fire. They were numerous, as follows:

(1) the necessity of uninterrupted maintainance of fire led to the first social division of labour between the sexes whereby the man had to secure the game, and the woman, consistent with her physiology, to watch the fire;

(2) the ability to cook food helped reduce the extent of infanticide previously widely exercised.

However, of particular interest to us is the effect mentioned in the next point, since there is a question of the influence of the discovery of fire upon the fate of aged persons. Here Krzywicki states: "A mature man, knowing his environment and having the experience of many years, was the object of respect in the primitive tribe. He knew where and when crops grew, how to catch fish, how to hunt game, etc. Thus, owing to his knowledge he was the first social link. But when he grew old his forces slackened and the memory of service and his stock of knowledge became useless. The sick old man was abandoned by his community". And thus:

(3) after the fundamental revolution caused by the discovery of fire, the situation of the aged changed rapidly. In Krzywicki's words: "with the discovery of fire the aged person found protection in it; he still had the strength to help women watch the fire".[1]

For the history of social relations, for historical demography, these considerations are of primary value. Here we have to do with the first, clearly distinguishable demographic consequences of the progress of civilization. One was the increase in the number of children, the second, the increase in the number of aged persons in a society. Of particular significance is the second consequence since it denotes the dawn of a new epoch characterized by the usefulness and, consequently, the toleration of the existence of old people.

Until now we have been dealing with suppositions without evidence. The question arises whether any evidence exists at all. Does science provide any numerical data that could throw some light into the darkness of the demographic beginnings of mankind?

Owing to recent researches, mainly archaeological, we can give many details on the topic of interest to us. We can even attempt to establish the course of development of the number of the aged in the earliest progress of mankind. Let us now proceed to examine these data. The work of Ilse Schwidetzky serves as a fundamental source of information about the order of mortality in prehistoric and early historical times, being a study in the scope of the "historical biology of population".

We learn from this work that anthropologists can determine approximately the age at death from excavated human skulls. This estimate is based, firstly on the teeth, and secondly on the skull seams.

For our work, of course, information about the number of aged persons among our prehistoric ancestors would be desirable and valuable. We learn from Ilse Schwidetzky's work that:

(1) among 20 known early palaeolithic men (Neanderthal men), as well as among 102 later palaeolithic men, not a single one has been found who was over 60 at the time of death;

(2) among 65 mesolithic men only one over 60 has been found;

(3) in the Silesian neolithic era, in the Austrian brass era and in the Swedish iron era, old people constituted 10 per cent of the total number of deceased;

(4) a higher proportion (the author does not state how high) of old people was found in the period after the migration of nations; this is demonstrated by the results of research on serial Franconian tombs.[2]

If the above data were considered sufficient for generalizations concerning the share of aged persons in the number of deceased, such an assumption naturally being subject to reservations, then the following apparently logical inferences, could be drawn:

(a) at the beginning of mankind's history the examples of survival to old age were extremely rare (by old age we mean an arbitrarily assumed age of over 60);

(b) along with the evolution of civilization the number of such cases grows more frequent.

These conclusions seem to point to the existence of a very close causal connection between the frequency of survival to old age and the level of civilization. Ilse Schwidetzky has no doubts on this. These are her remarks on the problem: "Es gibt... eine Abhängigkeit der Sterblichkeit von der Zivilisationshöhe... Die geringere Lebensgefährdung zivilisierter Völker kann sich dabei in der Senkung der Säuglings-und Kindersterblichkeit wie in einer Verlängerung der Lebensdauer, also in der Zunahme der höheren Altersklassen, auswirken. Insbesondere für die letztere haben wir aus frühgeschichtlicher Zeit zwar nicht statistisch umfangreiche, aber eindeutige Belege."[3]

This statement may be summarized thus: with the progress of civilization the danger to human life decreases and, consequently, life expectancy increases.

The same conclusions have been reached by other anthropologists and particularly by the Frenchman Henri V. Vallois who, at the Second Palaeontological Congress, spoke about the life expectancy of prehistoric man, and the German Hans Weinert, author of *Menschen der Vorzeit*, published in 1930.

It follows from the information given by the French anthropologist that among 187 tested skeletons, partly of Neanderthal men, mainly representatives of the stone age, only in three cases can survival to 50 yr be assumed. "Longevity," states Vallois "as we know it today, is a later phenomenon, possible only in the conditions of our civilization. Owing to it, only present-day man has achieved such a great age. There was no place in prehistoric society for people with inferior vitality."[4]

Weinert takes the same view: "We have not a single skull which could be recognized as senile... Senile bone remnants do not preserve too well; however, we can assume that among Neanderthal men old people were rarely encountered."[5]

Similar conclusions may be drawn from a comparative analysis of the numbers denoting the average age at death; the higher the form the higher is the average age of the deceased.

Extremely interesting researches in this field have been conducted by J. L. Angel, writer of "The Length of Life in Ancient Greece" (*J. Gerontol.*, 2, 1947).

Using archaeological discoveries, namely preserved human skulls, Angel determined the average age at death achieved by Greeks in various historical epochs. In the light of these data the average age of deceased Greeks was as follows:

AVERAGE AGE OF GREEKS AT THE TIME OF DEATH IN ANCIENT TIMES

Epoch	Average age at death
Neolithic—early bronze age	31·8
Roman times	38·5

Source: Researches of J. L. ANGEL (see SCHWIDETZKY: Das Problem des Völkertodes, Stuttgart, 1954, pp. 90–91).

The progress is quite evident: from the neolithic early bronze epoch to Roman times the average age of the deceased increases in Greece by 6·7 yr. There is no doubt that this increase accompanied the general progress in civilization, in which the Greeks participated to a large extent. It is also unquestionable that there is here not only a parallelism but also a causal relation between the two phenomena: the increase in the average age of Greeks was conditioned by the progress of civilization in ancient Greece.

It would be interesting to ascertain what kinds of relations play a role here. An attempt to answer this question was made by a demographer of the Metropolitan Life Insurance Company, who with reference to Angel's work states: "The increasing average age at death, as indicated in this survey, may well be related to advances in living conditions and in nutrition which are indicated by clues in archeological findings. In addition, the emergence of medical science undoubtedly contributed to the advance in longevity over that of prehistoric times."[6]

Ludwik Krzywicki found the cause of the increase in life expectancy in the relaxation of the custom of eliminating the aged unproductive people. Does this view contradict the interpretation quoted above by the American demographer?

In our opinion there is no contradiction. Both researchers ascribe to living conditions a decisive role in extending human life; with the improvement of these conditions, life lengthens. True, the new, more humanitarian relation to old people mentioned by Krzywicki is due to economic reasons. To the historically earliest and thus far most important factor in the growth of life expectancy is added, with time, another, no less important factor: the development of medical art.

A low average at death is a feature of the structure of deaths by age discussed earlier. This resulted not only from the high mortality rate of children and especially infants, not only from the great number of casualties among people at the vigorous age (as demonstrated by the great number of crushed human skulls) but also—and this is most significant to us at the moment—from the small number of people old at death. We have explained that in the structure of deaths in the primitive world this group was in any case non-existent since there was no place for unproductive people in ancient societies. And if, in the course of time, the average age at death is increasing, this is not without influence on the factors of interest to us—the proportion of aged persons among those dying. Thus, the average age at death is increasing mainly on account of the increase in the number of old people in society. It is highly probable that the appreciable increase in the number of old people began only as societies reached the later stages of civilization.

While for prehistoric times the archaeological findings present the only accessible source of information about age at death, in historical times, right from their beginning, the number of such sources increased. We mean specific information about age at death in the form of various kinds of inscriptions. The most important are:

(1) labels attached to mummies,
(2) epitaphs.

The famous English mathematician Karl Pearson undertook a very interesting attempt to reconstruct the human life expectancy in ancient Egypt. As statistical material for this research he used the labels attached to mummies. The results of these studies were made public in his work: "On the Change in Expectation of Life in Man During a Period of circa 2000 Years" in the first volume of the journal *Biometrica* of 1901–02. Pearson stated that the life expectancy of an infant in Egypt in Roman times was 22 yr.[7] Not without reason have American demographers stressed that such a mortality rate is not known today even in the most backward countries.[8]

The same result—22 yr—was obtained by W. R. Macdonell who explored the average life expectancy in ancient Rome and its provinces ("On the Expectation of Life in Ancient Rome and in the Provinces of Hispania and Lusitania, and Africa", *Biometrica*, **19**, 1913). Unlike his predecessor, Macdonell used material gathered from the collection *Corpus Inscriptionum Latinarum* in the library of the Berlin Academy and containing information on age at death of some thousands of Roman citizens at the beginning of the Christian Era.

The agreement between the results obtained by Pearson and Macdonell seems to indicate their reliability. But Macdonell's results for the Roman provinces may, and even must, raise some doubts, for according to his computation, the average life expectancy in Hispania and Lusitania (the two provinces were treated jointly) should be a little over 35 yr, and in Africa more than 45. On this account the American demographers make the following remark: "This figure is certainly open to question, as it is not far from that prevailing in the United States at the beginning of this century."[9]

The scepticism expressed in this answer really concerns only the provincial data (the strictly Roman data do not give rise to such reservations). However, in our view it is difficult thus to separate the results of research conducted by the same method and based on the same material; if the results are somewhat doubtful, then the whole cannot be regarded as reliable. There must be something wrong: either the method or the material. In this case, probably both.

Considering all the studies made on life expectancy in ancient times the demographer of the Metropolitan Life Insurance Company draws the reasonable conclusion that in this epoch the life expectancy of the infant oscillated between 20 and 30 yr.[10]

Of course, one may contest this or that method of computation; one may disagree with one or another result, but it cannot be denied that the average length of life at the dawn of history was extremely low and that only a negligible number of infants survived to old age.

In the prehistoric and early historical epoch there were few aged persons. The world of that time was a world without old people.

3. THE MIDDLE AGES

If there is reason to speak about the paucity of statistical material from ancient times, then this must be said still more emphatically about the Middle Ages, that brought a nearly total decline of population statistics.

Statistical material that could throw light on the darkness of the Middle Ages is not available in sufficient quantity. We must therefore avail ourselves of non-statistical material containing life expectancy. Such sources may be found in the literature of the Middle Ages.

(a) De Contemptu Mundi

As typical documents of the era, two literary works from the Middle Ages may be quoted. One is the work: *De contemptu mundi* originating from the beginning of the 13th century (published about 1208). Its author was Pope Innocent III (1161–1216), one of the leading personalities of the period.

The problems of demography were unknown to him. However, incidental to his considerations, he makes remarks of significance to historical demography. Such is his statement that *few people reached forty years of age and those reaching sixty were rare exceptions.*

The above information undoubtedly throws some light on the mortality rate in this little epoch of the Middle Ages: it confirms the short life expectancy of the times.

The causes of this phenomenon were, first of all, the economic and hygienic conditions. In addition there were many victims of political and religious persecution.

The same Innocent III ordered the extermination by fire and sword of the adherents of the anti-Popist movement of Albigenses and Waldenses. On the Vatican's orders the South of France, the center of this religious movement, was drowned in blood.

Old chronicles mention the terrible fate of the inhabitants of the French town of Béziers—a town of 20,000, large for those times. It was completely exterminated. The commander of the Papal army, the Abbot Arnold of the Cistercians, shouted in his religious fanaticism: "Kill all the people, the Lord will recognize his own souls."

It was obvious that many people could not survive to old age under such conditions.

In the light of our present, still inadequate, knowledge about the demographic conditions of the Middle Ages, the statement of Innocent III about the small number of persons surviving to old age seems undoubtedly realistic. Even the author of *De contemptu mundi* did not survive to old age. Innocent III died at 55.

(b) Miroir de Mariage

Let us examine the next document. This is a poetic work entitled *Miroir de Mariage,* written about 1400. The author was Eustache Deschamps (1330–1415), the best French poet of the 14th century.

Deschamps, like Innocent III, touched only incidentally on the length of human life. He stated that people grew old rapidly. Women at the age of 30 were already beginning old age, and for men old age commenced at 50. The author added that 60 yr was the normal end of human life.

And, too, a digression to the fact of a purely personal nature would be useful. Whoever knows the life story of the author of *Miroir de Mariage* is aware that it abounded in failures and that one cause of his troubles was his unfortunate marriage. Under the influence of his failures Deschamps became an irreconcilable woman-hater.

Thus, *Miroir de Mariage*, like other works by Deschamps is not impartial evidence as far as women are concerned. On the contrary, it is a libel against women.

Against the background of this silhouette of the poet a doubt may arise whether his statement that 30-year-old women were already senile should be taken seriously. We suspect that this information is more a product of his feelings than a true observation of life.

On the other hand, there is no reason to doubt the correctness of the poet's observations about men: the statement about the early death of men, we believe, is consistent with the sad reality of those times.

We should still like to call attention to the detail that Deschamps was 70 years old when he wrote his *Miroir de Mariage*. This makes his observations concerning the short life expectancy of men more reliable.

It is interesting that the German scholar Paul Herre, who devoted a special study to the creative activity of old people, draws attention on the great rarity of such events in the Middle Ages. "Tatsächlich haben wir aus den mittelalterlichen Generationen nur von sehr wenigen Menschen Kenntnis, die in diesem Alter noch mit grossen Leistungen aufwarten konnten."[11]

Herre points out that in the Middle Ages a serious regression of human life expectancy took place. As one of the causes the author mentions the decline of the medical arts. This statement, not supported by objective evidence, cannot be treated on the same level as information of the documentary type. But this does not mean that its value is questionable. This side of the problem is not yet quite clear.

Herre states further that with Germans and Romans survival to 70 yr was rather rare.

The information gathered here, although originating from various sources, shows fundamental agreement and permits the statement that in the Middle Ages the number of persons surviving to old age was still very low.

(c) Retrospective Life Tables for Medieval England

Speaking about the mortality conditions in the Middle Ages, we should consider those works which attempt to enlighten these conditions by retrospective statistical research. Such is the work of J. C. Russell on the medieval demography of England.[12]

AVERAGE LIFE EXPECTANCY OF AN INFANT
IN MEDIEVAL ENGLAND

Life table	Average life expectancy
For people born before 1276	35·28
For people born in 1276–1300	31·20
For people born in 1301–25	29·84
For people born in 1326–48	30·22
For people born in 1349–75	17·33
For people born in 1376–1400	20·53
For people born in 1401–1425	23·78
For people born in 1426–50	32·75

Source: JOSIAH COX RUSSELL, British Medieval Population, p. 186.

Utilizing the materials extant concerning the inheritance of property and, in addition, materials pertaining to the deaths of monks, Josiah Cox Russell made eleven life tables for medieval England. From these tables we extract the most characteristic figures concerning the average life expectancy of an infant. The figures contained in the tables concern men only.

There is a large spread of figures for the average life expectancy of an infant:

minimum . . . . 17·33 yr

maximum . . . . 35·28 yr

The first of these figures is exceptional, since it applies to the time of a plague (the black death epidemic) in England.

The second figure is under suspicion as to its exactness: it can be assumed to be too high for the 13th century. In any case, it is surprising that it should exceed the average life expectancy of the children of English kings computed by Russell as 30·7 yr.

The Polish reviewer of Russell's work, Dr Egon Vielrose, made some noteworthy observations as to the accuracy and utility of the computations contained in this work.[13] He stated:

(1) Russell's figures are not quite accurate since they are based on incomplete data about the deaths of infants;

(2) if some necessary corrections were introduced, the average life expectancy expressed by the mean for the epoch investigated would be not more than 26·5 yr, and, under less favourable assumptions, only 24·3 yr;

(3) these figures, although concerning the landed proprietors, are

equivalent to the life expectancy of the whole population of the country, since otherwise the actual rapid growth of population in medieval England would not be possible;

(4) the difference in the scope of the demographic conditions could not be great in the Europe of those times (many demographers share this opinion). If this is so, then from the data characterizing the conditions of one country, conclusions may be drawn approximately as to the conditions prevailing in other countries. From this the reviewer concludes that Russell's work can have great value for studies of Polish demography in the Middle Ages.

We can agree with all the reviewer's remarks. However, in the most important points we share the view of Dr Vielrose: by reducing Russell's figures we shall be nearer the truth.

Can it be ascertained that there was an increase in the average life expectancy in the Middle Ages as compared with antiquity?

The answer to this question is not easy. The maker of the English retrospective life tables states that in Roman times the average life expectancy in England was 30·3 yr. Since the English table for men born before 1276 shows 35·28 yr, it may be inferred that an increase in life expectancy followed. The same estimates are found by the demographers of the Metropolitan Life Insurance Company.[14]

We have agreed, however, that the result of Russell's computations (35·28) should be reduced. Under this condition it becomes more difficult to accept the thesis about the increase in the average life expectancy in the Middle Ages. In any case, if we assume that human life gained in longevity, these gains would be rather small.

The conclusion is self-evident: medieval England was a country with a rather low life expectancy. If this assertion is true with regard to England then it is undoubtedly still more justified with respect to the vast areas of the European continent. There is no doubt that this implies a small number of old people.

The Middle Ages, like antiquity, were part of a demographic epoch given the name of "demographic youth", which is characterized by a mass phenomenon of premature deaths and an insignificant proportion of the aged among the living.

4. ORDER OF DYING IN THE LIGHT OF THE FIRST LIFE TABLES

The earliest life tables, except for the table prepared by the Roman lawyer Ulpian, originate from 17th century. The best known tables are Graunt's for London, and Halley's for Wroclaw. With time, the historic–statistical sources will be enriched by retrospective life tables which increase our knowledge about mortality conditions many centuries past.

(a) Graunt's Tables

John Graunt (1620–74) has an important place in the history of statistics as one of its founders. "Thus he, more than any other man, was the founder of statistics," writes Walter F. Willcox in the introduction to the American edition of Graunt's work (1939).

Speaking about Graunt's merits, the Soviet historian of statistics M. Ptucha mentions Graunt's construction of the life table. In this respect Graunt was a pioneer.

The scientific value of this first life table, the exactness of its computations, are another matter. In this regard Graunt's table leaves much to be desired.[15]

Nevertheless it is worth while examining this earliest attempt to register the order of a generation's dying. This is Graunt's table:

LIFE TABLE FOR THE CITY OF LONDON AS COMPUTED BY J. GRAUNT (ABOUT 1660)

Age (yr)	Number surviving	Age (yr)	Number surviving
0	100	46	10
6	64	56	6
16	40	66	3
26	25	76	1
36	16	86	0

Source: H. WESTERGAARD. Contributions to the History of Statistics, P. S. King & Son, London, 1932, p. 22.

In the above table we have only an age column (x) and a column of survivors (l_x), and this not for every age. However, the number of persons surviving to old age which interests us, can be read from this table.

We learn from the column l_x that from every 100 infants there survived at:

56 yr . . . . 6 persons
66 yr . . . . 3 persons

By we can compute the number of persons surviving to 60 yr: approximately 4·6.

The meaning of the result obtained is clear: among persons constituting the generation observed, 95·5 per cent or the overwhelming majority died before attaining old age. Such an unfavourable order of mortality is not to be found in any known life tables.

Of course, the accuracy of the result stated is more than problematic. However, we are at liberty to assume that such an unfavourable order of dying could result only from a very high rate of mortality. We mean to say that the faulty methodological bases of Graunt's computation may have helped overstress the mortality rate, but the real situation must also have been bad.

We are convinced that the "life table" presents the situation in London in too pessimistic a light. If so, in order to obtain a picture closer to reality, we should raise the proportion of persons surviving to old age. We think that the number of persons surviving to 60 yr (interpolated earlier) may be doubled. In other words, we assume that an old age of 60 yr was achieved by 9–10 per cent of the total number of infants. Such is our evaluation, and the only support we can provide is the conformity of our estimate to all we know about mortality in the epoch considered.

(b) Halley's Table

The exceptionally pessimistic table of Graunt is opposed by a table very optimistic for those times (end of the 17th century), which is also better from the methodological view point. This is the life table shown below for the town of Wroclaw prepared by the famous astronomer and demographer Halley.

ORDER OF MORTALITY IN THE LIFE TABLE FOR THE TOWN OF WROCLAW (1687-91) COMPUTED BY E. HALLEY

Age (yr)	Number of persons	Age (yr)	Number of persons
1	1000	35	490
2	855	40	445
3	798	45	397
4	760	50	346
5	732	55	292
10	661	60	242
15	628	65	192
20	598	70	142
25	567	75	88
30	531	80	41
33	507	84	20
34	499		

Source: RAYMOND PEARL, *Introduction to Medical Biometry and Statistics*, third edition, Philadelphia and London, 1941, p. 27.

It appears from the table quoted that old age was reached in Wroclaw in the period investigated by Halley (at the end of the 17th century) by 24·2 per cent of the total number of infants. We obtain these results on the assumption that old age is counted from 60 yr. If we were to assume that the beginning of old age is 65 yr the percentage of infants surviving to old age would be reduced to 19·2.

Most characteristic is the great difference between the results obtained by the English astronomer for Wroclaw and by his less experienced predecessor Graunt, for London. Thus the generation observed was reduced to one quarter of its original number, in the Wroclaw table at 60 yr; in the London table as early as 26 yr. In the light of these data the Wroclaw table may be called *very good*, and the London table *very bad*.

The question arises whether both computations are not affected by serious deficiencies and whether the errors are not divided—one *plus*, the other *minus*.

We maintained a critical attitude to the extremely uncertain computations of Graunt. The same attitude should be taken toward Halley's computations despite the fact that methodologically the latter is incomparably superior to the former. It is evident that only a faultless method can define a true picture of the mortality conditions. However, such a qualification cannot be ascribed to Halley's method. While incomparably better than the primitive method of Graunt, it is still far from accurate (statistical practice has long abandoned Halley's method as incorrect). Thus, the life table computed for Wroclaw can only be accepted with great reservations.

The supposition that the proportion surviving to old age, i.e. 60 yr, is greatly exaggerated seems to be well founded. Let us be cautious and assume that this proportion is not 25 per cent, but only 20 per cent. It would still be a proportion more than twice the corresponding value assumed for the London table. In the light of the data assumed the number of persons surviving to old age (60 yr) varied in this period within the limits of 9–10 per cent as a *minimum*, and 20 per cent as a *maximum*.

(c) Retrospective Geneva Tables

Using the research of his many predecessors, the Swiss demographer Eduard Mallet made interesting retrospective computations illustrating the evolution of length of life of the inhabitants of Geneva over some centuries (16th to 19th).

The exceptional cognitive value of these computations induces us to quote a part of Mallet's computations. The initial values—from the 16th century—are extremely low. Later ones are somewhat better, although far from optimistic.

Let us analyse the figures of interest to us, on the numbers of infants surviving to old age.

ORDER OF MORTALITY IN LIFE TABLE FOR GENEVA COMPUTED FOR THE 16TH, 17TH AND 18TH CENTURIES

Age (yr)	Numbers of persons surviving to the end of each period		
	16th century	17th century	18th century
0.	100·00	100·00	100·00
1.	74·08	76·28	79·88
4–5.	55·65	59·00	66·84
6–10	48·06	52·40	61·09
11–15	43·54	48·72	58·61
16–20	38·89	44·86	55·92
21–30	29·87	37·29	49·39
31–40	20·59	29·65	42·75
41–50	14·34	22·34	35·41
51–60	8·58	14·95	25·94
61–70	4·08	8·06	14·53
71–80	1·18	2·45	4·52
81–90	0·23	0·37	0·50

Source: W. BICKEL, Bevölkerungsgeschichte und Bevölkerungspolitik der Schweiz seit dem Ausgang des Mittelalters, Zürich, 1947, p. 292.

In the light of the above computations, out of 100 infants in Geneva there survived to 60 yr:

in the 16th century . . . . 8·6
in the 17th century . . . . 14·9
in the 18th century . . . . 25·9

From these figures it is also evident that the order of mortality improved from century to century. This improvement may be qualified as very essential, since the proportion of survivors to old age increased threefold in that time.

However, despite these advances, the proportion of survivors to old age remained low; in fact the majority of infants—and their number was not small—died before attaining old age.

It is not inappropriate to quote what the well-known German physician and statistician, Dr Prinzing, stated while discussing the life expectancy of German women of past centuries in one of his works. He said that in the 16th century in Germany, out of 100 live girls born only 20 reached 60 yr.[16]

The author mentions that this number is based on a life table, but what table cannot be ascertained. If it concerns the middle class then it is probably limited to rich town patricians. In our view it is a sheer impossibility that the figure stated by Prinzing could characterize the mortality conditions of the total town population.

5. THE SITUATION IN THE 18TH CENTURY

The material of the 18th century is much richer: besides figures characterizing mortality for this century there is information about the economic conditions at the basis of the order of mortality. Let us begin with France.

(a) Order of Mortality in France

According to Necker (1732–1804), in the France of his time a quarter of the whole population died before reaching 3 yr; the second quarter, before achieving 25 yr; the third, before attaining 50 yr. Thus, only a quarter of the infants survived to 50 yr.

J. M. Kuliszer mentions that Necker's data are confirmed in life tables computed by French statisticians of the 18th century. According to the table of Dupré de Saint-Maur, based on data for Paris (1767) 24·2 per cent of infants survived to 50 yr. Assuming that, among 50-year-old persons, two-thirds survived to 60 yr (a very optimistic assumption) we obtain more or less 16 persons surviving to old age— 60 yr—out of 100 infants.

The mortality conditions for the whole of France were not much better. This is indicated by the feudal conditions which strangled the economy of the country.[17]

From the work of the late 18th century statistician, Arthur Young, who even before the French Revolution travelled all over France, J. M. Kuliszer, a responsible scholar, obtains the following description of the economic conditions of France: "The economic condition of the peasants was miserable in the Middle Ages—and did not seem to improve. Of course, there were also rich peasants, but this was exceptional... a phenomenon that struck Arthur Young was the lack of footwear. The people did not wear stockings or shoes, and often not even canvas covering, although they could boast of walking barefoot on well-built roads. Nutrition was not much better. Since wheat and rye were sold to cover taxes and other duties for landlords, there remained only the worse kinds of cereals such as barley and oats that were not accepted by the landlords. Meat was rare and served only on holidays. Such was the state in normal years, and it is therefore not surprising that during years of famine the peasants lived on grass; epidemics of typhus, dysentery and smallpox did not die out. When crops failed, one–quarter or one–fifth of the people lived by begging and in many regions the number of deaths exceeded that of births."[18]

In view of such living conditions it is not astonishing that Necker gave only one–quarter as the fraction of French infants surviving to 50 yr or in our computation that not more than 16 per cent of infants, much less than in Geneva, survived to 60 yr.

J. M. Kuliszer also refers to the table of Duvillard in which the number of survivors to 50 yr was 29·7 out of 100 infants. According to our assumption the proportion of persons surviving to 60 was about 20 per cent. This is a much more optimistic result than that stated earlier. Although Duvillard's table originates from the first years of the 19th century—1806, to be exact—still, the author, as was shown at the Hygiene Congress in Berlin in 1907 by two experts, Émile Levasseur and Marcel Huber, used the materials of his predecessors to a large extent. There is sufficient reason to classify, as 18th century, the proportion of people surviving to old age shown in Duvillard's table.

Let us return to the report by Arthur Young. He states that one day during his ramblings across France he met on the road a bent woman who appeared to be 60 yr. Asked about her age, she answered that she was 28 yr old. He learned from the ensuing talk that she had seven children and lived in poverty.

The case described by Young seems to be characteristic for French conditions of the period preceding the French Revolution. Such is the opinion of the French historian, Marcel R. Reinhard, who, generalizing the observations of the English statistician, speaks of the then premature physical wearing out of the French people ("L'usure était précoce...").[19]

(b) Order of Mortality in Germany

The miserable situation of the French people has been mentioned. That of the German people was no better. Friedrich Engels characterized the economic conditions of Germany at the end of the feudal period in these words: "Germany was one rotting and decomposing mass. No one felt well. Handicrafts, trade, industry and agriculture were reduced to very little. The peasants, traders and craftsmen suffered twofold pressure: from the bloodthirsty government and the bad state of trade. The noblemen and princes asserted that their incomes should not be lower than their expenditures. Everything was bad and in the country there reigned general dissatisfaction... Everything rotted, staggered to the point of breakdown. No recovery was to be hoped for since there was no power in the nation capable of removing the decomposing corpses of anachronistic institutions."[20]

The demographic conditions paralleled the economic conditions. In Germany, as in France, the order of mortality was not optimistic. The German statistician of the 18th century, Süssmilch, author of the life table based on Brandenburg material, stressed with some astonishment the conformity of his computations with the data of the French table established by A. Déparcieux on the basis of lists of deaths among the monks of the Benedictine monastery. He wrote: "I never expected such harmony between the monks in Paris and our peasants of Brandenburg. I was astonished when I discovered it, and the exceptional satisfaction on account of God's order was for me a prize for my toil" (according to *Göttliche Ordnung*, part II).

That fine historian of statistics, the Dane H. Westergaard, questioned the above considerations: in the light of modern ideas the notion of harmony, referred to by the author of *God's Order*, is not great. On the basis of the probabilities of death taken from the two tables, Westergaard proved that the German conditions were worse than the French.[21]

In view of this it seems likely that in Germany—as well as in France—the number of persons surviving to 60 yr, computed on the basis of tables, at best oscillated around 20 yr. In other words, about 80 per cent of the total number of deaths occurred in the period preceding old age.

(c) Order of Mortality in the Netherlands and Sweden

Conditions in the Netherlands and Sweden developed better, but not well during the same period (18th century).

Some idea about the order of mortality in the Netherlands is given by the table computed by Kersseboom based on Dutch data from before 1742 (this should not be confused with the London table of the same author based on the list of dead for London).

ORDER OF MORTALITY IN THE NETHERLANDS ON THE BASIS OF KERSSEBOOM'S TABLE OF 1742

Age (yr)	Number of survivors	Age (yr)	Number of survivors
0.	1000	30	507
1.	804	40	432
2.	768	50	362
3.	736	60	273
4.	709	65	225
5.	688	70	175
10.	639	80	72
15.	611	90	8
20.	584	95	1

Source: F. A. ZUBELEWICZ, *Rachunkowość handlowa w ważniejszych jej zastosowaniach* (*Trade Accountancy in Its Most Important Applications*), Warsaw, 1846, pp. 342–3, in an appendix titled: "Rachunki odnoszące się do zabezpieczeń na życie" (Accounts Dealing with Life Insurance) by Józef Słomiński.

The above table enables us to state that from 1000 infants only 273 survived to old age (60). And if we raise the lower limit of old age to 65, the number of survivors to old age drops to 225 out of 1000 new-born infants. These figures are not very high—not even good—but considering the period, they are rather encouraging. It is also important that specialists rate the Kersseboom table very highly for the exactness of its computation. The well-known historian of statistics, Harald Westergaard, characterizes the author as follows: "... sein Verdienst ist... sehr erheblich. Seine Schlüsse sind im allgemeinen vollkommen korrekt, und seine Verwendung des Leibrentenmaterials zur Aufstellung von Überlebenstafeln zeugt von Klarheit und Schärfe."[22]

Let us take a quick look at the mortality conditions in Sweden. In 1766 the secretary of the Swedish Academy of Sciences, Per Wargentin (the follower of Elvius), published a life table for Sweden based on statistical material from 1755 to 1763. We learn from this table that out of 1000 infants only 293 persons survived to 60 yr.

If we consider this figure in relation to the period we must consider it as very good. It may be that the primacy of Sweden in the evolution of favourable mortality conditions dates from those times.

(d) Summing up the Results

Summing up our considerations, we obtain the following approximate picture of mortality conditions of 18th century Europe:

NUMBER OF PERSONS SURVIVING TO 60 YR IN THE LIGHT OF LIFE TABLES FROM THE 18TH CENTURY

Object of observation	Period of the table	Number of persons surviving (per 1000 infants)
Paris	1767	ca. 160
France	end of 18th century	ca. 200
Brandenburg	1742	ca. 200
Geneva	18th century	259
Netherlands	1742	273
Sweden	1755–63	293

Source: Computed by the author.

If we disregard Paris with its unusual proportion of persons surviving to old age we have the spread of the indices we are interested in from 20 to 30 per cent. It seems that these figures provide a true picture of the mortality rates in 18th century Europe. They state that 70–80 per cent of all deaths occurred before old age.

6. INCREASE IN THE NUMBER OF PERSONS SURVIVING TO OLD AGE IN THE 19TH CENTURY

In the history of mortality conditions the 19th century opens a new epoch characterized not only by transformations in the social and economic conditions but also revolutionary advances in medical knowledge and a great development of sanitary facilities.

About what proportion of infants attained old age, and thus what proportion died old, we shall learn from a number of statements of which the first will reveal relations in some European countries near mid-century. The small number of countries represented in the statement is due to the fact that only a few countries established life tables which might be a basis for our computations.

In the above statement Russia is characterized by its extremely low number of persons surviving to old age. This is connected with the exceptionally unfavourable mortality conditions in tsarist Russia.

The Russian demographer Novoselsky (*O smertnosti i prodolzhitelnosti zhizni w Rossii*, Petrograd, 1916) states that in comparison with other countries Russia had an extremely high mortality rate of persons up to 15 yr. Also in the adolescent years and the productive age the mortality rate in Russia was higher than in other countries, although the differences were not so great as with persons below 15. But in old age, mainly over 80 yr, the Russian indices were exceptionally

NUMBER OF PERSONS SURVIVING TO 60 YR IN THE LIGHT OF LIFE TABLES FROM THE MID-19TH CENTURY

Country	Period of the table	Number of persons surviving to 60 yr per 1000 infants	
		male	female
European Russia	1862	24·9	27·2
Belgium	1841–50	33·6	35·4
England	1838–54	35·6	38·4
France	1840–50	37·0	39·1
Sweden	1841–55	35·8	44·4
Norway	1856–65	46·6	50·7

Source: Life tables of the given countries.

low. Novoselsky qualified the mortality conditions in Russia as being *typical for agricultural countries with backward sanitary, cultural and economic conditions.*

A comparative analysis of mortality rates in various countries made by Novoselsky put Russia in first place for mortality of infants. We meet a similar fact to the one stated above: the number of infants surviving to 60 yr is lowest in Russia. However, some reservation should be made here: although the Russian conditions were very poor, they were still not at the peak of bad mortality conditions. Here and there, especially outside of Europe, conditions were still more primitive but they were not published for lack of statistics.

The highest proportion of persons surviving to old age is to be found in the north of Europe: in Norway and Sweden. We shall not decide which comes first; the Norwegian figures are higher but were made ten years later than the Swedish.

The spread between the minimum and maximum figures in the above statement is very great: the Norwegian figures are nearly twice as high as the Russian.

Worthy of attention is the fact that in the first half of the 19th century a state of balance between deaths up to 60 yr and after 60 yr was still not reached. Even the Scandinavian countries had not achieved this state although they approached it more than other countries.

Let us now consider the proportions of deaths at the turn of the present century.

The first striking fact is the important increase in the number of countries having available data. It is an evident sign of the evolution of demographic statistics; the number of countries where life tables are computed was growing.

It is characteristic that the spread in the figures quoted is great, although our statement concerns countries of only one continent, Europe. The oscillations of our indices are within the limits: 28·4–54·7 per cent for males, and 30·7–60·2 per cent for females. The Dutch figures, the highest in our statement, are twice the Russian, or lowest figures. We see now that to treat Europe as a uniform demographic organism would be false.

NUMBER OF PERSONS SURVIVING TO 60 YR AT THE TURN OF THE 20TH CENTURY

Country	Period covered by tables	Number of persons surviving to 60 yr per 100 infants	
		males	females
European Russia	1896–97	28·4	30·7
Spain	1900	30·3	34·1
Bulgaria	1899–1902	36·6	36·1
Austria	1901–1905	36·4	39·8
Czechoslovakia	1899–1902	35·8	41·3
Italy.	1899–1902	44·0	43·4
Germany.	1891–1900	38·3	44·8
England	1891–1900	40·9	43·4
France	1898–1903	43·2	49·4
Belgium	1891–1900	43·5	50·3
Norway	1890–1900	49·8	55·6
Sweden	1891–1900	51·0	56·4
Denmark.	1901–1905	54·7	60·2

Source: Life tables of selected countries as given in the *Demographic Yearbook 1953*, United Nations, pp. 304–323.

The fact that the demographic conditions in Russia were distinguished by the lowest percentage of deaths at old age is nothing new: we have observed this earlier when discussing figures from the middle of the past century. During the 34–35 yr dividing the two Russian tables we note only a slight improvement in the death structure of the tsars' state; in the years 1896–97 about 70 per cent of all deaths occurred earlier than old age.

During the same period, the conditions in the North of Europe, Denmark, Sweden and Norway were quite different. In these countries, for the first time in the history of mankind, the deaths of old people (over 60) began to exceed the deaths of persons in lower age groups.

In our opinion, this was one of the important events in the history of demographic relations.

The primacy of the northern countries has ceased to be open to question. It is clear that they have outstripped the rest of Europe in the struggle with premature death.

And yet not so long ago—at the end of 19th century—statements about the exceptional improvement in mortality conditions in the north of Europe were viewed with disbelief. The German statistician Georg von Mayr doubted the truth of information about the record-breaking length of life in Sweden. He wrote the following remarks: "Zu dem schwedischen Ergebnis kann ich mich der kurzen Anmerkung eines Zweifels an der vollen Richtigkeit nicht enthalten. Die auffallend hohe Leblichkeit der schwedischen Greise... könnte hiernach recht wohl zu einem gewissen Bruchteil nur eine statistische Täuschung sein, davon herrührend, dass für die Ermittlung der Sterbewahrscheinlichkeit der höheren Altersklassen eine zu hohe Besetzung der Altersklassen mit Lebenden angenommen ist".[23]

It may be that an innate conservatism did not allow Mayr to observe the transitory character of traditional demographic systems. And yet, with the passing century, these systems, too, completed their existence.

It should still be stressed that everywhere, in countries with "good" and "bad" life tables alike, some shifts in the structures of deaths by age have occurred; everywhere the proportion of deaths occurring in old age increased.

With reference to Germany, Johannes Rahts was the first to call attention to this fact. In confronting the results of the first three German life tables, i.e. the table of Becker for 1871–80 and his own two tables for 1881–90 and 1891–1900, Rahts demonstrated the progressive decrease in the number of deaths before 60 yr in order to draw the conclusion that the living conditions of the population in Germany had been much improved in the last thirty years: "Man erkennt besonders durch Vergleichung der Zahlen der Gestorbenen, dass sich die Lebensverhältnisse im Deutschen Reich während dieser 30 Jahre wesentlich gebessert haben", wrote Rahts.[24]

It seems that the decline in the number of deaths of persons before 60 can, and even should be treated as proof of an improvement in hygienic conditions. However, it would be unsafe to draw conclusions as to the improvement in living conditions as a whole. In our opinion, it is possible but not necessary that such a correlation exists.

7. BEFORE THE FIRST WORLD WAR

Let us now consider the structure of deaths from old age in the period preceding the First World War.

(a) European Countries

NUMBER OF PERSONS SURVIVING TO 60 YR IN THE LIGHT OF LIFE TABLES BEFORE 1914

Countries	Period covered by table	Number of persons surviving to 60 yr per 100 infants	
		male	female
Denmark.	1911–15	59·7	64·7
England and Wales	1901–10	47·6	54·2
England and Wales	1910–12	52·1	58·7
Finland	1901–1910	44·2	49·3
France	1908–13	46·5	54·5
Germany.	1901–1910	43·8	50·8
Germany.	1910–11	47·7	54·0
Iceland	1901–1910	46·2	55·6
Italy.	1901–1911	44·9	46·6
Netherlands	1900–1909	53·6	57·3
Norway	1901/02–1910/11	55·8	60·0
Spain	1910	39·4	42·8
Sweden	1901–1910	56·5	60·4
Switzerland	1910–11	49·7	56·6

Source: Life table of the various countries (according to the *Demographic Yearbook 1953*, United Nations, pp. 304–323).

Among the European countries included in our statement the highest proportion of persons surviving to old age are in:

(a) for males:

    1. Denmark   1911–15   59·7%

    2. Sweden   1901–1910   56·5%

    3. Norway   1901/02–1910/11   55·8%

(b) for females:

    1. Denmark   1911–15   64·7%

    2. Sweden   1901–1910   60·4%

    3. Norway   1901/02–1910/11   60·0%

The primacy of the northern countries is incontestable, although there appear serious competitors as candidates to priority, to mention only the Netherlands.

While for males the maximum proportion of persons surviving to old age was nearly 60 per cent, this level was exceeded for females.

In Denmark nearly two-thirds of the total number of deaths of women occurred in old age.

The lowest indices in our statement are for Spain, namely:

for males . . . . 39·4%

for females . . . . 42·8%

that is, around 40 per cent.

We do not wish to assert that Europe did not have worse figures at this time. The lack of life tables for many countries, especially for those backward in the demographic field, does not permit such an assertion. But without regard to the conditions that may have existed elsewhere, the figures given for Spain must be recognized as discreditable for Europe, particularly for Spain itself. These figures prove great backwardness in the battle with premature deaths.

(b) Countries outside Europe

Let us have a look at countries outside Europe.

The statistical material to be analysed is the more interesting as it contains minima and maxima not observed in Europe. The absolute extremes are to sought outside Europe.

Here is the material at our disposal.

NUMBER OF PERSONS SURVIVING TO 60 YR IN THE LIGHT
OF LIFE TABLES BEFORE 1914

Countries	Period covered by tables	Number of persons surviving to 60 yr per 100 infants	
		male	female
Argentina	1914	42·0	46·1
Australia	1901–1910	56·8	63·2
British Guiana	1910–12	14·2	20·7
India	1901–1911	11·2	12·2
Jamaica	1910–12	33·0	37·1
Japan	1909–1913	42·1	43·1
New Zealand	1906–1910	63·3	67·2
(without Maoris)	1911–15	65·8	69·3
Trinidad and Tobago	1910–12	28·8	34·3
U.S.A..	1909–1911	48·3	54·2

Source: Life tables of the various countries (according to the *Demographic Yearbook 1953*, pp. 304–323).

We have here two extremes: on the one hand New Zealand eclipses the countries of northern Europe, outstripping them in the reduction of premature deaths and, on the other hand, India, having a formidably high proportion of such deaths.

More should be said in an analysis of the mortality conditions in India.

We learn from the table quoted that in the years 1901–1911 the number of persons surviving to 60 in India was 11–12 per cent. In other words, among the stationary population premature deaths (considered as deaths before the age of 60) constituted nearly 90 per cent of the total number. Let us add that such a small percentage of people in India survived to the age of 60 at a time when in New Zealand two–thirds of the total number of deaths occurred in old age.

The question arises whether the period when these data were obtained was not exceptionally unfavourable for India in regard to sanitary or economic conditions, was perhaps a period of epidemic or famine. This question is the more appropriate since India has often been afflicted by terrible calamities of famine and plague. It suffices to mention "the Great Indian Famine" of 1876–8, the 10 yr famine of 1891–1900, particularly acute in 1898–1900; the bubonic plague that ravaged a vast area of the country in 1896. The Indian statistician S. P. Jain, from whom these facts are taken, states that "the decade 1901–1910 was comparatively normal".[25]

The Indian demographer, a professor at the University in Baroda, S. Chandrasekhar, wrote after the Second World War about the tragedy for his people in the tremendous number of premature deaths which basically could have been prevented: "It is a tragedy because medical progress in India is largely an illusion in comparison with that in other countries. Thousands of cases which now result in death are preventable and curable".[26] Indeed, one can only call this terrible number of premature deaths a national tragedy.

In our statement India is not an isolated problem: a similar death structure by age occurs in British Guiana. Over 85 per cent of the men and 80 per cent of the women inhabiting this territory die before reaching old age.

It should be remembered that our knowledge about the demographic conditions of colonial peoples is limited by a lack of statistical materials. It is quite possible that the mortality rates known from Indian tables are not the worst.

8. THE SITUATION BETWEEN THE TWO WORLD WARS

The years between the two world wars—and especially the Thirties—provide such rich statistical material on mortality rates, life tables being used as a popular tool for measuring these conditions, that we are compelled to limit our analysis to the extreme values, i.e. to the highest and lowest proportions of persons surviving to an old age of 60.

Below are the maxima for the Thirties:

(a) for men;

(1) New Zealand (without Maoris)	1935–8	73·5%
(2) Denmark	1936–40	72·3%
(3) Sweden	1931–40	71·0%
(4) Norway	1931/32–40/41	70·5%
(5) Australia	1932–4	69·9%

(b) for women:

(1) New Zealand (without Maoris) . . .	1935–8	78·1%
(2) Norway	1931/32–40/41	75·9%
(3) Australia	1932–4	75·6%
(4) Denmark	1936–40	75·3%
(5) Sweden	1931–40	74·5%

Thus the maximum proportion of persons surviving to old age for both sexes exceeded 70 per cent; for men it was 73·5 per cent, for women 78·1 per cent. In both cases New Zealand has the best record. In Europe the northern countries: Denmark, Sweden and Norway top the list.

We have demonstrated for each sex five countries having the highest proportion of persons surviving to old age. Thus, our statement does not cover countries having a good but not the best proportion of deaths at old age: the U.S.A., Switzerland, Israel, Iceland, Germany, England, the Netherlands and Canada.

Let us discuss the other extreme of demographic conditions.

The proportions of persons surviving to old age noted in the Twenties and Thirties are:

(a) for men:

(1) India	1921–31	14·9%
(2) British Guiana.	1920–22	17·9%
(3) Trinidad	1920–22	25·2%
(4) Mexico	1930	26·6%
(5) Jamaica	1920–22	26·9%

(b) for women:

(1) India	1921–31	13·2%
(2) British Guiana.	1920–22	24·2%
(3) Mexico	1930	30·0%
(4) Guatemala	1939–41	31·7%
(5) Trinidad	1920–22	31·9%

The worst mortality rates are for India: no other country keeping demographic statistics has such a low proportion of persons surviving to old age. Quite understandable and fully justified is the statement made in 1931 by the Indian demographer B. K. Sarkar at the International Demographic Congress in Rome. "Nella statistica comparata di mortalità l'India apparirebbe come uno cimitero dell'umanità".[27] Indeed, in the light of comparative figures, the India of that time made the impression of a "cemetery of mankind".

A pecularity of Indian conditions is the fact that the numbers of women are decimated quicker than those of men: 14·9 per cent of the men and only 13·2 per cent of the women survive to the age of 60. This is connected with the particularly difficult living conditions of women.[28]

9. AFTER THE SECOND WORLD WAR

We submit below the data concerning the period after tne Second World War.

According to the life tables, the maximum proportions of persons surviving to old age in Europe were as follows:

(a) for men:

(1) German Democratic Rep.	1956–7	82·9%
(2) Sweden	1951–5	82·0%
(3) Denmark	1951–5	80·9%
(4) the Netherlands	1947–9	80·5%
(5) Norway	1946–50	79·1%

(b) for women:

(1) Sweden	1951–5	86·6%
(2) the United Kingdom	1956–8	86·0%
(3) Czechoslovakia	1958	85·5%
(4) Denmark	1951–5	85·4%
(5) Norway	1946–50	84·6%

Thus, we note further important achievements in the battle against premature deaths: the maximum number of deaths in old age is 83 per cent for men, 87 per cent for women.

As far as minima are concerned, among European countries (according to the *Demographic Yearbook*) the lowest proportion of persons surviving to old age is in Portugal for men, and in Yugoslavia for women.

These minima are:

for men	59·8%
for women	67·3%

PERSONS SURVIVING TO 60 YR AS SHOWN BY LIFE TABLES

(a) European countries

Country	Period covered by tables	Persons surviving to 60 yr per 100 infants	
		male	female
Austria	1949–51	68·6	77·7
Belgium	1946–9	67·3	77·2
Bulgaria	1956–7	73·0	79·7
Czechoslovakia	1958	76·9	85·5
Denmark.	1946–50	78·0	81·7
Denmark.	1951–5	80·9	85·4
Finland	1950–51	65·6	79·8
France	1950–51	69·9	79·8
France	1952–6	71·9	82·4
Federal German Republic . .	1949–51	72·8	80·2
German Democratic Republic ·	1956–7	82·9	83·6
Ireland	1945–7	66·3	68·5
Ireland	1950–2	72·5	76·4
Italy.	1950–53	72·0	78·8
Netherlands	1947–9	80·5	83·9
Norway	1946–50	79·1	84·6
Poland	1952–3	64·1	73·6
Poland	1955–6	69·1	78·3
Portugal	1949–52	59·8	68·9
Romania	1956	69·7	75·6
Sweden	1946–50	79·6	83·6
Sweden	1951–5	82·0	86·6
United Kingdom	1956–8	78·0	86·0
England and Wales	1956–8	78·4	86·4
Scotland	1956–8	74·6	83·6
Northern Ireland	1956–8	77·5	84·7
Yugoslavia	1952–4	62·9	67·3

Source: Demographic Yearbooks for 1953 and 1954 and statistical yearbooks of the various countries.

It should not be overlooked that these minima are higher than the maxima given for the period preceding the First World War. This is a proof of the great and highly desirable changes that have taken place in mortality over the last half century.

Let us now analyse the countries outside Europe.

Outside Europe the image of mortality is greatly diversified. We find very high, along with very low, numbers of persons surviving to old age. The high figures are close to some European figures, the low are not to be found in modern Europe. These maxima are:

(a) for men:

(1) Israel (Jews only)	1953	78·5%
(2) New Zealand (European descent)	1950–52	78·2%
(3) Canada	1950–52	74·4%
(4) U.S.A. (white population)	1950	73·5%

(b) for women:

(1) New Zealand (European descent)	1950–52	84·1%
(2) U.S.A. (white population)	1950	83·6%
(3) Israel (Jews only)	1953	83·0%
(4) Canada	1950–52	81·8%

Thus, as in Europe, the maximum proportions of persons surviving to old age approach 80 per cent for men and nearly 85 per cent for women.

However, more characteristic are the minima found in non-European countries:

(a) for men:

(1) Mauritius	1942–6	15·9%
(2) India	1941–50	22·0%
(3) Belgian Congo (Afr. pop.)	1950–52	27·6%

(b) for women:

(1) India[29]	1941–50	21·3%
(2) Mauritius	1942–6	22·5%
(3) Belgian Congo (Afr. pop.)	1950–52	31·5%

For India we observe some improvement in mortality conditions as compared with 1921–31, when the proportion of persons surviving to old age was 14·9 per cent for men and 13·2 per cent for women. However, a new and terrible phenomenon appears in Mauritius where 80 per cent of the population dies before reaching old age.

Can the structure of deaths on the island of Mauritius be considered the worst mortality conditions at the present time? Probably not. We assume there are still worse conditions, and if we do not know anything about them it is only because there are no life tables.[30]

To visualize the spread between the proportions of numbers of persons surviving to old age, the maxima and minima should be compared:

(a) for men:

maximum 82·9%
minimum 15·9%

(b) for women:

> maximum 86·6%
> minimum 21·3%

Thus for men the maximum is five times the minimum, for women it is four times.

NUMBER OF PERSONS SURVIVING TO 60 YR AS SHOWN IN RECENT LIFE TABLES

(b) Non-European countries

Country	Period covered by tables	Number of persons surviving to 60 yr per 100 infants	
		male	female
Africa:			
Belgian Congo (African pop.) .	1950–52	27·6	31·5
Union of South Africa (Asian descent).	1945–7	46·6	44·8
Union of South Africa (European descent).	1945–7	69·1	76·5
Mauritius	1942–6	15·9	22·5
North America:			
Canada	1950–52	74·4	81·8
Costa Rica	1949–51	60·0	
El Salvador.	1949–51	48·5	53·1
U.S.A., total population . . .	1949–51	71·2	80·9
white population. . .	1950	73·5	83·6
coloured population .	1950	55·8	61·9
Barbados	1945–7	46·6	55·6
British Honduras	1944–8	39·4	46·6
Jamaica	1945–7	48·4	54·9
Trinidad and Tobago	1945–7	49·6	54·6
South America:			
Argentina	1947	59·6	68·4
Brazil Fed. distr.	1949–51	45·9	58·1
British Guiana	1945–7	42·4	49·0
Asia:			
Ceylon.	1952	64·3	62·3
India	1941–50	22·0	21·3
Israel (Jews only)	1953	78·5	83·0
Japan	1953	68·2	73·5
Siam	1947–8	44·9	52·0
Oceania:			
New Zealand European population	1950–2	78·2	84·1
Maoris	1950–2	52·5	53·0

Source: Demographic Yearbook for the years 1953 (pp. 304–323), and 1954 (pp. 627–629).

10. DEMOGRAPHIC FORECASTS

While in the past centuries premature deaths before old age were
an overwhelming majority, today a large number of the infants born
attain maturity and die in old age. This evolution is not yet accomplished; the battle with diseases which cause premature deaths (in
the broadest meaning of the term) is still going on. In this connection
we support the standpoint of the Belgian actuary, J. Gabriel, who,
when asked "What are the perspectives for the future?" answered as
follows: "Elles ne peuvent qu'être encourageantes quoiqu'on ne puisse
bien entendu envisager une amélioration sans fin de mortalité."[31]

In the works of modern demographers we encounter specific attempts
to unveil the hidden future. These attempts are undertaken by means
of hypothetical life tables. We shall not be in error if we treat them
as forecasts of the future development of mortality conditions.

The computation of hypothetical life tables was begun in 1934 by
the American demographers Louis L. Dublin and Alfred J. Lotka.
The purpose of the first such table—according to its authors—was to
demonstrate the final limit of longevity that can be achieved at the
present state of medical and hygienic knowledge. In other words,
the authors intended to establish a table demonstrating the best conditions of mortality for those times or, an *optimum table.*

As a starting point for their computations Dublin and Lotka made
use of New Zealand life tables for women for the period 1931–2,
which were considered as extremely good for that time (the average
life expectancy of an infant, according to these tables, was 66·4 yr).
Moreover, they utilized the life tables of the U.S.A. for 1930 and the
experiences of the great American insurance companies. They assumed
that the best results then shared by selected population groups would
in time become a common phenomenon. However, they did not
anticipate future advances in medical knowledge and hygiene. This
life table was published in the journal *Human Biology* (No. 1, 1934,
article entitled "Longevity in the United States") and repeated in *Population* for February, 1934.

The optimum table computed by Dublin and Lotka determined the
average life expectancy of an infant (for both sexes together) as not
quite 70 yr (exactly 69·9). As compared with the state of things thus
far described by U.S. statistics (1901: 49·2 yr, 1930: 59·7 yr) this
denoted a considerable advance. The forecasts of the American demographers mentioned above are very near to their realization: according to the table for 1951 for the white population, the average length

of life of men in the U.S.A. is 66·6 yr; of women, 72·6 yr. In some other countries, the average computed for both sexes together exceeds 70 yr (the Netherlands; Sweden; the white population of New Zealand).

In 1941, i.e. seventeen years after the publishing of the optimum table of Dublin and Lotka, in the office for demographic analysis of the Metropolitan Life Insurance Company, a new hypothetical table was made.

The average length of life of an infant—an optimum one under existing conditions—was determined this time as 70·8 years.[32] As compared with the previous table we notice a small change: the optimum life expectancy of infants increases by about 1 yr.

Thus the optimum proportion of persons surviving to old age (60 yr) has not been greatly affected by this change: we can establish it at about 80 per cent.

Dublin, Lotka and M. Spiegelman point to the fact that in the life table for 1946 for the white population of the U.S.A. the average life expectancy of women was only half a year lower than the above stated optimum value.[33] We do not consider this comparison to be justified. One may, and even must, compare the real with the hypothetical characteristics, but only for homogenous groups. However, the American demographers compare the real characteristics *for women* (of course higher) with the hypothetical characteristics for *both sexes together*. Such "lessons in optimism" are not fully correct.

Further optimum life tables are found in the work of the American statistician P. K. Whelpton entitled *Forecasts of the Population of the United States, 1945–1975*, published in 1947 by the Bureau of the Census in Washington.

Whelpton computed two pairs of such tables: one pair on the basis of American material, the second based on world material.

The basis for the computation of the first pair of tables was the American statistical data for 1940 on mortality among the white population in particular states of the U.S., arranged by sex and age. The optimum tables—one for men, the second for women—were constructed by Whelpton on the basis of the *lowest* probability of death that he found for each age in the material. It became evident that in the mortality tables constructed by this method the average length of life of an infant is 5–6 yr greater than those shown in official American life tables for the same period, that is 6·4 yr higher for white men and 5·3 yr for white women.

The second pair of tables has been drawn up from the lowest

probabilities of death taken from world statistical material. As compared with the official American life tables for 1940, for the white population Whelpton obtained results 6·6 yr higher for men and 4·4 yr higher for women.

Besides optimum tables Whelpton made perspective computations up to 1975, based on three different assumptions:

(a) high mortality assumptions;
(b) low mortality assumptions;
(c) medium mortality assumptions.

It should be explained that according to the first of these hypotheses the mortality rate, rising gradually, would attain the level of 13·5 per thousand in 1975; according to the second it would hover around 10 per thousand, and according to the third would be 11 per thousand about 1960 and 12 per thousand in 1975.

How are these hypotheses connected with the process of population aging going on in the United States? Dublin, Lotka and Spiegelman give the following answer: "As the proportion of aged persons in the population rises, the high death rates of that period of life will assume increasing weight in the total mortality picture. In the case of the 'low' assumptions, the reductions in the age-specific death rates within the period up to the year 1975 are sufficient to offset the effect of the aging of the population."[34]

Thus, independently of the hypothesis assumed, the general picture of mortality will be formed under a strong, although often invisible, influence of the population aging process.

What is the proportion of persons surviving to old age in Whelpton's computations?

In the light of perspective computations based on low mortality assumptions the proportion of persons surviving to the age of 60 will, in the U.S.A., reach a level in 1975 not yet met there, namely about 85 per cent (per 100 infants of the white population).

The evolution of the number of people surviving to 60 years has been as follows:

1901 . . . . not quite 50%
1946 . . . . not quite 75%
1950 . . . . about   76%

The above figures concern the whole population of the United States. For the exclusively white population these figures would be higher. It may be assumed that in 1951 the number of people surviving to old age among the white population was 79 per cent.

From these figures it seems probable that the level of 85 per cent would be reached earlier than would appear from Whelpton's forecast. It is the more probable since the life tables for some European countries—for instance Norway, Sweden, Great Britain—for many years show over 80 per cent of the population surviving to 60 yr.

It remains to discuss the hypothetical life table, the "Table de survie biologique" by the French demographer J. Bourgeois-Pichat.

In constructing this table, Bourgeois-Pichat wished to determine the limit approached by the systematically increasing value l (number of persons surviving to old age) in contemporary life tables. The Bourgeois-Pichat computation is based on the hypothesis that infectious diseases (tuberculosis, etc.) will be exterminated, while the degenerative diseases (cancer, heart diseases, etc.) will not increase.

The number living is given in this table as:

at birth	10,000
at 10 yr	9885
at 20 yr	9875
at 30 yr	9846
at 40 yr	9770
at 60 yr	9036
at 80 yr	4999

According to this table for 10,000 infants, 9036 or 90·4 per cent will survive to 60 yr.

It is interesting that late old age (80 yr) will be reached by half of the total number of infants.

Is the author not too optimistic? In the opinion of Alfred Sauvy there exists a chance of a considerable lengthening of human life, even much greater than assumed by Bourgeois-Pichat. "Il est vrai," writes Sauvy, "que les meurtriers les plus rebelles comme le cancer peuvent un jour trouver leur maître. Il ne saurait donc être question d'imposer une limite véritable à la vie humaine."[35]

If we draw the lesson of previous experience we see that there is no reason to treat the Bourgeois-Pichat forecast as unreal. We are witnessing an astonishing and uninterrupted advance in science and technique. We can anticipate that, in the future as in the past, life will outstrip the boldest demographic forecasts.

REFERENCES

1. L. Krzywicki, *Ludy. Zarys antropologii etnicznej (Nations Outline of Ethnic Antropology)*, Warsaw, 1893, p. 47.

2. I. Schwidetzky, *Das Problem des Völkertodes. Eine Studie zur historischen Bevölkerungsbiologie.* Ferd. Enke Verlag, Stuttgart, 1954, p. 90.

3. *Ibid*, p. 90.

4. As quoted by A. L. Vischer, *Das Alter als Schicksal und Erfüllung. III. Ausgabe.* Bruno Schwabe und Co. Verlag, Basel, 1955, p. 69.

5. *Ibid.*, pp. 69–70.

6. "Longevity from Ancient to Modern Times", *Stat. Bull.* (Metropolitan Life Insurance Company), 1947, No. 10.

7. W. F. Willcox, *Studies in American Demography*, Ithaca, New York, 1940, p. 59.

8. "It is unlikely that even the most backward area of the world of today has a mortality record much worse than that established in the center of civilization 2000 years ago" (Dublin, Lotka, Spiegelman, *Length of Life*, 1949, p. 30) (see below.)

9. Dublin, Lotka and Spiegelman, *Length of Life. A Study of the Life Table*, Revised edition, The Ronald Press Company, New York, 1949, p. 30.

10. "While the ingenuity and enterprise of Pearson and other investigators of early records are to be commended, probably the only conclusion to be drawn with any great degree of accuracy is that, in antiquity, the average length of life may have been somewhere between 20 and 30 years" ("Longevity from Ancient to Modern Times," *Statistical Bulletin* 1947, No. 10).

11. P. Herre, *Schöpferisches Alter*, II Ausgabe, Leipzig, 1943, pp. 18–19.

12. J. C. Russell, *British Medieval Population*, University of New Mexico Press, Albuquerque, 1948.

13. *Roczniki Dziejów Społecznych i Gospodarczych (Annal of Social and Economic History)* 1953, Vol. 15, Poznań, 1955, PWN, pp. 388–90.

14. "This figure (35·28 E.R.), which represents at best the situation among the more favored economic classes, may be indicative of some gain in longevity since the beginning of the Christian Era" (*Stat. Bull.* 1947, No. 10).

15. The well-known American demographer, Frank Lorimer, defends the computation method used by Graunt and considers it "a brilliant conception" in conditions of a total lack of information about the age of the deceased. (F. Lorimer, "The development of demography", in a joint work, *The Study of Population, an Inventory and Appraisal*, edited by P. M. Hauser and O. D. Duncan, University of Chicago Press, Chicago, 1959, pp. 126–7).

16. F. Prinzing, *Die Sterblichkeit in der bürgerlichen Bevölkerung Deutschlands seit den Zeiten der Karolinger*, in the work by A. Lindheim: *Saluti senectutis*, Leipzig and Vienna 1909, p. 206.

17. From the work of the American demographer Thompson we extract the following information: Dupré de St. Maur computed that in France before 1750 only 540 children out of 1000 born survived to 5 yr, and only 484 to 10 yr (*Population Problems*, McGraw-Hill Publications in Sociology, 3rd edition, New York and London 1924, p. 220). The above data, although fragmentary, leave no doubt that the tempo of dying in France of the mid-18th century was very rapid.

18. J. M. Kuliszer, *Dzieje gospodarcze Europy zachodniej (The Economic History of Western Europe)*. Polish edition, Vol. 2, pp. 79–80.

19. M. R. Reinhard, *Histoire de la Population Mondiale de 1700 à 1948*, Éditions Domat-Montchrestien (no date or place of publication given).

20. K. Marx and F. Engels, *Collected Works*.

21. H. Westergaard and H. C. Nybolle, *Grundzüge der Theorie der Statistik*, II. Ausgabe, Gustav Fischer, Jena, 1928, pp. 40–41.

22. *Ibid.*, p. 38.

23. G. von Mayr, *Statistik und Gesellschaftslehre*, 2 Band, Freiburg im Breisgau 1897, p. 292.

24. J. Rahts, "Sterbetafeln", in a joint work *Die Statistik in Deutschland*, 1 Band, 1911, p. 464.

25. S. P. Jain, "Mortality Trends in India". *Proceedings of the World Population Conference*, 1954, Vol. 1, United Nations, New York, 1955, p. 441.

26. S. Chandrasekhar, *India's Population. Fact and Policy*, New York, 1946, p. 73.

27. B. K. Sarkar, "I quozienti di natalità, di mortalità e di aumento naturale nell'India attuale nel quadro della demografia comparata," *Actes du Congrés International des Études sur la Population*, Vol. 6, Rome 1934, p. 573.

28. "La condition de la femme, pour des raisons de coutume et de religion est particulièrement mauvaise aux Indes. Conséquence: la mortalité féminine y est supérieure à celle de tout autre pays" (G. Bouthoul, *La Surpopulation dans le Monde*. Payot, Paris, 1958, p. 9).

29. Using data from 1941–50, H. F. Dorn calls attention to the fact that "in India slightly over one-half of newborn female infants are alive at age twenty; only three in ten survive to the end of the reproductive period". (H. F. Dorn, "Mortality," in a collective work, *The Study of Population, An Inventory and Appraisal*, edited by P. M. Hauser and O. D. Duncan, University of Chicago Press, 1959, pp. 457–8).

30. Those who travel like to tell about the many old people met among primitive peoples. Critical anthropologists put no credence in these reports. Moreover, A. L. Vischer (*Das Alter als Schicksal und Erfüllung*, p. 70) believes that the chances of meeting aged people among primitive peoples are slim, since length of life is primarily dependent on social factors and these are not of the best.

31. J. Gabriel, "Évolution et tendances actuelles de la mortalité en Belgique", *Proceedings of the World Population Conference, 1954*, United Nations, New York 1955, p. 95.

32. "A lesson in optimism", *Stat. Bull.* (Metropolitan Life Insurance Company) No. 11, 1941.

33. L. I. Dublin, A. J. Lotka and M. Spiegelman, *Length of Life*, revised edition, Ronald Press Company, New York, 1949, pp. 167–168.

34. *Ibid.*, p. 170.

35. A. Sauvy, *L'Europe et sa Population*, pp. 54–5. The same idea is developed by the author in *De Malthus à Mao Tsé Toung, le Problème de la Population dans le Monde*. Éditiën Denoël, Paris, 1958, pp. 51–52.

CHAPTER 7

The Normal Length of Human Life

IN RESEARCH on population aging we should not overlook the biometric function of the life table which shows the mean length of life of aged persons, or the normal length of human life.

In this chapter we shall deal with this biometric function, first giving the method of computing the normal length of life and then its historical evolution.

1. METHOD OF COMPUTING NORMAL LENGTH OF LIFE

(a) Historical Note

Let us begin with a question that since time immemorial has preoccupied the human mind and which concerns the ordinary mortal as well as the researcher.

This question is: *How long should a man live?*

The same question sometimes occurs in another form. For instance: *How long could a man live if diseases and all kinds of harmful circumstances did not exist?* Or, *what length of human life has been determined by nature?*

It must be stated that the above question (whether so formulated or not) is outside the field of demography, especially demographical statistics. The problem of the natural length of life, or the age nature fixed for man, is the incontestable domain of the natural scientists.

But one may be confronted by still another question: *What is the usual, normal limit of human life?*

This question concerns, not a natural, but a normal length of human life or, according to the terminology in use—the normal life expectancy. Thus, it is evident that only statistical observation can supply the material on which to base an adequate answer.

A knowledge of statistics and of demography—and both originate from political arithmetic—is concerned with the problem of the expectation of human life from the moment of birth. But political arithmetic came into being relatively late. As the date of its origin

140

we can assume the year 1662, when it appeared in the work of the first political arithmetician, the Englishman Graunt. His work bore the title: *Natural and Political Observations upon the Bills of Mortality*.

Of course, statistics was necessary for a scientific answer to the question concerning life expectancy. However, the question itself and the attempts to answer it are as old as the world.

A short review will be given here of these attempts which we may term primitive and, by their nature, highly uncertain estimates of the normal length of life, found in preserved religious and philosophical literature.

One of the oldest and best-known writings concerning the length of human life is the Ninetieth Psalm from the Old Testament:

"The days of our years are threescore years and ten

And if by reason of strength they be fourscore years,

Yet is their strength labour and sorrow;

For it is soon cut off, and we fly away."

It states that at the time of the king and prophet David the normal length of human life amounted to 70–80 yr.

Exactly the same time (70–80 yr) was the normal length of life determined by the Chinese wise men, King Solomon, the Greek historian, Herodotus and the old Hindu law makers of the Upanishads. There were still other estimates of life expectancy.

The Greek poet Mimnermus of the 7th century B. C., complaining of the vanity of human life, mentioned that death reaches man when he is sixty years old. This assertion was opposed by the greatest of the seven Greek sages, Solon, who stated that the limit of human life should be set at 80 yr.

Now we have not two but three values characterizing the normal length of life in antiquity: 60, 70 and 80 yr. Of course they have no relation to the mathematical precision which is required in contemporary statistics.

It may be of interest that the estimate of the psalmist found adherents among the statisticians of the 19th and 20th centuries.

The German statistician Max Haushofer spoke of this estimate with some respect: "eine Schätzung, die für ihre Zeit sehr vernünftig genannt werden kann".[1]

The imaginative German statistician Gottlieb Schnapper-Arndt (1847–1904), whose course of social statistics can, even today, be recommended as a thrilling lecture, was astonished about the similarity of the results of the investigations on life expectancy in his times (70–75 yr) to the estimate of the psalmist. Under this impression he wrote: "Und damit wären wir denn glücklich unter Anwendung eines gigantischen Verwaltungsapparates und mit den Hilfsmitteln der höheren Mathematik zu der Weisheit des Psalmisten... wieder zurückgelangt."[2]

In our opinion this attitude is unjustified. Even if the results of the two observations do agree (but not quite corresponding to reality), it must be remembered that the comparison of the results of researches based on exact statistical observations with the primitive estimate of the psalmist has not and cannot have any real value.

Thus, in no case can such a detail be raised to the level of a statistical document. In the Ninetieth Psalm we can see only a proof of the interest shown ages ago in the normal limit of human life.

There exists still one source of approximate and generally incorrect estimates of length of life—popular beliefs. Some Germans believed that the length of life of various beings can be constructed as a mathematical scheme. According to this scheme the normal length of human life was predicted as 81 yr.

Among Polish folk there is a belief in a symbolic "two axes" or 77 yr. This is supposed to be the limit beyond which human life does not extend.

Of course, these estimates cannot claim to be statistical documents. Against the proverbial authority of "folk wisdom" we can quote the attitude of the German philosopher Artur Schopenhauer (1788–1860) who, in his aphorisms (*Aphorismen zur Lebensweisheit*) sharply criticized the nonchalant generalizations besed on a primitive and shallow look at daily experience. The psalmist's estimate, pseudo-mathematical schemes of length of life, are merely such nonchalant generalizations.

The creators of scientific statistics and demography, the first political arithmeticians—Graunt, Petty and Halley—although greatly interested in the duration of human life did not pay any attention to the problem of the normal limit of life. Also, nothing new was contributed by the famous Berlin minister Johann Peter Süssmilch, the author of a two-volume work entitled: "Göttliche Ordnung in den Veränderungen des menschlichen Geschlechts aus der Geburt, dem Tode und der Fortpflanzung desselben erwiesen" (1740). In accordance with his theocratic assumptions, Süssmilch considered the order of mortality to be invariable and, in this connection, that the law of mortality formulated by the psalmist was still in force.

It is interesting that the initiative towards undertaking research on life expectancy, and finding a measure that would enable a definition of its value, did not originate from the statisticians, but from natural scientists. Flourens in France, Josef Majer in Poland and Tarchanov in Russia were pioneers in this field.

Pierre Jean Marie Flourens (1794–1867), the excellent French physiologist, published in 1854 the work entitled: *De la longévité humaine*. In this work Flourens mentioned the normal duration of life (according to his terminology "la vie ordinaire") as one of the four basic measures of the length of human life. He defines the normal life as the age commonly (communément) reached by those who escape accidents which shorten human life. Flourens meant that the normal duration of life is approximately an average life of aged persons ("c'est en quelque sorte la vie moyenne des vieillards").

It should be conceded that in this formulation there is not only a germ but a full conception of human life expectancy as a mathematical measure of length of life. We shall soon ascertain that Wilhelm Lexis, who has been regarded as the creator of the above measure, did nothing more than assume one of the averages, namely the model of the age of persons deceased in old age, as the measure of a normal length of life.

Also the result of Flourens's computations—"La durée ordinaire est à peu près de 75 ans"—should be acknowledged as fully reliable: in the middle of the past century the normal length of life in France was undoubtedly about 75 yr.

Flourens's work was published in 1855 in German translation and in the author's own country had many editions (the fifth French edition was in 1872).

In Poland, the idea and method of research on life expectancy was developed by the Cracow physiologist Josef Majer (1808–99).

Many years before Wilhelm Lexis, who began the modern method of computing life expectancy, Majer formulated the conception of this measure as an "average of the duration of life of persons who have achieved old age".[3]

We have mentioned the investigations of Flourens. The question arises whether Majer did not sometimes profit from the contributions of his French colleague who enjoyed such a great scientific authority. We may assume that this was possible. However, this circumstance should not diminish the importance of the work of the Cracow scientist, which brought new ideas to Polish scientific literature.

The works of the above researchers and of the Russian Ivan Tar-chanov (1846–1908) cleared the way for the proper method of comput-ing life expectancy. This was achieved by the German statistician and excellent methodologist, Wilhelm von Lexis.

(b) The Concept of Wilhelm von Lexis

A good augury for finding a method of measuring the normal length of life was the application of the theory of statistics. This is the achieve-ment of Wilhelm von Lexis. In 1877 von Lexis stated his conception of the normal duration of life as the age at which occurs the greatest concentration of deaths of aged persons (in his work *Zur Theorie der Massenerscheinungen in der menschlichen Gesellschaft*). A quarter of a century later he returned to the same problem in his paper, "Abhand-lungen zur Theorie der Bevölkerungs- und Mortalitätsstatistik" (1903).

Tracing the curve of deaths by age, von Lexis observed certain regularities. The curve shows two peaks: one at the very threshold of human life, i.e. in infancy; the second in old age, somewhere between 65 and 75 yr. Between these two maxima occurs one minimum at about 10 yr.

Accordingly von Lexis divided the curve of deaths into parts, separating out the deaths of aged persons, beginning with 60 yr. In this period of life the deaths follow a fairly regular course in the shape of a bell (the normal distribution).

In the opinion of von Lexis only deaths in old age can be treated as normal. Therefore to determine the normal human age we should eliminate the deaths of children unfit for life (0–9 yr) and premature deaths (10–59 yr) and then base the computation on deaths in old age (60 yr and over).

The regularity of the curve of deaths in old age, with its clearly defined peak, led von Lexis to the conclusion that the age in which the largest number of deaths at old age occur is the normal end of life in keeping with the "typical organism" of man.

The measure suggested by von Lexis has found wide application in research on the duration of life. It appears in demographic literature under different names: "die normale Lebensdauer", "das Normalalter", "vita normale", "normal length of life", etc.

The technique of computation of the normal duration of life by von Lexis's method is as follows: from the column d_x of the life table we find the greatest number of deaths in old age; the age corresponding to this number is the normal duration of life.

Here are a few examples of the application of the von Lexis's method.

**NORMAL DURATION OF LIFE OF THE JAPANESE
ACCORDING TO THE MORTALITY TABLE FOR 1921—25**

Men		Women	
age	number of deaths	age	number of deaths
68	1808	73	1784
69	1831	74	1796
70	1831	75	1793
71	1802	76	1773

Source: Japanese mortality table No. 4, Tokyo 1930.

In the above table the maximum of deaths for men occurs in the years 69 and 70, for women at 74 yr. Thus, according to von Lexis's method, we can state that in the years 1921–5 the normal life duration of Japanese was 69–70 yr for men, and 74 for women.

Let us make the same use of the mortality table of the Federal German Republic:

**NORMAL DURATION OF LIFE IN THE F. G. R.
ACCORDING TO THE MORTALITY TABLE FOR 1949—51**

Men		Women	
age	number of deaths	age	number of deaths
75	3056	77	3603
76	3120	78	3661
77	3152	79	3670
78	3150	80	3624
79	3116	81	3521

Source: General table of mortality of the Federal German Republic 1949–51, Wiesbaden 1953.

According to this table the normal duration of life for men is 77 yr, for women 79 yr.

A difference between the Japanese and German tables is quite evident: the normal duration of life for Japanese in 1921–1925 differed by 7–8 yr for men and 5 for women from those of the F.G.R. in the years 1949–51. The difference in time at which the data were gathered does not cancel the value of our comparison. We only wish to show that at different times and places the normal duration of life is different.

Thus, the thesis about the invariability of the normal duration of life preached by the minister-statistician Süssmilch, adherent to the idea of "God's order" in demographic phenomena, must be dropped. What is more, the investigation of changes occurring in the normal duration of life becomes indispensable.

Wilhelm von Lexis has given us a convenient instrument for measuring the normal length of life and, at the same time, defining differences in its level with time and space.

What more can be said about the theoretical value of this instrument?

The critics have many objections. Numerous researchers point out that it is unjustified to assume as normal an age at death which has been computed on the basis of the totality of deaths in old age, i.e. not only normal but premature ones.

Such objections hit at the cognitive value of von Lexis's measure. The author of this measure expressed the view that the normal age at death computed by his method corresponds to the "organic type" of man. This assertion is rather unfortunate and, consequently, we share the opinion of critics contesting the cognitive value of von Lexis's measure understood in the above sense. Let us add that this criticism of the measure proved fruitful since it led to the construction of new measures basing the computation of the normal duration of life only on normal deaths.

If we reject the incorrect qualification of von Lexis's measure as characteristic of the "organic type" of man, we should still consider whether it does not have a definite and sensible cognitive value as one measure of the duration of life. This cannot be denied: the normal duration of life computed by von Lexis's measure is the mode in an age when most people die in old age and it is also a descriptive parameter of all deaths in such an age. In this sense we may even speak of it as a *normal age*.

But this still does not solve the question of the value of von Lexis's measure as a characteristic of all deaths in old age. In our opinion, this value is nevertheless rather small. The weakness of von Lexis's measure is that it does not concern the number of deaths corresponding to the age which is considered as normal. The age of 75 yr chosen on the basis of, say, 1500 deaths would by equally representative as that age computed from 3000 deaths (where $\Sigma d_x = 100,000$).

Therefore, when considering the value of von Lexis's measure we reach the conclusion that this measure cannot be ascribed great importance. Its necessary and unconditional complement should be the maximum deaths in old age. We consider it justified to state that from the two elements involved here—the maximum number of deaths in old age and the age at which the maximum is reached—von Lexis has given fundamental importance to the element of lesser importance. Better and worse demographic conditions differ considerably more as to the maximum number of deaths in old age than as to the normal age.

(c) The Method of Josef Majer

Josef Majer took an interest in the computation of the normal duration of life in connection with the figures given by Flourens which the Cracow physiologist objected to as not conforming with reality.

Flourens thought that a life duration of from 80 to 100 yr would be regarded as normal. The Polish scholar did not agree. "The very rarity of such cases," objects Majer, "contradicts the notion of the usual." We see that the Cracow physiologist used the term "usual length of life" (the term "normal length of life" originated later) and thus the view cited deals with the usualness of surviving to a given age.

As we see, the frequency of deaths at a definite age was important to Majer. "The usual duration of life...," wrote Majer, "should be called its limit in the year of old age in which the greatest mortality occurs."[4]

Thus, in principle, Majer supported the theory of von Lexis.

However, the Cracow physiologist took into account the difficulties connected with application of von Lexis's method, namely the poorly arranged or disarranged series of values of d_x in mortality tables. How was he to proceed in such cases?

Majer suggested the following solution: "Since oscillations are frequent this term should be regarded as an average length of life of persons entering an old age of 60 yr."

The method suggested by the Polish scholar, which we shall call the Majer method, can be given by the following formula:

$$\text{normal duration of life} = 60 \text{ yr} + e^0_{60}$$

where: e^0_{60} is the average further duration of life for persons of 60 yr.

An example where the Majer method can by applied is easily found.

In the Japanese mortality table for 1921–1925 mentioned above, the average further duration of life of persons of 60 yr is:

for men. . . . . 11·9 yr
for women . . . . 14·1 yr[5]

Thus, the normal duration of life computed by the Majer method is:

for men . . . . 71·9 yr

for women . . . . 74·1 yr

The question arises: how do the results of computations made by the von Lexis and Majer methods compare?

To answer this question we shall again use the Japanese, German, and Polish mortality tables already quoted.

This is the normal duration of life in Japan computed on the basis of the mortality table of this country for the years 1921–5:

NORMAL DURATION OF LIFE IN JAPAN 1921–5

Method of computation	Normal age	
	men	women
von Lexis's method	69–70	74
Majer's method	71·9	74·1

Source: Author's computation based on the Japanese life table No. 4.

It appears that there are no great differences between the results of computation by different methods: the difference for men is a few years; for women the results are almost identical.

Also, insignificant differences result from comparison of the normal values of life duration obtained by the above two methods for the Federal German Republic on the basis of the life table for the years 1949–51. The proof is evident in the following statement:

NORMAL DURATION OF LIFE IN THE F. G. R. 1949–51

Method	Normal age	
	men	women
von Lexis's method	77	79
Majer's method	76·2	77·5

Source: Author's computation based on the life table for the Federal German Republic, 1949–51.

This time the difference for men does not exceed 0·8 yr and for women 1¹/₂ yr.

It may be pointed out that higher values have been obtained by von Lexis's method both for men and for women. Previously, in the Japanese life table, higher values were obtained by Majer's method.

Let us consider the normal duration of life in Poland as computed by the two different methods.

For Poland we shall state the data based on two life tables: for 1927 (for both sexes together); and for the years 1931–2 (for each sex separately).

NORMAL DURATION OF LIFE IN POLAND,
1927 AND 1931–2

Period	Sex	Normal age computed by the method		Difference in years
		of von Lexis	of Majer	
1927.	m. plus f.	74	74·4	0·4
1931–2.	m.	72–73	73·7	0·7–1·7
	f.	75	75·1	0·1

Source: Author's computation on the basis of Polish life tables for 1927 and 1931–32.

In the tables previously discussed (Japanese and West German) the differences in the results of the computations made by the two methods were insignificant. In the last case these differences were close to zero.

These examples show that in a number of cases Majer's method and von Lexis's method lead to approximate if not identical results.

This conformity of results obtained by different methods should not astonish us since it is a logical consequence of the normal distribution of the set d_x in the life table; the normal duration of life as computed by Majer's method hides an arithmetic average of the same set for which von Lexis computes the mode. As the theory of statistics teaches us, the more a distribution approaches the normal, the smaller is the difference between the arithmetic mean and the mode.

There are still other facts: between the results found by Majer's method and by von Lexis's method a discrepancy sometimes occurs. As an illustration we state below data based on the old Russian life tables:

NORMAL DURATION OF LIFE IN EUROPEAN RUSSIA,
1874–83 AND 1896–7

Years	Normal age computed by the method of		Difference in years
	von Lexis	Majer	
1874–83	63–64	71·5	7·5–8·5
1896–7	68	74·1	6·1

Source: Author's computation based on Russian life tables for 1874–83 and 1896–7.

Thus the differences are great, amounting to from 6 to 8 yr depending of the period. It is necessary to considered why they arise.

It would not be strange to look for the causes of these differences in the faulty methods computing the life tables. The primitive method of computing, and not only of Russian life tables, was well known.

However, in this case there is no reason to be suspicious on this point: the Russian life table for the years 1874–83 (for the Orthodox population in European Russia) was made by talented statistician and professor of the University of Berlin, Wladyslaw Bortkiewicz who, in his youth when studying the theory of statistics, specialized in the method of drawing up life tables.

The causes of these differences must lie elsewhere.

We have already mentioned the work of Nowoselski on the specific conditions of mortality in ancient Russia. These investigations revealed a characteristic fact: in Russia a high mortality rate of children was accompanied by a very low mortality rate of aged persons.

Some details should be examined here.

The period of old age is counted conventionally from the age of 60 yr. But it is not from this age that the relatively low probabilities of death so characteristic for the old Russian life tables are dated. The specific character of these tables becomes evident much later, somewhere about 70 yr, and appears in full beginning at 80 yr.

From this follow some essential results:

(1) the normal duration of life computed by von Lexis's method is relatively low since its level is determined by the maximum numbers of deaths and these occur in the ages between 60 and 70;

(2) the normal duration of life computed by Majer's method is incomparably higher since its length is determined by the further average duration for persons of 60 yr; thus, not only the high numbers of deaths between 60 and 70 but also the low numbers over 70 and the very low over 80 are significant.

The difference between the results of the computations made by the two methods is due to the fact that the von Lexis method does not take into account the course of the death curve after passing the peak while the Majer method considers its course up to the very end, i.e. to the highest age contained in the life table.

We have dwelt on this problem since it throws some light not only on the mortality conditions in old Russia but also on the value of two different measures of the normal duration of life which we shall use in our considerations. Our conclusions are as follows:

(1) in principle neither the von Lexis measure nor the Majer measure presents an adequate characteristic of mortality conditions in general; these are mainly measures of life duration of old people;

(2) the meaning of the two measures is approximate but not identical;

(3) since each of them has its own meaning it should be recognized that, in principle, both methods have their uses.

(d) The Method of Karl Freudenberg

In recent times, demographers have been more frequently concerned with other methods of computing the normal duration of life which differ not only in computation but also in idea. We have in mind a method suggested by Professor Karl Freudenberg of Berlin. It differs from the quasi-classical method of von Lexis in that the normal duration of life is not computed from all deaths occurring in old age, but only from those which are considered *normal*.

The normal duration of life thus conceived can be calculated only if statistics of deaths according to causes are available. Besides, a scientific division into normal and premature deaths is necessary.

This new conception and method of finding the normal duration of life were presented by Professor Freudenberg in his work: *Die Gesetzmässigkeit der menschlichen Lebensdauer*, published in 1934. The author used as working materials both life tables and records of deaths classified by causes.

The following conclusions reached by Freudenberg as a result of an analysis of the life duration in Germany merit special attention:

(1) the computation of the normal life duration of the German population in 1932–4 found by parametric calculation provides numerical values higher than those obtained by numbers mechanically adjusted. By the latter method the author obtained 75·8 yr for men and 76·9 yr for women; parametric computation yields 79·9 yr and 80·9 yr respectively;

(2) the results of parametric calculation differ only a little from the computation of "normal age" on the basis of the statistics for causes of death. This led Freudenberg to the conclusion that the normal duration of life of the German population, by both computations, is 80 or somewhat over 80 yr.

"On revient toujours à son premier amour." Twenty years after publishing this work, Freudenberg returned to the problem of mortality in old age, publishing a new work in this field in the journal *Schweizerische Zeitschrift für Volkswirtschaft und Statistik*.[6]

In his new work the author presents his conception of the normal duration of life computed on the basis of the statistics for causes of death and submits practical examples of the application of his methods, using materials contained in the *U.N. Demographic Yearbook* for 1953.

What are the possibilities for application of Freudenberg's method? They are not very great. We have pointed out at the beginning that it can be used only when there are precise and properly differentiated statistics of death.

Of course, many countries have such statistics today. In Germany their beginnings go back to the nineties of the last century. But they were very modest beginnings: only a few more important causes of death were listed; there were only four age groups; the sex of the deceased was not considered. In addition, the accuracy at that time was open to question.[7]

In many countries such shortcomings are today things of the past. But not everywhere. Professor Freudenberg states that the computation of the normal age by his method is already impossible for southern Europe and all the more so for tropical countries, owing to the lack of statistical material on which his computation should be based.

A somewhat modified Freudenberg's method is used by the Swiss Statistical Office. The modifications in method introduced by the Swiss statisticians consist in some corrections to the system of normal causes of death assumed by the Berlin professor.[8]

In comparison with von Lexis's method the computations in Freudenberg's method usually produce higher numerical results. For the years 1939–44 the above–mentioned Swiss computations showed values for normal life duration of 84-5 yr. This is not surprising: in Freudenberg's method premature deaths are eliminated and these as a rule occur in a less advanced age.

Some authors consider Freudenberg's measure more accurate than von Lexis's. We do not share this opinion. In our view, it is a question of two different characteristics, each having its own meaningful content. Consequently, they are not in competition.

Freudenberg thinks that for comparison of normal life age in various countries his method is better suited than the classical von Lexis method. "The comparing of normal ages in various territories," says Freudenberg, "has some value only if the statistics are equally reliable. However, one should not base one's computation on the normal age which is obtained directly from the life tables since they are still mostly influenced by premature deaths" (*op. cit.*, p. 457).

We agree fully with the first part of the above statement: only fully reliable data can be compared. The second part seems to be unconvincing because, sometimes, a characteristic that does not overlook premature deaths may be more useful. For our considerations the values of normal life duration based on the totality of deaths in old age are more instructive than those referring only to "normal" deaths.

It should also be stated that Freudenberg's method is not backed by the authority of the biological sciences. Freudenberg reckons part of the deaths in old age among normal deaths while the biologists reduce normal deaths to quite exceptional cases.

What deaths do the biologists recognize as normal?

The Soviet biologist Nagorny speaks about a life cycle that finds its natural epilogue or its end as a result of the action of internal factors of the organism itself and adds: "It is a cycle that ends with a physiological death in old age, not in a death caused by external factors strange to the life process".[9]

The German philosopher Schopenhauer defines as natural those deaths that follow without disease, not accompanied by suffering ("ohne Krankheit, ohne Todeskampf, ohne Röcheln, ohne Zuckung, bisweilen ohne zu erblassen; welches die Euthanasie heisst").

How often do such normal deaths occur?

Nagorny quotes American statistics for 1900–10 which show that, in 98 cases out of 100, death was caused by diseases, accidents, etc. Only in two cases was death due to old age. Premature deaths thus made up 98 per cent and normal deaths only 2 per cent of the total.

But even this insignificant percentage of normal deaths is contested by the biologists. "Often a death which we deem to be a consequence of aging," says Nagorny, "actually has other causes." The author refers to research by L. Aschoff (1938) who performed autopsies on 400 corpses of persons over 65 years of age, seemingly deceased in consequence of old age. On this basis he stated that disease was the real cause of death in all cases, without exception.

In the light of these facts Nagorny's statement becomes conceivable: that "physiological" death has not yet been found, either in man or in animals. Thus, all deaths, including those currently called "natural death", are produced by the action of external factors strange to the life process; it is not old age but disease that ends human life.

We should not close our eyes to the fact that the views of biologists given above throw some doubt on Freudenberg's theory which, in spite of these views, reckons most deaths occurring in old age as normal deaths. It seems that the scientific foundations of Freudenberg's theory are not yet crystallized.

(e) Other Methods of Determining Normal Age

Freudenberg's method is not the last method of computing normal age. Other methods have been suggested. One is the method of H. Kracke which appears in the literature of statistics.

H. Kracke stated his method in a work he prepared for printing, entitled: *Bemerkungen zur Verteilung der Sterbefälle nach den Deutschen Allgemeinen Sterbetafeln von 1871 bis 1951.* According to Professor Freudenberg who read the manuscript, Kracke's method is based not on statistics of the causes of death but on mortality tables. The starting point of Kracke's statements is the historical development of mortality in each particular year of life and extrapolation of the death curve to the asymptotic value at which it is assumed only normal deaths will remain. In this way Kracke reaches the conclusion that the normal duration of life in Germany was 80·6 yr.

Theoretically still another conception of determining normal life from mortality tables may by envisaged. Owing to the undoubted relation between the normal and the average duration of life, some measure of the relation between the average further duration of life and normal age may be constant.

This idea is suggested by the life tables of some countries (England, France, Germany) in which the normal age is followed by a further duration of life of 5–6 yr. Thus without any greater risk the normal duration of life may be determined as the age which, in life tables, is followed by five or six years further expectation of life.

Naturally, this would be a less precise measure to be used only in special cases when other, more accurate measures of normal life duration fail.

The vicissitudes of particular methods of computation of the normal life duration vary. Thus:

(1) Majer's method, despite its simplicity, has not been recognized;
(2) von Lexis's method became very popular and is still widely used today;
(3) Freudenberg's method, which is in the first stages, seems to be one that will achieve full recognition.

2. EVOLUTION OF NORMAL DURATION OF LIFE

(a) In Antiquity

It hardly seems justified to begin a historical outline of the development of normal life duration from primitive estimates found in ancient writings. We are not attracted by the example of those authors who, following the psalmist, Chinese sages and Herodotus, assume that the normal age in antiquity was 70–80 yr.

But this does not mean that we should completely renounce the attempt to reconstruct a normal life duration in antiquity. On the contrary, we want to undertake such an attempt, but on the basis of another source: the life table established by the Roman lawyer Ulpian.

Of course, we are aware that Ulpian's table is an uncertain source of statistical information. In our opinion it is more a historical relic that has no claim to being a statistical document. However, it may assumed that this source, with all its deficiencies, has a greater value than the free estimate of the psalmist.

Let us have a look at this interesting relic of ancient culture.

AVERAGE FURTHER DURATION OF LIFE IN ULPIAN'S TABLE (3RD CENTURY A.D.)

Age	Average further life duration	Age	Average further life duration
0–20	30	44–45	15
20–25	27	45–46	14
25–30	25	46–47	13
30–35	22	47–48	12
35–40	20	48–49	11
40–41	19	49–50	10
41–42	18	50–55	9
42–43	17	55–60	7
43–44	16	60 and over	5

Source: DUBLIN, LOTKA, SPIEGELMAN, *Length of Life*, pp. 30–31.

From this table we note two values of the average further duration of life: one for the age 50–55 yr, the second for the age of 60 yr and over. The first of these is 7 yr, the second 5 yr. If we apply to these numbers Majer's method of computing the normal age, then we obtain for ancient Rome a normal duration of 65–67 yr.

We previously expressed the hope that the Ulpian table would prove to be a more reliable source of information as to the normal length of life in antiquity than the estimate of the psalmist. The numbers we obtained seem to confirm our hope: the normal age computed on the basis of the Ulpian table appears to be closer to the truth.

(b) The Middle Ages

From the Middle Ages some estimates of the normal age have also been preserved in the form of literary works. Let us recall what Deschamps said in the beginning of the 15th century—that people aged very quickly: a woman of 30 and a man of 50 was old, and the age of 60 yr was the normal limit of human life. We have already criticized the information given by the French poet.

Could we not learn more about normal length of life in the Middle Ages as we did for antiquity, by means of life tables?

There are no life tables available from the Middle Ages; no such research was done in that epoch. But there do exist some retrospective computations made in our times.

In 1948 there appeared a highly interesting work by J. C. Russell on the population conditions in medieval England.[10]

It contains some retrospective life tables computed by the author. We shall note from these tables the average further length of life of 60-year-olds in order to determine by Majer's method the normal length of life.

NORMAL LENGTH OF LIFE IN MEDIEVAL ENGLAND

Year of birth	Average further length of life of 60-year-olds	Normal length of life
before 1276	9·42	69·4
1276–1300	8·30	68·3
1301–1325	9·29	69·3
1326–1348	10·81	70·8
1348–1375	10·90	70·9
1376–1400	9·98	70·0
1401–1425	10·47	70·5
1426–1450	13·71	73·7

Sources: (1) J. C. RUSSELL, *British Medieval Population*, p. 186: (2) author's computation by Majer's method.

The above results seem to be quite realistic, particularly if we eliminate from the computation the last value (73·7 yr) that differs greatly from the typical level. With this correction our computation would show a normal age of 68–71 yr for England in the period of the late Middle Ages.

In relation to the result obtained for ancient Rome this shows an increase in the normal length of life of 3–4 yr. We do not see here anything improbable. On the contrary, it is natural that English tables established many hundreds of years later than the Ulpian tables and based on material referring to the more privileged classes of English society, should show an increase in the normal length of life.

(c) The 19th Century

Next in our historical sketch of the evolution of the normal age we shall analyse the estimate of Christopher Bernoulli from the first half of the 19th century. Bernoulli was the first to define the normal length of life as the age at which the number of deaths due to old age is the highest; he estimated this age generally as 75 yr.

The Bernoulli estimate being localized neither as to time nor place cannot be of great significance for us. Moreover, it may be supposed that it is somewhat exaggerated for the first half of the 19th century.

Our opinion is based on the following facts:

(1) in Sweden, from the life table from the years 1816–40, the normal life duration, computed as the modal age of deceased aged persons, was 72 yr, and in Norway the same normal age was still noted in the second half of the century (1856–65);

(2) in France in the years 1817–32 the normal duration of life computed from data given by Demonferrand, by Majer's method was 73·2 for women and 73·3 for men;

(3) the normal age in England computed in the same way for the years 1838–54 from Farr's life table was 73·5 for men, and 74·3 yr for women.

Thus, for the first half of the 19th century values for the normal duration of life are found within the limits of 72 and 74 yr. It is evident that these data concern countries most advanced in hygienic conditions: only such countries felt the need of life tables. Thus we may consider that we have to do only with the *best* results in normal life duration.

In the second half of the 19th century the number of countries collecting regular population statistics (together with population censuses) and computing life tables by modern methods, was greatly increased. We shall not quote the many figures now available; we shall limit ourselves to the most characteristic.

Prominent European demographers of the second half of the 19th century, when they examined their observations, determined the typical normal length of life as follows:

Bodio. . . . . 70–71 yr
Bertillon (father) . . . . 73 yr
von Lexis . . . . 71–72 yr

The maximum values were much higher. In Sweden at the end of the century (1891–1900) the normal length of life was 78 yr. It was one of the highest, if not the highest, value for the normal length of life in the world.

(d) The 20th Century

In the 20th century we are witnessing a further increase in the normal length of life.

For the first time there appear on the statistical scene such values as 80 yr and over. These record-breaking values are for the moment the privilege of women. These are the highest values thus far achieved for the normal duration of life of women:

MAXIMUM VALUES OF THE NORMAL LENGTH OF LIFEOF WOMEN

Country	Period	Normal age (yr)
Norway	1945–8	82
Sweden	1946–50	81

Source: Life tables of the given countries.

Thus, the Scandinavian countries (Norway and Sweden) are first in the world as to the length of life of women (the same is true of the normal age of men).

The normal age of women in the Federal German Republic approaches this limit; judging from the life table of this country from the years 1949–51 it was 79 yr.

It would be more difficult to say what is the *average* normal length of life typical of modern conditions. It seems that, in the light of recent life tables of the economically developed countries, this age may by 75–76 yr.

The values of normal life duration as discussed above have been determined by means of the generally accepted von Lexis method. If we use Majer's method the picture becomes richer but also somewhat different. It is richer because of the abundant material on the average further duration of life of 60-year-old persons to be found in U.N. statistical and demographic yearbooks, different since, as we know, the results of the two computations do not always agree.

NORMAL DURATION OF LIFE COMPUTED BY J. MAJER'S METHOD (HIGHEST VALUES)

Country	Period covered	No. of years
Men:		
Norway	1946–50	78·4
Netherlands	1947–9	77·5
Denmark	1946–50	77·1
Sweden	1946–50	77·0
Women:		
Norway	1946–50	79·4
U.S.A., white population	1951	79·1
Canada	1950–2	78·6
New Zealand, European pop.	1950–2	78·5
England and Wales	1952	78·5
Netherlands	1947–9	78·2
Israel	1950–1	78·2

Source: U.N. statistical and demographic yearbooks for 1952 and 1954.

From the above review it can be shown that the maximum normal length of life for men is 77–79 yr; for women, 78–80 yr. The higher numbers for women conform to the generally known greater longevity of women.

It is worth while stressing the achievement of Norway, which has a record normal life duration both for men and women. The length of life called long by the psalmist is today Norway's norm for the whole population. Many countries are already within reach of this standard.

Of course, it would be interesting to find the conditions at the other demographic pole—in countries with the worst life tables. However, we prefer to renounce the attempt to reconstruct this picture by Majer's method, since this method is useless for societies where only an insignificant part of the population survives to 60.

When investigating the evolution of the normal length of life over the centuries we cannot use Freudenberg's method, for its application would require statistical materials unknown in past centuries. However, we can use his method to compute the normal age more recently.

NORMAL LENGTH OF LIFE IN CERTAIN COUNTRIES
COMPUTED BY FREUDENBERG'S METHOD, 1953

Country	Normal age (yr)
Iceland	85
Norway	84
Sweden	82
Denmark	82
Netherlands	82
Belgium	81
France	81
Federal German Republic	81
Switzerland	80

Source: *Schweizerische Zeitschrift für Volkswirtschaft und Statistik* 1955, No. 4, p. 453.

For a long time the northern countries have shown a high normal length of life, Sweden and Norway belonging traditionally to the countries with the highest normal age.

This time the number of northern countries with the highest achievements in extending human life is increased by Iceland. What is more, this country far outdistances other countries in the normal duration of life, according to Freudenberg's comparison.

This fact has great significance for investigations on the different normal ages in various countries. There has long been a contest between the adherents and opponents of the theory that climate plays the most important role in influencing the normal duration of life.

Some statisticians refer with particular liking to natural influences, especially to the climate, as exerting a decisive influence on longevity. In order to prove the thesis they make tables for countries with different geographical and climatic conditions and, from differences in normal length of life (such differences undoubtedly do exist) they draw conclusions about the decisive importance of climate. In these statements the economic and social differences in the countries are omitted, thus avoiding the unpleasant social inequality with regard to death.

The old climatic theory is being revived by some modern authors in a more ingenious form. Attention is called to the influence exerted by an increase of heat on the biologic processes (H. Linser: *Das Problem des Todes*. Vienna, 1952). In Freudenberg's opinion it is not good hygienic conditions that determine the high normal age in northern countries, but the climate which is healthful for the aged.[11]

When confronted with reality the climatic theory encounters many difficulties that the Berlin statistician cannot avoid. One difficulty is supplied by Iceland which, with unchanged climate, has been transformed within 100 yr from the country with the *lowest* to the country with the *highest* normal age. Let us add that within these hundred years Iceland rose from terrible poverty and now occupies one of the first places among civilized countries of the world.

The normal age of Icelanders, computed by Freudenberg's method, is 85 yr. It may be recalled that identical results were obtained in the computation of the normal duration of life for the Swiss by a somewhat modified method of the Berlin statistician. Thus far the age of 85 yr is the maximum value of normal length of life.

(e) Prospects for the Future

One can speak about prospects for the future only when it is made clear that the normal length of life is not invariable but may be subject to change in time and in space. This is our standpoint.

We know that this view is not shared by all demographers. We learn from the history of demography that the invariability of the normal length of life was upheld primarily by the German demographer of the 18th century, Johann Peter Süssmilch. He asserted with deep conviction that the mortality conditions prevailing in his time did not differ greatly from those of ages before and that, in particular, the normal duration of life did not change much over the centuries.

Being absorbed with the idea of "God's order" (such was the title of his book) Süssmilch tried to find this order in various demographic phenomena. He found it everywhere: in the number of victims of epidemics, in the order of mortality in such groups as French monks and Brandenburg peasants; in the number of children born dead; in the repetition of unfortunate accidents and, finally, in the invariability of normal life duration.

These are the words in which the Berlin minister formulated his thesis about the invariability of demographic phenomena in time and space: "So war die Dauer des Lebens schon vor 3000 Jahren, und zwar im Orient, eben so, wie sie noch jetzt ist. So wie die Menschen in Deutschland geboren werden, leben und sterben: ebenso geschiehts in Finnland, Schweden, Engelland, Holland und Frankreich" (*Die göttliche Ordnung*).

We do not intend to reiterate our critical appraisal of the above

11

thesis already expressed elsewhere. We want only to repeat the conclusion: "Limited by his theological attitude, Süssmilch was unable to foresee that changes of a human nature would be expressed in future by other proportions and other quantities than those which he observed himself and which he defined as unchanging. The author of *Die göttliche Ordnung* was unable to comprehend the future progress of mankind."[12]

However, we would be unjust to Süssmilch if we were to lose sight of the conditions in which he lived and worked. Süssmilch was a writer of the 18th century, chiefly from its first half—and so he was of the epoch in which human minds were under the strong impression of religious metaphysics that saw in social processes and in demographic phenomena a sign of God's order or something perfect and constant. We stated previously, in defence of the 17th century English statistician Gregory King, that he was a child of his epoch: the same should be said about Süssmilch.

Among those who watched mankind's development with some scepticism should be included the German statistician of the second half of the 19th century, Dr Ernst Engel. This level-headed and thoroughly educated researcher, free of religious fanaticism, asserted in the seventies of the past century that the decline of mortality, so largely publicized by demographers, was nothing but an illusion. This same Engel contested the thesis of the increasing length of human life. For him, not only the normal but also the average length of life was open to question.[13]

The invariability of the normal length of life was supported in the beginning of the 20th century by the German statistician Gottlieb Schnapper-Arndt. Impressed by the results of research by Lexis, he admired the wisdom of the psalmist and of the "father of German population science", Süssmilch, who, without any administrative apparatus and without the assistance of higher mathematics, managed to determine the normal duration of human life without error.

Was this computation really without error?

Can it be considered a proof of the correctness of the psalmist's estimate, that another researcher, equipped with modern scientific-statistical apparatus based on mathematics, arrived at the same results over a thousand years later?

Can this coincidence of results be considered a proof of the constancy of the normal life duration?

In our opinion, there is no doubt that all these questions should be answered by "No". The psalmist's estimate can by no means be recognized as accurate and, if it does not differ from the result obtained at the end of 19th century by Lexis, then it is but another argument for the imperfection of the psalmist's estimate. For it is highly improbable that the advances in medicine and hygiene achieved within many centuries by such scientists as Avicenna, Vesalius, Bacon of Verulamium, Harvey, Malpighi, Leeuwenhoek, Cuvier, Albrecht v. Haller, Jenner, Pasteur, Virchow, Behring, Koch and many others should have had no influence on the normal length of human life.

The thesis about the invariability of normal length of life finds its strongest opposition in the subsqent series of life tables. They provide, if not a proof, then at least a serious indication that the normal length of life is not a constant and that its line of development is basically increasing.

What we do not doubt is the extreme slowness of the increase in the normal length of life.

With the changes in living conditions, improvement in the socio-economic situation of the population, not so much the normal age but the number of persons reaching that age undergoes a change. The normal length of life itself changes extremely slowly, which may lead many a researcher to doubt whether such a process exists at all.

It seems that, using the existing series of life tables, we can today dissipate these doubts and state that the evolution of the value of the normal of life is characterized by an increasing trend. Thus, not only does the number of deaths at normal age increase but the normal age itself rises slightly. This fact implies nothing that could embarrass the naturalists: the progressing increase in the normal duration of life may be regarded as a shrinking of the interval between the normal and natural length of human life. It seems to be beyond doubt that the evolution of mortality conditions tends in this direction.

Can we, then, yield to the temptation to sketch the future evolution of the normal length of life and guess the point to which this evolution will lead? We do not want prophecy. Nor do we want to assert that the normal age of man will rise to infinity. However, some prospects seem to be sufficiently clear.

Thus, it seems beyond doubt that countries where the normal length of life now lags behind the maximum level reached by Norway and Switzerland will, in the next few years, undergo a reduction, if not complete removal, of their demographic lag or backwardness.

11*

It may also be expected that countries with the highest normal length of life—the northern countries, Switzerland, and some others—will in the next years be the scene of further advances in this field. We have in mind no great changes, such as Stefan Szulc dreamed about, which would cause the shifting of the normal life duration upward by a dozen or even dozens of years.[14]

Sound computations allow us to anticipate a more modest increase of at best several years in the normal length of life. We should not forget that at such a late age it is not so easy to extend the duration of human life even a little.

Many years ago Carl Ballod expressed the view that a greater increase in the normal age should not be expected. His reasoning was as follows: if the population of a country as well off as New Zealand does not differ very greatly in mortality level from the agricultural population of Prussia then it is doubtful whether the normal length of life can ever be extended beyond 80 yr.[15]

Thus far the facts seem to support the thesis of the Latvian demographer: the maximum values for the normal length of life are not much higher than 80 yr. However, even this fact is not proof. We do not think that in every situation one can predict the future from the past.

Let us recall one fact. In many laboratories and research institutes scientists are working devotedly to discover a means to fight the human affliction of cancer. The defeat of this dangerous enemy would undoubtedly contribute to a considerable increase in the normal length of life. And yet not only cancer harasses the aged and it is not only against this disease that scientists are working.

We adopt a moderate optimism based on a belief in the progress of mankind.

3. NUMBER OF DEATHS AT NORMAL AGE

Let us recall the definition of the normal age: the normal age or normal length of life is the age in later life during which the greatest number of deaths occur.

Thus the basis for determining the normal length of life is the maximum concentration of deaths. The actual number is, in principle, of no importance: it suffices that it is the greatest in a given life table. In practice, we find a large spread of the maximum number of deaths that have served as bases for determining the normal age.

Many researchers pay attention to the normal age only, losing sight of the death concentration at this age. Such an attitude is not reasonable. We cannot ignore how great a number of deaths is characteristic of the normal length of life at a given age.

This circumstance has a particular importance for investigations on the process of population aging. If, from this point of view, the increasing of the normal age is very significant, more important still is the increase in the maximum number of deaths accompanying this age. Even if the normal age, as Süssmilch imagined, were stable, then the fact itself of the increase in the number of deaths at that age would have considerable importance for transformations in the structure of the population age in general, and aged persons in particular.

The number of deaths determining the normal age of a given population interested Stefan Szulc. His deep and incisive mind did not allow him to overlook what is most essential for the normal length of life.

In one of his last works Stefan Szulc submitted some numbers characterizing the normal age of the population ot former Russia, Sweden, and Norway, and showing what maximum numbers of deaths were connected with each. The data provided by Szulc are concerned with women only. Thus, the object of investigation is not so much a maximum but the absolute maximum.

We give below data taken from this demographer.

MAXIMUM NUMBERS OF DEATHS OF WOMEN ACCORDING TO THE LIFE TABLES OF CERTAIN COUNTRIES

Country	Period of table	Age of maximum number of deaths	Maximum number of deaths
European Russia	1874–83	63–64	1240
Sweden	1816–40	72	1830
,, ...	1891–1900	78	2460
,, ...	1946–50	81	3810
Norway	1856–65	72	2130
,, ...	1901–10	79	2460
,, ...	1945–48	82	3630

Source: *Przegląd Statystyczny (Statistical Review)* 1955, No. 2, p. 90.

The above table shows that not only does the age of greatest concentration of deaths increase, but the number of these deaths does, too. The maximum number of deaths of aged persons becomes more pronounced and higher.

Thus, in Norway the number of deaths, which is the basis for the normal length of life, has increased since the middle of the last century by about 70 per cent. A still greater increase in the maximum number of deaths of the aged can be observed in Sweden. It doubled. If we compare the limiting values: the highest Swedish number of deaths, for the years 1946–1950, and the lowest Russian number for the years 1874–83, then we see that the upper limit is three times the lower.

The above considerations concern the female population.

For men not covered by the above statement the age maxima are, as a rule, lower than for women (except for Japan). This is shown in the next statement.

For men there is also a considerable spread of maximum deaths in old age although it is less than for women.

MAXIMUM NUMBERS OF DEATHS OF MEN AND WOMEN ACCORDING TO LIFE TABLES OF CERTAIN COUNTRIES

Country	Period of table	Normal age		Maximum number of deaths	
		men	women	men	women
Japan	1921–5	69–70	74	1831	1796
Poland	1931–2	72–73	75	2130	2320
U.S.A. (white population) . .	1939–41	75	78	2777	3203
Fed. German Republic . . .	1949–51	77	79	3152	3670

Source: Life tables of the countries.

There is still one problem that should be noted: to what degree the two quantities, the normal age and the maximum number of deaths in old age, correspond to one another.

Even from the Szulc table we could see that to the same normal age not always the same maximum number of deaths corresponds. In Sweden in the years 1816–40 the maximum number of deaths for women occurred at 75 yr; the normal age of women in Norway in the years 1856–65 was identical. But the maximum number of deaths corresponding to this age differed: 1830 in Sweden and 2130 in Norway.

The same fact appears in our statement where we happen to deal with a normal age of 75 yr. Thus, in the Polish table for 1931–2, this age corresponds to 2320 deaths (for women), and in the U.S. table for 1939–41 for the white population, to 2777 (for men).

Let us compare the above maximum numbers of deaths for the same normal age of 75 yr:

Condition	Normal age	Maximum number of deaths
A	75 yr	1830
B	75 yr	2130
C	75 yr	2320
D	75 yr	2777

The above table shows that the normal age, not accompanied by information about the number of deaths in that age, is of little importance. One and the same normal age may imply a quite different number of deaths. It suffices to point out that in condition D the maximum number of deaths is 50 per cent higher than in A. It is evident that the weight of the normal age is greater the higher is the maximum number of deaths corresponding to it.

We should still add that the values of normal age and maximum numbers of deaths in old age are increasing at a non-uniform rate: the increase in the first is small and in the second much greater.

On account of the disproportionate increase in the normal age and the maximum number of deaths, demographers draw the conclusion that the limit of human life as determined by nature can be raised only slightly. This is the opinion of the demographer from the Federal German Republic. These are his words: "Die Tatsache, dass sich das Sterblichkeitsmaximum bei den alten Leuten nur wenig verschoben, aber ständig vergrössert hat, ist ein weiterer deutlicher Beweis dafür, dass die dem menschlichen Leben gezogenen natürlichen Grenzen sich nicht wesentlich verändert haben."[16]

This conclusion would be reasonable if the normal limit of life were equivalent to its natural, i.e. physiologically conditioned, limit. Such was the view of older researchers as to the essence of the normal age; this opinion was shared by Christopher Bernoulli, and some years later by Wilhelm von Lexis.

But this view was strongly opposed by physiologists. We have mentioned that Joseph Majer opposed Bernoulli's thesis that the age of 75 yr is the *natural* limit of human life. Man should live not 75 yr, but 100–110 yr, according to the Polish physiologist.

Similarly, Tarchanov opposed the thesis of von Lexis according to which the normal age computed from the life tables (72–3 yr) is the "natural" limit of human life. The Russian physiologist determined the natural human age at 100 yr.

As to our opinion, we share the view of these two physiologists that the normal age should not be identified with the natural age. In our understanding the *normal* length of life is an empirical value, while the *natural* length of life is a theoretical norm, determined by natural science and thus independent of the real, better or worse, state of mortality conditions prevailing at a given time and place.

We pass over the question of what should be this theoretical, natural length of life, that Majer and Tarchanov determined as 100–110 yr, and which the great naturalist Ilja Mechnikov raised to 150 yr.[17] We can only complain that we have been deprived by nature of the optimism expressed by Mechnikov, Bogomolets[18] and other authors about the possibility of extending life to 150 yr.[19]

In the light of our assumptions we cannot share the opinion of the West German demographer who asserts that "the natural limits to human life have changed only slightly." It must be said that the life tables give no reason for such a conclusion.

In our opinion the tables give information only about the normal duration of life and say nothing about its natural limit. Our conception of the normal length of life prevents it from being a measure of changes in the physiological norm for duration of life.

REFERENCES

1. M. HAUSHOFER, *Lehr- und Handbuch der Statistik*, Vienna, 1882, II Ausgabe, p. 182.
2. G. SCHNAPPER-ARNDT, *Sozialstatistik, Vorlesungen über Bevölkerungslehre, Wirtschafts- und Moralstatistik.* Leipzig, 1912, p. 159.
3. J. MAJER, "Długowieczność" ("Longevity"), *Encyklopedia Powszechna S. Orgelbranda* (*S. Orgelbrand's General Encyclopedia*), Warsaw, 1861.
4. J. MAJER, *Trwanie życia w Krakowie na zasadzie wykazu zmarłych w latach 1859–1868 obliczone co do ludności chrześcijańskiej* (*Longevity in Cracow on the Basis of Lists of the Dead among the Christian Population for the Years 1859–1868*) Cracow, 1881, p. 31.
5. H. SAITO, *Sur la Table de Mortalité des Japonais*, No. 4, XIX Session de l'Institut International de Statistique, Tokyo, 1930, pp. 7–12.
6. K. FREUDENBERG, "Die Sterblichkeit in hohen Lebensaltern", *Schweiz. Z. Volkswirtsch u. Stat.*, Jahrgang 91, No. 4, December 1955.
7. K. FREUDENBERG, "Grundzüge der Sterblichkeitsentwicklung nach dem Alter während eines Zeitraums von 80 Jahren für Deutschland". *Proceedings of the World Population Conference, 1954*, United Nations, New York, 1955, p. 77.
8. *Schweizerische Volkssterbetafeln* 1931/41 and 1939/41, Bern, 1951.

9. A. NAGORNY, *Starenie i prodlenie zhizni* (*Aging and the Extension of Life*), Moscow, 1950.

10. J. C. RUSSELL, *British Medieval Population.* University of New Mexico Press, Albuquerque, 1948.

11. K. FREUDENBERG, "Die Sterblichkeit in hohen Lebensaltern", *Schweiz. Z. Volkswirtsch. u. Stat.* 1955, No. 4, p. 459.

12. E. ROSSET, *Historia statystyki* (*History of Statistics*), University lecture typescript, pp. 31–32.

13. Engel's thesis was opposed as unfounded by the Latvian C. BALLOD in his work, *Die mittlere Lebensdauer in Stadt und Land,* Leipzig, 1899.

14. The Polish demographer stated: "We should like the normal life to be extended not by a few but by scores of years. We should like people to preserve as long as possible their full force and ability to work. It seems possible..." (S. SZULC, "Zagadnienie przedłużenia życia ludzkiego w oświetleniu demografii," (The Problem of Extending Human Life in the Light of Demography), *Przegląd Statystyczny* (*Stat. Rev.*) 1955, No. 2, p. 103.

15. C. BALLOD, *Die mittlere Lebensdauer in Stadt und Land,* 1899, p. 58.

16. "Allgemeine Sterbetafel 1949/51". *Statistik der Bundesrepublik Deutschland,* Band 75. Stat. Bundesamt, Wiesbaden, 1953.

17. E. METCHNIKOFF, 1) *Essais Optimistes,* A. Maloine, Paris, 1907; 2) *Études sur la Nature Humaine. Essai de Philosophie Optimiste,* Masson, Paris, 1905.

18. A. BOGOMOLETZ (*Prodlenie zhizni.* Kiev, 1938) states: "This is the normal duration of life in the given stage of human development and science permits a determination of 125–150 yr. However there is no basis for considering these figures as final" (p. 91).

19. This problem has recently been analysed again by the Soviet scientist S. Strumilin in the article: "In the Cosmos and on the Earth," published in the journal *New Times* of February 10, 1961. He predicts that human life will lengthen to 150 yr probably even to 200 yr. According to this author mankind tends toward a stationary state and this will be a consequence of the lengthening of human life since, in a society having many aged persons, the death rate will equal the birth rate

Part III

POPULATION AGING TRENDS

CHAPTER 8

Population Structure by Age in Different Time Periods

IF A RESEARCHER wants to trace the evolution of a demographic phenomenon over a longer period of time and if there is no continuous statistical material available, he has no other choice but to select times for which he has the necessary data and to analyse the dynamics of the phenomenon in these time periods.

The number of periods of time does not much depend on the researcher. The decisive factor is the possession of the proper statistical material.

Our quest for sources, mainly handbooks of vital statistics and statistical and demographic journals, has enabled us to define the following periods:

(1) the earliest period about 1850;
(2) the years 1861–75;
(3) the turn of the 20th century;
(4) the years preceding the outbreak of the First World War;
(5) the last years before the Second World War;
(6) recent times.

The earlier the period of time, the fewer statistical materials are available and the less can be said about the age structure of the population. A truly rich statistical material—rich in geographical range—is only available for the sixth period. Recognition should be given to the great service rendered by the United Nations Organization and particularly to its Statistical Office which, with great care, gathers, elaborates and publishes data on the demographic relations of the great and small, developed and backward countries of the world.

The data from various periods of time will be used to analyse the dynamics of the aging process.

1. THE EARLIEST PERIOD (ABOUT 1850)

In the middle of the past century only a few countries could boast of knowledge about the age structure of their populations. They were

172

the countries that made population censuses and listed in them the ages of those registered.

From the paper recently published by the U.N. Department for Social and Economic Problems on the aging of societies, we extract the information about the age structure of the population of seven countries in the following table:

POPULATION STRUCTURE BY AGE OF SEVEN EUROPEAN COUNTRIES ABOUT 1850

Country	Year of population census	Age group		
		0–14	15–64	65+
		years		
France	1851	27·31	66·23	6·47
Belgium	1846	32·33	61·80	5·87
Norway	1855	34·92	69·33	5·75
Denmark	1850	33·08	61·46	5.45
Sweden	1850	32·87	62·36	4·78
Netherlands	1849	33·38	61·86	4·75
Great Britain	1851	35·48	59·88	4·64

Source: *The Aging of Populations and Its Economic and Social Implications,* United Nations, New York, 1956, pp. 91–168.

Leaving aside the question of whether the figures contained in the above statement represent a state of old age or only of population aging, we should call attention to the differences that occur in the age structure of the seven countries considered here.

A first glance at the figures which interest us reveal that among the countries investigated a special place is held by France:

(a) as having the smallest proportion of children (0–14 yr);

(b) as having the largest proportion of persons in the productive age (15–64 yr);

(c) (and this is perhaps most characteristic) as having the highest proportion of aged people (65 yr and over).

Without applying any test it may be said that in the middle of the 19th century France was the most advanced European country as far as demographic old age is concerned.

If France were omitted, the differences between the remaining countries listed would be negligible. The indices for the number of children (0–14 yr) would vary within the limits from 32·33 per cent (Belgium) to 35·48 per cent (Great Britain). Also, the proportions of persons in the productive age (15–64 yr) would then lie between 59·33 per cent (Norway) and 62·36 per cent (Sweden). Of course, it should not be overlooked that, in the given case, we are dealing here with the culturally and economically most advanced European countries of that time. Naturally, among such countries the differences could not be over large.

When considering the number of aged persons in the societies listed we can identify three categories of countries:

(a) France, far ahead, with a very high proportion of aged persons, unknown in any other country;

(b) countries with 5–6 per cent of old people—Belgium, Norway, and Denmark;

(c) countries numbering 4·5–5 per cent aged—Sweden, the Netherlands, and Great Britain.

These figures give a picture of the demographic situation in the most advanced countries in the middle of the 19th century. Later, these figures were shared by other countries and were no longer a curiosity.[1] In the middle of the last century, however, these figures expressed the highest demographic old age then known.

2. THE YEARS 1861–75

The next period of time for which we have more comprehensive statistical material on the age structure of the population covers the sixties and seventies of the 19th century.

For demographic research this period has great importance in that it coincides with the end of the previous demographic epoch: in many European countries,—e.g. England, Austria and Sweden—the epoch of high fertility then approached its end.

The gathering and ensuring of data on the age profile of the population in this interesting period was the work of two less known, or more accurately, forgotten statisticians: the Frenchman Maurice Block (1816–1901) and the German Hans von Scheel. Block, the author of numerous papers, in 1878 published a handbook of statistics entitled: *Traité théorique et pratique de statistique*. The second of these statisticians, von Scheel, after some changes, published the work of the French statistician as: *Handbuch der Statistik des Deutschen Reiches*. The following data have been taken from the German edition of Maurice Block's work, in other words, from Block–Scheel.

The age classification used in this work has thirteen groups, of which the first six are 5 yr groups (0–5 yr, 5–10 yr up to 25–30); the next six are 10 yr groups (30–40 yr, 40–50, up to 80–90), and the last group—the thirteenth—comprises the population above 90 yr.

For our purpose such a detailed age classification is not needed. The division of the population into three principal groups would be sufficient:

(a) children,

(b) adults,

(c) aged people.

In the Block–Scheel classification three larger age-groups correspond to this division:

(a) 0–15 yr;

(b) 15–60 yr;

(c) 60 yr and over.

However, since we shall deal later with other classifications and time periods, in many of which the group of children and adolescents will include not 15 but 20 yr, we shall separate out the ages 15–20. This will make future comparisons easier.

Let us analyse the figures themselves:

AGE STRUCTURE OF THE POPULATION OF CERTAIN COUNTRIES IN THE YEARS 1861–75

Country	Year	Of 1000 people, those in the age class:			
		0–14	15–19	20–59	60 and over
Canada	1861	429	117	408	45
Hungary	1869	370	95	485	50
U.S.A.	1871	387	105	457	51
European Russia	1867	380	102	459	59
Austria	1869	338	93	503	66
England	1871	361	96	468	75
Germany.	1875	348	95	481	76
Scotland	1871	367	100	452	81
Sweden	1870	340	91	487	82
Netherlands	1869	334	92	490	84
Italy.	1870	324	90	498	88
Switzerland	1870	316	84	511	89
Denmark.	1870	333	93	485	89
Norway	1865	360	94	457	89
Ireland	1871	328	116	463	93
Belgium	1866	317	88	495	100
France	1872	271	84	529	116

Source: (a) MAURICE BLOCK and HANS VON SCHEEL, *Handbuch der Statistik*, p. 236, (cited from Haushofer); (b) for Russia: W. DE LIVRON: *Statisticheskoye Obozreniye Rossiiskoi Imperiyi*, St. Petersburg 1874, p. 31.

Let us call attention to both normal and abnormal facts.

Two normal facts appear:

(1) the proportion of children (0–14 yr)—except for the extreme values—lies within the limits of 30–40 per cent, thus it is very high;

(2) the proportion of old people (60 yr and over)—again except for the extreme values—is 5–10 per cent, which is not very high.

From this general background the French conditions stand out very distinctly. Let us recall that France was the country in which the "demographic revolution" took place first. The decline in births commenced as early as the first half of the 19th century, which was when other European countries had an increasing birth rate.

A statistician should not ignore that rare and particular phenomenon. As experience shows, new forms and new conditions sometimes appear, first as sporadic but distinctive phenomena. Among demographic phenomena this principle has great significance.

We shall see how a demographic situation that is exceptional at one time is often a token of what may become fairly general. This is especially true of characteristics reflected in figures on the natural evolution of mankind.

This function of "demographic barometer" was fulfilled long since by the French birth numbers: they make it possible to forecast with a high degree of probability the future development of demographic conditions in other countries.

Here are two interesting comments:

(a) "la France est le premier pays où a été pratiqué largement la limitation des naissances dans les mariages"—wrote the French demographer Louis Henry;[2]

(b) "jene frühzeitige Kinderbeschränkung macht Frankreich zum besonders reizvollen Studienobjekt. Denn dort haben sich längst Wirkungen gezeigt, die anderswo noch bevorstehen", wrote the German journalist Ernst Kahn.[3]

Let us also consider the French figures as a forecast of the future of a large number of countries.

The following facts should be particularly stressed:

(1) in the seventies of the last century France was the only country in Europe—and probably in the world—in which children of ages 0–14 years constituted less than 30 per cent of the total population;

(2) besides Switzerland, France also had the lowest percentage of young people of 15–19 yr;

(3) the proportion of adult population (of ages from 20–59) was

higher in France than in any of the other countries included in the table;

(4) France also had the highest proportion of aged persons (60 yr and over).

Of course, it would not be reasonable to ascribe all the properties of the French age pyramid to the decline in the birth rate. The formation of this age pyramid was undoubtedly influenced by other factors too, although it can be ascertained that none of them played anything like the role of the decline in births. All four features characterizing France's age profile were formed under the overwhelming influence of the decline in the birth rate.

An antithesis of these French conditions in the Europe of that time were the contours of the age pyramid in Hungary and Russia.

Unlike France, in these two countries can be observed:

(1) a particularly high proportion of children; and

(2) a particularly low proportion of old people.

Thus we have compared two poles of demographic conditions: *the pole of old age* represented by France, and *the pole of youth* represented by Hungary and Russia.

We have said that societies having in their populations 8–10 per cent of persons over 60 yr should be considered as approaching the stage of aging.

There are eight such societies in the table by Block and Scheel:

**COUNTRIES WHICH IN THE YEARS 1861–75 WERE
APPROACHING THE STATE OF AGING**

1. Ireland	5. Italy
2. Norway	6. Netherlands
3. Denmark	7. Sweden
4. Switzerland	8. Scotland

We have further agreed that societies having 10–12 per cent of their members over 60 will be counted as *aging*, and those having a still greater proportion of people of that age, as *old*.

Using this convention we can state the following facts:

(1) in 1866, by achieving an index for the number of old age persons (60 and over) of 10 per cent, Belgium entered a considerably advanced phase of the process of population aging;

(2) this process was still more advanced in France; with 11·6 per cent of the population over 60, France stood nearly at the threshold of demographic old age;

(3) the conventional limit of old age (12 per cent of the population over 60 yr) had nowhere been reached;

(4) the process of aging of the population, however, proceeded so rapidly that France could be expected to reach old age in the seventies.

A few words remain to be said about countries outside Europe.

Among non-European countries two included in the table were Canada and the U.S.A.

The age pyramid of the United States was shaped under the influence of immigration. This is the reason why the proportion of old people was so low (5·1 per cent).

As to Canada—this country occupies a particular place in the table being analysed.

Canada stands ahead other countries in the large numbers of children and young people: in 1861 tnis country had 42·9 per cent children between 0 and 14 yr, and 11·7 per cent young people between 15 and 19. Thus, children and young people constituted jointly 54·6 per cent of the total population or the majority of the society. In this respect Canada is a unique country in this report.

Considering the population structure with regard to the number of adults and old people we observe the exceptional position of Canada as the country with the lowest proportion of these population groups: 40·8 per cent of adults and 4·5 per cent of old people, the lowest given.

Of course, one must realize the accidental character of this priority; if our investigation were to encompass a greater number of countries and if, especially, we succeeded in acquiring data concerning the structure of societies with a natural fertility rate, then there could be no talk about the "primacy" of Canada.

For some countries we use, besides those given in brackets, other age classification: 0–14 yr, 15–64 yr and 65 yr and over.

We submit these figures in the table on page 179.

Here the sequence of countries according to the number of old people does not differ from the previous: first place as to the advancement of the aging process is held by France, closely followed by Belgium and Norway, and then Denmark, the Netherlands, Sweden, Switzerland, etc.

Let us recall that previously—when discussing the demographic situation in Europe in the middle of the 19th century—the highest proportion of persons of 65 and over amounted to 6·47 per cent; now, after twenty years, in the same France, it is 7·41 per cent.

And further: in the middle of the 19th century only three countries

POPULATIONS OF CERTAIN COUNTRIES ACCORDING TO AGE IN THE SIXTIES AND SEVENTIES OF THE 19TH CENTURY

Country	Year of census	Age group in years		
		0–14	15–64	65+
In the sixties of the 19th century:				
France	1861	27·12	66·20	6·89
Belgium	1866	31·68	61·99	6·33
Norway	1865	36·04	57·71	6·23
Netherlands	1869	33·39	61·08	5·52
Sweden	1860	33·51	61·27	5·22
Denmark	1860	33·68	61·08	5·20
Switzerland	1860	29·55	65·34	5·11
Great Britain	1861	35·69	59·63	4·68
Portugal	1864	33·91	61·42	4·67
Italy	1861	34·18	61·65	4·19
Austria	1869	33·84	62·24	3·92
In the seventies of the 19th century:				
France	1872	27·06	65·54	7·41
Norway	1875	34·40	59·50	6·10
Denmark	1870	33·37	60·78	5·81
Switzerland	1870	31·47	62·98	5·54
Sweden	1870	34·05	60·51	5·43
Italy	1871	32·46	62·43	5·11
Portugal	1878	33·78	61·49	4·73
Great Britain	1871	36·18	59·03	4·79
Spain	1877	32·39	63·43	4·18

Source: The Aging of Populations and Its Economic and Social Implications, United Nations, New York 1956, pp. 91–168.

had over 5 per cent the population at the age of 65 and over; now seven countries have this proportion of old people, and two of them have over 6 per cent of the population in old age.

These facts undoubtedly demonstrate that in the period concerned, i.e. in the fifties, sixties, and seventies of the 19th century, the process of population aging continued in many European countries.

3. AT THE TURN OF THE CENTURY

The next period of time to be considered is the turn of the present century. While the sixties and seventies previously considered still belonged to the epoch of high fertility, now we shall observe quite different conditions. The dawn of the new century found many European countries in a state of demographic depression, in some cases twenty years old, and in some countries even thirty. This showed itself in a more and more rapid decline in the birth rate.

For the period concerned some material of interest was gathered by Edward Byron Reuter. In his work entitled *Population Problems* we find data about the age structure of eight countries: the U.S.A. and seven European countries (England, Germany, France, Ireland, Sweden, Italy and Serbia).

We have succeeded further in gathering from other sources similar data for nine other countries which could not be considered in the previous table.

Reuter's data, which are the basis of our statement, are classified in four age groups:

(a) below 15 yr;
(b) 15–39 yr;
(c) 40–59 yr;
(d) 60 yr and over.

We shall reduce these four age groups to three by combining the two middle ones. This modification is necessary since for the countries that we have added to the report of this demographer we do not have the same division into age groups.

On page 181 there are the data for twelve countries of Europe and five outside Europe.

Let us consider the most characteristic items in the above table. On the one hand is France, with the greatest number of old people on the other hand Puerto Rico, with the greatest number of children. Using the traditional terminology we can speak here about the *oldest* and the *youngest* society. Let us compare these two extremes; this will give us a picture of the spread in conditions in the age structure of the population at the threshold of the 20th century.

None of the elements of the age structure of the population of France had an equivalent in any other country.

Then France is exceptional for:

(1) the lowest proportion of children (0–14 yr);
(2) the highest proportion of adults (15–59 yr);
(3) the highest proportion of old people (60 yr and over).

Thus, each of the French figures in the table is unique for the time.

It would seem that the same could be said about the figures characterizing the population structure of Puerto Rico: we have here not

POPULATION AGE STRUCTURE OF CERTAIN COUNTRIES
AT THE TURN OF THE CENTURY

Country	Year	% of population at the age of		
		0–14	15–59	60 and over
Puerto Rico	1899	439	521	40
Serbia	1900	419	537	44
Cuba	1899	367	587	46
British India	1901	385	564	51
Poland*	1900	393	545	62
European Russia	1897	385	546	69
Austria	1900	352	576	72
England	1901	324	602	74
U.S.A.	1900	334	591	75
Hungary	1900	356	568	76
Germany	1900	348	574	78
Japan	1903	335	583	82
Czechoslovakia*	1900	342	571	87
Italy	1901	341	562	97
Ireland	1901	304	587	109
Sweden	1900	324	557	119
France	1901	261	615	124

* Within the 1938 borders.

Sources: (a) E. B. REUTER, Population Problems, p. 32, (b) Zagadnienia demograficzne Polski (Problems in the Demography of Poland), Warsaw, 1936, p. 15, (c) other sources.

only the highest number of children, but also the lowest number of adults and of old people. This is true, but on the other hand we should not forget that the indices for the island owe their exceptional character to the fact that our investigations do not include countries with a still greater number of children and a still smaller number of adults or old people. That such countries existed there is no doubt.

But even so the spread of conditions is great. From the table it can be seen that the proportion of children in Puerto Rico is nearly twice (1·7 times) the French proportion. For old people the proportion is three times as great in France as on the island.

Let us add some other indices. For every 100 adults (15–59 yr) France had 42 children (0–14 yr), and Puerto Rico had 84, or twice as many. For every aged person (60 yr and over) France had two children, Puerto Rico eleven.

These figures lead us to call France a country of old people, and Puerto Rico a country of children. All other figures in our table lie

between these extremes, gravitating either to the "young" or the "old" type of population.

It should be stressed that the differences in the numbers of children and of old people is wider this time than formerly: the proportion of children previously varied between 271 and 429 per thousand, while in this table it varies from 261 to 439; the proportion of children was between 45 and 116 per thousand; here it lies between 40 and 124 per thousand.

It is not difficult to perceive that we have to deal here with facts of a double nature:

(a) the increase in the maximum proportion of children and the decline in the minimum proportion of the aged are apparent, since they result from widening the circle of societies covered by the investigation;

(b) conversely, the decline in the minimum proportion of children and the rise in the maximum proportion of old people are *real* and demonstrate the action of the new demographic trend, namely the trend towards the aging of societies.

We have assumed the conventional limits which permit the determination of the significant points in the demographic development of societies: the threshold of aging and the threshold of old age. Let us apply this convention to the figures now being considered.

In the approach to aging (8–10 per cent of persons at the age 60 yr and over) we find three countries:

(1) Japan, numbering 8·2 per cent old people (1903);

(2) Bohemia, numbering 8·7 per cent old people (1900); and

(3) Italy with 9·7 per cent old people (1901).

In the phase of aging (10–12 per cent of persons at the age of 60 and over) are two countries:

(1) Ireland with a proportion of old people of 10·9 per cent (1901);

(2) Sweden with 11·9 per cent old people (1900).

If we note that Ireland and Sweden were previously almost in the forefront of aging, then their present inclusion among aging societies is a striking token of the advancing process of population aging.

Finally, France—and this is also characteristic—crossed the threshold of old age at the beginning of the current century (12·4 per cent old people in 1901). Not only in the history of population conditions in France but in the world, is this the first crossing of the limit which we have regarded as the beginning of demographic old age.

The above facts are in full harmony with the character of the new demographic epoch which is characterized by the widening decline in the fertility rate. Together with the progressive decline in the fertility rate, the number of aging societies in Europe increases, and France, as the leading country, opens a new chapter in the history of demographic conditions as the first to cross the threshold of demographic old age.

As to the territory of Poland, we must use this term in relation to the then political situation. When the country was partitioned among its neighbours this territory presented a picture of demographic youth, shown by the high proportion of children and young people while the number of aged persons was relatively low.

Below is the list of indices based on an age classification which shifts the beginning of old age by 5 yr.

POPULATION DISTRIBUTION OF CERTAIN COUNTRIES ABOUT 1900

Country	Census year	Age groups			
		0–14	15–44	45–64	65+
Argentina	1895	40·35	47·23	10·47	1·95
Australia	1901	35·20	48·75	...	ca.2·0
Ceylon	1901	43·43	44·48	10·01	2·03
Brazil	1900	45·03	43·48	9·38	2·11
India	1901	38·58	46·60	...	ca.2·3
New Zealand	1901	33·38	48·95	13·59	4·06
U.S.A.	1900	34·47	47·74	13·72	4·07
Great Britain	1901	32·55	47·90	14·86	4·69
Germany	1900	34·79	45·03	15·30	4·88
Austria	1900	34·40	44·54	16·08	4·98
Canada	1901	34·55	46·39	13·99	5·07
Bulgaria	1900	40·20	40·38	14·29	5·13
Portugal	1900	33·79	43·31	17·18	5·72
Switzerland	1900	31·03	46·39	16·79	5·84
Netherlands	1899	...	...	...	6·01
Italy	1901	34·12	42·17	17·55	6·16
Belgium	1900	31·72	46·02	16·07	6·18
Denmark	1901	33·94	43·31	16·10	6·66
Norway	1900	35·55	41·17	15·37	7·91
France	1901	26·13	45·27	20·41	8·20
Sweden	1900	32·44	42·19	17·00	8·37

Source: *The Aging of Populations and Its Economic and Social Implications*, United Nations, 1956, pp. 91–168.

This classification of data about the age structure of the population reveals a larger number of countries with a high proportion of aged

persons, thus with a considerably advanced process of population aging.

This statement is supported by the following facts:

(1) there are now seven countries with a proportion of old people amounting to over 6 per cent, while in the previous time period of the sixties and seventies there were only four: Sweden, Denmark, Italy and the Netherlands;

(2) in the previous time period only one country (France) showed over 7 per cent of the population at the age of 65 and over; now we have three such countries: France, Norway and Sweden;

(3) the highest *maximum* share of old people in the total population of that time was 7·41 per cent (France in 1872); it is now exceeded by Norway with nearly 8 per cent, and France and Sweden with over 8 per cent of the population at the age of 65 and over.

However, in order to avoid a distortion of the true picture of demographic conditions of that time it should be added that in Western Europe, besides countries showing a rapid rate of population aging, there were also others where this process was stopped at the turn of the century. Great Britain is obviously in this category since in 1871 she had 4·79 per cent of persons of 65 and over while thirty years later had no more than 4·69 per cent.

The same may be said about Germany which in 1875 had 7·6 per cent of persons 60 and over and a quarter of a century later had 7·8 per cent at this age. For a period of twenty-five years this increase is negligible.

Thus we may say that western and northern Europe entered the new century partly under the impetus of rapid population aging (Sweden, France, Norway), and partly with stagnation in this field (Great Britain, Germany). Particularly interesting is the fact that the inhibition of the process of population aging occurred precisely in those countries which soon led in the development of this process.

4. BEFORE THE FIRST WORLD WAR

One of the periods of time marked out for our research covers the years preceding the outbreak of the First World War.

The need to isolate the period before the First World War as a separate time period follows from the fact (and we shall return to this later), that war is a source of deep perturbations in demographic conditions. Besides, in order to determine the demographic consequences of the war one should be acquainted with the demographic conditions prevailing in the period immediately preceding the war.

For this new time period we use data arranged in three age groups:
0–14 yr, 15–64 yr, 65 and over. This division will frequently be used.

**POPULATION OF CERTAIN COUNTRIES ACCORDING TO AGE
ABOUT 1910 (PER THOUSAND)**

Country	Census year	Age groups		
		0–14	15–64	65+
Argentina	1914	384	593	23
India	1911	385	591	24
Greece	1907	383	576	41
U.S.A.	1910	321	636	43
Australia	1911	318	639	43
New Zealand	1911	313	640	47
Canada	1911	331	623	47
Germany	1910	341	609	50
Bulgaria	1910	397	551	52
Spain	1900	353	613	52
Great Britain	1911	308	640	52
Austria	1910	348	599	53
Switzerland	1910	313	630	58
Portugal	1910	344	597	59
Netherlands	1909	345	594	61
Belgium	1910	305	631	64
Italy	1911	340	595	65
Denmark	1911	336	597	66
Norway	1910	354	568	78
Sweden	1910	317	599	84
France	1911	258	658	84
Ireland	1911	293	602	105

Source: Various publications.

Let us analyse the two most characteristic series of figures: the
column for children (0–14 yr) and the column for the aged (65 and
over).

In the children's age column the indices lie within the limits:

minimum . . . . 25·8%
maximum . . . . 39·7%

The country with the least proportion of children is France; the
country with the highest proportion of children is Bulgaria. Thus,
the Bulgarian proportion is one and a half times as great as the French.

A still larger spread of indices may be observed in the group of
old age where the extreme values are:

minimum . . . . 2·3%
maximum . . . . 10·5%

The least number of old people is in Argentina, the greatest in Ireland. The process of population aging in the latter country is interesting since its cause was the mass emigration of the Irish, but not the aged. On the other hand, Argentina is a country of broad immigration. Since, among immigrants as a rule young people prevail, the population in the productive age is strengthened by immigration. The age structure of immigrants makes the high rate in countries of immigration quite understandable. The only age group receiving no immediate benefit from immigration is that of the aged. The age distribution of the population of Argentina corresponds fully to these principles.[4]

Comparing the indices contained in this table with those of previous time periods, we note the further progress of population aging. As an illustration it should be mentioned that:

(1) in Austria the proportion of old people (65 and over) had increased from 3·92 per cent in 1869 to 5·27 per cent in 1910;

(2) in Denmark the proportion of old people increased from 5·45 per cent in 1950 to 6·62 per cent in 1911;

(3) in France the proportion of old people increased from 6·47 per cent in 1851 to 8·36 per cent in 1911;

(4) in Great Britain the proportion of old people increased from 4·64 per cent in 1851 to 5·22 per cent in 1911;

(5) in Italy the proportion of old people increased from 4·19 per cent in 1861 to 6·50 per cent in 1911;

(6) in the Netherlands the proportion of old people increased from 4·75 per cent in 1849 to 6·12 per cent in 1909;

(7) in Sweden the proportion of old people increased from 4·78 per cent in 1850 to 8·44 per cent in 1910.

These examples suffice. They give a clear picture of the rising trend of the indices for the number of old people in Europe. They are also characteristic of the progress of the aging process of European communities.

The figures from the period preceding the outbreak of the First World War also permit us to ascertain the existence and progress of population aging outside Europe.

A few examples serve to support this thesis.

(1) in the U.S.A. the proportion of old people (65 yr and over) increased from 4·07 per cent in 1900 to 4·30 per cent in 1910;

(2) in New Zealand the proportion of old people increased from 2·96 per cent in 1891 to 4·73 per cent in 1911.

At the same time, and this is very interesting, there was an increase in the proportion of aged people (65 and over) in underdeveloped countries:

(1) in Argentina the percentage of old people increased from 1·95 per cent in 1895 to 2·31 per cent in 1914;

(2) in Ceylon the percentage of old people increased from 2·03 per cent in 1891 to 2·30 per cent in 1911.

The above facts express a general trend of transformations in the distribution of the population age and, therefore, support the conclusion that *not only Europe but also other parts of the world have changed their demographic features underlying the process of population aging, which has gradually extended to the underdeveloped countries. On the eve of the outbreak of the First World War — although the demographers did not perceive it—the process of population aging had already become an essential feature of contemporary demographic conditions.*

5. BEFORE THE SECOND WORLD WAR

For the period between the two world wars, especially in its final years, data on the distribution of the population age in many European countries were compiled by the French demographer Adolphe Landry.

In this fifth time-period the age classification is not the same as in earlier periods.

The division into the age groups is the following:

(a) 0–19 yr: age of children and adolescents ("enfance et adolescence");

(b) 20–59 yr: adults ("adultes");

(c) 60 yr and over: old people ("vieillards").

The number of countries covered by the statement of the French demographer is fairly large: Landry included eleven countries from Europe alone.

We here extend Landry's data to include figures for Denmark, Poland and from Latin America, Venezuela, Colombia, Mexico and Peru which are interesting for their un-European demographic conditions.

The extendend data are given in the table on page 188.

If we compare the extreme values (minima and maxima) occurring in the above statement it appears that the variations differ in different columns.

AGE DISTRIBUTION OF THE POPULATION OF CERTAIN
COUNTRIES IN THE THIRTIES OF THE 20TH CENTURY

Country	Year	Per 1000 general population		
		0–19	20–59	60 and over
India	1931	490	470	40
Venezuela	1941	514	442	44
Columbia	1938	523	427	50
Mexico	1940	514	435	51
Peru.	1940	516	420	64
Romania	1930	466	468	66
U.S.S.R.	1939	451	483	66
Turkey	1935	480	452	68
Japan	1935	465	460	75
Poland	1931	431	491	78
Canada	1931	417	498	85
U.S.A..	1940	345	551	104
Netherlands	1939	375	520	105
Hungary	1939	359	535	106
Italy.	1936	377	514	109
Denmark.	1935	342	546	112
Germany.	1939	319	557	124
Switzerland	1940	304	568	128
Great Britain	1938	300	568	132
Sweden	1935	308	560	138
Belgium	1938	306	552	142
France	1936	302	551	147

Source: Various publications.

The spread of figures denoting the proportion of children and adolescents (0–19 yr) is great:

minimum . . . . 30·0% (Great Britain, 1938)
maximum . . . . 52·3% (Colombia, 1938)

It follows from these figures that, while in Great Britain the children and adolescents constituted less than one third of the total population, in Colombia their share exceeded half of the total population. Colombia is not the only country in the table in which the children and adolescents constitute the majority of the society. In Venezuela, Mexico and Peru the same phenomenon may be observed. Nearly half the population are children and adolescents in India, Turkey, Romania and Japan. Closely behind them follow the U.S.S.R. and Poland.

Relatively small is the spread between the indices for the number of adult population (20–59 yr):

minimum . . . . 42·0% (Peru, 1940)
maximum . . . . 56·8% (Great Britain, 1938)

It should be noted that in this group the lowest indices characterize the countries of Latin America, while the highest are met in West European countries, Switzerland having an index not lower than the British maximum.

In the group of old people (60 yr and over) again there is a large spread of indices:

minimum . . . . 4·0% (India, 1931)
maximum . . . . 14·7% (France, 1936)

As we see, in France the proportion of old people was about 3·5 times as great as in India.

If the data are restricted to Europe, the differences are not so great. For instance, in pre-war Romania the number of old people was less than half the number in France.

The classification scheme used in our analysis allows us to identify the countries with different degrees of advancement in population aging.

Let us begin, as previously, with the countries situated in the approach to aging (8–10 per cent of the population at the age of 60 and over). This time this group is represented by one country only, Canada, which in 1931 had 8·5 per cent of old people.

It seems as if the world were divided into two opposite demographic camps: a camp of young societies, the other a camp of aging or already old societies, without an intermediate group to represent the "approach to aging". Of course, the reservation should be made that in this case we have to do only with impressions which are not sufficiently supported by statistical data.

In the group of aging societies (10–12 per cent of old people) this time we find:

(1) the U.S.A. with a proportion of old people of 10·4 per cent (1940);
(2) the Netherlands with 10·5 per cent old people (1939);
(3) Hungary with 10·6 per cent old people (1939);
(4) Italy with 10·9 per cent old people (1936);
(5) Denmark with 11·2 per cent old people (1935).

The above-mentioned countries have already appeared in time periods previously analysed. Thus, we can observe the evolution of the population aging process over about 70 yr preceding the outbreak of the Second World War.

From these five countries—three, i.e. the Netherlands, Italy and Denmark—show a constant but rather slow increase in old age indices. In the other two, Hungary and the United States, show a constant but violent increase in the proportion of old people.

To avoid misunderstanding it should be reiterated that we are considering the proportion of persons at the age of 60 and over.

In the Netherlands the percentage of old people increased as follows:

1869 . . . . 8·4%
1939 . . . . 10·5%

From a country which in 1869 was in the approach to old age, the Netherlands was transformed within 70 yr into an aging country.

The same may be observed in Italy where the evolution of old age indices was as follows:

1870 . . . . 8·8%
1901 . . . . 9·7%
1936 . . . . 10·9%

The degree of advancement of the population aging process as measured by the proportion of old people is in Italy slightly greater than in the Netherlands, but the rate of the development of this process is nearly identical, and slow in the two countries.

In Denmark the proportion of old people (60 yr and over) increased over the same period as follows:

1870 . . . . 8·9%
1921 . . . . 10·3%
1935 . . . . 11·2%

The dynamics of the increase in the proportion of old people in Denmark does not deviate in its principal features from its evolution in the Netherlands and Italy. Denmark, being in 1870 at the approach of old age, in the first twenty years of the 20th century entered the phase of proper aging. The course of events here was also rather gentle.

A quite different picture is given by the Hungarian statistics from which we extract the following old age indices:

1869 . . . . 5·0%
1900 . . . . 7·6%
1939 . . . . 10·6%

In Hungary the proportion of old people became twice as great in the period considered. From a country that was definitely young demographically in 1869, Hungary was transformed within seventy years into a country considerably advanced towards demographic old age.

A similar course of events took place in the United States, as demonstrated by the old age indices stated below:

1871 . . . . 5·1%
1900 . . . . 7·5%
1940 . . . . 10·4%

Here the proportion of old people also doubled. Here, too, seventy years brought a transition from clear demographic youth to a distinct state of aging.

The appearance of the United States in the list of aging societies is the more remarkable since, for the first time, we observe a considerable progress of the process of population aging outside Europe.

A special group is constituted by societies having over 12 per cent of old people (60 yr and over), called old societies.

The number of these societies increased considerably: while in the time-periods previously considered the only representative was French society, now our table has six countries with over 12 per cent of old people.

This is a review of these countries:

COUNTRIES HAVING OVER 12% OF OLD PEOPLE (60 YR AND OVER) IN THE YEARS 1935–40

1. France	4. Great Britain
2. Belgium	5. Switzerland
3. Sweden	6. Germany

In the light of the above old-age indices and the list of old societies, France is the country most advanced in old age: in no other country is such a high proportion of old people (14·7 per cent in 1932) to be found.

However, Belgium, with 14·2 per cent of old people in 1938 was quite near to the record French level and Sweden, with 13·8 per cent in 1935 was not far behind.

The above countries — France, Belgium, and Sweden — were leading in the world as to the degree of demographic old age achieved.

Among the "old" countries the youngest was Germany at that time. Before the First World War, in 1910, Germany had no more than 7·7 per cent of the population at the age of 60 and over. Spain and Bulgaria were then the demographically youngest countries.

Directly before the Second World War (1939) the proportion of old people in Germany had increased to 12·4 per cent. In less than thirty years this proportion increased by 60 per cent. Professor Waszak, a student of demographic conditions in Germany wrote: "... in the age structure of the population in Germany in the period 1910–39 such changes occurred that the numerical relations between particular age groups were no longer regarded as normal for a biologically long-lived nation".[5] Indeed, Germany, until recently a demographically young country, now appeared as a demographically old country.

We made a reservation as to whether such a picture is given by the old age indices in the above table. The reservation was necessary since we are operating with fragmentary data and we cannot be sure whether the figures are actually different, plus or minus.

Is it possible that the highest proportion of old people given here— i.e. the French proportion of 15 per cent—might be surpassed by a still higher index of another country.

It is not only possible but even probable. We have in mind Ireland which in the previous time period already advanced to the fore of countries with the largest group of old people. That this reservation is valid is fully supported by further considerations dealing with the same material up to the Second World War but with a different scheme of classification.

We shall now consider the conditions from the thirties of the current century once again—this time on the basis of the popular age classification scheme: 0–14 yr, 15–64, and 65 and over.

In the new arrangement we have to deal with a different group of countries: some have been eliminated, new ones included.

Twelve new countries have been included: Brazil, Chile, Egypt, Bulgaria, Yugoslavia, Portugal, Greece, Australia, New Zealand, Austria, Norway and Ireland. Some of them, like Chile and Egypt,

POPULATION OF CERTAIN COUNTRIES BY AGE ABOUT 1930

Country	Census year	Age groups (in years)		
		0–14	15–64	65+
India	1931	400	578	22
Brazil	1940	425	551	24
Chile	1930	379	587	34
Egypt	1937	392	572	36
Turkey	1935	414	547	39
Romania	1930	349	608	43
Japan	1930	366	587	47
Poland	1931	334	617	49
Bulgaria	1934	355	593	52
Yugoslavia	1931	346	601	53
U.S.A.	1930	294	652	54
Canada	1931	316	628	56
Portugal	1930	320	618	62
Netherlands	1930	306	632	62
Greece.	1940	330	607	63
Australia	1933	275	660	65
New Zealand	1936	255	679	66
Switzerland	1930	246	685	69
Italy.	1936	306	619	74
Germany.	1933	235	691	74
Great Britain	1931	242	684	74
Denmark.	1935	254	671	75
Belgium	1930	230	694	76
Austria	1934	237	684	79
Norway	1930	285	632	83
Sweden	1930	248	660	92
France	1931	230	677	93
Ireland	1936	276	627	97

Source: Various publications.

appear for the first time in our considerations. Thus our demographic knowledge has been enriched.

The list is led this time, too, by India as the country with the lowest percentage of old people: the statistics of that country for 1931 show not more than 2·2 per cent of the population at the age of 65 and over. Close behind India come the countries of Latin America from the previous table: Venezuela, Columbia, Mexico and Peru. This time some countries of Latin America are included in addition: Brazil and Chile (the others have been excluded from the field of observation).

All these facts on the whole give a particular youth to Latin America. Demographically young countries not only have a small proportion of old people; they are also characterized by a high proportion of children. In our table appear only three countries with large proportions of children: Brazil, Turkey and India. These are the indices for the number of children (0–14 yr) in these countries:

Brazil	42·5%
Turkey	41·4%
India	40·0%

The table shows further that in Europe the greatest number of children was found in the Balkan countries, especially Romania, Bulgaria and Yugoslavia. In these countries the indices of the numbers of old people were not very high.

It is interesting that among these countries is Poland with its rather peculiar conditions: in Poland the proportion of children was lower than in Balkan countries which would indicate that the process of population aging made greater progress; but, at the same time, Poland had a low proportion of old people, from which a quite opposite conclusion might be drawn. The difficulties of interpretation would be removed if we were to use a bilateral index (to be discussed later), which would enable us to ascertain the progress of population aging.

In the lower part of the table are countries most advanced in the process of population aging: Belgium, Sweden and France, which also occupied a similar place in the preceding statement and Austria, Norway and Ireland which did not appear in that statement.

The figures on Ireland are instructive. As compared with other countries having a considerable proportion of old people, Ireland has a relatively large number of children and a relatively small number of adults. This is connected with the fact that the main factor of changes in the population structure of Ireland was emigration, which caused serious gaps among the adult population of that country.

The percentage of old people in Ireland is one of the highest we have met in the period between the World Wars (1919–39). At the end of this period only a few slightly higher maximum numbers of old people (65 and over) were observed:[6]

Latvia	9·9%
Belgium	9·9%
France	9·8%

We now have a full picture of the spread of proportions of old people in the years between the World Wars: the numbers of aged persons lay within the limits of 2·2 per cent (India) to 9·9 per cent (Latvia). This statement must be made with the reservation that only countries having more or less reliable data about the population structure by age are considered.

6. AFTER THE SECOND WORLD WAR

We pass on to the next time period which is the period of recent years. The data comprising this period are interesting for two reasons, firstly with regard to the still distinct traces not only of one but of two world wars and, secondly, on account of present applicability of the figures from recent years.

These figures are given below.

AGE STRUCTURE OF THE POPULATION IN CERTAIN COUNTRIES AFTER THE SECOND WORLD WAR

Country	Year	Number per 1000 inhabitants in the age groups		
		0–19	20–59	60 and over
Brazil	1950	525	433	42
India	1951	479	467	54
Egypt	1947	481	459	60
Argentina	1947	408	526	66
Israel (Jewish pop.)	1953	399	532	69
Yugoslavia	1952	412	503	85
Poland	1955	395	520	85
Canada	1951	378	509	113
Netherlands	1953	375	505	120
U.S.A.	1950	343	536	121
Australia	1951	336	540	124
New Zealand (European pop.)	1953	359	506	135
Federal German Rep.	1952	307	552	141
Sweden	1950	293	558	149
Austria	1952	291	550	159
England and Wales	1950	284	557	159
France	1950	291	542	167

Source: Various publications.

With regard to demographic "youth", i.e. a large number of children, low productive population and small number of old people, the first place is occupied by Brazil. The age structure of the Brazilian population is so specific that it is worth some closer analysis.

The proportion of children and adolescents (0–19 yr) is extremely high: the children and adolescents here constitute more than half of the total population of the country—a phenomenon rarely met today. Neither in India nor in Egypt—countries with an extremely large number of children—has the share of children and adolescents (0–19 yr) in the total population reached 50 per cent. Still less can the Brazilian conditions be compared to the conditions prevailing in the neighbouring Argentina, where the proportion of children and adolescents to the total population is 40 per cent.

It has already been stated that the high proportion of children and adolescents is normally accompanied by a small number of old people. Brazil follows this principle—persons at the age of 60 and over constitute hardly 4·2 per cent of the total population. Such a low percentage of old people is hardly ever met today. Even India, regarded until recently as a "cemetery of mankind", not to speak of Egypt or Argentina long ago exceeded such a low proportion of old people.

On the other hand our interest is fixed on three countries: France, England with Wales and Austria, where the situation is diametrically opposed to that in Brazil. In these countries a record low proportion of children and adolescents and a record high proportion of old people is to be noted. The share of children and adolescents has fallen below 30 per cent: in France and Austria to 29·1 per cent, and in England with Wales even to 28·4 per cent.

The following data give some idea of the increase in the number of old people in these countries: in England with Wales and in Austria the share of persons of 60 and over in the total population approaches 16 per cent; in France this figure has already been exceeded. The French percentage is the highest in the world.

Let us compare the extreme values.

In the column for children and adolescents (0–19 yr) the extremes are:

minimum . . . . . 24·4% (England and Wales, 1950)
maximum . . . . . 52·5% (Brazil, 1950)

The difference is great: England with Wales has only one-half the number of children in Brazil.

Less striking are the differences in the column for the adult population (20–59 yr):

minimum . . . . . 43·3% (Brazil, 1950)
maximum . . . . . 55·8% (Sweden, 1950)

If we add that England and Wales have a nearly identical proportion of adult population (55·7 per cent) it is clear that a minimum proportion of children and adolescents accompanies a maximum proportion of adults and, conversely, a maximum proportion of children and adolescents corresponds to a minimum proportion of adults.

In the column of old people (60 years and over) the spread of indices is extremely large:

minimum . . . . . 4·2% (Brazil, 1950)

maximum . . . . . 16·7% (France, 1950)

The highest, French, is four times the lowest, Brazilian, proportion of old people. In other words, for one aged person in Brazil there are four old people in France.

The result is that the exceptional character of the age distribution in Brazil is apparent at every step and the community, is to use a popular term, ultra "young" while, on the other hand, France, Sweden and England are representatives of advanced demographic "old age".

Let us look now at the particular old age groups.

On the verge of aging (8–10 per cent of persons at the age of 60 and over) we now find Poland and Yugoslavia. In both countries per 100 persons in general there are 8·5 aged persons.

We wish to call attention to the fact that the age pyramids in Poland and Yugoslavia have until recently shown particular demographic youth. The process of population aging has caused these youngest European societies to reach the verge of aging.

The next group of aging societies (10 to 12 per cent of persons 60 and over) is this time nearly empty. Only one country is represented, Canada, in which the number of old people increased from 8·5 per cent in 1931 to 11·3 per cent in 1951.[7]

There is a certain logic to this "depopulation" of the group of the aging societies: since in the previous time period the verge of aging was empty, it is natural that in this time period the group of aging societies should be empty.

It is thus reasonable that the countries which in the previous time period supplied the group of aging societies should be found in the next group of old societies: the U.S.A., the Netherlands, Hungary and Italy. In the new table there are only two of them—the U.S.A. and the Netherlands—both of which naturally appear in the group of old societies. It may be supposed that the two remaining countries, if data about the proportion of old people were available, would also be found in this group of societies.

The number of old societies has grown considerably since 1939. At the outbreak of the war the number of countries qualified for this category (12 per cent and more of old people) was nine or ten; now there are eighteen. This is their list:

COUNTRIES HAVING AT LEAST 12% OF AGED PERSONS (60 YEARS AND OVER) IN 1953

1. France	7. German Dem. Rep.	13. Denmark
2. Belgium	8. Scotland	14. New Zealand
3. England and Wales	9. Norway	15. Australia
4. Austria	10. Northern Ireland	16. Netherlands
5. Ireland	11. Switzerland	17. Italy
6. Sweden	12. Federal Germ. Rep.	18. U.S.A.

Western and northern Europe are almost wholly covered in this list. Outside of Europe three countries are included: New Zealand, Australia and the U.S.A.

7. MOST RECENT STATISTICAL DATA OF THE U.N.

The various international reviews, especially the U.N. demographic yearbooks today, cover broad statistical material concerning the proportion of the population in the productive age in various countries of the world.

From this material we have computed the proportions of children (0–14 yr), adults (15–64 yr), and old people (65 and over) for a number of countries representing various levels of economic and demographic development.

These proportions will be the object of our further consideration. Although they are computed for all countries by the same method (based on the international age classification), it should be remembered that the comparability of statistical data does not depend only on that. However, an essential condition of comparability is the concurrence of data in time and uniform accuracy. This last requirement is not fulfilled by world-wide data, as has previously been pointed out.

We must thus make the reservation that we must operate with statistical materials of unequal value. It is evident that their value will decrease for countries outside Europe. Here and there, particularly on the peripheries of the world, the statistical material may be without any value.

One remark still seems necessary. In international reviews, especially as comprehensive as the one represented here, there often is a similarity or even identity of figures which actually have quite different meanings. Thus, the interpretation of figures expressing a different economic and social reality must be handled with special care.[8]

We pass over to numerical data which will be considered in a normal sequence: children—adults—old people. The indices of numbers of children over the world are as follows:

PROPORTION OF POPULATION AT THE AGE OF 0–14 YR AS SHOWN BY RECENT DATA

Country	Year	Per cent of population at the age of 0–14 yr
South Africa (Asian pop.)	1951	47·5
New Zealand (Maoris)	1953	46·5
American Samoa	1950	46·3
Fiji Islands	1958	46·0
Philippines	1959	45·9
British Guiana	1958	44·6
Cambodia	1959	44·6
Taiwan	1958	44·5
San Domingo	1950	44·5
Peru	1955	44·1
Federation of Malaya	1957	43·8
Paraguay	1950	43·8
Costa Rica	1957	43·7
Nicaragua	1950	43·3
Puerto Rico	1950	43·2
Pacific Islands	1958	42·9
Singapore	1957	42·8
Ecuador	1950	42·5
Algeria (Moslem pop.)	1953	42·5
Trinidad and Tobago	1958	42·4
Réunion	1956	42·3
Thailand	1959	42·3
Iran	1956	42·2
Guinea	1955	42·1
Columbia	1951	42·1
Venezuela	1950	42·0
Brazil	1950	41·9
Mexico	1950	41·8

Country	Year	Per cent of population at the age of 0–14 yr
Greenland	1951	41·8
Panama	1950	41·6
El Salvador	1950	41·2
South Korea	1955	41·2
Ceylon	1955	40·7
Honduras	1950	40·6
Guadeloupe and dep.	1956	40·4
Mauritius	1952	40·2
Martinique	1956	39·9
Turkey	1956	39·9
Nepal	1954	39·2
Albania	1955	39·1
Egypt	1947	38·1
Haiti	1950	38·0
Jamaica ex. dep.	1956	38·0
Maldive Islands	1946	37·8
India	1951	37·5
Burma	1954	37·4
Malta and Gozo	1957	37·4
Chile	1952	37·3
Gold Coast	1952	36·5
Bechuanaland	1946	36·5
Israel	1958	36·0
People's Rep. of China	1953	35·9
Barbados	1958	34·9
Cyprus	1958	34·5
Iceland	1957	34·2
Canada	1959	33·4
Poland	1958	32·9
Bermuda	1950	32·7
New Zealand	1958	32·1
Kuwait	1957	31·9
Union of South Africa (white pop.)	1956	31·9
Hawaii	1950	31·2
Japan	1958	31·0
U.S.A.	1959	31·0
Argentina	1947	30·7
Finland	1958	30·7
Yugoslavia	1957	30·2
Netherlands	1958	30·1
Australia	1958	29·9
Portugal	1958	29·5
South West Africa	1951	29·2

Country	Year	Per cent of population at the age of 0–14 yr
Northern Ireland	1958	28·8
Czechoslovakia	1957	27·7
Romania	1956	27·5
Bulgaria	1958	26·4
Denmark.	1957	26·4
Algeria (White pop.)	1953	26·4
Greece.	1958	26·3
Italy.	1951	26·2
Spain	1950	26·2
Norway	1957	26·1
Hungary	1958	25·7
France	1958	25·7
Scotland	1953	24·9
Switzerland	1958	24·1
Ireland	1951	23·7
Sweden	1957	23·6
England and Wales	1958	22·8
Belgium	1957	22·6
Austria	1954	21·6
Fed. German Rep.	1957	21·2
German Dem. Rep.	1958	20·6
Luxembourg	1958	19·4

Source: *Demographic Yearbook* (1953, 1954, 1955, 1959) U.N. and others.

The number of countries having many children has increased considerably in this table: 36 countries have a proportion of children exceeding 40 per cent. Of course, this does not mean a rejuvenation of mankind; on the contrary—the population is aging. The increase in the number of countries showing a high proportion of children is a product of the development of statistics which cover more countries and the new ones have many children.

We now have an excellent opportunity to consider what countries enjoy a demographic youth.

The leading representatives of demographic youth are the inhabitants of the South African Union of African origin and the Maoris who are the remnants of the indigenous population of New Zealand. The other representatives of demographic youth are *the poorest and most backward peoples of the world* who are usually oppressed both by native and foreign exploiters. The large number of children here goes hand in hand with hunger for large masses of the populations Josué de Castro expressed the view that "it is not overpopulation that is the cause of death by starvation of people in many parts of the world but, on the contrary, hunger is a cause of overpopulation".[9] More essential for us is the fact that the demographic youth is a consequence of natural, uncontrolled fertility accompanied by a high mortality which decimates the population before old age.

Would it not be more reasonable to speak of demographic primitivism than of demographic youth?

We do not want to omit another fact. In the last table (page 199) there appeared new maximum proportions of children in the total number of population.

Let us recall the previous maxima.

(1) in the time period 1861–75 the highest proportion of children was given for Canada: 42·9 per cent (1861);

(2) in the time period covering the turn of the century the first place as to number of children was occupied by Puerto Rico: 43·9 per cent (1899);

(3) in the time period 1930–40 Turkey took the lead: 41·4 per cent (1935).

We have already pointed out that in a statistical wasteland—a lack of population censuses—we have to deal with *apparent* maximum proportions of children; we do not know the *real* maxima which are characteristic of primitive countries.

Today, owing to the progress of statistical civilization, we are in an incomparably better situation. Today we can prove that the proportions of children previously regarded as maximum were not so. The true maxima are 46 per cent and even 47 per cent, again with the reservation that there may be higher proportions in countries whose age structure is unknown to us. Fortunately the number of such countries is diminishing.

Ten years ago Marcel Reinhard expressed the view that the population of India is one of the youngest in the world, perhaps the youngest ("...la population hindoue est l'une des plus jeunes du monde, peut-être la plus jeune"). The imprudence of this conclusion is evident. Besides, not only ten but even fifty years ago, the Indian figures did not support the statement we find in the work of the historian of world population.

Let us have a look at those countries in which the proportion of children is the lowest, or at countries demographically old. These are, as a rule, highly developed countries, industrially and in urbanization. Naturally, they also have a highly developed culture.

In countries at the top of demographic old age the proportion of children is not much over 20 per cent. In one case this proportion is below 20 per cent (Luxembourg). It is interesting that among the countries with the highest number of children are both the Federal German Republic and the German Democratic Republic. It would appear that the inspiration to increase the number of children, implanted by the Third Reich, was not very deeply rooted in German society: today Germany has fewer children than in the twenties when F. Burgdörfer feared for his country the sad fate of a nation without young people (Volk ohne Jugend).

Let us now consider the age group of 15–64 yr.

The following table shows what the proportion of this population is in the world.

PROPORTION OF POPULATION AT THE AGE OF 15–64 YR AS SHOWN BY THE LATEST DATA

Country	Year	Population 15–64 yr (%)
Union of South Africa (Asian pop.)	1951	50·3
Fiji Islands	1958	50·9
New Zealand (Maoris)	1953	51·1
Philippines	1959	51·3
American Samoa	1950	51·3
British Guiana	1958	52·1
Pacific Islands	1958	52·2
Paraguay	1950	52·5
San Domingo	1950	52·6
Puerto Rico	1950	52·9
Peru.	1955	52·9
Taiwan	1958	53·0
Cambodia	1959	53·1
Federation of Malaya	1957	53·4
Costa Rica	1957	53·4
Iran	1956	53·8
Nicaragua	1950	53·8
Ecuador	1950	54·0
Trinidad and Tobago	1958	54·1
Réunion	1956	54·3
Algeria (Moslem pop.)	1953	54·4
Guinea	1955	54·6
Mexico	1950	54·8
Albania	1955	54·8

Country	Year	Population 15–64 yr (%)
Guadeloupe and dep.	1956	54·9
Singapore	1957	55·0
Panama	1950	55·2
Martinique	1956	55·2
Thailand	1959	55·2
Honduras	1950	55·4
Venezuela	1950	55·4
South Korea	1955	55·5
Brazil	1950	55·7
Malta and Gozo	1957	55·8
El Salvador	1950	55·9
Greenland	1951	56·1
Mauritius	1952	56·6
Turkey	1956	57·1
Ceylon	1955	57·4
Nepal	1954	57·9
Haiti	1950	58·0
Jamaica ex. dep.	1956	58·1
Iceland	1957	58·1
Bechuanaland	1946	58·2
Chile	1952	58·7
Cyprus	1958	58·7
Egypt	1947	58·8
India	1951	58·9
Barbados	1958	59·1
Canada	1959	59·1
New Zealand	1958	59·1
Israel	1958	59·3
People's Rep. of China	1953	59·7
Burma	1954	59·8
U.S.A.	1959	60·3
Ireland (Republic)	1951	60·4
Maldive Islands	1946	60·9
Bermuda	1950	61·2
Netherlands	1958	61·2
Northern Ireland	1958	61·4
Union of S. Africa (white pop.)	1956	61·4
Poland	1958	61·5
Australia	1958	61·7
Gold Coast	1952	62·0
Finland	1958	62·3
France	1958	62·8
Portugal	1958	63·1
Japan	1958	63·5

Country	Year	Population 15–64 yr (%)
Norway	1957	63·5
Denmark	1957	63·5
Yugoslavia	1957	63·7
Hawaii	1950	64·8
Argentina	1947	65·2
Scotland	1953	65·2
Sweden	1957	65·2
South West Africa	1951	65·3
England and Wales	1958	65·4
Hungary	1958	65·6
Italy	1951	65·7
Kuwait	1957	65·7
Belgium	1957	65·7
Greece	1958	65·8
Switzerland	1958	65·9
German Democratic Rep.	1958	66·0
Algeria (white pop.)	1953	66·1
Romania	1956	66·1
Bulgaria	1958	66·3
Spain	1950	66·6
Austria	1954	66·7
Czechoslovakia	1948	68·0
Federal German Rep.	1957	68·6
Luxembourg	1958	70·2

Source: Demographic Yearbook (1953, 1954, 1955, 1959) and others.

Also in the middle age group there is a distinct correlation between the demographic indices and the degree of economic development. The underdeveloped countries, as a rule, have a low proportion of adults and, conversely, the developed countries have high values for this proportion. The economic importance of these differences results from the fact that the adult population is potentially the productive population and that this population has to support the unproductive elements.[10]

The lowest proportion of population at the productive age in our table is 50·3 per cent. This proportion is for the Asian population of the Union of South Africa. A slightly higher proportion (50·9 per cent) is to be found for the Fiji Islands. Next are the indigenous New Zealand Maoris; the people of the Philippines; American Samoa; British Guiana; the Pacific Islands, etc. In these societies the proportions of adults or productive population lie within the limits of 51–52 per cent. There are few working people here and, at the same time the burden of supporting unproductive elements, mainly children, is exceedingly great.

Let us consider now the other pole of the conditions under investigation. It is the maximum proportion of the productive population and is to be found in the western world. Here the extreme, in Luxembourg reaches the level of 70·2 per cent. This is the highest proportion of persons at the productive age which has ever been noted in world statistics. Only once have we encountered such a high number. According to Eva M. Hubback[11] in England and Wales, in 1939, the proportion of persons in the age group 15–64 to the total number of population was 70 per cent.

Should we expect to see a still higher proportion of persons of productive age in the future? The answer should be sought for in demographic forecasts. In one of them, denied by history, we met a proportion of productive population surpassing 70 per cent. It is the German pre-war demographic forecast made by Friedrich Burgdörfer.[12] He predicted that in 1950 there would be in Germany in 1950 70·7 per cent of persons at the age of 15–64, and in 1955 there would be 71·3 per cent. In the Federal German Republic the proportion of the population of that age is now nearly 69 per cent and is the highest in the world. It denotes a considerable reduction of the burdens connected with supporting unproductive elements. However, it cannot be said that such a state of affairs is an ideal society: experience shows that over a longer period of time the extremes are undesirable. The demographic extremes cannot pretend to the role of a social ideal.[13]

Let us now discuss old people.

The proportions of old people are shown in the table below.

PROPORTION OF THE POPULATION AT THE AGE OF 65 AND OVER AS SHOWN BY RECENT DATA

Country	Year	Population of 65 and over (%)
Maldive Islands	1946	1·3
Ghana	1952	1·3
Greenland	1951	2·0
Singapore	1957	2·15
Union of South Africa (Asian pop.)	1951	2·2

Country	Year	Population of 65 and over (%)
Cambodia	1959	2·3
New Zealand (Maoris)	1953	2·4
American Samoa	1950	2·4
Kuwait	1957	2·4
Brazil	1950	2·4
Thailand	1959	2·5
Taiwan	1958	2·5
Venezuela	1950	2·6
Federation of Malaya	1957	2·8
Philippines	1959	2·8
Burma	1954	2·8
Nepal	1954	2·85
Costa Rica	1957	2·9
El Salvador	1950	2·9
San Domingo	1950	2·9
Nicaragua	1950	2·9
Peru	1955	3·0
Columbia	1951	3·1
Fiji Islands	1958	3·1
Egypt	1947	3·1
Algeria (Moslem pop.)	1953	3·1
Mauritius	1952	3·2
Panama	1950	3·2
Guinea	1955	3·3
British Guiana	1958	3·3
Trinidad and Tobago	1958	3·3
South Korea	1955	3·3
Réunion	1956	3·4
Mexico	1950	3·4
Turkey	1956	3·4
Ecuador	1950	3·5
Ceylon	1956	3·6
India	1951	3·6
Paraguay	1950	3·7
Jamaica (ex dep.)	1956	3·9
Puerto Rico	1950	3·9
Haiti	1950	4·0
Hawaii	1950	4·0
Iran	1956	4·0
Honduras	1950	4·0
Chile	1952	4·0
Argentina	1947	4·1

Country	Year	Population of 65 and over (%)
People's Rep. of China	1953	4·4
Guadeloupe and dep.	1956	4·7
Israel	1958	4·7
Martinique	1956	4·9
Pacific Islands	1958	4·9
Bechuanaland	1946	5·3
South West Africa	1951	5·5
Japan	1958	5·5
Poland	1958	5·6
Barbados	1958	6·0
Bermuda	1950	6·1
Albania	1955	6·1
Yugoslavia	1957	6·1
Romania	1956	6·4
Union of South Africa (white pop.)	1956	6·6
Cyprus	1958	6·8
Malta and Gozo	1957	6·8
Finland	1958	7·0
Iceland	1957	7·2
Spain	1950	7·2
Bulgaria	1958	7·3
Portugal	1958	7·4
Canada	1959	7·5
Algeria (white pop.)	1953	7·5
Czechoslovakia	1948	7·6
Iceland	1957	7·7
Greece.	1958	7·9
Italy.	1951	8·1
Australia	1958	8·4
U.S.A..	1959	8·7
Hungary	1958	8·7
Netherlands	1958	8·7
New Zealand	1958	8·8
Northern Ireland	1958	9·8
Switzerland	1958	10·0
Denmark.	1957	10·1
Scotland	1953	10·1
Federal German Rep.	1957	10·2
Luxembourg	1957	10·4
Norway	1957	10·4
Irish Rep.	1951	10·7
Sweden	1957	11·2

Country	Year	Population of 65 and over (%)
France	1958	11·5
Belgium	1957	11·7
Austria	1954	11·7
England and Wales	1958	11·8
German Democratic Rep.	1958	13·4

Source: *Demographic Yearbook* (1953, 1954, 1955, 1959) and others.

There are countries where the proportion of old people is so low that one should rather speak about the non-existence of old people. In the above table are populations in which less than 2 per cent of the people are 65 and over. These are Ghana and the Maldive Islands.

Thus, we have in the mid-20th century examples of societies wholly void of old people. We realize that such cases of extreme demographic primitivism appear in a greater number than shown in the U.N. statistics.

Leaving the above facts aside we must state that the proportion of old people remains within the limits of 2–13·4 per cent. Thus, in the oldest populations the number of old people is nearly seven times the number in the youngest populations.

An analysis of the age distribution of the population has now been made to the most recent times and thus our first task in the analysis of age structure at various time periods has been fulfilled. The review has shown highly differentiated demographic conditions, from the most primitive (a complete lack of old people) to biological degeneration (lack of children).

8. CONCLUSIONS

Our investigations have made it possible to determine the spread of indices for the various age groups over the world.

As to the proportion of children (0–14 yr) we have stated the following extremes:

minimum . . . . 19·4%
maximum . . . . 47·5%

The maximum is one and a half times the minimum.

Values near the minimum occur in highly developed European societies and those around the maximum in non-developed societies

For the age group 15–64 yr (productive population) we have the following extreme values:

minimum . . . . 50·3%

maximum . . . . 70·2%

This time the picture is reversed: for non-developed societies the indices of population at the productive age are low, while in highly developed societies these indices are high.

This state of affairs is understandable: in non-developed societies with their high fertility rates and resultant large numbers of children the proportion of productive people in the population cannot be large. Conversely, in developed countries where unlimited fertility has been controlled, the fewer the children, the higher is the percentage of the remaining age groups in the population.

As to the aged (65 and over) we have noted a large spread between the lowest and the highest indices of their number. The proportion of old people in the German Democratic Republic (13·4 per cent) is ten times as high as a similar proportion in the [Maldive Islands (1·3 per cent).

The minima stated above are extremely low. Societies having one or two old persons for every 100 inhabitants are indeed societies without aged persons. It appears reasonable to assume that there are many such societies. In many non-developed societies not having been studied by demographers, one can assume similar low indices of old people. A lack of the aged is the most revealing sign of demographically primitive conditions.

At the other pole of demographic conditions are societies with a large number of old people.

The countries of western, middle and northern Europe lead in this respect: their proportions of old people surpass 11 per cent which is without precedent in the history of demographic conditions. They are countries of old people.

This review of international conditions has shown that the number of such countries is steadily increasing:

(1) in the time period 1861–75 no country could be classified as old; even France could not be regarded as such although it was near to that state;

(2) at the turn of the century France appeared as the first and, for the moment, the only "country of old people";

(3) before the First World War three countries had appeared in a similar role: Ireland, France and Sweden;

(4) before the Second World War the "countries of old people" were increased by Belgium, England, Switzerland, Germany and Latvia, and possibly by others unknown to us;

(5) at present the U.N. statistical data allow us to speak about 18 countries which are qualified for the above category; besides the countries already mentioned there are: Austria, the German Democratic Republic; Scotland; Norway; Northern Ireland; the Federal German Republic; Denmark; New Zealand; Australia; Italy; the U.S.A.

In many other countries not qualified to appear in this category the process of aging is already much advanced. These are all those countries we have qualified as aging countries or those on the verge of old age. What is more, the countries which are still young are under the influence of the aging process.

Naturally, one can evaluate the process of aging of populations as a rather limited phenomenon, as does the U.N. demographer.[14] But one can also take another point of view and consider the new phenomenon as just beginning and one which may become the dominant condition in the field being investigated. We are inclined to adopt the latter viewpoint and, unlike the U.N. demographers, to accept a wider scope for the process of population aging.

The following conclusion seems to be justified and necessary for the understanding of new trends in demography: *we are witnessing profound changes in the demographic features, not only of Europe but perhaps of the world; these features have changed and are further changing under the influence of the aging process.*

REFERENCES

1. Indeed, still today—thus, after a lapse of above 100 yr—in many a European country the proportion of old people has not reached the level it had in Belgium, Norway or Denmark, not to mention France, at about 1850. The non-European countries (with some few exceptions) were still further behind. On this point the U.N. demographer makes the following remark: "It will be seen that the population of Western Europe included about 5 per cent of old people towards the middle of the last century, a substantially higher proportion than that obtaining today among many populations of the world" (*The Aging of Populations and Its Economic and Social Implications.* United Nations, New York, 1956, p. 11). While a number of countries in Europe and outside Europe even today have not reached the proportion of old people possessed by some countries in Western Europe in the middle of the past century, contemporary statistics do give a number of cases showing a considerably larger proportion of old people, sometimes even twice as large, as that which was a record 100 yr ago.

2. *Population*, Paris, 1954, No. 2, p. 198.

3. E. KAHN, *Der internationale Geburtenstreik*, 1930, p. 46.

4. At the beginning of this century Argentina had a population of little more than 5,000,000 (in 1900 5,106,000). The population is now 20,000,000 (in 1958 20,248,000). This quadrupling of the population in such a short time was a result of immigration which was most intensive in the first decade of the 20th century (1900–10). The immigrants were Europeans, chiefly Spaniards.

5. S. WASZAK, *Perspektywy demograficzne powojennych Niemiec* (*Demographic Prospects for Post-war Germany*) Poznań, 1947, p. 467.

6. *Wirtsch. u. Stat.*, organ of the Statistical Office of the Reich, Berlin, 1940, No. 2.

7. J. BEAUJEU-GARNIER (*Géographie de la Population*, p. 297) pointing out that Canada is on the way to becoming old ("la population canadienne est sur la voie du vieillissement"), recalls that in 1881 this country had only 6·4 per cent of its people in the age group of 60 and over. Let us here also recall that in 1861 there were only 4·5 per cent in that age group.

8. The mathematician Pascal stressed that an interpretation adequate to one situation may prove faulty with regard to another ("vérité en-deçà, erreur au-delà"). Developing this idea, the French writer A. TOULEMON writes: "What is true for China need not be true for Italy; what is true for France is not true for Australia; from continent to continent, from sea to sea, from frontier to frontier, the demographic conditions are different..." (A. TOULEMON, *Histoire des Doctrines de la Population*, Éd. Berger-Levrault, Paris, 1956, p. 153).

9. J. DE CASTRO, *The Geography of Hunger*.

10. This problem is analysed by the American economist P. F. Drucker whose work is known to us from the German edition: "Amerika in den nächsten zwanzig Jahren", as published in *Harper's Magazine*, 1955.

     Following this author, the same topic is dealt with by the Swiss economists C. GASSER and F. KNESCHAUREK, *Struktur und Entwicklungsprobleme der schweizerischen Volkswirtschaft*, 1957.

11. E. HUBBACK, *The Population of Britain*, Pelican Books, London, 1947, p. 42.

12. F. BURGDÖRFER, *Volk ohne Jugend*, 1939, p. 135.

13. E. ROSSET, "Proporcja ludności nieprodukcyjnej jako problem społeczny i ekonomiczny" (The Proportion of Unproductive Population as a Social and Economic Problem), *Zeszyty Naukowe Uniwersytetu Łódzkiego* (*Scientific Notes of the University of Lodz*), Lodz, 1960.

14. In the U.N. publication devoted to the problem of the aging of societies the following view is presented: "The modification of the age structure of populations is a relatively recent phenomenon and has not yet affected many countries. All the underdeveloped countries, for instance, have very similar age compositions and where figures are available they show that the age composition has hitherto varied very little. The aging of populations at the apex of the pyramid is therefore a characteristic of the developed countries" (*The Aging of Populations and Its Economic and Social Implications*, United Nations, New York, 1956, p. 21).

CHAPTER 9

The Evolution of the Age Structure of the Population in Some Countries

A COMPARATIVE study of the youth or age of populations in different time periods having been made in the preceding chapters, we shall now proceed to examine the dynamics of the changes in the age composition of populations.

The subject of this chapter is the evolution in the structure of populations in eleven countries—France, Great Britain, Sweden, Belgium, the Netherlands, Australia, the Philippines, Ceylon, Argentina, Brazil and Poland.

1. THE EVOLUTION IN THE AGE STRUCTURE OF THE FRENCH POPULATION

When studying the evolution in the aging of populations the researcher is bound to turn his eyes towards France, the country which is a symbol of demographic old age, the country of "well-preserved old people".

We shall examine the evolution in the age structure of the French population under several variants of age classification.

The first of these, widely used in statistics (though perhaps not in France), divides the population into three groups—children (from 0–14), the productive population (from 15–64), and aged people (65 and over).

The evolution in the age structure of the French population as divided into these groups is given in the table on page 214.

During the hundred years since the mid-19th century, when the first figures given in the table were collected, the population of France has been affected by two parallel processes:

(1) a decline in the number of children (0–14), and

(2) an increase in the number of aged people (65 and over).

In other words, the aging of the French population has been proceeding from both ends, from below and from above; or, to use the terminology of the United Nations, from the base and at the apex.

213

AGING PROCESS OF POPULATION

EVOLUTION IN THE AGE STRUCTURE OF THE FRENCH
POPULATION 1851–1958

Year	Total	Age groups		
		0–14	15–64	65+
1851	100·0	27·3	66·2	6·5
1861	100·0	27·1	66·2	6·7
1872	100·0	27·1	65·5	7·4
1881	100·0	26·7	65·2	8·1
1891	100·0	26·2	65·5	8·3
1901	100·0	62·1	65·7	8·2
1911	100·0	25·8	65·8	8·4
1921	100·0	22·7	68·2	9·1
1931	100·0	23·0	67·7	9·3
1950	100·0	21·7	66·5	11·8
1955	100·0	23·6	65·0	11·4
1958	100·0	25·7	62·8	11·5

Source: *The Aging of Populations and Its Economic and Social Implications*, New York, 1956 and other publications.

The losses in the number of children have equivalent gains in the number of the aged. Thus, during the hundred years between 1851 and 1950 the proportion of children decreased from 27·3 to 21·7, or by 5·6, while that of aged people increased from 6·5 to 11·8, or by 5·3.

No marked change could therefore be expected to have taken place in the proportion of the medium group, which represents the productive population. In fact, while in 1851 the proportion of persons aged 15–64 was 66·2 per cent, the corresponding figure in 1950, a hundred years later, was nearly the same: 66·5 per cent.

The figures for 1955 and 1958 disclose a new trend. Its features are:

(1) a growing increase in the proportion of children (0–14), and

(2) a slowdown in the growth of the proportion of old people (65 and over).

One can hardly indulge in prophecies as to the future development of this trend which, contrary to the preceding one, may result in rejuvenating the population. However, it would be hazardous to attach one's hope to this new demographic tendency, so untypical of modern times.

The intensity of the changes in the age structure of populations is another important aspect of the problem. These changes may be larger or smaller.

Judging from the table above, during the last one hundred years the changes in the age structure of the French population were not very large. The reasons are clear enough. As compared with other European countries which now belong to the "aged" category, the aging of the French population began much earlier. It is not enough to say that France is an "aged" nation; it is necessary to add that her aging started long before it did elsewhere. Since her population was already "old", no radical changes tending towards further aging of the population could be expected to occur. This explains the slow rate of evolution in the age structure in France.

This can be illustrated by some additional figures. In 1881, the percentage of children (0–14) was:

> in Great Britain . . . . 36·5%
> in Sweden . . . . 32·6%
> in France . . . . 26·7%

The lowest proportion of children at the bottom of demographic depression has been empirically established at some 20 per cent; consequently, France had less than 7 points to lose while Sweden's losses could amount to nearly 13 and Britain's to more than 16 points. In fact, this is what actually happened in these countries. Late in the 1930s they had only a little more than 20 per cent of children under fifteen. France approached this minimum level at a slower pace than the other countries as she had a much shorter way to go than they.

French data for the recent years display a shift in the evolution of the age structure of the population; the proportion of children, which from time immemorial was invariably on the decline in France, has stopped shrinking and has even slightly increased.

We shall try to find out when this shift took place, and why.

The turning point in the age distribution of the French population came in 1946 when for the first time France noted an increase in the proportion of children and adolescents, both in absolute and relative figures. Whence came this increase? "Par suite de la reprise de la natalité, notre population jeune augmente depuis 1946, en valeur absolue," says the French demographer Jean Fourastié.[1] He is certainly right; the number of children has risen mainly due to an increased birth rate. But not only owing to that. The effects of the successful fight with infant mortality must not be underestimated. France has more children not only because more and more of them are born but also because fewer and fewer of them die.

All this notwithstanding, France cannot escape a further increase in the proportion of old people in the years to come, and, consequently, further progress in the aging of her population: this is borne out by population forecasts.

Not that this detracts from the importance of the shift in France's demographic situation. To realize its meaning in full, it would be helpful to estimate the future age structure in France on the assumption of the very low birth rates of the years before the last war; the figures thus found would make it quite plain how much France owes to her new, post-war trend in birth rates.

The evolution in the age structure of the French population can be examined from the angle of a different age classification. The variant generally accepted in France divides the population into three groups: 0–19, 20–59 and 60 and over. The figures obtained for these groups date back to the 1851 census and, even earlier than that, to Moheau's estimates made in 1778.

The 1851 census was not the first in France; she had conducted censuses since half a century earlier. But it was in 1851 that a question about age was first included. Hence, the 1851 census supplied the earliest official data on the age structure of the French population.

Estimated figures covering still earlier periods are contained in Moheau's *Recherches et considérations sur la population de la France*, written in 1778.[2]

Here are tabulated data on the evolution in the age structure of the French population during the last 180 yr.

EVOLUTION IN THE AGE STRUCTURE OF THE FRENCH POPULATION 1778–1957

Year	Total	Age groups		
		0–19	20–59	60 and over
1778	100·0	42·6	50·3	7·1
1851	100·0	37·0	53·1	9·9
1872	100·0	35·5	52·9	11·6
1881	100·0	35·4	52·3	12·3
1901	100·0	34·6	53·0	12·4
1911	100·0	33·9	53·5	12·6
1921	100·0	31·6	54·6	13·8
1936	100·0	30·2	55·1	14·7
1947	100·0	29·8	54·0	16·2
1956	100·0	31·1	52·6	16·3
1957	100·0	31·3	52·3	16·4

Sources: JEAN DARIC, *Vieillissement de la population et prolongation de la vie active*, p. 19, and JEAN-CLAUDE CHASTELAND and LOUIS HENRY, "La Situation Démographique" *Population*, Paris 1956, No. 4, p. 746.

Let us examine the column under the 0–19 age group.

It shows that:

(1) from 1778 to 1947, or for 170 yr, the proportion of children and adolescents in France was dwindling continually;

(2) from the initial 40 per cent and more, the proportion of young people up to 19 dropped to 30 per cent, falling still lower in the period which can be considered the bottom of the demographic depression in France;

(3) due to the continual increase of several years standing, the proportion of young people increased, to reach 31·3 per cent in 1957, equalling the 1922 level;

(4) a decade has elapsed since it began, but the effects of the new trend are too insignificant to presage impressive gains in the number of children and adolescents in the near future.

The next age groups, comprising the adult population (20–59), reveals small fluctuations in recent years:

minimum . . . . 52·3
maximum . . . . 55·1

The category we are most interested in is the aged group (60 and over).

According to Moheau, by the end of the 18th century the aged constituted 7·1 per cent of total population. The proportion may have been somewhat exaggerated, but for the sake of this study let us assume that it is correct. Even so, it can be seen that during the first 150 years of uninterrupted growth, the proportion of aged persons in France doubled, and now, after another thirty years, it has nearly trebled in relation to the figure given by Moheau.

How can this be reconciled with the fact, noted earlier in this chapter, that the number of children and adolescents in France is on the increase?

At any given moment, the age structure of a population is the resultant of past as well as present events. The age composition is, so to speak, a living monument to all the demographic facts accumulated in the course of the previous one hundred years. Under the circumstances, it may happen that various age groups within a given population are subject to divergent tendencies; while a rejuvenating trend gains the upper hand in one or more age groups, an opposite trend may prevail in the remaining groups.

The present demographic situation in France is a conglomerate of such contrasting tendencies: parallel to the growth in the number of young people up to 19, which tends to a rejuvenation of the population, there is an increase in the number of old people (60 and over) which is a symptom of the aging of a population. Each of the two tendencies has its own origins: the former sprouted recently; the latter is a repercussion of a more distant past.

According to future estimates prepared by the French demographer Marcel Croze, the two opposite tendencies will continue to co-exist during the next several years.[3]

Croze forecasts that by 1966 the proportion of young people (0–19) will amount to 33·3 per cent, but the proportion of old people (65 and over) will also increase and reach 12·1 per cent. The situation is to change by 1971, when the proportion of young people is expected to shrink to 31·6 per cent while that of old people will increase to 12·7 per cent. This would mean full recurrence of the aging process.

Let us try to outline the chronology of the aging of the French population in accordance with the scale we have suggested.

The aging process seems to have commenced early in the 19th century. Fifty years later, that is, a hundred years ago, France reached the phase of aging. And since the late 1870s, or for eighty years now, she has been in the phase of old age.

Should another scale of rating the aging process be adopted, we would obtain a different chronology of the process. But whatever the scale adopted, France will keep her top place among aging or aged nations as the country where the aging process made its earliest start.

Another way of establishing the chronology of the aging of populations is to refrain from differentiating its phases and simply to find out when the proportion of old people began to rise in the given area. Such was the method used by Marcel Reinhard in his comprehensive study of the modern history of world populations (1700–1948).

According to the French historian the aging of the French population began in the first half of the 19th century. In the years between 1800 and 1850 the proportion of persons over forty increased in France from 27 per cent to nearly 33 per cent and that of persons over 60 from 7 per cent to 10 per cent.[4]

All this brings us to the following conclusions:

(1) the aging of the French population began a long time ago; France is ahead of all other nations in this respect;

(2) the aging process in France has reached dimensions unknown anywhere else; for decades, France has represented the most advanced phase in the aging of populations;

(3) the shift in birth rates recently noted in France has reduced but not halted the great increase in the proportion of the aged;

(4) the present proportion of the aged in France has not yet reached the top of the curve; on the contrary, according to calculations made by French demographers, a further increase in the proportion of old people is forthcoming; in other words, the aging of the French population is expected to continue.

2. THE EVOLUTION IN THE AGE STRUCTURE OF THE BRITISH POPULATION

Since in no other country has the aging of the population been so rapid as in Great Britain, it is but just and proper to examine the evolution in the age structure of the British population following that of France.

A century of population development is illustrated by the accompanying table.

EVOLUTION IN THE AGE STRUCTURE OF THE BRITISH POPULATION 1851–1958

Year	Total	Age groups		
		0–14	15–64	65 and over
1851	100·0	35·5	59·9	4·6
1861	100·0	35·7	59·6	4·7
1871	100·0	36·2	59·0	4·8
1881	100·0	36·5	58·9	4·6
1891	100·0	35·1	60·1	4·8
1901	100·0	32·5	62·8	4·7
1911	100·0	30·8	63·9	5·2
1921	100·0	27·9	66·0	6·0
1931	100·0	24·2	68·4	7·4
1939	100·0	21·4	69·6	9·0
1951	100·0	22·2	66·8	10·9
1953	100·0	22·4	66·4	11·2
1958	100·0	22·8	65·4	11·8

Source: *The Aging of Populations and Its Economic and Social Implications* (United Nations, New York, 1956, p. 141) and other publications.

The column of the 0–14 age group shows that:

(1) in the years between 1851 and 1881 the proportion of children was constantly increasing;

(2) 1891 marked the beginning of a decrease in the proportion of children which reached its low point of 21·4 per cent in 1939;

(3) the post-war years have brought a slight increase in the proportion of children.

This brings us to several important conclusions.

From 1871 to 81 the proportion of children (0–14) was 36 per cent or more. Such a high percentage of children was even then very rare in western Europe. In the 1870s and 1880s Britain still belonged to those nations with an abundance of children.

But what happened in the subsequent years has no equivalent in any other European country. During the three decades between 1881 and 1911, Britain's proportion of children dwindled from 36·5 to 30·8 per cent, and in the next three decades, between 1911 and 1940, from 30·8 to 21·1 per cent. The drop in the proportion of children, drastic as it had been in the first thirty years, was further accelerated in the next thirty years. Within six decades Britain turned from a country rich in children into one of those with the lowest proportion of children.

In 1940, the proportion of children in Britain amounted to 21·1 per cent. It may be interesting in this connection to see what was the development of birth rates in Britain. The table below contains the pertinent data for the years from 1936 to 47.

BIRTH RATES IN GREAT BRITAIN (PER 1000 INHABITANTS)
1936–47

From 1936 to 41		From 1942 to 47	
year	births per thousand	year	births per thousand
1936. . . .	14·8	1942 . . .	15·6
1937. . . .	14·9	1943 . . .	16·2
1938. . . .	15·1	1944 . . .	17·7
1939. . . .	14·8	1945 . . .	15·9
1940. . . .	14·1	1946 . . .	19·2
1941. . . .	13·9	1947 . . .	20·5

Source: Statistics of natural movement of the British population.

The striking facts revealed by the table are:

(1) Britain's birth rates between 1936 and 1941 were extremely low (births under 15 per thousand are among the world's lowest);

(2) the low point of demographic depression in terms of births was reached in 1940 and 1941;

(3) the turning point came in 1942; it was then that the decline in births was replaced by an increase.

These facts make it clear why Britain had the lowest percentage of children in 1940 and 1941. Then the proportion of children was a little more than 20 per cent, or so low as to be rarely encountered, not only in Britain but in world-wide demographic statistics. It is no less clear that after 1941, when the bottom of the demographic depression had been left behind, the children's age group (0–14) was bound to gain in strength. It actually did, as shown by the 1951, 1953 and 1958 figures.

As to the economically productive population (15–64), its proportion is inversely related to that of the children (0–14); when the former is on the increase the latter declines, and conversely. From 1881 to 1941 the proportion of working-age population was rising; since 1941 it has been shrinking.

Britain's productive population reached its high mark in 1941, when it amounted to 70 per cent—the highest proporcion of adult population ever noted the world over.

We are now coming to the post-productive age group—the aged.

In the mid-19th century the proportion of old people in England was not very high. In 1851, Britain had 46 persons aged 65 and over to every one thousand inhabitants (the corresponding figure in France for the same year was 65).

It is remarkable that this not very high proportion of old people in Great Britain remained stable for several decades. In 1901, it was 47 per thousand, or nearly the same as in 1851.

The conclusion is that in the second half of the 19th century the symptoms of the aging of the British population were not yet easy to discern. True, they could be detected in the last two decades of the 19th century, but only in the decline of the number of children (0–14); the proportion of the aged remained as it had been for some time.

We know that Britain's highest proportion of children was recorded in the 1881 census. That was the year of the demographic peak in that country. Let us see what has happened since then.

The proportion of the aged (65 and over), which was 4·6 per cent in 1881, rose to 9·0 per cent in 1939 (nearly twice as much as in 1881) and to 11·8 per cent in 1958 (nearly two and a half times as much as in 1881). It is amazing how rapid was the pace of the aging process in a country which had resisted it for so long.

It may be helpful to compare the British figures with the French statistics which are usually regarded as classical. The comparison is made for the proportion of aged persons in the two countries in 1881 and in 1953.

The table indicates that Great Britain, where in 1881 the proportion

COMPARATIVE EVOLUTION IN THE PROPORTION OF THE AGED IN GREAT BRITAIN AND IN FRANCE 1881 AND 1958

Country	Percentage of persons aged 65 and over	
	1881	1958
Great Britain	4·6	11·8
France	8·1	11·5

Source: Computed by the author.

of aged persons was little more than one half of that in France, has now outstripped France in this respect.

The aging of the population began in Britain much later than in France. However, within a few decades Britain joined the nations where the aging process was most advanced. The differences in aging between Britain and France, so large some time ago, have been levelled out. Britain today is the more advanced of the two as regards demographic age; she is now amongst the nations most affected by the aging of the population.

3. THE EVOLUTION IN THE AGE STRUCTURE OF THE SWEDISH POPULATION

We shall now examine the situation in the country which takes just pride in being the first to have built up demographic statistics and in diligently collecting statistical data. This is Sweden, the home country of Per Wargentin.

As we know from the preceding chapters, the aging process in Sweden is in an extremely advanced stage. To analyse the development of the age structure of the Swedish population we shall study the data covering the last one hundred years (1850–1957),[5] contained in the table on page 223.

Let us now proceed to analyse the evolution in the proportion of each of the three age groups.

In 1850, which is the initial year under examination, Sweden still had rather a high percentage of children; the 0–14 age group comprised one-third of the total population. In 1870, or twenty years later, the proportion of children reached 34·1 per cent, the highest figure for the last one hundred years in Sweden.

But the next forty years, from 1870 to 1910, brought a steady decline in the proportion of Swedish children. The decline was initially slow: from 34·1 per cent in 1870, the percentage of children shrunk to 31·7 per cent in 1910.

EVOLUTION IN THE AGE STRUCTURE OF THE SWEDISH POPULATION 1850–1957

Year	Total	Age groups		
		0–14	15–64	65 and over
1850	100·0	32·9	62·4	4·8
1860	100·0	33·5	61·3	5·2
1870	100·0	34·1	60·5	5·4
1880	100·0	32·6	61·5	5·9
1890	100·0	33·3	59·0	7·7
1900	100·0	32·4	59·2	8·4
1910	100·0	31·7	59·8	8·4
1920	100·0	29·3	62·3	8·4
1930	100·0	24·8	66·0	9·2
1940	100·0	20·4	70·2	9·4
1950	100·0	23·4	66·3	10·3
1952	100·0	23·6	66·0	10·4
1957	100·0	23·6	65·2	11·2

Source: Various publications.

It was after 1910 that the declining trend rapidly accelerated. The 1930 census registered a mere 24·8 per cent of children under 15, or one-fourth instead of the previous one-third of the total population.

Low as it was, the proportion kept diminishing. It dwindled to 21·2 per cent in 1938, according to contemporary statistics, and the 1940 census revealed an unprecedented low in the proportion of children—20·4 per cent, or even less than in England. Judging from available data, no equally low percentage of children has been recorded in world statistics.

Such a drastic decline in the proportion of children was obviously the effect of the sudden decrease in Sweden's birth rates after 1910. In the mid-19th century Sweden had 33 births per thousand inhabitants; by 1909, which was the year preceding the sharp decrease in fertility, birth rates dropped to 26 per thousand and in 1933 to as little as 13·7 per thousand.

To quote Dr Ernst Höijer, Director-General of the Central Statistical Office in Stockholm, the 1933 birth rate was "terrifyingly low" ("eine erschreckend niedrige Zahl").[6] In fact, such low birth rates are practically unheard of in world statistics even during demographic depressions. Austria is the only country to have had once, in 1935, a still lower birth rate (13·2 per thousand).

The years after 1933 brought symptoms of improvement in Sweden's demographic situation.

The first symptom, one of essential importance, was the increase in marriages. For many decades Sweden had extremely low marriage rates (slightly above six per thousand). In 1933, there were seven marriages to one thousand inhabitants, or as many as in the mid-19th century. Marriage rates kept rising: 7·76 per thousand in 1934, 8·20 in 1935. Commenting on these figures, von Ungern-Sternberg says that the rise in marriage rates in Sweden was "evidently the result of an unusual economic boom" ("offenbar infolge des aussergewöhnlichen Anstiegs der wirtschaftlichen Konjunktur").[7]

The increase in fertility was the next symptom of a change in the demographic situation in Sweden.

It began rather inconspicuously; the 1934 low was 13·67 per thousand, and the next year the birth rate rose to 13·76. But the tide kept rising as the years passed by: the 1939 figure was 15·4, and that of 1942, 17·7. From 85,000 in 1933, the number of births increased to 113,600 in 1942—the highest figure in Sweden since 1922.

Dr Höijer notes the connection between the increase in marriages and in births; more marriages resulted in more births.

To bear this out, the Swedish statistician quotes the following data. The number of women in the reproductive age (15–45) increased by 80,000 in round figures, while the number of married women in the same age group increased by 156,000. This is an evidence, says Dr Höijer, of a growing propensity to marry. Particularly large was the increase in the number of married women in younger age groups, whose fertility rates are the highest.

"Es kann daher nicht abgestritten werden, dass Eheschliessungen in jungen Jahren der hauptsächlichste Grund für die Zunahme der Geburten waren," notes Dr Höijer.[8]

Hence, the increase in the number of young married couples was, in Dr Höijer's opinion, the essential factor contributing to the increased birth rates.

Lower infant mortality, of course, played its part, too. But in the case of Sweden it was of no great significance since infant mortality in that country had been low even before the rising demographic tide began, as indicated by the following figures:

1935–39	4·32%
1950	2·10%
1954	1·85%
1958	1·58%

It is worth noting that Sweden today has the lowest infant mortality rate in the world.

The new demographic policy pursued by the Swedish government with the aim of encouraging marriages and births proved to be a powerful incentive. The reader will find relevant information in the work written by the Director of the Swedish Statistical Office, quoted here.

The improvement in Sweden's demographic situation, expressed in increased marriage and birth rates and in further decline in infant mortality, could not but influence the age structure of the population. This is illustrated by the table inserted earlier in this chapter. By 1952 the proportion of children under 15 in Sweden grew to 23·6 per cent, restoring its 1932 level. In other words, the Swedish nation managed to make up for its demographic shortcomings in the previous two decades.

Let us now examine the fluctuations in the proportion of adult population (15–64) in Sweden.

Between the years 1880 and 1910 the number of Sweden's adult population was on the decline. This is the more significant as the proportion of children in the same period also decreased. While decline in the proportion of children was the effect of dropping birth rates, the proportion of adult population dwindled as a result of mass emigration.

For Sweden was once a nation of emigrants. It was between 1880 and 1910 that the greatest number of Swedes left their home country. "Die Auswanderung hatte ihren Höhepunkt in den 80er, 90er Jahren und im ersten Jahrzehnt des laufenden Jahrhunderts erreicht," says von Ungern-Sternberg. Emigration cut down the ranks of the adult population; within fifty years, from 1861 to 1910, migrations brought Sweden a net loss of 500,000 men and 420,000 women, most of them certainly in the productive age group.[9]

After 1910, emigration from Sweden grew smaller and immigration to Sweden larger. The migration balance, formerly adverse, became favourable. From a country of emigration Sweden turned into a country of immigration.

The German scientist quoted above says that in the years 1931–3, Sweden's population increased by 25,000 owing to immigration. These were mainly re-emigrants from the United States and Canada. "There is no doubt," says von Ungern-Sternberg, "that immigration outnumbered emigration because the situation and living standards in

Sweden were deemed attractive and there was no reason to leave the country."[10]

Following these changes in migration tides, the proportion of adult population, formerly on the decrease, began to increase. By 1940 it hit an unprecedented record of 70·2 per cent. By 1952 it dropped as a consequence of the rise in the proportion of children on the one hand and that of old people on the other.

This brings us to the oldest age group.

The proportion of the aged (65 and over) has been continually growing in Sweden. In 1850 it comprised 4·8 per cent of the total population. By 1958 it reached 11·2 per cent, which means that during the period under study the proportion of old people in Sweden more than doubled. This is the yardstick of the development in the age structure of Swedish population; this is also the yardstick of progress in its aging process.

Such was the evolution in Sweden's proportion of children, adult population, and old people during the last one hundred years.

This change can also be shown in indices. Taking the 1850 proportions as 100, the 1958 indices are:

```
          0–14 age group . . . . . . . . . .  72
         15–64 age group . . . . . . . . . . 105
         65+   age group . . . . . . . . . . 233
```

Thus the proportion of children between the years 1850 and 1958 diminished by 28 per cent that of the adult population increased by 5 per cent and that of the aged by 133 per cent.

These figures clearly indicate the main trend in the development of the age structure of the Swedish population; they bear witness to an advanced aging of the population.

4. THE EVOLUTION IN THE AGE STRUCTURE OF THE BELGIAN POPULATION

Belgium, being one of the countries where the aging of the population has made the greatest progress, is a most attractive object of study for the demographer. Not so long ago, Professor Tulippe, author of an interesting study on the aging of the Belgian population, repeatedly quoted in this work, gave vent to his apprehension that if no adequate preventive measures were taken Belgium's depopulation would be imminent. The danger of depopulation, according to Professor Tulippe, lies in the existing age composition.

Let us examine the development of the age structure of the Belgium population which gives rise to such fears.

EVOLUTION IN THE AGE STRUCTURE OF THE BELGIAN POPULATION 1846–1957

Year	Total	Age groups			
		0–14	15–20	21–64	65+
1846. . . .	100·0	32·3	61·8		5·9
1856. . . .	100·0	30·3	64·1		5·6
1866. . . .	100·0	31·7	62·0		6·3
1880. . . .	100·0	33·5	11·0	49·2	6·4
1890. . . .	100·0	32·8	11·7	49·2	6·4
1900. . . .	100·0	31·7	11·4	50·6	6·2
1910. . . .	100·0	30·5	11·0	52·1	6·4
1920. . . .	100·0	25·0	11·8	56·8	6·5
1930. . . .	100·0	23·0	9·7	59·8	7·6
1947. . . .	100·0	20·6	9·2	59·5	10·7
1957. . . .	100·0	22·6	65·7		11·7

Source: *Population Studies* (London 1954, No. 2, p. 154) and United Nations publications.

The table discloses the following obvious symptoms of the aging of Belgium's population:

(1) a constant decrease in the proportion of children (0–14), which dropped from one-third of total population in 1880 to one-fifth in 1947;

(2) a decline in the proportion of adolescents (15–20) from 11 per cent in 1880 to 9·2 per cent in 1947;

(3) an increased proportion of adults (21–64) from 49·2 per cent in 1880 to 59·5 per cent in 1947; and

(4) an extremely sharp upsurge in the proportion of old people (65+) from 5·9 to 11·7 per cent (1846–1957).

What were the factors which brought about such a radical change in the demographic structure of Belgium?

Cicely Watson sees its main causes in birth decline and war losses: "The decline in births and the losses due to two wars have unbalanced the Belgian age structure, and led to an increase in the proportion of older people."[11]

We must add, however, that the influence of the two factors—the decline in births and the war losses—upon the aging process was partly counterbalanced by immigration.

Fernand Hebette says that Belgium is gradually changing from a country of emigration into one of regular immigration. The change began more than twenty-five years ago, and was engendered by the rapid aging of Belgian population.[12]

A closer glance at the different stages in the demographic evolution of Belgium will enable us to shed more light upon the aging of her population.

The characteristic facts are:

(1) the lowest proportion of older people is to be found, not unexpectedly, in the earliest census figures (1846, 1856), though even then the percentage of older people was, relatively speaking, not very low (the respective figures for Great Britain in the same years were between 4·6 and 4·7 per cent);

(2) the period between 1886 and 1910 saw virtual stabilization of the proportion of older people; the index recorded in four successive censuses was never below 6·2 nor above 6·4 per cent;

(3) beginning from the famous Quetelet Census in 1846 and ending with 1910, the proportion of children (0–14) varied only little, either plus or minus; Professor Tulippe was right to note a certain stabilization of the demographic situation in Belgium between 1880 and 1910 ("la situation démographique est restée pratiquement inchangée de 1880 à 1910");

(4) the turn in Belgium's demographic situation came after the First World War, when the number of children (0–14) decreased to 25 per cent; for the time being the number of older people remained unchanged;

(5) by 1930 the proportion of children dropped to 23 per cent and that of old people increased to 7·6 per cent; symptoms of aging were by then noticeable both at the base and the apex of the age pyramid;

(6) 1947 brought a catastrophic low in the proportion of children (20·6 per cent) and an unprecedented high in the proportion of the aged (10·7 per cent);

(7) 1957 marked a slight increase in the proportion of children and a further rise in that of old people.

Neither at the bottom nor at the top of the age pyramid does Belgium's demographic situation resemble what it was in the past. More than that: it differs a great deal from what is the rule in other European countries. Watson has good reason to say that unbalanced proportions are characteristic for the present age composition of the Belgian population. It was Tulippe who voiced alarm at the danger of such an age structure for the future of the nation ("... s'il n'intervient pas une augmentation de la natalité ou une immigration massive, il faut appréhender une diminution de la population de la Belgique dans les prochaines décades").[13]

What is involved, therefore, is the danger of depopulation resulting from the advanced aging process of the population. Not that the danger is unavoidable; it might be prevented by an increase in fertility or by mass immigration.

5. THE EVOLUTION IN THE AGE STRUCTURE OF THE DUTCH POPULATION

The demographic situation of the Netherlands differs greatly from that of Belgium. Though the aging process has made some progress in the Netherlands (growing proportion of older people), its pace is much slower than that in Belgium.

The table below shows an age structure which has been praised by German demographers as normal and sound; it is moreover, one rarely encountered. What are its characteristic features?

The most important feature is the high (for west-European standards) and stable proportion of children. The period under study covering more than a hundred years, brought little change in the proportion of children (0–14) in the Netherlands. A possible interpretation is that the aging of the Dutch population finds no stimuli in reduced birth rates and, therefore, does not occur "from the base".

EVOLUTION IN THE AGE STRUCTURE OF THE DUTCH POPULATION 1849–1958

Year	Total	Age groups			
		0–14	15–44	45–64	65+
1849. . . .	100·0	33·4	45·5	16·3	4·7
1859. . . .	100·0	32·5	46·5	16·1	4·9
1869. . . .	100·0	33·4	44·3	16·8	5·5
1879. . . .	100·0	35·1	42·7	16·7	5·5
1889. . . .	100·0	35·2	42·3	16·5	6·0
1899. . . .	100·0	...	...	...	6·0
1909. . . .	100·0	...	...	...	6·1
1920. . . .	100·0	32·6	45·4	16·1	5·9
1930. . . .	100·0	30·6	46·0	17·1	6·2
1938. . . .	100·0	28·6	46·8	17·9	6·7
1940. . . .	100·0	27·9	46·9	18·3	7·0
1950. . . .	100·0	29·3	43·8	19·2	7·7
1953. . . .	100·0	29·8	42·6	19·5	8·1
1958. . . .	100·0	30·1	41·0	20·2	8·7

Source: Wirtschaft u. Statistik, 1940, p. 167, and United Nations publications.

But one would be mistaken to think that the Dutch population is not affected by the aging process. It is, as is proved by the two following facts:

(1) the rapid increase in the proportion of persons in the older productive age group (45–64) in recent decades,

(2) the steady increase for more than a century in the proportion of persons of post-productive age (65+).

We are not familiar with Dutch population forecasts, but judging from J. G. Sleeswijk's statement at the Second International Congress of Gerontologists in St. Louis in 1951, the Netherlands' proportion of older people (65+) is expected to increase within the next twenty years to 1,120,000, reaching some 10 per cent of the total population or three times as much as at the beginning of the 20th century.[14]

There is no need to look for more eloquent evidence of the aging process.

6. THE EVOLUTION IN THE AGE STRUCTURE OF THE POLISH POPULATION

When proceeding to a comparative study of the age structure of the Polish population in different periods, the researcher faces an obstacle of basic importance. The difficulty lies in the territorial incomparability of the available data.

Given the present knowledge of Poland's demographic past—an admittedly insufficient knowledge, by the way—the obstacle is insurmountable. This is the reason why the statistics quoted below include data for different areas—in one case it is the Kingdom of Poland, in another Galicia or the Prussian–occupied part of Poland. Only since 1918, the year when the Polish State regained its independence, do the data cover the whole territory of Poland. But even these are often hard to use in a comparative study in view of the fact that Poland's frontiers were altered after the Second World War.

The earliest available data give the age structure of the population of the Kingdom of Poland in 1848. Few nations collected any information on their age composition in those distant years,[15] and, although the 1848 figures may seem inaccurate or incomplete, the very fact that they do exist is so extraordinary as to be worth noting; we believe it is of great importance for the history of statistics and of Polish culture.

The age structure of the population of the Kingdom of Poland in 1848 was:[16]

0–19 age group	45·4%
20–59 age group	51·2%
60+ age group	3·4%

Let us begin by examining how reliable these figures are.

Efficient though it was, the statistical machinery of the then Governmental Committee for Internal Affairs could not avoid errors in statistics. After all, in mid-19th century the population of the Kingdom of Poland was mostly illiterate. And illiteracy of those questioned entails inaccuracy and errors in replies, particularly to questions on the age of the questionee.

This is self-evident. The point is, did those errors work both ways, or were they all in the same direction? If the latter, it would imply a grave systematic error in statistics.

The cautious researcher must consider the possibility of such an error. Should this be the case, the problem would arise whether the proportion of old people—since this is the one we are most interested in—was biased in plus or minus.

Let us assume that the statistics under examination contain a systematic error which reduces the proportion of older people. Even so, and even after introducing the necessary corrections into the official data, we receive a proportion of old people equal to, or only slightly above, that existing in demographically backward countries. The conclusion is that *in the mid-nineteenth century, the population of the Kingdom of Poland had an unusually low proportion of old people, which is a typical symptom of extreme demographic backwardness.*

It is particularly interesting to trace the age structure of the Polish population at the turn of the 20th century. For two reasons: firstly, it is common usage to start from the turn of the century when comparing data at different periods and to establish on this basis the dynamics of population movements; secondly, the demographic shift—or, to quote A. Landry, "the demographic revolution"—began in Poland precisely at the turn of the century.

Research by Stefan Szulc yielded an age structure of the Polish population about 1900 as:[17]

        0–14 age group . . . . 39·3%
        15–64 age group . . . . 57·1%
        65 + age group . . . . 3·6%

These figures indicate that at the beginning of the 20th century, prior to "the demographic revolution" which took place in Poland much later than in western Europe, children up to 14 constituted nearly 40 per cent of the then population of Poland.

The percentage of old people was very small, falling far short of the figures in western Europe for those years.

232

About 1900, the proportion of persons aged 60 and over was 6·2 per cent; the figure was valid for the Polish areas in their entirety as well as for the smaller territory of the Kingdom of Poland.

By comparing the 1900 figure with that for the Kingdom of Poland in 1848 (3·4 per cent) we can see that by the end of the 19th century the proportion of the aged rose far above the extraordinary low recorded in mid-19th century statistics.

But it was still low, only a little higher than in India (5·1 per cent in 1901) and lower than in European Russia (6·9 per cent in 1897).

Only in the western part of Poland, then partitioned into three, did there exist a noticeable trend towards modernizing the demographic situation; the rest of the country, despite the progress attained continued to have a low proportion of old people until the end of the 19th century.

The figures quoted above show that by the beginning of the 20th century the Polish population was not yet affected by the aging process, though its first symptoms could be discerned in the part of Poland occupied by Prussia.

We shall now examine the long-term evolution in the age structure of the Polish population until the most recent years.

Different age classifications having been used in statistics of different areas and periods. We shall use a variant having three age groups: from 0–14, from 15–59 and 60 and over.

AGE STRUCTURE OF THE POLISH POPULATION
IN THE YEARS 1848–1958

Area	Year	Number of persons in different age groups per 1000 inhabitants		
		0–14	15–59	60+
Kingdom of Poland	1848	...	...	34
Galicia	1869	354	603	43
,,	1900	389	552	59
Kingdom of Poland	1897	393	546	61
Prussian-occupied Poland	1900	401	523	76
Poland	1921	354	574	72
,,	1931	334	588	78
,,	1949	283	636	81
,,	1958	329	581	90

Source: Census figures and estimates.

This table is an interesting statistical document of the development in age structure of the Polish population during the last 110 yr.

One may have one's doubts as to the complete reliability of certain figures in the table—firstly, because the early census data may not have been accurate and, secondly, because the material presented does not always pertain to the same areas, which detracts from the comparative value of the figures quoted.

Nevertheless, the table reveals in full the main development trend: constant and systematic increase in the proportion of old people to the total population of Poland. Whatever the margin of error and inaccuracy in the statistics, the trend has manifested itself. It must have been very strong indeed if it managed to find its way through a multitude of various errors, possibly including systematic ones.

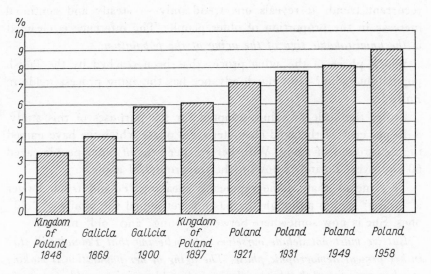

FIG. 3. Evolution in the aging of the population in Polish areas 1848–1958. Percentage of population aged 60 and over.

Let us see what are the changes in the proportion of each age group.

The 0–14 age group shows characteristic fluctuations: after an initial increase, the proportion of children begins to diminish. The turning point coincides with the turn of the century. While the second half of the 19th century saw a growing proportion of children in relation to the total population, since the beginning of the 20th century we have witnessed the reverse. The declining proportion of children is the effect of the birth decline which began in Poland in the early years of this century.

The number of adult population (15–59) changed in the inverse ratio. When the proportion of children increased, that of adults decreased; when the proportion of children dwindled there came a rise in the percentage of the adult population. The development trend prevailing in Poland, as revealed in statistics, has thus been the same as elsewhere. It will be remembered that, as a rule, index numbers of the adult population are not subject to large fluctuations; the rule is also corroborated by Polish statistics.

The last column in the table, that of the aged, shows changes in no way resembling the two previous ones; instead of two intermittently recurrent trends it reveals one trend only—a steady and continual increase in the proportion of older people. The inference is clear; it is *the unmistakable sign of the aging of the population.*

Which phase of the aging process has been reached by the Polish population today? How much advance has the aging process made in Poland?

Under the scale of values adopted for the purposes of this study, 8–10 per cent of the aged characterizes a phase which we have named the foreground of aging. With her 8·5 per cent of older people (aged 60 and over) Poland is now in the foreground of aging.

This means that, demographically speaking, Poland is no longer a "young" nation although she has not yet joined the family of "old" ones. She is now somewhere between "young" and "old" nations.

But we must not delude ourselves into believing that Poland will stay in her present demographic phase. The aging of her population is making steady progress, and the phase of demographic old age is inexorably approaching for Poland.

If we assume that the proportion of aged people in Poland will continue to increase at the same rate, Poland will reach the phase of aging in the early 1970s, when she is expected to pass the conventional lower limit of the aging phase (10 per cent of the population aged 60 and over).

Under the same assumption, the conventional level of demographic old age (12 per cent of the population aged 60 and over) will be reached by Poland before the end of this century.

But the assumption that the rate of increase in the proportion of older people will remain unchanged is arbitrary and doubtful. It is much more probable that it will accelerate, in which case Poland will much sooner join the family of "old" nations.

Let us now see what are the changes in the proportion of persons aged 65 and over. In 1958, it was 5·6 per cent, or as much as in Yugoslavia in 1953.

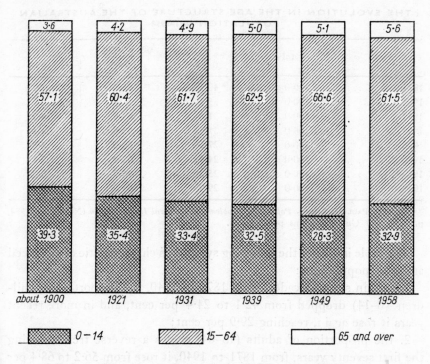

FIG. 4. The age structure of the Polish population between 1900 and 1958 (in percentages).

Poland's proportion of old people (aged 65 +) is amongst the lowest in Europe. So is that of Yugoslavia. The above brings us to the conclusion that Poland has not escaped the aging process, though its roots are not yet deep in this country. In the first half of the 20th century the age structure of the Polish population changed considerably; the population has markedly aged, though not so much as to make Poland a demographically "old" country. Let it be noted once again that Poland's place today is between the "young" and "old" nations.

7. THE EVOLUTION IN THE AGE STRUCTURE OF THE AUSTRALIAN POPULATION

The aging of populations has advanced not only in Europe and North America. Oceania, the world's youngest continent, has also been affected by it.

Here is a table illustrating the evolution in the age structure of the population of Australia, the largest island on our globe.

THE EVOLUTION IN THE AGE STRUCTURE OF THE AUSTRALIAN POPULATION 1871-1958

Year	Total	Age groups		
		0–14	15–64	65+
1871	100·0	42·1	56·2	1·7
1901	100·0	35·2	...	circa 4
1911	100·0	31·8	63·9	4·3
1921	100·0	31·8	63·8	4·4
1933	100·0	27·5	66·0	6·5
1940	100·0	24·4	68·4	7·3
1947	100·0	25·2	66·7	8·0
1958	100·0	29·9	61·7	8·4

Sourc e: PAUL H. LANDIS, *Population Problems. A Cultural Interpretation* (New York, 1954, p. 471), and United Nations publications.

The table indicates the following symptoms characteristic of advanced aging of populations:

1. within seven decades, from 1871 to 1940, the proportion of children (0–14) dropped from 42·1 to 24·4 per cent, and in more recent years it rose agai 1, reaching 29·9 per cent;

2. the proportion of adults (15–64) shows a reverse trend; during the first seventy years, from 1871 to 1940, it rose from 56·2 to 68·4 per cent and in the 1950s it diminished to 61·7 per cent;

3. the proportion of aged persons (65 +) has been steadily and continually on the increase. It was 1·7 per cent in 1871, at the beginning of the period under study, and by 1958 it increased to 8·4 per cent, five times the previous figure.

The striking fact about the evolution in the age structure of the Australian population is that the 1871 figures are typical of extreme demographic youth, while statistics for the latest years indicated the advanced old age of the population.

The reasons for this sudden switch from one extreme to the other seem evident. The Australian population owes its extraordinary youth in the 1870s to immigration, and its old age in the 1940s and 1950s to a decline in the birth rate.

Thus far we have been examining the situation in highly developed countries. Notwithstanding their demographic divergencies they have one thing in common—the aging of their populations. Naturally, the aging process has made different progress in different countries, but we do not know of a single developed country which has not been affected by it.

Let us now turn to the underdeveloped countries, which can be regarded as the opposite pole in social, economic, and demographic relations. We are aware of the difficulties facing the student of population problems in these countries; statistical data are scarce, having been collected only very recently, and are far less accurate than in the case of highly developed countries. But whatever the difficulties, we must not be dissuaded from trying to survey the demographic situation in underdeveloped areas. Here again, we shall endeavour to examine it from the point of view of the aging of populations.

8. THE EVOLUTION IN THE AGE STRUCTURE OF THE PHILIPPINE POPULATION

A country where the old are very few, the Philippines, offers an interesting object of study. The statistics available cover only eight years, from 1949 to 56. They were presented by Dr Leon M. Gonzales, Head Statistician of the Philippine Republic, at the 30th Session of the International Institute of Statistics in Stockholm (8–15 August, 1957).

Scanty as it is, we shall try to analyse this material. The demographic situation of underdeveloped countries is so important and so little known that under no circumstances can one afford to disregard any data supplied.

The table on page 238 contains absolute figures quoted in Dr Gonzales's report, as well as relative figures (age structure percentages) computed by the author of the present work.

The table shows that the population of the Philippines is on the increase; from 19·5 million in 1949 it grew to 22·3 million in 1956, mainly owing to improved sanitary conditions. As Dr Gonzales said, "Improved sanitary conditions propelled by public health safeguards and superior medical techniques helped tremendously in arresting the incidence of epidemics or the spread of contagious diseases from one region to another. Notable health safeguards which proved their indispensability to the favourable growth of the population include: hospital rehabilitation, malaria control, rural health unit establishments, health education of the people, water supply, improved toilet facilities, etc."

AGE STRUCTURE OF THE PHILIPPINE POPULATION 1949–56

Year	Total	Age groups				
		0–1	2–13	14–20	21–65	66+
Absolute figures (in thousands)						
1949.........	19,509	1070	6870	2979	8018	572
1950.........	19,880	1190	6611	3300	8222	557
1951.........	20,259	1211	6679	3200	8619	550
1952.........	20,646	1230	6577	3406	8879	554
1953.........	21,039	1251	6589	3468	9191	540
1954.........	21,440	1275	6462	3644	9374	685
1955.........	21,849	1301	6330	3815	9728	674
1956.........	22,265	1328	6297	3928	10,013	699
Proportion of total population						
1949.........	100·0	5·5	35·2	15·3	41·1	2·9
1950.........	100·0	6·0	33·2	16·6	41·4	2·8
1951.........	100·0	6·0	33·0	15·8	42·5	2·7
1952.........	100·0	5·9	31·8	16·5	43·1	2·7
1953.........	100·0	5·9	31·3	16·5	43·7	2·6
1954.........	100·0	6·0	30·1	17·0	43·7	3·2
1955.........	100·0	5·9	29·0	17·5	44·5	3·1
1956.........	100·0	6·0	28·3	17·6	45·0	3·1

Source: DR LEON M. GONZALES, *Post Censal Population of the Philippines, 1949–1956* (report at the 30th Session of ISI in Stockholm, August 8–15, 1957), and the author's calculations.

Along with the numerical increase of the population, its age structure began to change. "The age composition of the population is always in a constant state of change," says Dr Gonzales.

Let us see how far these statements are borne out by the data furnished.

Judging from the table above, official statistics in the Philippines recognize five age groups:

(a) infancy (0–1),
(b) childhood (2–13),
(c) adolescence (14–20),
(d) adults (21–65) and
(e) the aged (66+).

The first of these groups, infancy, shows a constant increase in absolute figures: from a little over a million in 1949 to 1·3 million in 1956, according to Philippine statistics. The increase is less noticeable in relative figures; except for the rather large rise in 1950 against the previous year, the proportion of infants was alternately 5·9 per cent and 6·0 per cent, indicating no definite trend in either direction.

The number of children (2–13) dropped from nearly 6·9 million in 1949 to 6·3 million in 1956. The decline is still more marked in relative figures: the proportion of children diminished from year to year, shrinking from 35·2 per cent in 1949 to 28·3 per cent in 1956.

The group of adolescents (14–20), on the contrary, was steadily on the increase and grew from 2,979,000 in 1949 to 3,928,000 in 1956, or by nearly one million in a few years. The rise in the proportion of adolescents is also reflected in relative figures.

The same applies to the adult population (21–65) which grew constantly and gained two million in eight years (10,013,000 in 1956 as against 8,018,000 in 1949). Here again, the rising tide is repeated in relative figures.

Finally, the aged group develops along a fluctuating line; in the years 1949–53 it was on the decline, and in the remaining three years (1954–6) the number of aged persons was comparatively high. It is noteworthy that by 1956 the Philippines had nearly 700,000 old people as compared with 540,000 only three years earlier (in 1953).

The reader will bear in mind that these are estimates. Since we are not in a position to judge their accuracy we must take into account a margin of error, perhaps of a large error. Nevertheless, Philippine statisticians deserve praise for their understanding of the importance of information on the age composition of the population.[18]

The above estimates, if accurate, forecast demographic "modernization": the aging of the Philippine population seems to be forthcoming in the not too distant future.

9. THE EVOLUTION IN THE AGE STRUCTURE OF THE CEYLONESE POPULATION

Ceylon draws the demographer's attention as the first underdeveloped country to have stepped onto the path of modernization of demographic relations.

We have in mind sanitary measures taken in Ceylon to protect the life and health of the population, measures which have resulted in a radical reduction of mortality. DDT, used on a nation-wide scale, helped in the fight against malaria and infant diarrhoea. Launched in 1946, the DDT campaign was so successful that within one year death rates dropped from 20·3 to 14·3 per thousand. Since 1947, Ceylonese statistics have registered still lower death rates.

However, Ceylon's battle against death was not coupled with modernized birth control. Like other economically and demographically underdeveloped countries, Ceylon had extremely high fertility rates before the last war. Nothing changed in this respect after the end of the war. More than that; except for 1954, post-war birth rates exceed the pre-war level.

Here are the data on the natural movements of the Ceylonese population during the last thirty-eight years.

NATURAL MOVEMENT OF CEYLONESE POPULATION 1920–58

Years	Births	Deaths	Natural increase
	per 1000 inhabitants		
1920/1924	38·5	28·9	+ 9·6
1930/1934	37·8	22·4	+15·4
1950	40·4	12·6	+27·8
1951	40·5	12·9	+27·6
1952	39·5	12·0	+27·5
1953	39·4	10·9	+28·5
1954	36·2	10·4	+25·8
1958	35·5	9·7	+25·8

Source: United Nations publications.

The table clearly indicates Ceylon's one-sided demographic modernization, which is virtually confined to death rates.

A study of the long-range dynamics of the natural changes in the Ceylonese population reveals that:

(1) birth rates remained stable until recently,

(2) death rates have been reduced to one-third of the 1920–4 figure,

(3) the natural increase rate has nearly tripled as against the 1920–4 figure.

Ceylon's natural increase rates for recent years are among the highest in the world. The American sociologist Hertzler notes that the latest rates of natural increase in Ceylon have reached "an unprecedented level".[19] This is obviously the direct effect of one-sided modernization of demographic relations in that country.

A tremendous mortality decline led to a proportionate increase in average length of life in Ceylon. Thus, while expectation of life at birth for babies born in 1920–22 was:

for males . . . . 32·72 yr
for females . . . . 30·67 yr

the respective figures for the post-war years are:

	M. (yr)	F. (yr)
1945/1947	46·79	44·72
1949	56·07	54·79
1950	56·36	54·83
1951	56·09	53·98
1952	57·6	57·3

Life expectancy for the older age groups is also much longer; the reader interested in this aspect of the problem is advised to consult our sources of information.[20]

The American demographer Earl Huyck has made an interesting and not incorrect remark that the indices of mean length of life in Ceylon place her in the category of the well-developed rather than of the underdeveloped areas of the world.[21] However, this is in blatant contrast with the otherwise backward demographic situation of the country.

It is reasonable to expect similar one-sided demographic developments in other underdeveloped areas.[22] This makes it the more important for the demographer to study in detail what has been happening in Ceylon. Such is, at least in our understanding, the intention of the work by Irene B. Taeuber, who sees Ceylon as a demographic laboratory ("Ceylon as a Demographic Laboratory: Preface to Analysis", *Population Index*, October 1949).

Let us now examine the age composition of the Ceylonese population which is the main object of our interest.

Ample material has been furnished by Ceylonese statisticians on the age structure of the population for the last seventy-five years. Seven censuses were held in Ceylon within that period, the earliest in 1881 and the latest in 1953; in between those two, population censuses took place in 1891, 1901, 1911 and 1946. The data on the structure of the population are available for those in-between years and are given in the table on page 242, along with estimates for 1955.

The table reveals the following interesting facts:

(1) until 1946 the proportion of children was slowly but steadily

AGE STRUCTURE OF CEYLONESE POPULATION 1891–1955

Year	Total	Age groups			
		0–14	15–44	45–64	65+
1891. . . .	100·0	43·4	44·5	10·0	2·0
1901. . . .	100·0	42·2	46·4	.	.
1911. . . .	100·0	40·9	45·9	10·9	2·3
1921. . . .	100·0	39·4	47·0	11·2	2·4
1946. . . .	100·0	37·2	47·2	12·1	3·4
1955. . . .	100·0	40·7	45·2	12·2	1·9

Source: *The Aging of Populations and Its Economic and Social Implications* (United Nations, New York, 1956, p. 111) and other publications.

decreasing; as compared with more that than 43 per cent in 1891, it dropped to a little above 37 per cent in 1946;

(2) the proportion of the active population (15–64) was simultaneously growing, but the rate of increase for the older productive age group (45–64) was far higher than that of the younger group (15–44);

(3) the proportion of aged persons grew continually, reaching 3·4 per cent in the 1940s as compared with 2 per cent by the end of the 19th century. 1946 brought a change in the age-structure development.

Instead of declining, the proportion of children began to increase; the growth in the number of old people was arrested (although the figure of 1·9 per cent for 1955 seems erroneous).

The peculiar feature in the case of Ceylon is that death rates have been sharply reduced while fertility remains very high. This obviously slowed down the aging of the population. To be more precise, the Ceylonese pattern of demographic modernization may even result in a certain rejuvenation of the population. But this is a temporary phenomenon. When demographic modernization reaches the stage of birth control—an inevitable development, we dare to say—a reverse process will ensue and the aging of the population will begin.

10. THE EVOLUTION IN THE AGE STRUCTURE OF THE ARGENTINE POPULATION

Censuses are infrequent in Argentina and statistics illustrating the evolution of the age structure of her population are far from exhaustive.

The only data available for a comparative study are those furnished by the three censuses held in Argentina, the first in 1895, the second in 1914, and the third in 1947, stretching over a period of fifty-two years.

During that time the age structure of the Argentine population developed as follows:

AGE STRUCTURE OF THE ARGENTINE POPULATION 1895–1947

Year	Total	Age groups			
		0–14	15–44	45–64	65+
1895. . . .	100·0	40·3	47·2	10·5	1·9
1914. . . .	100·0	38·4	48·6	10·6	2·3
1947. . . .	100·0	30·8	49·0	16·2	3·9

Source: United Nations publications.

The table proves that the age structure of the Argentine population is unstable; it displays the following changes:

(1) a shrinking proportion of children; it dropped from 40 per cent by the end of the 19th century to less than 31 per cent half a century later;

(2) a slight increase in the proportion of the younger productive age group (15–44); during the same period it rose from 47·2 to 49 per cent;

(3) a much larger increase in the proportion of the older productive-age group (45–64) from 10·5 to more than 16 per cent;

(4) the largest increase in the old-age group (65+) from 1·9 to 3·9 per cent.

These figures are unquestionable evidence of the aging of the population. To use the accepted terminology, the Argentine population has aged both from the base and at the apex.

Argentina has the lowest proportion of children and the highest proportion of old people among Latin American countries. This is an indubitable proof that Argentine conditions are more favourable for the aging of the population than are those in any other country of Latin America.

11. THE EVOLUTION IN THE AGE STRUCTURE OF THE BRAZILIAN POPULATION

A short glance at the situation in Brazil reveals that she represents the opposite demographic pole in Latin America. While Argentina's age structure has been somewhat modernized, Brazil has the youngest—or, as one might put it, the most backward—age composition on that continent.

The only comparative data for Brazil are those collected in three censuses—in 1900, 1940 and 1950. The 1910 census figures are of no avail since a different age classification was used and, therefore, they cannot be compared with those obtained in the remaining three censuses. The data received in the three censuses in Brazil are:

AGE STRUCTURE OF THE BRAZILIAN POPULATION 1900–50

Year	Total	Age groups			
		0–14	15–44	45–64	65+
1900. . . .	100·0	45·03	43·48	9·38	2·11
1940. . . .	100·0	42·54	44·81	10·25	2·40
1950. . . .	100·0	41·85	44·95	10·74	2·46

Source: United Nations publications.

The age structure of the Brazilian population has two peculiar features—an exceedingly large percentage of children and an excessively small proportion of old people, the former so high and the latter so low as to be rarely encountered anywhere else today. The two are an evidence of Brazil's extreme demographic youth.

But even this unusually young population has certain symptoms which may presage the imminent advent of the same developments that other and more developed nations have lived through and left behind, and which have resulted in the aging of populations.

We have in mind two trends, weak but easy to trace. They are:

(1) the gradual decrease in the proportion of children (0–14) and

(2) the gradual increase in the proportion of the older productive-age group (45–64) and of the aged (65+).

There is every reason to state that Brazil's age structure is stable; an age composition whose index numbers over a period of fifty years vary within the small span of 0·35–3·18 points, can be considered stable. It is of particular significance that symptoms of the forthcoming aging of the population can be detected even in so stable a structure. For they are the harbingers of the aging process in a nation which can certainly be regarded as the classical representative of demographic youth.

As indicated by the statistics examined in the previous chapters, in the highly developed countries the aging of the populations is far advanced and is gaining further momentum; we can see now that in the underdeveloped countries, though their populations as yet are far from reaching the phase of aging, the seeds of the aging process are easily discernible.

This corroborates the forecast of the United Nations demographer that the underdeveloped countries will soon enter the phase of aging.[23] Our analysis discloses that in the underdeveloped countries, at least in those which have more or less reliable statistics, demographic relations are being brought up to date. So far this has been a one-sided modernization (reduction of mortality with no equivalent decline in fertility), but it is reasonable to believe that it will not long remain so. The second half of the 19th century saw *demographic revolution* in the highly developed west European countries, a revolution brought about by decline in birth and mortality rates. The future historian of demographic relations will perhaps classify the mid-20th century as the era of the birth of the *second demographic revolution*, this time in the underdeveloped countries. It will not be basically different from the first; its symptoms will be a weakening of the demographic rhythm, a decline in mortality and birth rates. And it will lead to the same development, so well known to us, in the age structure—to the aging of populations.

REFERENCES

1. J. FOURASTIÉ, "La croissance des classes jeunes et le problème de l'emploi," *Population*, Paris, 1956, No. 1, p. 14.
2. The name of Moheau used to be regarded as the pseudonym of the Baron de Montyon, a French intendant renowned for his philanthropic work (1733–1820). Such was also the belief of the British demographer C.F.McCLEARY (*Population: Today's Question*, London, 1938, pp. 133–4). But it was denied by L. CHEVALIER (*Démographie Générale*, Paris, 1951, p. 37); Moheau is the authentic name of the author of the first French work on demography; he was secretary to the famous philanthropist. The French demographer E. LEVASSEUR (*La Population Française*, 1899) praises Moheau's book as "the foundation of modern demography".
3. M. CROZE, "Chronique de démographie", *J. Soc. Stat.*, Paris, June, 1956, p. 58.
4. M. R. REINHARD, *Histoire de la population mondiale de 1700 à 1948*, Editions Domat-Montchrestien, Paris, 1949, p. 203.
5. D. S. THOMAS (*Social and Economic Aspects of Swedish Population Movements 1750–1933*, New York, 1941) quotes statistics on the age structure of the Swedish population for earlier years (1750–1800, and 1800–50). We have not used these data as it does not seem advisable to resort to structure characteristics based on averages for such lengthy periods.
6. E. HÖIJER, *Die Bevölkerungsentwicklung in Schweden im Vergleich mit der Deutschlands*, Kieler Vorträge gehalten im Institut für Weltwirtschaft an der Universität Kiel, Jena, 1943, p. 4.
7. R. VON UNGERN-STERNBERG, *Bevölkerungsverhältnisse in Schweden, Norwegen und Dänemark*, Berlin 1937, p. 20.
8. E. HÖIJER, *Die Bevölkerungsentwicklung in Schweden...*, *op. cit.*, p. 17.
9. *Allg. Stat. Arch.*, 1916/1917, 10. Band, p. 264.

10. R. von UNGERN-STERNBERG, *op. cit.*, p. 17.

11. CICELY WATSON, "A Survey of Recent Belgian Population Policy", *Population Studies*, London, 1954, No. 2, p. 154.

12. F. HEBETTE, "L'évolution démographique de la Belgique", *Population*, Paris, 1954, No. 1, p. 86.

13. O. TULIPPE, *Le Vieillissement de la Population Belge*, p. 4.

14. J. G. SLEESWIJK, "The Social Consequences of Aging in the Netherlands", *J. Gerontol.*, Vol. 6 Supplement to No. 3, pp. 150–151.

15. *The Aging of Populations and Its Economic and Social Implications* (United Nations, New York, 1956, p. 12) names only six countries which by 1850 had some data on the age structure of their populations; they are Belgium, Denmark, France, Great Britain, the Netherlands and Sweden.

16. L. WOLSKI, *Materyały do statystyki Królestwa Polskiego*, (*Materials on the Statistics of the Kingdom of Poland*), Biblioteka Warszawska (Warsaw Library) 1850, Vol. 2, p. 207.

17. S. SZULC, *Ruch naturalny ludności w Polsce w latach 1895–1935* (*The Natural Movement of the Population in Poland in 1895–1935*), p. 13.

18. "It is of vital importance to know the number and characteristics of the population... Information on the age structure of the population is essential for many purposes... These age structures are of vital significance in demographic, economic and sociological analyses." (Dr Gonzales).

19. J. O. HERTZLER, *The Crisis in World Population. A Sociological Examination with Special Reference to the Under-developed Areas*, Lincoln, University of Nebraska Press, 1956, p. 77.

20. *Statistical Yearbook 1955*, Prepared by the Statistical Office of the United Nations, New York, 1955, p. 52.

21. E. HUYCK, "Differential Fertility in Ceylon", *Population Bull. U.N.O.* No. 4, December 1954, United Nations, New York, p. 22.

22. Such developments have actually taken place in many of these areas. In Taiwan, mortality has been so reduced as to approach the lowest level known in statistical practice (8·1 per thousand in 1954) but fertility has stayed very high (44·5 per thousand in 1954). As a result, Taiwan's natural increase is fantastic (36·4 per thousand in 1954). The effect is that the population of Taiwan has been further *rejuvenated* (the proportions of persons aged 60 and over was 4·2 per cent in 1950 as against 4·8 per cent in 1940 and 4·5 per cent in 1905). These changes must by no means be attributed solely to natural changes in the population; migrations must have played their part, too. Besides, there is always the possibility of large errors in the statistics from which we draw our conclusions.

23. "For the time being, thanks to the advances of medical science and to economic and social development, the under-developed countries are experiencing a reduction of mortality without any decline in fertility. There is thus a rejuvenation from the base, the apex of the pyramid remaining unchanged. It is reasonable to suppose, however, that mortality will not continue to decline indefinitely without leading to a decline in fertility, which will give rise to heavy aging from the base and at the apex. It can therefore be forecast that in the under-developed countries a phase of rejuvenation will be followed by a phase of heavy aging" (*The Aging of Populations and Its Economic and Social Implications*, United Nations, New York, 1956, p. 3).

CHAPTER 10

Prospects for the Aging Process in the Light of Demographic Forecasts

1. GENERAL REMARKS

We have studied the trends of development in the aging of populations in the past and present. We shall now proceed to examine its prospects for the near and more distant future.

As noted in the first part of this work, the future development of the composition of populations by sex and age can be estimated on the basis of demographic forecasts.

They may or may not live up to their name; often enough, they are not intended to predict actual developments in the future but to outline the pattern of events which would ensue should a certain situation, theoretically assumed, continue to prevail for a long period of time.

The question is: can one expect that such forecasts, sometime *purely hypothetical*, can truly portray the future course of the aging of populations?

Statisticians and demographers know what can and what cannot be expected from demographic forecasts.

Dr Egon Kern, the Austrian statistician we have quoted earlier, says: "Diese Aussagen über die künftige Entwicklung der Überalterung lassen sich deshalb mit voller Bestimmtheit machen, weil sie in Struktureigentümlichkeiten der heute bereits lebenden Bevölkerung wurzeln. Freilich lässt sich solcherart nur die Entwicklungsrichtung, nicht aber auch das jeweilige genaue Ausmass der Überalterung voraussagen, da dieses auch bereits von der zukünftigen Entwicklung der strukturbestimmenden Faktoren, die aber unbekannt sind, mit beeinflusst wird."[1]

Kern's statement is correct. Uncertain as population forecasts are in view of their dependence on not always realistic assumptions, the least uncertain element in them is the future development of the number of old people. This is obvious, since future aged persons are already alive when population forecasts are being prepared. If the datum level is known it is much more probable that the forecasts will prove accurate. No such forecasts can be expected, of course, to estimate accurately the future number of any group of the population, even the oldest. One of the reasons is that migrations, which also have a bearing on the proportion of old people, are disregarded in most forecasts.[2]

It is true, however, that development trends in the aging of populations can be traced many years in advance. Sufficient basis for this is supplied by demographic forecasts.

There is an immense variety of future estimates of population movements for different countries. They are prepared not only at statistical offices but also in scientific institutes and sometimes by individual researchers. A fraction of this wealth of data will be used in this work to depict the future prospects of the aging of populations.

2. BURGDÖRFER'S FORECAST FOR GERMANY

Let us begin with the estimates prepared by Burgdörfer for the German Reich years ago; though out of date, they are still extremely interesting to examine. The practical value of the German demographer's calculations have been brought to nothing by historical events, but as an effort to assess the consequences of a steady decline in the birth rate they retain some theoretical importance even now. What was the essence of Burgdörfer's estimates?

Between the years 1925 and 1935 the number of old people (65+) in Germany increased from 3·6 million to 4·5 million,[3] gaining 900,000 within one decade.

Burgdörfer's forecast was that by 1946 Germany would have six million, and by 1960 more than seven million old people. The fruit of the years of high birth rates—the 1870s, 1880s and 1890s—was expected to reach old age in the present period. The climax was to come about 1980, when the population born in the last year prior to the First World War would reach old age. The number of old people in Germany would then total 9·5 million, having more than doubled within half a century (1930–80).

Burgdörfer prepared estimates of the future age structure of the German population up to the year 2000.

On page 249 are his figures.

As pointed out by Burgdörfer himself, in 1925 one out of every seventeen persons in the German Reich belonged to the post-productive age group (65+), but by the end of the 20th century that age group would include every seventh and—under Variant B—every sixth Ger-

ments of structure are mainly the changes in fertility and elements of conjuncture in mortality ("Les éléments de conjoncture concernent plutôt la mortalité et les éléments de structure concernent plutôt la fécondité"). The theory put forth by the French demographer is admittedly in keeping with the pattern of changes in the number of population in the post-productive age groups: birth rates in the past form the element of structure which determines the number of old people.

We shall now make a comparison between future estimates for the Federal German Republic and Burgdörfer's forecast for the German Reich.

The comparison discloses that the aging of the German population has followed the pessimistic rather than the optimistic variant of Burgdörfer's forecast. Under his optimistic variant (Variant A), the proportion of old people was to reach 14 per cent by 1980. But in the new estimates for the German Federal Republic the same proportion is expected to be attained as early as in 1972. The aging of the population has thus been accelerated in relation to the estimates in Burgdörfer's Variant A.

The new estimates are closer to Variant B, which anticipated a more rapid rate of growth in the proportion of the aged than did Variant A.

4. DEMOGRAPHIC FORECASTS FOR AUSTRIA

After the Second World War, the Austrian Central Statistical Office (Österreichisches Statistisches Zentralamt) prepared future estimates of the age structure of the Austrian population up to 1980.

The figures obtained in the 1951 census in Austria were taken as datum level, and future estimates were made with the assumption that reproduction and mortality rates would remain unchanged.

Dr Egon Kern, who used it for the purposes of a methodological study (mentioned earlier in this work), points out the unusual value of this forecast; this is because Austria, in contradistinction to a number of other countries and the Federal German Republic in particular, was not an area of large-scale immigration after the last war. This, says Dr Kern, makes it much easier to have a clear and lucid picture of how the elements of the pyramid of age are interconnected and interrelated ("weshalb die Zusammenhänge klarer und übersichtlicher zutage treten").

This alone would be a sufficient reason to make a thorough study of Austria's latest population forecast. Another and, in our opinion

no less important reason impelling us to do so, is Dr Kern's excellent
and penetrating commentary on these estimates. We shall take the
liberty of quoting his comments further on in this work.

Here are the figures.

ESTIMATED CHANGES IN THE AGE STRUCTURE
OF THE AUSTRIAN POPULATION TO 1980

Year	Total	Age groups		
		0–17	18–64	65+
Males				
1910	100·0	36·0	58·5	5·5
1951	100·0	29·2	61·3	9·5
1975	100·0	25·8	61·5	12·7
1980	100·0	25·2	62·5	12·3
Females				
1910	100·0	34·9	58·6	6·5
1951	100·0	24·4	64·1	11·5
1975	100·0	22·0	60·7	17·3
1980	100·0	22·1	60·2	17·7

Source: EGON KERN, "Die Frage der Überalterung", *Allg. Stat. Arch.*, 1957, 41. Band, fasc. 1, p. 34.

The table little resembles the ones inserted earlier in this chapter
or those we are going to examine on the next pages.

Its peculiar features are, firstly, an age classification rarely encountered in statistics (18 yr as the demarcation line between adolescence and adulthood) and, secondly, differentiation of data for males
and females.

It is of the greatest importance to have these figures separated,
since indices and their movements are different for the two sexes.
The differences become striking by the end of the period under study
in the five years between 1975 and 1980, when the development
trends of male and female indices are expected to follow opposite
directions.

What are the estimates for the evolution in the proportion of each
age group?

The proportion of children and adolescents (0–17), on the decline
for several years now, will continue to decrease for a long time. The
percentage of males in this age group is expected to shrink systematically
until the end of the period under study (1980); from 29·2 per cent
in 1951, the proportion of boys is to diminish to 25·8 per cent in

1975 and to 25·2 per cent in 1980. The percentage of girls, on the contrary, is to stop diminishing by 1975 and show a slight increase from then on. From 24·4 per cent in 1951, the proportion of girls is expected to drop to 22·0 per cent in 1975 but will rise to 22·1 per cent five years later.

There are characteristic differences in fluctuations of the adult population (18–64). While the proportion of men in this age group is on the increase (from 61·3 per cent in 1951 to 62·5 per cent in 1980), the percentage of women is on the decline (from 64·1 per cent in 1951 to 60·2 per cent in 1980).

But it is the oldest group (65+) whose proportion is the yardstick of the advance made by the aging of the population.

The proportion of this age group will rise considerably; from 1951 to 80 it will grow from 9·5 to 12·3 per cent for males and from 11·5 to 17·7 per cent for females.

The two remarkable things about this age group are the large difference between the proportion of males and of females and the shift from increase to decline in the percentage of males by the end of the period under study.

The reason for the differences noted has been explained by Kern who says that: "Die grossen Differenzen, die hierbei zwischen den Werten der beiden Geschlechter auftreten, sind nicht nur auf die höhere mittlere Lebensdauer der Frauen, sondern vor allem auch auf den Umstand zurückzuführen, dass die für das Jahr 1951 massgebenden männlichen Jahrgänge durch den ersten, die für das Jahr 1975 und 1980 massgebenden Jahrgänge durch den zweiten Weltkrieg erhebliche Einbussen erlitten haben" (*op. cit.*, p. 34).

Thus, men are outnumbered by women in the old-age group not because life expectancy for females is greater but because the male population suffered heavier losses in the two world wars. Were it not for the wars and their toll, paid mostly by men (war casualties among women are far fewer), the difference in the proportion of old men and old women would not be so large.

But what is still more interesting is the reversal of the rising tide in the proportion of old people in relation to the total population. It goes without saying that such a reversal would mean the end of the aging process and the beginning of a rejuvenation of the population.

The above table clearly displays such a shift in the male population: the proportion of males in the post-productive age group (65+) will reach 12·7 per cent in 1975 and drop to 12·3 per cent in 1980. The reduction, small as it is, denotes an important symptom of new demographic relations.

No similar shift is revealed in the estimates for the female population; however, this does not necessarily mean that such a shift is non-existent. Kern believes that it probably does exist but cannot be noticed as the maximum point on the curve representing the proportion of females aged 65 and over lies between the years 1975 and 1980.

All things considered, can it be stated that in actual fact the aging of the Austrian population will be checked and that this is really to be expected in the mid-1970s?

Certainly yes, says Kern in reply to this question, and adds the following interesting statement: "Die erste Feststellung, die wir hierbei machen können, ist, dass das gegenwärtige Ansteigen der Überalterung eine vorübergehende Erscheinung ist, die, ungefähr vom Jahre 1975 an, wieder von einem Rückgang der Überalterung abgelöst wird" (*op. cit.*, p. 40). The Austrian statistician sees the present intensification in the aging of the population as a transitory stage, and believes that the reverse tide will begin in Austria about 1975.

How far will the aging process retreat and how long is its retreat expected to last?

According to Austrian statisticians, the rejuvenation of the Austrian population will be somewhat accelerated after 1980, as by that time the oldest group will comprise the scanty population born in the years of dearth–during the First World War. By the turn of the century the proportion of old people is expected to plunge to its lowest level, following which it will rise again.

Events of the past will thus influence the future, and the effects of years of plenty and of dearth in births will reverberate decades later.

5. DEMOGRAPHIC FORECASTS FOR FRANCE

P. Depoid has prepared population forecasts for France, in two variants, up to the end of the 20th century.

The first variant assumes unchanged fertility (at the 1935–7 level) and unchanged mortality (at the 1933–8 level). The second variant assumes unchanged fertility, as in Variant A, and a decline in mortality (down to the level of Dutch mortality rates in 1931–40).

Here are the figures obtained by the French demographer.

**ESTIMATED CHANGES IN THE AGE STRUCTURE
OF THE FRENCH POPULATION 1947–2000**
Depoid's forecast

Year	Total	Age groups		
		0–19	20–59	60+
Variant A				
1947	100·0	29·8	54·0	16·2
1960	100·0	28·3	54·7	17·0
1980	100·0	27·7	55·4	16·9
2000	100·0	27·9	53·6	18·5
Variant B				
1947	100·0	29·8	54·0	16·2
1960	100·0	28·2	54·6	17·2
1980	100·0	27·3	54·7	18·0
2000	100·0	27·3	52·6	20·1

Source: JEAN DARIC, *Vieillissement de la population et prolongation de la vie active*, p. 27.

Both variants forecast further progress in the aging of the French population. By the end of the century the proportion of old people in France will reach 18·5 per cent under Variant A and 20·1 per cent under Variant B. In other words, by that time one in every five Frenchmen will be in the old-age group.

As early as in 1930, Burgdörfer predicted that unless the situation improved by immigration, France could not escape depopulation; in another thirty years, said Burgdörfer, the French population would diminish by two million.[5] After the last war, in 1948, Alfred Sauvy calculated that if fertility remained as low as before the war, the French population would total:

    in 1955 39,778,000
    in 1970 38,086,000
    in 1985 35,648,000
    in 2005 32,389,000

Sauvy's comments on these figures are: "Le vieillissement précède la décroissance de la population."[6] It is indeed so; the aging of the population is followed by a reduction in its total number.

According to other estimates, made on the basis of a more optimistic assumption (15 per cent increase in fertility beginning from 1945, mortality unchanged), France's population will number:

    in 1955 40,600,000
    in 1970 40,100,000
    in 1985 39,420,000
    in 2005 39,010,000

In this case, too, the population is expected to keep diminishing for some time. Why? Because of the aging already acquired ("du fait du vieillissement déjà acquis"), says Sauvy. An increase in fertility by as much as 25 per cent above the pre-war rates, assuming unchanged mortality and no migrations, would be needed for the French population to equal its pre-war number by 1980. These figures indicate how deeply the demographic situation of France has been affected by the protracted aging process of her population.

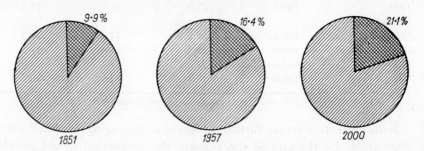

FIG. 5. The aging of the French population.
(Percentage of persons aged 60 and over.)

In 1956, the French *Institut National de la Statistique et des Études Économiques* published *Tableaux de l'Économie française* which contain future estimates for France up to 1970.[7]

The data given therein have been used in part to prepare the following table.

ESTIMATED CHANGES IN THE AGE STRUCTURE
OF THE FRENCH POPULATION 1955–70

Year	Total	Age groups		
		0–14	15–64	65+
1955	100·0	23·9	64·6	11·5
1960	100·0	25·8	62·8	11·4
1965	100·0	24·6	63·5	11·9
1970	100·0	23·3	64·2	12·5

Source: The author's calculations based on material in *Zeszyty Ekonomiki Pracy* (*Notes on Labour Economics*) 1956, No. 2.

According to the table, the proportion of children (0–14) is expected to increase only until 1960; in subsequent years the rising trend is to be replaced by a descending one. By 1970 the percentage of children will have dropped somewhat below the 1955 figure.

The evolution in the proportion of adults (15–64), though following a reversed course, will have similar effects. In 1955–60 the percentage of adults in relation to the total population will decrease, but in the next decade it will rise again and by 1970 will nearly recover its 1955 level.

The only change which will have essential bearing upon France's age structure during the fifteen years is the increase in the proportion of old people—from 11·5 per cent in 1955 to 12·5 per cent in 1970.

It ought to be kept in mind that these figures denote a higher percentage of old people than has ever been known in statistical practice; the highest proportion of persons aged 65 and over registered hitherto is that of France in 1953: 11·4 per cent.

Thus, the population forecast we have just examined anticipates an unprecedented high in the proportion of old people in France in the coming years. The percentage of the aged is expected to increase at the expense of the proportion of children and adults.

The figures quoted below, taken from the same forecast, illustrate the increase in the total number of the population and in that of old people.

France's population is expected to reach:

in 1955	43,247,000
in 1960	44,350,000
in 1965	45,138,000
in 1970	45,846,000

Hence, the estimated increase in France's population in the years 1955–1970 is 6 per cent.

The number of old people (65+) is expected to total:

in 1955	4,951,000
in 1960	5,070,000
in 1965	5,347,000
in 1970	5,749,000

Accordingly, while the total population will increase during the fifteen years by 6 per cent, the group of old people will increase within the same period by 16 per cent, or two and a half times.

The problem of how to find means of subsistence for the five million old people in France is urgent and hard to solve even today. But it is bound to grow more and more pressing in the years to come, since the number of old people is continually increasing while the costs of their livelihood have to be covered by relatively smaller group of earners.

It may be helpful to see what number of adults corresponds to each aged person, i.e. the average number of people supporting one old person.

THE NUMBER OF ADULTS (20–59) TO EACH AGED PERSON (60+) IN FRANCE 1851–2000

1851–1901	1921–1954	1960–2000
1851 ... 5·4	1921 ... 4·0	1960 ... 3·3
1881 ... 4·3	1931 ... 3·7	1980 ... 3·0
1901 ... 4·3	1954 ... 3·3	2000 ... 2·6

Sources: 1. JEAN DARIC, *Le Vieillissement de la population en France et ses conséquences économiques et sociales*, pp. 95–96. 2. JEAN DARIC, *Vieillissement de la population et prolongation de la vie active*, p. 27

A hundred years ago France had more than five persons in the productive-age group (20–59) to each old person (60+). Today it is no longer five but only 3·3 adults who have to pay the living costs of one aged person. And, according to Depoid's estimates, the number of persons in the productive age as against each old person will further diminish; by 1980 it will be three, and by the turn of the next century only 2·6 adults will have to support one old person.

The French statistics quoted are an indication, or rather sound a warning, of what can be the effects of incessant progress in the aging of populations. Statistics show that a hundred persons in the productive age are now furnishing the means for maintenance of thirty-three old people, and that in the future, in case the "optimistic" variant of the population forecast under examination comes true, the same number of adults will have to bear the burden of supporting some forty old people.

The Paris monthly *Regards* has depicted rather outspokenly the sad plight of old people in France.[8] The monthly describes "the unfathomable misery" (*l'insondable détresse*) of old people, caused mainly by demographic facts—by the unbalanced equilibrium in the proportion of old people to earners.

One cannot evade the question: what is in store for the aged in the years to come, when their number will be incomparably larger and when their livelihood will depend on a relatively still smaller group of active workers?

This is, indeed, one of the crucial questions inherent in the aging of populations.

6. DEMOGRAPHIC FORECASTS FOR THE BRITISH POPULATION

Before the last war numerous long-range forecasts of population changes were made in Great Britain with the aim of warning the nation of the fatal effects of the "birth strike", if protracted indefinitely. We shall examine one of these forecasts, prepared by Dr Enid Charles for the century between 1935 and 2035.[9]

Had Britain's fertility rates stayed at the extremely low level of the year 1931, drastic reduction of the population would have been the inevitable effect after some time.

The following figures give a notion of the expected reduction of the population in this hypothetical case:[10]

1935	40,600,000
1940	40,900,000
1945	40,900,000
1950	40,700,000
1960	39,500,000
1980	34,600,000
2000	28,500,000
2035	19,900,000

Dr Charles also calculated the future estimates for the British population proceeding from another and more pessimistic assumption, i.e. a further decline instead of the stabilization of fertility.

In that case, the population of Great Britain would number:[11]

in 1940	40,655,000
in 1975	31,452,000
in 2035	4,426,000

Having studied the estimates for the year 2000 the British writer W. J. Thorne gave vent to his doubts as to whether calculations made so far ahead could be taken seriously. He thought they amounted to little more than guesses.[12]

Had these estimate been intended to predict the actual course of events in a distant future, we should have been inclined to agree with W. J. Thorne. But he is definitely wrong when it comes to forecasts of a purely hypothetical type, aimed at disclosing the consequences of prolonged predominance of certain unfavourable trends in population movements. This being the aim of Dr Charles's forecast, we cannot question its value.

True enough, the danger of depopulation in Britain, demonstrated by Dr Charles, has now been forestalled owing to increased birth rates in that country. But when showing to the nation the extent of the calamity to be brought about by a sharp decline in fertility, the demographer was prompted by nothing else but a desire to ward off this disaster. Neither is there any doubt as to the fact that, had the decrease in fertility continued and had it not been checked in time, it would have led to disastrous depopulation of Britain, just as foreseen by Dr Charles.[13]

What would be the change in Britain's age composition if fertility and mortality remained at their 1931 level?

The British population would age incredibly; within sixty or seventy years old people (60+) would outnumber children and young people (0–19).

This is revealed by the following figures quoted from Dr Charles's forecast:

FUTURE ESTIMATES OF THE AGE COMPOSITION OF THE POPULATION OF ENGLAND AND WALES 1935–2035

Year	Total	Age groups		
		0–19	20–59	60+
1935	100·0	30·7	56·8	12·5
1955	100·0	25·0	58·4	16·6
1975	100·0	22·8	55·3	21·9
1995	100·0	22·5	53·9	23·6
2015	100·0	22·4	54·1	23·5
2035	100·0	22·4	54·2	23·4

Source: *Political Arithmetic, A Symposium of Population Studies,* Edited by Lancelot Hogben, London, 1938, p. 98.

The table reveals:

1. an appalling decline in the number of children and adolescents (0–19) for the first forty years, followed by a slowdown in the rate of reduction and eventually by stabilization in the proportion of children and adolescents;

2. an increase in the number of adults (20–59) during the first two decades, followed by a decrease over the next forty years and by a slight increase in the last four decades;

3. a huge increase in the proportion of old people (60+) during the first sixty years, preceding a slight decrease in the last forty years.

Before the last war, by 1935, the age of 60 yr or more was reached by one in every eight Britons. According to the estimates now under examination, as a result of the expected evolution in the age composition of the British population, by the turn of the next century every fourth Britisher will have joined the ranks of old people.

But the most striking fact is that in the latest stage of the period under study, children and adolescents will be outnumbered by old people. The spectre of a nation without youth, with which Burgdörfer used to frighten his German compatriots, would thus materialize in Britain.

We shall now take up the forecast for the British population made immediately after the end of the last war for the period from 1944 to 1989, and published by W.A.B. Hopkin (later of the Royal Committee for Population).

The age classification adopted in Hopkin's estimates differs from the usual pattern. The population is divided into the following categories:

1. children;
2. working age;
3. pensionable age.

Since the pensionable age for men and women differs in Great Britain, categories 2 and 3 include unequal male and female age groups, i.e.:

(a) category 2 (working age) comprises men aged from 15 to 64, or born within fifty years of each other, and women aged from 15 to 59, or born within forty-five years;

(b) category 3 (pensionable age) comprises men aged 65 yr and over and women aged 60 yr and over.

Hopkin's estimates are show in the table on page 262.

The following interesting facts are revealed by the table:

1. it is expected that the proportion of children (0–14) might drop below 20 per cent; no such low proportion has hitherto been recorded in this age group in Britain or any other country;

2. the proportion of the pensionable group will be on the increase until the end of the period under study; this is particularly significant in view of the reliability of the future estimates for this age group (since it is composed of persons who were already alive and whose exact number was known when the forecast was made).

The estimates translated into absolute figures, not quoted here, give rise to further reflections. Here are two of them:

1. within the years 1944–89 the population of England and Wales

AGE COMPOSITION OF THE POPULATION OF ENGLAND AND WALES IN 1944 AND ITS ESTIMATED EVOLUTION IN 1944–1989

Year	Total	Age groups		
		children	working age	pensionable age
		0–14	m. 15–64 f. 15–59	m. 65+ f. 60+
1944	100·0	20·5	66·9	12·6
1949	100·0	20·8	65·7	13·5
1954	100·0	21·0	64·9	14·1
1959	100·0	20·5	64·6	14·9
1964	100·0	19·6	64·6	15·8
1969	100·0	19·0	63·9	17·1
1974	100·0	19·0	62·7	18·3
1979	100·0	19·2	62·0	18·8
1984	100·0	19·4	61·5	19·1
1989	100·0	19·3	61·5	19·2

Source: CARLTON WALLACE, How to Retire Successfully, Evans Brothers Limited, London, 1956, p. 15.

is expected to diminish by 1,644,000, including a reduction by 875,000 in the number of children and by 3,311,000 in the working-age group;

2. the number of persons of pensionable age is to increase by 2,452,000—from 5,396,000 in 1944 to 7,848,000 in 1989.

Should this forecast turn out to be accurate—and, as we said before, so far as old people are concerned there is every reason to believe so—Britain's demographic situation would be materially changed; the number of people of pensionable age would equal that of children, and Great Britain would become "a nation of pensioners" rather than "a nation of children".

This, by the way, is not the first forecast of such a demographic prospect for the British population.

In the preceding chapters, dealing with methodological problems, we mentioned the future estimates for Great Britain made in several variants by the Royal Committee for Population after the end of the last war, covering a period of one hundred years (1947–2047).

One of the medium variants in this forecast, examined by the British writer W. J. Thorne, has led him to the conclusion that by 2007, the age composition of the United Kingdom will be:

children (0–14) . . . . 19·2
adults (15–64) . . . . 65·1
the old (65+) . . . . 15·7
total 100·0.

The proportion of the aged, as calculated by Thorne and translated into absolute figures, means millions of persons of pensionable age (in a population of 50 million the old people would total 7,850,000). But the absolute number of old people is of little interest to Thorne. He says: "It is not the *absolute* number of the old that is important but the proportion of the old to the earners."[14] By the beginning of the 21st century, according to the figures quoted, the United Kingdom will have one old person for every four adults.

A much less favourable proportion of the aged to the earners is anticipated in Hopkin's estimates, mentioned earlier in this chapter; having adopted a different classification of working-age and pensionable-age groups, Hopkin's estimates show more than five in working age to one pensionable person in 1944, and only a little over three to one in 1989.

The British writer is understandably worried about who is going to feed the enormous army of people who can no longer work for their living.

7. DEMOGRAPHIC FORECASTS FOR SWITZERLAND

We know from Swiss writers that until very recently the problem of the future development of the population and its effects upon the national economy was outside the scope of interest of Swiss economists. It was in 1954 that the attention of scholars was drawn to the population forecast prepared by the Central Statistical Office in Switzerland, which gave the estimated age composition of the Swiss population in the two decades between 1951 and 1971. The data obtained in the census of December 1, 1950, were accepted as datum level. The estimates were made in three variants; the method adopted was biometric.

Leaving aside or the moment the two extreme variants ("optimistic" and "pessimistic"), let us examine the one which the authors regard as the most probable.

ESTIMATED EVOLUTION IN THE AGE STRUCTURE OF THE SWISS POPULATION 1951-1971

Year	Total	Age groups		
		0–19	20–64	65+
1951	100·0	30·6	59·8	9·6
1961	100·0	31·3	57·9	10·8
1971	100·0	28·3	58·2	13·5

Source: *Schweiz. Z. Volkswirtsch. u. Stat.* 1956, 92, No. 3, p. 303.

Let us examine the evolution within each age group.

The number of children and young people (0–19), following a temporary and insignificant increase, is considerably reduced in the second decade (1961–71). This seems to imply that Swiss statisticians do not expect a recurrence of the upsurge in births noted in the 1940s. As long as the population born in the fertile 1940s remains in the age of adolescence the proportion of the youngest group will stay relatively high. The situation will change when it reaches adult age; previously rising, the proportion of children and young people will begin to decrease.

The next group, comprising the economically active population (20–64), follows a reversed curve; it descends in the first decade and ascends in the second.

In contrast with the two previous groups the proportion of the old (65+) reveals one trend only—it keeps growing. Its increase is very large: from 9·6 per cent to 13·5 per cent of the total population. While in 1951 every tenth person in Switzerland belonged to the old-age group, twenty years later one in every seven or eight persons will be of the age of 65 yr or more.

In absolute figures, at the beginning of 1951 Switzerland had 452,200 people aged 65 and over and by 1971 their number will reach 700,000— i.e., 150 old people for every 100 that there were in 1951.

The Swiss demographer Wegmüller notes in this connection that:

1. beginning from the 1930s, progressive aging ("eine fortschreitende Überalterung") has been characteristic for the Swiss population;

2. the aging process will continue in the future.[15]

Under the quoted variant of future estimates for Switzerland the proportion of the three age groups will increase during the two decades as follows:

0–19 age group	by 16·0%
20–64 age group	by 7·5%
65 + age group	by 61·0%
average increase	15·0%

The increase in the group of aged is thus nearly four times as large as in the youngest and eight times as large as in the adult group.

These figures brought Dr Lütolf, a Swiss economist from St. Gallen, to the conclusion that "what is the most significant about the future estimates is not the over-all population increase—amounting to 15 per cent, it remains well within normal limits and probably will not lead to disturbing economic consequences—but that they anticipate a marked aging ("die ausgeprägte Überalterung") of the population. To put the matter in simple terms, during the next fifteen years there will be more and more persons to feed and relatively fewer and fewer persons economically active. This will certainly have a bearing upon the national economy..."[16]

Here are the estimates for 1971, computed on the basis of different assumptions.

ESTIMATED AGE STRUCTURE OF THE SWISS POPULATION IN 1971 (IN THREE VARIANTS)

Variant	Characteristic	Age groups		
		0–19	20–64	65+
I	Most probable	28·3	58·2	13·5
II	Most unfavourable	26·6	60·2	13·2
III	Most favourable	30·6	56·0	13·4

Source: *Schweiz. Z. Volkswirtsch. u. Stat.* 1956, 92, No. 3, p. 306.

Variants II and III (Variant I was examined earlier) assume different birth and mortality rates. The small proportion of children and adolescents (0–19) in Variant II and their large proportion in Variant III are the effect of the low birth rates assumed in the former and high birth rates assumed in the latter. Similarly, the proportion of old people under Variant II, assuming unchanged mortality, is smaller than under Variant III, which assumes a reduction in mortality rates.

We are coming now to the index of dependency.

Professor Wegmüller has calculated the estimates for the beginning, the middle and the end of the two decades relating to:

1. the number of children and adolescents (0–19) per thousand adults (20–64).

2. the number of old people (65 +) per thousand adults (20–64), and

3. the general index of dependency (die totale Belastungsziffer), which is the sum of the two previous figures.

The results of Professor Wegmüller's calculations are tabulated on page 266.

The old-age column is of the greatest interest to us. Each of the three variants shows a steady increase in the index of old people who must be provided with means of subsistence by the earners.

Under Variant I (the most probable one, according to the estimators), by 1971 every thousand adults will have to support 232 aged persons, as against 160 in 1951. Dr Lütolf believes that Variant III, and not

266   AGING PROCESS OF POPULATION

THE PROPORTION OF DEPENDENTS (CHILDREN AND OLD PEOPLE) TO THE ADULT POPULATION IN SWITZERLAND 1951-71

Variant	Year	Per 1000 adults (20–64)		
		children and adolescents (0–19)	old people (65+)	total
Variant I . . .	1951	511	160	671
	1961	541	187	728
	1971	485	232	717
Variant II . .				
	1951	511	160	671
	1961	528	185	713
	1971	441	218	659
Variant III . .				
	1951	511	160	671
	1961	563	190	753
	1971	547	240	787

Source: *Schweiz. Z. Volkswirtsch. u. Stat.* 1956, No. 3, p. 307.

Variant I, is the most realistic. Under Variant III, the ratio of dependency will grow still more burdensome: by 1971, Switzerland will have 240 old people for every thousand adults, or 50 per cent more than in 1951.

Switzerland can thus expect a disproportionate increase in the number of old people in the next few years. Characteristically, while the Swiss estimates predict 13 per cent of aged persons (65+) in 1971, the corresponding figure for France in 1970 is, according to *Tableaux de l'Économie française* quoted above, only 12·5 per cent; which means that in a not too distant future Switzerland will leave France behind in respect to the aging of its population.

One cannot but understand the Swiss economist who is so concerned about the effects of the aging process: as the number of old people increases, the costs of their livelihood become an ever heavier burden on the relatively smaller group of earners.

8. DEMOGRAPHIC FORECASTS FOR SPAIN

It sometimes happens that statisticians prepare population forecasts for other countries. Decades ago, for instance, future estimates for ten countries were made at the Statistical Office of the German Reich under F. Burgdörfer.[17]

For Spain, a population forecast was calculated at the French National Institute for Demographic Studies (l'Institut National d'Études Démographiques) by the distinguished French demographer J. Bourgeois-Pichat. Our information on this forecast is taken from J. Daric's work on the demographic evolution in Spain.

J. Bourgeois-Pichat assumes for the purpose of his estimates that:

1. mortality will stay at its 1950 level all during the thirty years (1950–80), and

2. the birth rate will slightly decrease.

With these assumptions, Spain's population (which, according to the census of 31 December, 1950, was 27,976,755) would total:

in 1955 . . . . 29·0 million
in 1960 . . . . 29·9 million
in 1965 . . . . 30·6 million
in 1970 . . . . 31·0 million
in 1975 . . . . 31·2 million
in 1980 . . . . 31·2 million

It is thus expected that the population will increase very slowly and will reach numerical stability by the end of the period under study.

It is interesting to examine the expected changes in the age structure of the population against the background of retrospective figures.

PAST AND FUTURE EVOLUTION IN THE AGE STRUCTURE OF THE SPANISH POPULATION (1900, 1950, AND 1980)

Year	Total	Age groups		
		0–14	15–64	65+
1900	100·0	33·5	61·3	5·2
1950	100·0	26·2	66·6	7·2
1980	100·0	21·1	69·6	9·3

Source: JEAN DARIC, "Évolution démographique en Espagne," Population, Paris, 1956, No. 1, pp. 89 and 100.

The table indicates that the past trends in the age structure of the Spanish population will continue to prevail in the future.

Thus:

1. the proportion of children (0–14) will further decrease,

2. the proportion of active population (15–64) will continue to increase, and

3. so will the proportion of aged persons (65+).

The three tendencies are typical of progressive aging of the population. In particular, the increase in the proportion of active population (15–64) is typical for the early phase of aging ("comme il arrive au début du vieillissement", to quote Daric).

The last column in the table shows that, by 1980, Spain will reach the phase of aging attained around 1950 in Denmark, the Federal German Republic and Switzerland—all of them nations where the aging of populations is relatively far advanced.

9. EUROPEAN FORECASTS OF THE O.E.E.C.

In 1953, the Organization for European Economic Cooperation (O.E.E.C.) requested its members to prepare demographic forecasts for the years 1961 and 1971 on the basis of the 1951 figures.[18]

For the purpose of these forecasts, populations were divided into three age groups:

1. children (0–14),
2. working age (men: 15–64; women: 15–59),
3. pensionable age (men: 65+, women: 60+).

The same age classification was used in the British estimates quoted earlier in this chapter.

The member nations of the O.E.E.C. prepared future estimates for their populations in three versions—optimistic, pessimistic, and medium. Migrations were not taken into consideration.

The medium versions submitted have been entered into O.E.E.C. population projections.

The accompanying table contains some of the O.E.E.C. figures which seem of particular interest to us (page 269).

The table indicates diverse rates of population increase in different countries.

Naturally, the leading places in absolute figures belong to countries with the largest populations. But Italy, due to her enormous natural increase (nearly seven million) is far ahead of all the other countries. The runners-up are France (3·8 million), Great Britain and Spain (2·9 million each), the Netherlands (2·71 million), the F.G.R. (2·4 million) and Portugal (2·28 million).

Owing to fluctuations in the rates of population increase, some countries are expected to drop to lower places on the list. According to the O.E.E.C. projections, the Federal German Republic will be overtaken by Italy and so will Belgium by Portugal.

In relative figures, the largest increase is noted in:

Portugal	+27·0%
the Netherlands	+26·6%
Ireland	+23·6%

EXPECTED INCREASE IN POPULATIONS OF FIFTEEN EUROPEAN COUNTRIES, MEMBERS OF O.E.E.C. 1951–71

Country	Population (in thousands)		Increase in 1951–1971	
	1951	1971	in thousands	%
Great Britain	50,500	53,400	+2900	+5·7
F.G.R.	47,800	50,200	+2400	+5.0
Italy.	46,400	53,300	+6900	+14·9
France	42,100	46,000	+3900	+9·3
Spain	28,100	31,000	+2900	+10·3
Netherlands	10,200	12,910	+2710	+26·6
Belgium	8650	9120	+470	+5·4
Portugal	8440	10,720	+2280	+27·0
Sweden	7040	7360	+320	+4·5
Austria	6930	6980	+50	+0·7
Switzerland	4720	5170	+450	+9·5
Denmark.	4290	4940	+650	+15·2
Norway	3280	3800	+520	+15·9
Ireland	2960	3660	+700	+23·6
Luxembourg	290	290	—	—
15 countries	271,700	298,850	+27,150	+10,0

Source: *Zeszyty Ekonomiki Pracy* (*Notes on Labour Economics*) 1956, No. 2, pp. 21–22 (table arranged by the author of the present work).

The countries where the aging process has made less progress have, of course, a speedier rate of population increase; they will gradually climb to the top of the list, outdistancing their nearest statistical neighbours.

Let us now proceed to examine the expected increase of the population in post-productive age (men aged 65 and over, women aged 60 and over).

The figures are tabulated on page 270.

Rarely does one encounter figures so impressive as these. They reveal a tremendous rate of increase in the number of old population. The table shows that the unprecedented growth of the old-age group, characteristic of recent years, will continue to exist in west European countries in years to come.

During the short period of two decades (from 1951 to 71) the fifteen countries listed in the O.E.E.C. projection will gain 12·86 million persons of pensionable age. By the end of the period under study they will total more than 45 million as against the initial 32·2 million old people. To every 100 aged persons in 1951, twenty years later there will be 140. Indeed, these are startling figures.

ESTIMATED INCREASE OF POPULATION OF PENSIONABLE AGE IN 15 EUROPEAN COUNTRIES, MEMBERS OF O.E.E.C. 1951–71

Country	Old people in thousands		Increase in 1951–1971	
	1951	1971	in thousands	%
Great Britain	6820	9620	+2800	+41·1
F.G.R.	5630	8600	+2970	+52·8
Italy.	4750	7000	+2250	+47·4
France	5950	7130	+1180	+19·8
Spain	2450	3210	+760	+31·0
Netherlands	990	1570	+580	+58·6
Belgium	1180	1630	+450	+38·1
Portugal	760	1120	+360	+47·4
Sweden	890	1240	+350	+39·3
Austria	940	1260	+320	+34·0
Switzerland	570	860	+290	+50·9
Denmark.	480	710	+230	+47·9
Norway	390	620	+230	+59·0
Ireland	380	450	+70	+18·4
Luxembourg	30	50	+20	+66·7
15 countries	32,210	45,070	+12,860	+39·9

Source: Zeszyty Ekonomiki Pracy (Notes on Labour Economics) 1956, No. 2, pp. 21 and 28 (arranged by the author).

Which countries are the leaders in the aging list?

In absolute figures obviously those with the largest populations, and first of all the Federal German Republic with the expected increase of nearly 3 million old people. Next come Great Britain (2·28 million) and Italy (2·25 million) followed by France (1·18 million).

Still in absolute figures, amongst the fifteen countries Great Britain has the largest number of old people; her pensionable-age group is expected to reach 10 million persons in the next few years. France is the second at the moment, but there is every reason to suppose that she will soon be outstripped by the Federal German Republic, considering the latter's amazing rates of increase in old population. In 1951, France totalled 320,000 more old people than the F.G.R.; but if the O.E.E.C. estimates are accurate, by 1971 the Federal German Republic will have almost a million and a half more than France.

The situation as depicted in relative figures is no less interesting. Leaving aside Luxembourg with her extremely small population, the top places among the remaining fourteen countries as regards population increase in the oldest group belong to:

Norway	59·0%
Netherlands	58·6%
F.G.R.	52·8%
Switzerland	50·9%

These are the four countries where the number of the aged is expected to increase most rapidly in the near future.

We shall now compare the increase in the number of old people and that of the total population in the O.E.E.C. countries.

As we have seen, during the twenty years between 1951 and 1971 the population of the fifteen member states of the O.E.E.C. is expected to increase by 10 per cent on the average. The number of old people in these countries will rise by almost 40 per cent. Consequently, the average increase in the number of the aged will be four times as large as that of total population.

But the average is far below the figures attained in several countries. In the case of the Federal German Republic the increase in the number of old people exceeds ten times that of the whole population; in Sweden, nearly nine times; in Great Britain and Belgium, more than seven times; in Switzerland, more than five times. In Austria, which does not expect a noticeable population increase, the number of old people will increase nearly fifty times as much.

There is a single country where the increase in the number of old people is expected to lag behind that of total population: it is Ireland, with a 23·6 per cent population increase and an 18·4 per cent rise in the number of the aged during the two decades. This is the only exception to the general rule that the number of old people increases much more rapidly than does the population as a whole.

The member states of the O.E.E.C. represent a zone where the aging of populations has reached an advanced phase. The symptoms examined above are typical of demographic old age.

This is a problem which the western countries will find more and more pressing in the coming years.

10. FORECASTS FOR THE UNITED STATES

Some thirty years ago, the distinguished American demographer P. K. Whelpton made a population forecast for the United States, assuming that birth, mortality and immigration rates will remain at their 1920 level.

By extrapolating the then development trends the American demographer obtained the following figures.

ESTIMATED AGE STRUCTURE OF U.S. POPULATION 1920–80

Age	Population in thousands		Percentage	
	1920	1980	1920	1980
0–19.	43,633	37,300	41·0	26·1
20–49.	46,328	61,600	43·6	43·1
50–69.	13,378	34,500	12·6	24·7
70+	2951	9500	2·8	6·7
Total	106,290	142,900	100·0	100·0

Source: *Actes du Congrès International des Études sur la Population*, Rome, 1931, Volume 7, p. 17.

Whelpton's estimates show that:

1. during the sixty years from 1920–80 the number of children and adolescents in the United States will decrease both in absolute numbers and in proportion to the total population;

2. the number of adults (20–49), while increasing in absolute figures, will remain the same as in 1920 in proportion to the total population,

3. the number of older people (50+) will increase both in absolute figures and in proportion to the total population.

Accordingly, the older group is the only one whose proportion is expected to increase. Characteristically, the largest increase is anticipated in the percentage of persons aged 70 and over.

These estimates are only as realistic as the assumptions, mentioned earlier, upon which Whelpton based his calculations. To quote his own words: "Here again it should be emphasized that the situation in 1980 will not be exactly as the table indicates, these data being presented simply to show what will result if immigration and birth and death rates continue recent trends on a basis that seems reasonable now."[19]

What situation does Whelpton have in view?

He means the situation as regards the evolution in the number of the total population. The future development of U.S. population may or may not follow the trend indicated in Whelpton's forecast, which is based on purely conventional assumptions.

However, as far as the proportion of age groups is concerned, the estimates can be regarded as much more exact.

In other words, Whelpton's estimate of further progress in the aging of the U.S. population is the least doubtful part of his forecast.

Another, and much more extensive, forecast for the United States population was subsequently prepared by W. S. Thompson and P. K. Whelpton; on the basis of the 1940 census figures they calculated the future development of the population until 1980. It is much more extensive in that the forecast comprises six variants (A, B, C, ... F) which make it possible to analyse diverse eventualities in the case of diverse trends in migration and birth and mortality rates.

The four variants we are going to examine are:

1. Variant A—medium fertility, medium mortality, no immigration surplus,

2. Variant B—medium fertility, medium mortality, annual immigration surplus of 100,000 persons,

3. Variant C—low fertility, high mortality, balanced migrations, and

4. Variant D—low fertility, medium mortality and balanced migrations.

The future estimates of the age structure of the U.S. population are given in the table on page 274, in four variants.

Opinions may differ as to which of the four variants is the most realistic. But in any case, it is quite probable that the actual development of the U.S. population will fluctuate within the upper and lower limits indicated in the table. What are these limits?

The proportion of children and adolescents (0–19), which was 34 per cent in 1940, will drop continually and, in 1980, reach

minimum 20·9%
maximum 26·1%

Thus during the forty years from 1940–80 the number of children and adolescents in proportion to the total population of the United States will diminish from one-third to one-fourth or even one-fifth.

The next two age groups taken together represent the productive population (20–64) which in 1940 amounted to 58·7 per cent of the total population of the United States. By 1980, its proportion will reach:

minimum 59·6%
maximum 63·7%

The proportion of productive population will thus increase, but not much.

AGE STRUCTURE OF THE U.S. POPULATION IN 1940
AND ITS EXPECTED DEVELOPMENT BETWEEN 1940 AND 1980

Year	Total	Age groups			
		0–19	20–44	45–64	65+
Variant A					
1940. . . .	100·0	34·0	38·9	19·8	6·9
1950. . . .	100·0	31·0	39·7	21·4	7·9
1960. . . .	100·0	29·3	37·4	23·3	10·0
1970. . . .	100·0	27·3	35·0	25·9	11·8
1980. . . .	100·0	26·0	33·7	25·9	14·4
Variant B					
1940. . . .	100·0	34·0	38·9	19·8	6·9
1950. . . .	100·0	30·9	39·9	21·3	7·9
1960. . . .	100·0	29·3	37·8	23·0	9·9
1970. . . .	100·0	27·3	35·4	25·7	11·6
1980. . . .	100·0	26·1	34·1	25·8	14·0
Variant C					
1940. . . .	100·0	34·0	38·9	19·8	6·9
1950. . . .	100·0	29·2	40·8	21·9	8·1
1960. . . .	100·0	26·2	39·2	24·4	10·2
1970. . . .	100·0	23·4	36·4	28·2	12·0
1980. . . .	100·0	21·5	34·0	29·7	14·0
Variant D					
1940. . . .	100·0	34·0	38·9	19·8	6·9
1950. . . .	100·0	29·2	40·7	22·0	8·1
1960. . . .	100·0	25·9	39·0	24·5	10·6
1970. . . .	100·0	23·0	35·7	28·3	13·0
1980. . . .	100·0	20·9	33·1	29·6	16·4

Source: W. S. THOMPSON, *Population Problems*, Third Edition, McGraw-Hill Book Company, New York and London, 1942, p. 288.

The most rapid changes are expected in the oldest group (65+). From 6·9 per cent of the total population of the United States in 1940 the proportion of old people is to rise by 1980 to:

> minimum 14·0%
> maximum 16·4%

The effects of the aging of the population are thus manifest: within four decades the proportion of old people in the United States will at least double.

It will be remembered that in his most pessimistic forecast of the future development of the German population, F. Burgdörfer estimated that by the year 2000 the proportion of the aged in his country would reach 16·7 per cent; the pessimistic variant of the American estimates presages nearly the same proportion (16·4 per cent) as early as in 1980. The inference is that the demographic situation in the United States is assessed more pessimistically than was years ago the situation in Germany by the German demographer.

But relative figures fail to disclose the gravity of the situation. To see it in full light let us pass from relative to absolute figures.

U. S. POPULATION AGED 65 AND OVER IN 1930–50 AND ESTIMATES FOR 1960–80

Actual population		Expected population	
year	number of aged	year	number of aged
1930	6,633,805	1960	14,818,000
1940	9,019,314	1970	17,995,000
1950	12,322,000	1980	22,051,000

Source: PAUL H. LANDIS, *Population Problems*: *A Cultural Interpretation*, second edition, New York, 1954, p. 87.

These are the crucial figures in the forecast. They show that the U.S. population is aging at a terrifying speed.

Let us try to analyse these figures.

In 1930, the number of old people in the United States was 6·6 million; by 1950, or twenty years later, it reached 12·3 million. Within two decades the number of old people increased by 5·7 million.

During the next two decades (1950–70) the oldest group is expected to increase from 12·3 to 18·0 million persons. According to Thompson's and Whelpton's calculation the number of old people is to increase by another 5·7 million during these twenty years.

In the last ten years, from 1970 to 80, the number of old people is expected to rise from 18·0 to 22·0 million; in other words, a single decade will add four million persons to the army of old people.

These data are not the product of the scholarly imagination; the men and women who will reach old age (65+) in 1980 are actually among us; their present number is not an unknown quantity. Hence, the future estimates are, in all probability, quite realistic.[20]

Should we consider the old-age group as consisting of persons aged 60 and over, as do statisticians in many countries—including France, which tops the list of aging nations—the situation would not change.

Here again the table on page 276 indicates an accelerated increase in the proportion of old people.

276

**EVOLUTION IN THE PROPORTION OF THE POPULATION AGED 60
AND OVER IN THE UNITED STATES 1860-2000**

Year	Source of data	Percentage of population aged 60+
1860.	census	4·3
1880.	census	5·6
1900.	census	6·4
1920.	census	7·0
1940.	census	10·4
1960.	estimates	13·5
1980.	estimates	17·1
2000.	estimates	18·8

Source: L. CHEVALIER, *Démographie générale*, Dalloz, Paris 1951, p. 521.

According to the French demographer Chevalier, the United States is some eighty years "behind" France in the aging of the populations; but this "gap" is to disappear within one generation.[21]

What was the cause of such excessive speed in the aging of the U.S. population?

For many decades, the proportion of old people in the United States remained very low because the country was receiving a steady, large influx of immigrants, mostly adolescents and young, active people; typically for any young society, the birth rate was high. But things have changed since then. Immigration has been cut back if not stopped altogether, and one or two children has become the rule in family planning. The gates were thus opened wide for victorious ingress of the aging process.[22]

The expected rapid development of aging of the U.S. population is but a further stage in this process.

We have so far examined the situation in highly developed countries. Being in the most advanced phase of the aging of populations, they are by definition objects of particular interest for the demographer. However, we are no less concerned with what is in store for the countries where the aging of populations has not yet become a problem. What are the prospects for these young nations? What is the expected development of their demographic situation in the next decades?

To find an answer to these questions let us analyse population forecasts for Central America, which might well be regarded as typical for the "underdeveloped", demographically young countries. The conclusions to be drawn from a study of their population problems can be generalized to embrace all those areas where economic under-development is coupled with demographic youth.

11. DEMOGRAPHIC FORECASTS FOR CENTRAL AMERICA (INCLUDING MEXICO)

Population estimates for Central America (including Mexico) have been prepared by the Population Division of the United Nations.[22]

As they raise the curtain on the future development of the countries which can be considered a reservation of natural demographic relations, these estimates are of unusual interest for the demographer.

As in many another underdeveloped country, the lag in vital statistics in Central America (including Mexico) exists only in respect of births. Deaths are subject to other laws in those countries; mortality being on the decline, it is evident that demographic relations in the underdeveloped countries have been somewhat modernized.

This dual character of the present demographic situation in the underdeveloped countries finds an excellent illustration in the vital statistics of some Central American countries, including Mexico, given in the table below.

VITAL STATISTICS IN SOME CENTRAL AMERICAN COUNTRIES INCLUDING MEXICO IN 1930–4 AND 1948–52

Country	Birth rate		Death rate		Rate of natural increase	
	1930–34	1948–52	1930–34	1948–52	1930–34	1948–52
Mexico	44·5	44·7	25·6	16·6	18·9	28·1
Costa Rica . . .	44·6	47·2	22·3	12·3	22·3	34·9
El Salvador . . .	43·3	47·4	23·0	15·7	20·3	31·7
Guatemala	51·1	51·7	26·2	22·3	24·9	29·4

Source: The Population of Central America (including Mexico), 1950–1980, United Nations, New York, 1954, p. 13.

Birth rates are astonishingly high—from 43 to 47 per thousand in Mexico, Costa Rica and El Salvador, and more than 50 per thousand in Guatemala.

The striking fact is that post-war birth rates in all four countries are much higher than they were before the last war. But we must not jump to the conclusion that birth rates have actually increased since the war. As the U.N. demographer points out: "... population growth in Mexico and Central America has not only been rapid, but has accelerated in recent years. The figures shown must be interpreted with some caution since they are not very accurate in all cases. Thus, the apparent slight increases in birth rates may in some instances have to be attributed to greater completeness of birth registration during the more recent period" (*The Population of Central America 1950–1980*, p. 13).

At any rate, the figures quoted display the trend in birth rates prevailing in Mexico and many other Central American countries until this very day.

This is not the case with death rates. Except for Guatemala, where the decrease in these rates is relatively small, the remaining three countries show a sharp decline in mortality in recent years. In Costa Rica, to take the most noteworthy example, death rates dropped from 23·3 per thousand in 1930–4 to 12·3 per thousand, or about half of the pre-war figure, in 1948–52. The U.N. demographer is justified in remarking that, while the birth rates may not be very accurate "the sharp decreases in death rates, on the other hand, reflect probably with fair accuracy the real decline in mortality" (*op. cit.*, p. 13).

A rapid rate of natural increase was the obvious outcome of these developments. In El Salvador, and particularly in Costa Rica, it mounted to astounding proportions, reaching 31·7 per thousand a year in the former and nearly 35 per thousand in the latter in the years 1948–52. When juxtaposed with these figures the pre-war natural increases, large as they appeared in those years (maximum 24·9 per thousand in Guatemala in 1930–34), seem quite small.

What are the prospects for the countries whose demographic situation is so peculiar?

U.N. demographers intended to reply to this question by preparing future population estimates for 1950–80. Theirs was not an easy task, considering the gaps in statistics and the inaccuracy of the data available. In the case of British Honduras the latest statistics on age and sex composition of the population dated back to 1946; in the case of Guatemala the researchers had to turn to the 1940 figures on the age and sex of the population.

To quote the forecasters, "the existence of these statistics... is no guarantee of their accuracy. Census enumerations may have been incomplete, at least in some areas. The reporting of ages at the census and of ages at death is often quite inaccurate. The registers of births are inexact to a varying degree... Despite such defects in the statistics and the necessity to adjust or supplement some of them, the general quantity and quality of population statistics in this area are now sufficient to permit the computation of useful estimates of future population, by sex and age, for every country and territory" (op. cit., pp. 6 and 7).

As a result, future population estimates for Central America including Mexico (Costa Rica, El Salvador, Guatemala, Honduras, Nicaragua, Panama and British Honduras) have been prepared for the period from 1950 to 80. Eleven such projections have been made, including general ones.

It is interesting to study the assumptions upon which these population estimates were based.

The future development of birth rates in that part of the world was a puzzle for the forecasters. It is not inconceivable that high fertility rates in Central America with Mexico might begin to decrease under the influence of such factors as urbanization, industrialization, general education, diversification of economic opportunities and reduction of infant mortality. To be more precise, there is no doubt as to the influence of these factors. What is unknown is their effect; there is no certainty as to whether their influence upon birth rates will lead to the same results as it did in Europe. Some experts, when commenting on the future development of birth rates in underdeveloped countries, express the belief that the force of habit might prove stronger than the factors tending towards birth decline and that, as a result, birth rates will be stabilized at their present high level.

In view of the divergences in expert opinions, the U.N. demographers deemed it advisable to assume three variants of expected birth rates—high, medium and low. The medium one seems to be the closest to reality.

No such alternatives had to be introduced for mortality rates whose development trend is but too evident. The authors of the estimates emphasize that "with the application of modern knowledge, declines in death rates in some countries may be even more rapid. Poverty of medical resources, on the other hand, may in some instances prove an impediment to such rapid progress" (op. cit., p. 8).

On page 280 is given a summary of population estimates for Central America, including Mexico.

The future age structure of the population of Central America (including Mexico) will thus largely depend on birth rates, i.e.:

1. if birth rates stay at their present high the proportion of children (0–14) will slightly increase (from nearly 43 per cent in 1950 to 45

PRESENT (1950) AND FUTURE (1980) AGE STRUCTURE OF THE
POPULATION OF CENTRAL AMERICA (INCLUDING MEXICO)

Year	Total	Age groups		
		0–14	15–59	60+
1950	100·0	42·56	52·77	4·67
1980 high . .	100·0	45·23	49·83	4·94
medium .	100·0	39·56	54·71	5·74
low . .	100·0	33·89	59·52	6·59

Source: *The Population of Central America (including Mexico), 1950–1980,* United Nations, New York, 1954, p. 20.

per cent in 1980) and so will the proportion of the population aged 60 or more (from 4·7 per cent in 1950 to 4·9 per cent in 1980),

2. if birth rates are somewhat reduced the proportion of children will drop to 40 per cent while that of persons aged 60 and over will rise to 5·7 per cent,

3. if birth rates are low the proportion of children will shrink to 34 per cent and that of older people will increase to 6·6 per cent.

It is characteristic that the proportion of persons aged 60 and more is going to increase in any case, whether birth rates are reduced or remain stable. Hence, the aging of populations is the inevitable prospect for Central America in the near future.

Naturally, nowhere in Central America can we apply the west European standards typical for the most advanced phase in the aging of populations.

Should the "medium" variant of future birth rates prove accurate— which we believe to be the most probable—by the end of the period under study (1980) the proportion of children (0–14) in Central America including Mexico would be twice as large as that in Belgium in 1950 (20·9 per cent) while the proportion of old people (60+) would be barely over one-third the respective figure for Belgium in 1950 (15·9 per cent).

The aging of populations in the underdeveloped countries has only just begun; many decades will pass before they reach the phase which we regard as demographic old age.

12. CONCLUSIONS

We have examined several population forecasts from the point of view of expected changes in the age composition. We shall now endeavour to sum up the results of our study.

The conclusions to be drawn from our analysis are:

1. during the coming decades the evolution in the age structure of European populations will be characterized by an increasing proportion of old people, i.e. by further aging of populations;

2. the increase in the number of old people will be out of proportion to that in the remaining age groups and in total population, thus reinforcing the aging trend which obtains in European populations;

3. demographic forecasts display a picture of advanced "old age"; by the end of the 20th century the proportion of persons aged 60 and more is expected to reach 20 per cent in France and more than 23 per cent in Britain; according to Burgdörfer, before the end of this century Germany will have almost 17 per cent of persons aged 65 and over;

4. Burgdörfer's forecast anticipates an extraordinary phenomenon: the number of old people (65+) is to exceed that of children (0–14); similarly, Dr Charles expects that the old (60+) will outnumber children and adolescents (0–19) in Britain;

5. hypothetical estimates prove that the aging of populations, if prolonged, must lead to depopulation; this is an imminent danger for western Europe where the aging of populations has made the most rapid progress;

6. Swiss economists foresee grave perturbations in the economic life of their country as a result of the advanced aging of the population;

7. judging from future estimates for Central America, with Mexico, the underdeveloped countries will not escape the aging of populations, though on a much smaller scale.

All this indicates that the aging of populations, a serious and complex demographic problem today, will become still more grave in the years to come.

REFERENCES

1. E. KERN, "Die Frage der Überalterung", *Allg. Stat. Arch.* 41. Band, Erstes Heft, 1957, p. 40.

2. With this reservation, Landis considers that estimates prepared for 65 yr are sufficiently accurate: "Since all those who will reach age 65 between now and the year 2019 have already been born, future estimates of the older population, ignoring immigration, can be made with good accuracy." (*Population Problems: A Cultural Interpretation*, New York, 1954, p. 103). If we replace "immigration" by "migrations", Landis's remark can be regarded as a general rule.

3. F. Burgdörfer, *Volk ohne Jugend*, 3rd edition, Heidelberg—Berlin, pp. 222–223.
4. L. Chevalier, *Démographie Générale*, Dalloz, Paris, 1951, p. 100.
5. F. Burgdörfer, *Volk ohne Jugend*, 3rd edition, pp. 397–399.
6. A. Sauvy, *La Population, ses Lois, ses Équilibres*, Presses Universitaires de France, 1948, p. 95.
7. They are quoted, in absolute figures, by A. Rajkiewicz in *Zeszyty Ekonomiki Pracy* (*Notes on Labour Economics*) 1956, No. 2, pp. 31–32.
8. "L'insondable détresse de vieux gens de chez nous", *Regards*, Paris, 1956, No. 409.
9. E. Charles, "The effect of present trends in fertility and mortality upon the future population of Great Britain and upon its age composition", in *Political Arithmetic*, London, 1938.
10. A. Sauvy, *La Population, ses Lois, ses Équilibres*, p. 82.
11. G. F. McCleary, *Population: Today's Question*, George Allen & Unwin Ltd, London, 1938, p. 105.
12. "When it comes to an estimate of what world population will be in 2000 the margin of possible error is so great that the published figures must be regarded as little more than guesses" (W. J. Thorne: *Your Future is Now*. Eyre and Spottiswoode, London, 1956, p. 16).
13. Years ago, we witnessed a dispute between Burgdörfer and the German writer E. Kahn. The latter, though not a demographer, made several statements whose aptness can be fully appreciated only now. Here is what he said about the prospect, disregarded by many authors, of a radical change in the then demographic trends: "Im Augenblick scheint alles für einen Rückgang der Bevölkerung zu sprechen. Welchen Umfang aber die Bewegung annehmen und wie lange sie dauern wird, kann niemand wissen, denn die Gewohnheit und die Anschauungen der Menschen sind ebensowenig vorauszusehen wie etwa die gerade für die Lebensaussichten so wichtige Entwicklung der Medizin; das muss immer betont werden" (*Der internationale Geburtenstreik*, Frankfurt a. M. 1930, p. 208). This change did take place in low fertility zones, in Great Britain and elsewhere.
14. W. J. Thorne *Your Future is Now*, Eyre and Spottiswoode, London, 1956, p. 19.
15. W. Wegmüller, *Die statistischen Grundlagen der Bevölkerungsprognose*, p. 304.
16. F. Lütolf, "Die volkswirtschaftlichen Konsequenzen der Bevölkerungsentwicklung in der Schweiz", *Schweiz. Z. Volkswirtsch. u. Stat.* 1956, 92. Band, No. 3, p. 308.
17. They covered three decades (1930–60) and assumed unchanged fertility and mortality rates in the ten countries. The results were published in Vol. 401 of *Statistik des Deutschen Reichs*, Part II, 1930.
18. The data quoted are taken from an article entitled "Deutschlands Altersaufbau in den kommenden Jahrzehnten im Vergleich zu anderen Ländern Europas", published in *Bundesarbeitsblatt* 1956, No. 10, and printed in Polish translation in *Zeszyty Ekonomiki Pracy* (*Notes on Labour Economics*) 1956, No. 2, pp. 16–30.
19. P. K. Whelpton, Calculation of Future Development of Population, *Actes du Congrès International des Études sur la Population*, Rome 1931, Vol. VII, Rome, 1934, p. 16.
20. Landis's estimates agree with Variant A in Thompson's and Whelpton's forecast. Other variants of their forecast contain similar figures: the expected number of old people in 1980 is 22,180,000 in Variant B and 22,050,000 in Variant D; only Variant C gives a smaller figure—18,994,000.

21. "La proportion actuelle est celle qu'avait la France vers 1860. Les États-Unis vont franchir en une génération le chemin parcouru par la France de 1860 à nos jours" (L. CHEVALIER, *op. cit.*, p. 522).
22. "Future population estimates by sex and age, Rapport I: The population of Central America (including Mexico), 1950–1980." *Population Studies*, No. 16, United Nations, Department of Social Affairs, Population Division, New York, 1954.

CHAPTER 11

Aging of the Population in the Productive Age

1. INTRODUCTORY REMARKS

Simultaneously with the general aging of the population which, as we already know, consists in a general increase in the proportion of old people in the total population—another and no less important demographic trend can be observed. This is a growing proportion of older elements in the *productive population*, that is, people in the productive age.

According to the French demographer Jean Daric, there is an essential connection between the aging of the productive population and the aging of the population as a whole. He sometimes even identifies these two processes, as when he declares: "To say that a population is aging is to say that the productive part of that population is aging."[1]

It is obviously incorrect to identify these two processes, for it would then be impossible even to give a separate definition of each. However, it cannot be denied that the aging of the productive population and the aging of the population as a whole are organically connected. This is due both to the origin of the phenomenon common to the two processes, and to its consequence: the general aging of the population is preceded by the aging of the productive section of that population.

As an instrument for measuring the extent or rate of the aging of the population as a whole, we have hitherto used the term "old-age coefficient" to define the ratio of old people to the total number of the population. By transposing the same idea to the aging of the population of productive age, we propose to use a measure expressing the percentage of the older part of the productive population to the productive population as a whole. Following the method of the French demographer, we shall take the ages 20–59 as the productive years, and the ages 40–59 as the older years of productive life (this measure is useful in that the productive period of life is divided into two equal parts, each consisting of twenty years, and giving twenty-year groups).

We thus arrive at the concept of a *coefficient of the aging of the productive population*.

Since, however, we have insufficient data to calculate such a coefficient for all countries and all periods, we shall not confine ourselves to this method alone, but shall use others as well to calculate the relative ages of the population.

2. THE PRESENT LEVEL OF AGING OF THE PRODUCTIVE POPULATION

It follows from these introductory remarks that the topic interesting us at present will be the age structure, not of the population as a whole, but of only a part of it, namely, the productive part. The structure of the population may be studied either as it exists at a given moment (the static view), or while changes take place in it (the dynamic view). Neither viewpoint should be neglected, as only the two taken together can give us a true picture of what we are examining.

Let us begin with the static view. We shall examine (as far as possible) the aging of the productive population as it is at present. Since the statistical data available are very profuse and very varied, we shall differentiate the various levels of aging of the productive population, and deal with each one separately.

(a) Countries with the Lowest Coefficients of Aging of the Productive Population

There are many countries with a low, or even very low, coefficient of aging of the productive population. Though a number of them appear in the statistical tables of the United Nations, yet not all countries with a low level of aging in the productive population are covered by statistical surveys, which means that in some cases the data needed to calculate the desired coefficients of aging simply do not exist.

In consequence it must be remembered that—as was the case in our discussion of the lowest level of aging of the general population— our remarks about the lowest level of aging of the productive population are subject to the reservation: *in so far as this can be established from the statistical data available.* Bearing this safeguard in mind we may now proceed to examine the lowest coefficients of aging of the productive population in the world.

We have before us a group of countries which have an exceptionally low percentage of people coming within the second half of the productive age (40–59). At the head of the list is Mozambique, which has an incredibly low proportion of productive population in this age group—barely a quarter of the total productive population between the ages of 20 and 59. The cause of this peculiar age structure of the productive population is not hard to find, for Mozambique is only one case of the most marked demographic primitivism. It is one of the countries noted for (1) natural fertility, (2) high mortality, (3) brevity of the period needed to double the population. Moreover, in such demographic conditions the age groups from later years are markedly stronger than the age groups born in earlier years. The countries given in the table below provide an example of maximum inequality between the older and younger age groups of the productive population. In the extreme example provided by Mozambique, the number of people in the first half of the productive period of life is *three times* as great as that of people in the second half.[2]

COUNTRIES WITH THE LOWEST COEFFICIENTS OF AGING OF THE PRODUCTIVE POPULATION, YEARS 1940–51

Country	Year	Total	Age group	
			20–39	40–59
Mozambique	1940	100·0	75·4	24·6
Philippines	1948	100·0	71·2	28·8
Dominican Republic	1950	100·0	70·5	29·5
Angola	1940	100·0	70·0	30·0
Nicaragua	1950	100·0	69·6	30·4
New Zealand (Maoris)	1951	100·0	69·5	30·5
Columbia	1950	100·0	69·3	30·7

Source: Calculated by the author.

An age structure of the productive population similar to that in Mozambique can also be observed in the Philippine and Dominican Republic. In both of these, persons aged 40–59 constitute less than 30 per cent of the total number of persons of productive age (20–59). The work of Dr Gonzales already cited provides us with data on the age structure of the population of the Philippines in recent years (1949–1956). These data, it is true, do not show us the separate successive stages of the productive period of life, but from the general tendency of demographic trends on the island it is safe to conclude that not only is a general aging of the population taking place, but also an aging of the productive population as well. This is due to the fact that at an earlier period, preceding the start of both these processes, the productive population of the Philippines was younger than is shown in our table.

This argument suggests the hypotheses that:

(1) in the "natural" state (i.e. in the most primitive demographic conditions), the ratio of population in the first to the second half of the productive age is 3:1;

(2) any aberration from this ratio, even if very small, is symptomatic of a tendency towards the aging of the productive population.

Therefore, although a country is still demographically young, it may conceal the germs of the process of aging of the productive population.

(b) Countries with Average Coefficients of Aging of the Productive Population

We now take a big step to a group of countries occupying a more central place as regards the coefficient of aging of the productive population. The countries in this group are given in the table below.

COUNTRIES WITH AVERAGE COEFFICIENTS OF AGING
OF THE PRODUCTIVE POPULATION 1941–51

Country	Year	Total	Age group	
			20–39	40–59
Canada	1951	100·0	59·9	40·1
Portugal	1950	100·0	59·9	40·1
Israel (Jewish population).	1951	100·0	59·8	40·2
Iceland	1950	100·0	59·3	40·7
Poland	1949	100·0	59·0	41·0
Tunisia (Europeans)	1946	100·0	58·4	41·6
Yugoslavia	1951	100·0	58·3	41·7
Italy	1949	100·0	58·0	42·0
Hungary	1941	100·0	57·8	42·2

Source: Calculated by the author.

The first point is to establish what values of this coefficient we consider as average. These are values near 40: this figure represents the arithmetic mean of the very low and very high values of the coefficient of aging of the productive population.

In this group we have countries in which, it is true, the productive population is not young, but neither is it yet old. We have put Poland in the middle position in this group, thereby qualifying her as the most typical representative of the intermediate (and probably transitional) phase of aging of the productive population. The present age structure of the productive population in Poland should satisfy all who advocate the principle of the "golden mean". The author is inclined to subscribe to the same principle.

The European countries most similar in age structure to Poland in this respect are Iceland and Yugoslavia, while of the non-European countries Israel (Jewish population) and Tunisia (Europeans) most closely approach the Polish pattern.

We have said of these countries that they already have the phase of demographic youth behind them. This statement is based on the traditional concept of demographic youth. Since we have already questioned whether it is correct to identify demographic primitivism with demographic youth, it may be advisable to think of quite another way of reckoning the process of population aging—for example we may use as our starting point that value at which a country ceases to be retarded demographically. In this case, Poland and the other countries given in the table could easily claim to be countries demographically young.

How would our table look if we were to change our criterion to the one mentioned above, that is, demographic youth?

In such a case the mean would not be, as heretofore, 40–41 per cent of the productive population in the second half of productive age, but approximately 45 per cent. Calculated in this way, the countries grouped around the mean are:

Ireland, 1951 . . . . 44·4%
Norway, 1950 . . . . 44·8%
Czechoslovakia, 1947 . . . . 45·0%
Denmark, 1950 . . . . 45·9%

The fact that in this calculation Czechoslovakia represents the average level of aging of the productive population instead of Poland is of little significance. Of great significance, however, is another fact that emerges—that in a narrower group of countries the differences in the size of the coefficient—high, intermediate, and low—almost disappear. Generally speaking, it can be said that in the advanced countries demographic differences are very much levelled out.

(c) Countries with High Coefficients of Aging of the Productive Population

We now come to a group of countries in which, as far as numbers are concerned, the differences between the numbers of the working population in the first and second halves of the productive age are reduced to a minimum.

The following table gives those countries in which the numbers of the two age groups approach or at least approached parity at the time of the census.

COUNTRIES WITH THE HIGHEST COEFFICIENTS OF AGING OF THE PRODUCTIVE POPULATION 1946–51

Country	Year	Total	Age group	
			20–39	40–59
Switzerland	1950	100·0	52·5	47·5
Great Britain	1951	100·0	51·6	48·3
Belgium	1947	100·0	51·4	48·6
France	1950	100·0	51·0	49·0
Fed. Germ. Rep.	1950	100·0	50·0	50·0
Austria	1951	100·0	48·1	51·9
Germ. Dem. Rep.	1946	100·0	46·0	54·0

Source: Calculated by the author.

The following sub-groups can be differentiated:

(1) the group in which the numbers in the second half of the productive age (40–59) are only slightly less than the numbers in the first half of the productive age (20–39); these countries are: Switzerland, Great Britain, Belgium and France;

(2) the Federal German Republic, where the two age groups are exactly equal;

(3) Austria and the German Democratic Republic, where an unusual and most unnatural state of affairs exists, in that the number in the second half of the productive age (40–59) is greater than in the first half.

This preponderance of older over younger age groups shown in the post-war censuses of Austria and East Germany would seem to point to war as an important cause of this unprecedented deformation of the age structure of the productive population. This supposition is fully confirmed by an analysis of the demographic conditions in Austria. It would be incorrect, however, to attribute this disproportion wholly to the influence of the Second World War. The effects of the First World War were also largely instrumental in bringing about this state of affairs. Other reasons for the post-war deformation of the age structure of the productive population cannot safely be ignored, either, since war was not the only cause.

It will be worth while to study the mechanism by means of which diverse factors affect the process of aging of the population of productive age.

War leaves its mark on the age structure of the population primarily because it takes a multitude of victims from among those who belong to the first half of the productive age. It should be noted, however, that the reduction of the ranks of young people by war is not the only, and frequently not even the most painful consequence of war.

The experience of the First and, partly, of the Second World War has shown that war brings in its trail a fairly marked, and sometimes even a sharp fall in the number of births. Thus war leads to a decimation of the ranks not only of people in their youth, but of children as well. The age pyramids of those countries which have been involved in wars therefore show two gaps, which for many years to come continue to affect the profile of the age pyramid.

The demographic consequences of the First World War will be discussed at length in later chapters of this book. In the meantime we shall confine ourselves to the statement that in some countries, particularly Germany and Austria, the First World War caused an enormous drop in the number of children. The "lean" war years could then be traced at higher and higher levels of the age ladder. It is not difficult to see that these "lean" year groups entered the age period which we have defined as the first half of the productive age (20–39) during the last five years preceding the outbreak of the Second World War, that is, in the years 1935–39. Since the end of the Second World War—this is the period for which the data quoted by us on the age structure of the productive population are cited— the "lean" year groups caused by the war continue to affect the profile for the 20–39 age group.

Apart from the drop in the birth-rate due to war, another factor has had a powerful influence on the formation of the age structure in general, and on the structure of the productive population in particular. This factor, which has been observed over many years, is, if it can be so described, the steady drop in the birth-rate in those countries governed by neo-Malthusian trends. Although a detailed analysis of this problem will be postponed to later chapters, it may be said here that all the countries in our table that have high coefficients of aging of the productive population (including Germany and Austria) have behind them a long period in which the birth-rate has been falling. Earlier, when we spoke of countries with an exceptionally high, i.e. *natural* fertility rate, we drew attention to the fact that more and more numerous young age groups were coming into the productive age. Now, in the case of those countries which, as Kahn so cleverly put it, have been affected by an "international birth strike", the converse can be noted—from a certain time on, the productive age group in these countries began to show a number of young people that was not only noticeably small, but growing smaller as time passed. Thus, after some years the "birth strike" began to exert a strong influence on the age structure of the productive population.

Let us examine Germany and Austria from this point of view.

Above, we quoted the age structure for the German Democratic Republic in 1946.

The younger group of the productive population (age 20–39) then consisted of those born in 1907–26, while the older productive age group (age 40–59) was comprised of those born in 1887–1906. Here, surely, we have a clear answer to the question: What was the cause of the numerical preponderance of the older group in the productive population? The main reason for this preponderance is that in 1946 this older productive age group was recruited from the years of abundant births, whereas the younger group was derived mainly from the "lean" years.

The same holds true for Austria. Since the data for Austria refer to 1951, the younger, less numerous group of people of productive age (20–39) comprises the groups born in 1912–1931, whereas the older, and numerically stronger group (aged 40–59) is made up of those born in 1892–1911. Here again, therefore, we have a numerical preponderance of that age group which is recruited from the years of "stronger" birth-rates.

In conclusion, then, it may be stated that:

(1) at the present moment the aging process of the productive population in the countries of Western Europe is exceptionally advanced;

(2) this is due to the fall in the birth-rate which for many years was a typical demographic phenomenon in the West;

(3) the present state of age levels of the productive population is due in very large measure to the two world wars, with their doubly destructive influence on demographic trends through mass destruction of young people, and reduction of the number of births.

3. AGING OF THE PRODUCTIVE POPULATION IN CERTAIN COUNTRIES

Up to now we have been dealing with the existing situation as regards the aging of the productive population. We shall now deal with the *dynamics* of this process. For this purpose we shall rely on the data of those countries which have long had population censuses.

Such studies covering many years throw fresh light on the aging of the population in the productive period of life. The value of our analysis should in no way be diminished by the fact that we shall be forced to depart from the uniform classification of age we have used hitherto—this time we shall make use of different divisions of the productive population into age groups, according to the sources from which the data are taken.

(a) France

We shall begin with France, which until recently was still the country with the biggest proportion of old people in the productive population.

We shall make only partial use of the wealth of statistical material available to us for this country. We shall examine only the changes which took place in the age structure of the productive population in the period 1901–1958.

The data providing the basis for our analysis of the age structure of the productive population in France are given below:

POPULATION OF PRODUCTIVE AGE (20–59) IN FRANCE IN THE YEARS 1901–58, DICIDED INTO TWO AGE GROUPS: 20–39 AND 40–59

Years	Total	Age group	
		20–39	40–59
1901	100·0	57·3	42·7
1911	100·0	57·0	43·0
1931	100·0	56·4	43·6
1950	100·0	51·0	49·0
1958	100·0	53·8	46·2

Source: Calculated by the author.

We can see from the above table that before the First World War (1901–11) the aging of the productive part of the population was present but scarcely noticeable. Likewise after the First World War, this trend was slight. Thus over the first three decades of this century the coefficient of aging of the productive population rose by barely one point (from 42·7 in 1901 to 43·6 in 1931).

If we consider that these coefficients were on a relatively high level at the beginning of the period we are examining, their slow rate of increase is to a certain extent understandable. Other factors might also have been influential, especially immigration.

A more marked rise can be noted after the Second World War. The coefficient for 1950 is more than 5 points higher than for 1931. This sudden aging of the productive population in France was the result of two concomitant factors—a decline in the birth-rate over a long period, and the two world wars.

In 1958—13 years after the end of the Second World War—the age coefficient of the productive population fell by almost 3 points as compared with 1950. This indicates, nevertheless, a marked rise as compared with the years between the world wars, especially as compared with the years preceding the First World War.

One other fact is worthy of note. At the beginning of the 20th century the age coefficient of the productive population in France was one of the highest if not *the* highest in Europe. Today, however, we should classify a coefficient of this level as near the mean. This fact alone is an indication of the great change that has taken place in the age structure of the productive population in Europe over the last fifty years—this section of the population has aged, and considerably so.

(b) Austria

We shall deal next with Austria as a country which now, as France once did, occupies one of the first places in the world as regards aging of the population of productive age.

Our analysis of Austria will deal with the period 1900–58 and within this period, apart from the first and last years (1900 and 1958), we shall consider five intermediate years: 1910, 1920, 1934, 1939 and 1951.

The relevent data are tabulated on page 294.

Before the First World War the aging of the productive section of the population in Austria advanced rather slowly: the age coefficient of the productive population rose from 39 per cent in 1900 to 39·5 per cent in 1910.

After the First World War, the proportions changed somewhat,

**POPULATION OF AUSTRIA IN THE PRODUCTIVE AGE (20–59)
DIVIDED INTO THE AGE GROUPS 20–39 AND 40–59
FOR THE PERIOD 1900–58**

Years	Total	Age group	
		20–39	40–59
1900	100·0	61·0	39·0
1910	100·0	60·5	39·5
1920	100·0	58·3	41·7
1934	100·0	58·1	41·9
1939	100·0	55·0	45·0
1951	100·0	48·1	51·9
1958	100·0	49·7	50·3

Source: Calculated by the author.

although not markedly, in favour of the older section of the productive population (from 39·5 to 41·7 per cent).

Between the wars (1920–34), the aging of the productive population came almost to a complete standstill. Towards the end of the inter-war period, however, there was a marked decrease in the proportion of people in the younger productive age group (20–39) and a corresponding increase in the proportion of the older group (40–59). The reason for this change to the detriment of the younger age group was that year by year there passed up to the older age group full groups born in years of high fertility, while its own ranks were not filled by corresponding numbers from below. In fact, quite the contrary—in the years just preceding the Second World War those coming up to fill the ranks of the younger productive group (aged 20–39) were the exceptionally poor year groups born during the First World War and now reaching maturity.

Another, and still more marked, reduction of numbers in the age group 20–39 (with a corresponding increase of numbers in the older age group 40–59) can be observed after the Second World War. The root of this may supposedly be sought in two factors—the loss of a large number of young people during the Second World War and, as before, the fact that the younger productive age group lost large numbers of 40-year-olds (born in fertile years) to the older age group, while the new year groups coming up from below were "lean" (those now coming to maturity having been born in infertile years with fewer births).

The outcome of all this was a most peculiar state of affairs in which the twenty older years had a decided numerical preponderance over the twenty younger years. The decline in the birth-rate and war were the decisive factors in producing these changes.

(c) The United States of America

We now come to the United States, which is an interesting country to study in that it gives a picture of an uninterrupted increase in the coefficient of aging of the productive population.

Here, however, our age classification is somewhat different from the one we have used so far. The table given below comprises 45, not 40 yr groups, that is, groups aged from 20–64. Thus in this classification the younger productive year groups are aged 20–44, while the older year groups are aged 45–64;

DISTRIBUTION OF THE POPULATION OF PRODUCTIVE AGE (20–64) IN THE UNITED STATES IN THE YEARS 1850–1958

Year	Total population of productive age	20–44	45–64
1850	100·0	78·2	21·8
1860	100·0	77·4	22·6
1870	100·0	74·8	25·2
1880	100·0	74·0	26·0
1890	100·0	73·8	26·2
1900	100·0	73·4	26·6
1910	100·0	72·8	27·2
1920	100·0	70·5	29·5
1930	100·0	68·6	31·4
1940	100·0	66·4	33·6
1950	100·0	64·9	35·1
1958	100·0	61·2	38·2

Source: Calculated by the author.

A mass of data is available, enabling us to trace changes in the age structure of the productive population for more than a hundred years.

The following facts are noteworthy:

(1) in the middle of the 19th century, persons comprising the second half of the productive population (aged 45–64) of the United States constituted only slightly more than one-fifth of the total number of people of productive age (20–64);

(2) twenty years later (1870), this older group constituted one-fourth of the total productive population;

(3) by 1940 this older section of the productive population now constituted one-third of the total productive population;

(4) the latest data (1958) show that the older productive group is now approaching 40 per cent of the productive population as a whole.

Constant and uninterrupted regrouping of the population of productive age can therefore be observed, the older age group constantly growing in strength at the.expense of the younger. In a word, the population of productive age is growing older.

(d) Switzerland

A gradual aging of the population of productive age can also be observed in Switzerland.

The Swiss statistician Dr Albert Koller applies the same limits to the productive period of life (age 20–64) as that used in the U.S.A., but he divides this period into three, not two, phases, each with 15 yr. Thus he differentiates the following age groups:

(I) 20–34
(II) 35–49
(III) 50–64.

The table given below shows the age structure of the productive population of Switzerland at the beginning and in the middle of the present century.

DISTRIBUTION OF THE POPULATION OF PRODUCTIVE AGE (20–64) IN SWITZERLAND IN THE YEARS 1900, 1950 AND 1958

Year	Productive population total	Age group 20–34	35–49	50–64
1900	100·0	46	32	22
1950	100·0	36	37	27
1958	100·0	36·6	34·1	29·3

Source: Calculated by A. Koller and E. Rosset.

It will be observed that over the period under consideration, covering almost sixty years, the younger fifteen ages (20–34) belonging to the total productive population have become seriously reduced, while the middle and the older age groups have grown in number. The most marked and most steady increase is to be seen in the proportion represented by the oldest of these age groups.

As Koller remarks in this connection, "die Hauptmacht der berufs-tätigen Personen ist somit älter geworden". It is true: the productive population of Switzerland is growing steadily older.

(e) The Netherlands

It is with particular interest that we now come to the study of the Netherlands, which, unlike the countries so far examined, is much less affected by the general process of the aging of the population. Hence the problem arises: what form does the aging of the productive population take in a country which has put up a long resistance to the general aging of the population?

The following table should provide the answer to this question.

DISTRIBUTION OF THE POPULATION IN THE PRODUCTIVE AGE IN THE NETHERLANDS, DURING THE YEARS 1849–1958

Year	Total popula-tion aged 15–64	Ages		
		15–29	30–44	45–64
1849	100·0	43·2	30·4	26·4
1859	100·0	42·4	31·9	25·8
1869	100·0	40·8	31·8	27·4
1879	100·0	40·8	31·0	28·2
1889	100·0	42·7	29·2	28·0
1920	100·0	42·8	31·0	26·2
1930	100·0	42·0	30·9	27·1
1940	100·0	39·5	32·4	28·1
1950	100·0	37·8	31·8	30·5
1953	100·0	36·5	32·1	31·4
1958	100·0	35·5	31·6	32·9

Source: Calculated by the author.

The numbers in the various age groups are not quite so uniform as one would expect. There are ups and downs. Certain trends, however, can be deduced:

(1) the youngest productive age group (15–29) shows a tendency to diminish. This group falls from 43·2 per cent of the total productive population in 1849 to 35·5 per cent in 1958;

(2) it would be difficult to establish any marked trend in the figures for the middle productive age group (30–44), except for a few ups and downs;

(3) there is, however, a distinct tendency for the numbers in the oldest age group (45–64) to rise. There was an increase from 26·4

per cent in 1849 to 32·9 per cent in 1958. This rise would have been even more marked if we had taken 1859 instead of 1858 as our starting point, since in that year the proportion of people aged 45–64 in the total number of persons of productive age was 25·8 per cent. Thus the Netherlands, too, is a country where the productive population is gradually growing older.

(f) Poland

From the fact that in recent decades there has been a gradual aging of the total population in Poland, too, it may be deduced that the productive part of Poland's population has also shown a tendency towards aging. These two processes, as we have said before, are very closely connected with each other.

PROPORTION OF PEOPLE AGED 20–39 AND 40–59 IN POLAND IN THE YEARS 1931, 1955 AND 1958

Year	Population aged 20–59	Age groups	
		20–39	40–59
1931	100·0	66·4	33·6
1955	100·0	57·4	42·6
1958	100·0	59·6	40·4

Source: Calculated by the author.

Although it occurred much later than in the countries of western Europe, the "demographic revolution" brought about by the victory of birth control over natural fertility—a revolution which, in practical terms, resulted in a decrease in the birth-rate—took place in Poland, too, but not until the turn of the century. In Poland the beginning of the new demographic era, the era of "controlled" births, can be regarded as dating from the beginning of the 20th century. The very fact that births began to be limited was an augury of future changes in the age structure of the adult, and, later, of the older population. The die was already cast.

The gradual aging of the population of productive age in Poland occurred as an inevitable consequence of the limitation of births. This is demonstrated in the table above, which gives a comparison of the figures for years not too far apart (1931 and 1955), which nevertheless show marked differences in the age structure of the population.

It appears that during a quarter of a century (1931–55), fairly marked changes took place in Poland among the population aged 20-59, in the form of a considerable rise in the proportion of people in the older age groups. Whereas these groups (aged 40–59) constituted one-third of the total adult population in 1931, by 1955 their proportion had risen to almost 43 per cent.

In recent years the proportion of the older section of the productive population in Poland has fallen to 40 per cent, but in the next few years is expected to return to the level of 42–43 per cent.[3] This would denote the stabilization of previous trends towards the gradual aging of the productive population.

(g) Egypt

We now come to a country that is exceptionally young demographically—Egypt.

In Egypt the number of old people is exceptionally small (those aged 65 or over account for no more than 3–4 per cent of the total population).

It is interesting to note the ratio between the older and the younger section of the productive population in such a young country. The following table shows their proportions.

PROPORTIONS OF POPULATION IN THE AGE GROUPS
20–39 AND 40–59 IN EGYPT, IN THE PERIOD 1917–47

Year	Total	Age groups (in years)	
		20–39	40–59
1917	100·0	66·2	33·8
1927	100·0	67·1	32·9
1937	100·0	65·1	34·9
1947	100·0	63·2	36·8

Source: Calculated by the author.

Even a casual glance at the above figures will suffice to show that changes, if any, have been slight. If, over the three decades reviewed above, the proportion of persons in the age group 20–39 fell from 66·2 per cent to 63·2 per cent, while the proportion of persons in the older age group, aged 40–59, rose correspondingly from 33·8 per cent, to 36·8 per cent then these changes can only be described as relatively small. However, it cannot be denied that both sets of figures do show a certain tendency—for the numbers in the younger group to fall, and for the numbers in the older group to rise.

It is not only in the advanced countries, then, that the productive population is becoming older. The same process can be seen, although on a much smaller scale, in a demographically young country like Egypt as well.

(h) India

In order to obtain a clearer picture of conditions in the demographically young countries, let us have a look at the data for the numerical strength of different sections of the population of productive age in India.

In this case, as in the case of Egypt, we shall take two age groups into consideration: those aged 20–39, and those aged 40–59. Not only do these countries show identical proportions between the age groups, but they also show a striking similarity in the proportion of old people (65 and over). In India in 1951 this proportion was 3·6 per cent.

Now let us examine the proportions of the age group 20–39 and the group 40–59 in such a demographically young country.

THE PROPORTIONS OF THE INHABITANTS OF INDIA IN THE AGE GROUPS 20–39 AND 40–59, IN THE PERIOD 1901–51

Year	Total	Age groups	
		20–39	40–59
1901	100·0	66·1	33·9
1911	100·0	66·7	33·3
1921	100·0	66·1	33·9
1931	100·0	68·3	31·7
1951	100·0	65·3	34·7

Source: Calculated by the author.

This time not only are there great changes in the age structure of the productive population, but there is not even any distinct trend visible. Over a long period the figures are more or less static, and it is only in the twenty years from 1931 to 1951 that one can trace a tendency for the numbers in the younger productive age group (20–39) to fall, and for the numbers in the older group (40–59) to rise.

It must be said, in conclusion, that in India the tendency shown in other countries for the age of the productive population to rise is practically non-existent. It is only in recent years that there have been some very small, hesitant signs of a change in this respect.

The question is whether there is any likelihood of an increase in the age of the productive population in India in the near future.

Dr Gilbert Étienne, who for many years has resided in India and who has taken a close interest in demographic and economic conditions in that country, rules out the prospect of India's fertility rate becoming much reduced within the next thirty years.[4] Although he admits that a moderate fertility rate in India is possible, he nevertheless thinks it likely to remain high. At the same time, appeals are being made for the adoption of birth control.[5] If these appeals find response in the community, then changes in the age structure of India may not be long delayed. Historical parallels make this prospect highly probable.

4. THE ECONOMIC AND SOCIAL ASPECTS OF THE AGING OF THE POPULATION OF PRODUCTIVE AGE

In view of the fact that the productive part of the population is growing older (a process which is far advanced in many countries), the attitude of the community to older workers is steadily gaining importance. We propose now to devote a few marginal remarks to this question.

I do not altogether agree with the views put forward by Gaston Bouthoul, the French sociologist, but some, I must admit, do throw light on the origin, if not on the genesis of the phenomena we are considering. We must place his views on the structure of modern societies in this category. According to Bouthoul, society is not monolithic. The nation consists of groups and individuals with different, and sometimes even diametrically opposed, mentalities. As Gustave Le Bon so rightly put it, there are representatives of all historical periods among us—people who mentally belong to the Middle Ages and others who are even palaeolithic in their way of thinking.[6]

It is not surprising, therefore, that even in civilized societies the most repulsive remnants of past ages still linger, and even find adherents and supporters. One such relic is the hatred or dislike sometimes felt for old people.

The numerous cases of suicide among old people condemned to toneliness and poverty are a serious blot on our civilization. Discrimination against older workers is no less reprehensible.

The economic consequences of this discrimination are well known: during times of economic crisis it is the older workers who fall the first victims under the axe of unemployment. Other consequences of this discrimination, however, should not be forgotten either, such as its permanently depressing effect on old people.[7]

It is therefore a matter of some moment whether the community shows sympathy and understanding towards old people, and old workers in particular, or the opposite. It is noteworthy that of late some changes for the better have been noted.

At the International Gerontology Congress which took place in St. Louis in 1951, the Dutch delegate, J. G. Sleeswijk, said: "There is little prejudice against employing older workers in the Netherlands. The Philips industrial concern, for instance, has so far had good experience with labourers aged 45–64; they are more conscientious and cause less accidents."[8]

The very fact that the virtues of older workers are extolled and this view supported by the industrial example quoted, may be regarded as proof that the prejudices against the older generation of workers are disappearing. The question arises whether this is a natural consequence of the demographic changes that have been taking place. Is it perhaps a result of the diminishing proportion of young people and the growing proportion of old people?

It would not be surprising if people began to attach more value to those whom they could not do without. On the other hand it may also be that the productivity of these workers has risen—it is possible that the physical and mental efficiency of the older generation of manual workers today is higher than it was in previous generations.

But even so, the problem would remain, whether factories are still as efficient when manned by increasing numbers of old people. Can old people keep pace with the younger workers? Are they equally efficient? This is a point which frequently occurs.

At the Gerontology Congress mentioned above where the Dutch delegate reported on the successful experience with older workers in factory jobs in his country, another European delegate, the French demographer, Jean Daric, referred to the diminished efficiency of older workers as a negative symptom accompanying the aging of the productive population. Daric (who has since died at an early age) was an expert on this problem. He declared: "Within the adult population an increase in the proportion of persons aged 40–59 can be observed, which is leading to a rise in the average age of the productive population, and this is having important consequences in the industrial sector, where the efficiency of production is directly connected with age."[9]

In speaking of the connection between productivity and the age of the workers, of course, Daric had in mind the *negative* effects of the aging of the productive population, a process which entails a rise in the proportion of people of lower efficiency.[10]

The same thought was expressed in the report of the Statistical Laboratory of the Catholic University del S. Cuore in Milan, which was presented by Professor Albino Uggè at the International Congress of Demographic Research held in Rome in 1931.

The report described how in the future the productive part of the population in Italy was likely to age and made the following comment:

"Questo fatto non è privo di importanza, date le moderne tendenze dell'industria ad utilizzare, di preferenza, la mano d'opera giovane e ad eliminare i lavoratori oltre un certo limite d'età. *Too old at forty!* è un principio che, specie all'estero, e in particolare modo in America, forma una direttiva che trova seguito. Se esso dovesse prevalere ed affermarsi su larga scala anche da noi, un lieve problema nescerebbe per il collocamento della mano d'opera."[11]

The statements made above are based on the assumption that efficiency decreases with age. But is this supposition correct? Is the brutal slogan *Too old at forty!* supported by scientific evidence?

Recent studies carried out in America encourage a different approach to the usefulness of older workers. Two research workers who put forward this view are Dr Leonard Himler and Dr Roy R. Grinker, whose special field is the vitality of middle-aged people. In the American magazine *Coronet* for March, 1957, we find the following information about this research: "In practically every industry, the responsible work is being done by men and women over 50, according to Dr Leonard Himler of the Committee of Industrial Psychiatry. Careful surveys by the Committee and other agencies show that workers over 45 are generally more valuable to their employers than workers under 45."

Thus, in the opinion of some research workers, the efficiency of industrial workers not only does not diminish, but actually increases with age. This does not mean that the employment of older workers is without its problems. "The real problem of the middle-aged man is not declining usefulness," says Dr Himler, "it's the defeatist and antagonistic attitudes that people have about aging."

It may be noted here that the above views are not so new as might appear. For similar views were expressed considerably earlier, in

1929, by the British economist Lionel Robbins, who in his "Notes on some probable consequences of the advent of a stationary population in Great Britain" (published in *Economica* April, 1929, p. 76) laid particular stress on the defeatist attitude of older workers, and their inability to adapt themselves to new conditions. Robbins pointed out that economic progress brings with it the expansion of some branches of production at the expense of others which involves the necessity for a redistribution of manpower. This redistribution involves migration not only from place to place but from one type of job to another. Meanwhile, older men and women are averse to changing their type of job, nor do they like moving their homes. It sometimes even happens that, faced with a choice between change of job or dwelling-place and loss of job, they prefer to stay where they are, and condemn themselves to unemployment and poverty. The aging of the labour force, concluded Robbins, is therefore a major barrier to economic adaptability.[12]

Dr Roy R. Grinker, who is known in the United States as an expert on the aging process, rehabilitates the usefulness of those aged over forty. "Middle age," he says, "is the most constructive and productive era of life... It is also a period of inventiveness and the time when a man is best able to try out new and original ideas." These words not only recognize the usefulness of older workers; they also imply condemnation of discrimination against older workers.

A new note can be detected in the statement that "the important thing is a man's ability, not his age."[13] This new approach to the question of the usefulness of older people in industry is also expressed in the view that many men and women reach the retiring age at a time when their long experience renders them perfectly capable of doing good work.[14] Let it be noted that this view is gaining in strength in the very country which before was dominated by the slogan *Too old at forty!*

This new approach to the older worker is to be found not only in theory, but also in practice. A. L. Vischer writes that some of the big concerns in America, such as General Electric and Ford, are tending to raise the proportion of their employees aged over forty to correspond with the changes that have taken place in the age structure of the population as a whole. It is also noteworthy that in the Ford works the management is now convinced that for jobs requiring systematic, steady work, as well as a real interest in the job, the best employees are those aged between 50 and 60.[15]

In the socialist countries there has never been any discrimination against older workers, and, happily, in the capitalist world as well, discrimination in the antihumanitarian form it has taken until now is also disappearing.

There is no doubt but that this new attitude has been instigated partly by demographic–economic changes, that is, changes brought about on the labour market by changes in the age structure of the productive population.

5. CONCLUSIONS

An analysis of facts and figures leads to the following conclusions, which have already been mentioned in the text, but which are summarized here:

(1) the aging process of the productive population is an inevitable concomitant and, in a certain sense, a forerunner of the aging process of the general population;

(2) the age structure of the productive population is affected by many factors, but one of these is of primary importance, namely, the trend in the birth-rate;

(3) the aging of the productive population is preceded by a fall in the birth-rate; conversely, a rise in the birth-rate augurs a fall in the age of the productive population;

(4) exceptional events, and war in particular (as can be seen from the experience of the last two world wars) exert no small influence on the structure of the population of productive age;

(5) the lowest known coefficient denoting the age of the productive population is to be found in the rural district of Chiapas in Mexico, where of every 100 persons of productive age (20–59), 77 belong to the first half of the productive period (20–39), and only 23 to the second half (40–59). A coefficient of aging of the productive population only slightly higher, 24·6 per cent, is to be found in Mozambique (1940); thus, in the case of the productive population of Mozambique, those in the younger age group are three times as numerous as those in the older group;

(6) at the other end of the scale, we came across the unexpected circumstance that in certain countries of central Europe, such as the German Democratic Republic and Austria, the older section of the productive population clearly preponderates over the younger section; we attributed this state of affairs to the coincidence of two factors causing the aging of the productive population—"lean" year groups (born in years when the birth-rate was low) coming forward to fill

20

the ranks of the younger age group of the productive population, and, secondly, the decimation of youth as a result of war;

(7) aging of the productive population is a process almost universally encountered today; it is even beginning to be observed in the demographically backward countries, where until now the process has been unknown;

(8) the aging of the productive population brings in its trail numerous consequences of an economic and social nature which are increasingly attracting the attention of economists and sociologists.

REFERENCES

1. "Dire qu'une population vieillit, c'est dire que la partie productrice de cette population vieillit" (J. DARIC, *Vieillissement de la population et prolongation de la vie active*, Paris 1948, p. 18).

2. If we were to examine the statistics for separate parts of the country, we should find even lower coefficients of aging of the productive population. According to a geo-demographical study by J. BEAUJEU-GARNIER (*Géographie de la Population*, Paris, 1956, p. 414) in Chiapas, one of the rural regions of Mexico, no more than 23 per cent of the total population of productive age (20–59) are in the older age group (40–59). It should be mentioned that the Chiapas region is one of the poorest and most backward in Mexico. According to the source quoted above, 65 per cent of the inhabitants of this region do not use footwear, and 70 per cent do not eat rye bread. Here, primitive demographic circumstances and economic retardation, both exceptionally well-marked, go hand in hand.

3. E. ROSSET, "Starzenie się ludności produkcyjnej w Polsce i w świecie" ("Aging of the productive population in Poland and in other parts of the world"), *Kultura i Społeczeństwo* (*Culture and Society*), Vol. 5, No. 1, 1961, Warsaw, p. 46.

4. G. ÉTIENNE, La Population de l'Inde. Perspectives démographiques et alimentaires, *Population*, Paris, 1957, No. 4, p. 669.

5. For example D. K. RANGNEKAR writes: "The economic and social implications of this trend are so serious that the urgency and vital significance of population control cannot be exaggerated" (*Poverty and Capital Development in India*, Oxford University Press, 1958, p. 279).

6. G. BOUTHOUL, *La Surpopulation dans le Monde*, Paris, 1958, p. 60.

7. A. J. ABRAMS, "Discrimination against older workers in various countries", in a joint paper "Old age in the modern world", *Report on the Third Congress of the International Association of Gerontology*, London, 1954, pp. 292, 293.

8. J. G. SLEESWIJK, "The social consequences of aging in the Netherlands", *J. Gerontol.* Vol. 6, Supplement to No. 3, pp. 150–151.

9. "On constate... à l'intérieur de la population adulte, un accroissement de la proportion des personnes âgées de 40 à 59 ans, ce qui conduit à une augmentation de l'âge moyen de la population productrice, laquelle a des conséquences importantes dans le secteur industriel où le rendement de la production est lié directe-

ment à l'âge" (J. DARIC, Le vieillissement de la population dans l'Europe de l'Ouest et son effet sur la population active, *J. Gerontol.*, Vol. 6, Supplement to No. 3, p. 77).

10. Even earlier, the negative effect of the aging of the productive population were pointed out by F. BOVERAT (*Le Vieillissement de la Population*, Les Éditions Sociales Françaises, Paris, 1946).

11. "Di alcuni riflessi economici e sociali del futuro sviluppo della popolazione italiana", Laboratorio di Statistica dell'Università Cattolica del S. Cuore in Milano, *Actes du Congrès International des Études sur la Population*, (édités par le Professeur Corrado Gini), Vol. 7, Rome, 1934, p. 94.

12. L. ROBBINS, "Notes on some probable consequences of the advent of a stationary population in Great Britain", *Economica*, April, 1929, p. 76.

13. P. H. LANDIS, *Population Problems: A Cultural Interpretation*, New York, 1954, p. 105.

14. J. KAPLAN, *Das Alter als soziales Problem*, Rascher Verlag, Zürich, 1956, p. 18 (translated from the English).

15. A. L. VISCHER, *Das Alter als Schicksal und Erfüllung*, Basel, 1955, p. 192.

CHAPTER 12

The Dependency of Non-productive Elements on Society

1. INTRODUCTORY REMARKS

We now come to a problem absorbing the attention of economists and politicians today—a problem which, because of its demographic basis, calls primarily for comment from the demographer. This is the new—or at any rate newly observed—problem posed by the dependency on the population of productive age of non-productive elements.

The population of productive age, that is, the adult population, cannot avoid the expense of supporting the non-productive elements, firstly, because they are obliged to maintain their children, and secondly because they must also pay their debts and maintain the old people who kept them yesterday.

Contemporary civilized societies proclaim that the fate of their non-productive elements is not a matter of indifference to them: he who cannot maintain himself has the right to expect help from the community. An illustration of this is the following declaration from the French Constitution:

"Tout être humain qui, en raison de son âge, de son état physique ou mental se trouve dans l'incapacité de travailler, a le droit d'obtenir de la collectivité des moyens convenables d'existence."

According to this declaration, everyone who is incapacitated, for example because of age ("en raison de son âge"), should receive his means of subsistence from the community.

However, it sometimes happens that the deed does not always fit the word, and it is interesting to note that so important a document as a State Constitution is not always an exception to this rule. Thus it happens that in France, the very country where the rights of the old and disabled are guaranteed by the Constitution, an enormous proportion of old people are living in utter misery, and, according to French sources, even dying from lack of food.[1]

This state of affairs is, in our eyes, a flagrant testimony to the moral

308

deterioration of modern civilized peoples.[2] In this case (as in several others) we support the views of that first-rate naturalist, Mechnikov, who, struck by the very large number of suicides among old people in western Europe at one time, spoke with bitter irony of the moral "progress" of our times, whereby modern civilized man does not kill the old people by his own hands, as his primitive forefathers did, but leaves it to the old people themselves to put an end to their lives.[3] If we were to say who is more blameworthy: the savage who buries his own father alive, or the civilized barbarian who in one form or another leaves old people to commit suicide, we should not be in doubt which of them deserves the more blame. The savage at least has the excuse that he is acting in accordance with the ethics of his tribe; the modern gerontophobe, who has the suicides of old people in large numbers on his conscience, does not even have this excuse.

2. METHODOLOGICAL PROBLEMS

Let us begin with problems of a methodological nature. The first question that arises is how to measure the dependency on society of these non-productive elements.

We must draw a difference here between measurements of two kinds: economic and demographic.

(a) Economic Measurements of Dependency

Economic measurements denote the cost to the community of maintaining its non-productive elements. As an illustration, the table on page 310 shows the expected cost, in the next ten years in France, of maintaining those children not yet old enough to work. These data have been taken from Variant A of a demographic prognosis for France for the years 1960–70.

The following facts which can be deduced from the above table should be noted, namely:

(1) children's needs vary according to their age. If we take the figure 100 as representing the needs of the oldest children (18 and over), then the needs of the youngest group (aged 0–3 yr) can be taken as only 26. Conversely, were we to take the needs of the youngest children as 100, then the index for the oldest children's needs would be 385. In a word, the oldest children's needs are almost four times as great as the needs of the youngest children. The needs of the intermediate groups of children have, of course, intermediate indices;

310   AGING PROCESS OF POPULATION

ESTIMATE OF NEEDS OF NON-EMPLOYED CHILDREN IN FRANCE 1960–70 IN OLD FRANCS

Age (yr)	Scale of needs (indices)	Annual individual needs in thous. old francs	No. of non-employed children in thousands		Total annual needs of children in 1,000,000,000 old francs	
			1960	1970	1960	1970
0–3	26	55	3273	3211	180	176
4–6	49	103	2430	2340	250	241
7–9	56	118	2402	2370	282	280
10–13 . . .	69	145	4324	2232	626	468
14–17 . . .	91	191	2221	3217	425	614
18 and over	100	210	200	274	42	58
Total . . .	—	—	14,850	14,644	1805	1837

Source: JEAN BÉNARD, *Vues sur l'économie et la population de la France jusqu'en 1970*, Paris, 1953, p. 52.

(2) in France the needs of one child are estimated at 55,000–210,000 old francs a year. It should be noted that the lower of these two sums equals an average clerk's monthly pay. Thus an older child's yearly needs will be equal to four months' pay of the same clerk;

(3) France has nearly 15 million children who are not wage-earners; their annual needs amount to the staggering total of 1,800,000,000,000 francs.

So far we have considered the needs of children. No less important are the needs of old people.

Demographers who are interested in this problem agree that the needs of old people are much greater than the needs of children. Here is some information on this matter.

At one time Friedrich Burgdörfer calculated that the costs of maintaining a child, an adult and an old person are in the ratio 3·5 : 7 : 6.[4] According to these figures, the cost of maintaining an old person is 71 per cent higher than that of maintaining a child.

Alfred Sauvy draws attention to the fact that the cost of maintaining a child is usually borne by the family, but that this is not so frequent in the case of the aged, and that family allowances for children are never as high as old age pensions.[5]

A few years ago the British economists Paish and Peacock published in the columns of *Economica* (November, 1954) the results of calculations according to which, in the financial year 1952–3 the cost of maintaining a person of pre-productive age (0–14) in Great Britain was £34 18s 0d whereas the cost of maintaining a person of post-productive age (men: 65+; women 60+) was £69 12s 0d. These same authors forecast that in the future the cost of maintaining one person of post-productive age will be £50 more than the cost of maintaining a child, since at the present time the difference between them is £35.[6]

Thus an old person's needs are greater than a child's needs. This circumstance is of great importance in view of the demographic trend towards a steady increase in the proportion of old people. In addition, there is a steady increase in the numbers of that section of the non-productive population whose maintenance is particularly costly.

(b) Demographic Measurements of Dependency

Demographers use three ratios of dependency:

(1) the ratio of dependency of children;
(2) the ratio of dependency of old people;
(3) the total ratio of dependency (of old people and children).

Since the maintenance of children and old people falls on the adult population, the following ratios of dependency are defined:

(a) the ratio of dependency of children is calculated as the ratio of children to adult population, expressed as a percentage;

(b) the ratio of dependency of old people is calculated as the ratio of old people to the adult population, expressed as a percentage;

(c) the total ratio of dependency is the sum of the two ratios described above.

The principle governing the construction of the ratios of dependency is, as we have seen, a simple one. Certain difficulties, however, are encountered in connection with the technique of calculating these ratios. One difficulty is to decide what limits to give to the productive period of life and from what year the non-productive years should be counted. Whereas French demographers take the years 20–59 (a total of 40 yr) as marking the productive period of life, their German counterparts extend this period to cover the years 15–64 (altogether 50 yr). The English and the Polish practice is to differentiate in this respect between men and women—the upper age limit of productive age for men is 65, and for women 60. These are the main systems of classification but, as we had occasion to point out elsewhere, there are many others besides.

According to the French age classification, the following formula gives the ratio:

(a) of dependency of children:

$$R_{dc} = \frac{N_{0-19} \times 100}{N_{20-59}}$$

(b) of dependency of old people:

$$R_{do} = \frac{N_{60+} \times 100}{N_{20-59}}$$

Where N_{0-19} = the number of people aged 0–19

N_{20-59} = the number of people aged 20–59

N_{60+} = the number of people aged 60 and over.

If we take the productive period of life to cover the ages 15–64, then the formula for calculating the ratios of dependency is as follows:

(a) for the ratio of dependency of children:

$$R_{dc} = \frac{N_{0-14} \times 100}{N_{15-64}}$$

(b) for the ratio of dependency of old people:

$$R_{do} = \frac{N_{65+} \times 100}{N_{15-64}}$$

Of course, in this case, too, the subscripts denote age.

The French demographer Marcel Croze divides the population into the following age groups:

(1) young people ("jeunes") aged 0–19;

(2) old people ("vieillards") aged 65 and over;

(3) adult population ("adultes") aged 20–64.

On the basis of this age classification Croze obtained the following ratios of dependency:

RATIOS OF DEPENDENCY OF YOUNG AND OLD PEOPLE IN FRANCE 1901–56

Year	No. per 100 persons aged 20–64		
	Young people (0–19)	Old people (65 and over)	Young and old people together
1901	60·5	14·4	74·9
1921	53·3	15·3	68·6
1936	50·4	16·4	66·9
1946	49·7	18·6	68·3
1956	54·3	20·2	74·5

Source: J. Soc. Stat., Paris, June, 1956, p. 56.

A point of essential methodological significance made by Croze[7] should be remembered, namely, that the ratio of dependency depends not only on the number of children and old people, but on the number of adults as well.

In research on the aging of the population, the coefficient expressing the ratio of old people to those of productive age is of primary importance. The importance of this index is due to the fact that, of the two sections of the non-productive population, that of post-productive age, that is the aged, is continually growing. It is they who cause the burden to increase steadily. This was pointed out by a member o f the Inter national Labour Office, who remarked, "En outre, le fardeau imposé à l'économie par les personnes à charge d'un âge avancé c'est-à-dire le rapport numérique entre la population ayant dépassé l'âge de trava-iller et la population en âge de travailler devient plus grand."[8]

Such ratios of dependency estimated for the years to come give an indication of the financial and other burdens awaiting the commun-ity in the future, in connection with the growth of non-productive elements.

Let us add to this the sociologist's point of view, all the more willingly since a sociological interpretation frequently provides the key to an understanding of the complicated mechanism of cause and effect in demographic phenomena.

Paul H. Landis raises the question of the connection which suppos-edly exists between the growing number of old people and the dimin-ishing number of births. His argument is interesting: "It is possible that a large grandparent quota (group above 50) in proportion to the parent quota in the population (the group in the reproductive ages 15–50) may have an effect on the birth rate. Because many families have an increased proportion of the aged to care for, due to the pro-longation of life, they may, in order to hold their standard of living, reduce the number of their offspring." Thus the greater burdening of the adult population owing to prolongation of life of the old parents may act as a brake on the production of more children.

If this assumption is correct, then, in Landis's opinion, it may be expected that "the development of pension plans probably tends to counteract this tendency".[9]

Ratios of dependency could play a useful role in statistical analysis of the connection mentioned by Landis.

314　　　　　AGING PROCESS OF POPULATION

3. THE DEPENDENCY OF NON-PRODUCTIVE ELEMENTS IN FIVE PEOPLE'S DEMOCRACIES

The data in the following table are taken from demographic forecasts made by United Nations statisticians, on dependency in five People's Democracies: Poland, the German Democratic Republic, Czechoslovakia, Hungary and Bulgaria.

NUMBER OF CHILDREN AND OLD PEOPLE PER 100 PERSONS AGED 15–59, IN THE YEARS 1950–70, ACCORDING TO UNITED NATIONS FORECASTS

Year	Poland	Germ. Dem. Rep.	Czechoslo-vakia	Hungary	Bulgaria
(a) *No. of children below 15, per 100 persons aged 15–59*					
1950. . . .	46	38	42	40	45
1960. . . .	59	37	49	45	42
1970. . . .	55	43	48	46	37
(b) *No. of persons aged 60 and over, per 100 persons aged 15–59*					
1950. . . .	15	26	19	18	15
1960. . . .	17	34	23	24	17
1970. . . .	20	41	26	29	22
(c) *Total ratios (a+b)*					
1950. . . .	61	64	61	58	60
1960. . . .	76	71	72	69	59
1970. . . .	75	84	74	75	59

Source: *Demographic Forecasts*, U.N. Statistical Office.

Two basic facts emerge from this table:
(1) the ratio of dependency of children is highest in Poland—this remains true for the years 1950, 1960 and 1970;
(2) the ratio of dependency of old people is lowest in Poland, although in 1950 and 1960 an equally low ratio can be observed for Bulgaria in 1970 Poland will be alone in having the lowest ratio of dependency of old people.

As far as the total ratios are concerned, 1960 is the peak year for Poland. In 1950 and again in 1970 Poland is outdistanced by the German Democratic Republic.

Let us quote still other ratios of dependency taken from a Polish demographic forecast for the years 1955–75, based on an international age classification.

DEPENDENCY OF CHILDREN AND OLD PEOPLE IN POLAND, 1955-75

Year	No. of persons of non-productive age, per 100 persons aged 15–64		
	0–14	65+	total
1955	49·4	8·7	58·1
1960	56·9	9·5	66·4
1965	55·5	10·6	66·1
1970	52·6	11·8	64·4
1975	51·6	12·8	64·4

Source: Polish demographic forecast for 1955–1975.

It should be borne in mind that the changes expected to occur in the number of children depend on suppositions concerning the future trend of the birth-rate. Thus, in this field, demographic prognoses are purely hypothetical.

The case is quite different as regards the ratios of dependency of post-productive elements. Such predictions are much more reliable.

The data quoted show that the dependency of old people in Poland will become steadily more marked. With every five-year period, the ratio becomes higher and higher. The increase in this index is considerable for, over the twenty years covered by the table, the dependency of the aged increases by nearly 50 per cent (8·7 to 12·8).

Different measures lead to different numerical results, but they all have one thing in common: no matter what kind of measure is used, the picture remains the same: the ranks of the aged steadily grow, while the ranks of those who have to feed them become steadily thinner. Therefore Poland, too, is faced with the problem which has been troubling politicians and sociologists in demographically "old" countries for years—that of providing for more and more old people.

A very characteristic state of affairs can be observed in the German Democratic Republic, where, as the table shows, in the next decade (1960–70) the number of persons of post-productive age will almost equal the number of people of pre-productive age.

Here is the core of one of the most important changes brought about by contemporary demographic trends. It can be summarized in the following comparison: our fathers worked to maintain their children; our children, on the other hand, and our grandchildren to an even greater degree, will have to work to maintain their old parents, and in many cases their grandparents as well. Analysis shows that this new state of affairs is not far off in Western Germany. But the same thing will happen in many other countries as well.

4. DEPENDENCY IN THE COUNTRIES OF WESTERN EUROPE

Let us examine the present situation and the prospects for dependency in the west European countries in the years 1951–71.

Let us have a look at the statistics published by the Economic Commission for Europe (O.E.C.E.) in its own publication: *L'Évolution Démographique en Europe Occidentale 1951–1971*, Paris, 1956.

Two kinds of dependency occur here: (1) dependency of children, and (2) dependency of persons of post-productive age. The appropriate ratios are calculated in relation to the productive population, that is, in this case, men aged 15–64 and women aged 15–59.

Let us examine these two coefficients separately.

The ratios of dependency of children have been calculated by O.E.C.E. for fifteen countries of western Europe (excluding Spain). These are given in the following table.

PAST, PRESENT AND FUTURE DEVELOPMENT OF DEPENDENCY OF PERSONS OF PRE-PRODUCTIVE AGE IN 15 COUNTRIES OF WESTERN EUROPE, 1951–71

Country	Dependency of children (0–14) per 100 persons of productive age		
	1951	1961	1971
1 Austria	35·8	32·3	32·4
2 Belgium	32·2	37·0	34·9
3 Denmark	42·2	40·0	38·7
4 Fed. Germ. Rep.	36·3	31·4	33·1
5 France	35·7	43·4	41·3
6 Greece	50·6	38·9	36·5
7 Ireland	49·4	51·3	47·9
8 Italy	41·1	38·0	35·3
9 Luxembourg	29·0	—	29·0
10 Netherlands	48·3	49·9	42·3
11 Norway	38·4	43·4	39·9
12 Portugal	48·0	46·5	46·6
13 Sweden	36·6	34·9	30·9
14 Switzerland	36·5	37·4	39·1
15 United Kingdom	35·0	35·9	31·6
15 countries	38·2	38·0	35·3

Source: L'Évolution Démographique en Europe Occidentale 1951–1971, O.E.C.E, Paris, 1956 p. 41.

Let us pick out the lowest and the highest figures in this table. In this way the deviations from the average will be more easily seen. We shall leave Luxembourg out of our analysis because of the slight importance of coefficients calculated for such a small demographic unit. The following ratios mark the extremes for the year 1951.

minima		*maxima*	
1. Belgium	32·2	1. Greece	50·6
2. United Kingdom	35·0	2. Ireland	49·4
3. France	35·7	3. Netherlands	48·3
4. Austria	35·8	4. Portugal	48·0
5. Fed. Germ. Rep.	36·3	5. Denmark	42·2

The picture is a logical one: on the one hand we have demographically old countries, with few children and therefore low ratios of dependency, and on the other hand demographically young countries with a fairly large proportion of children and therefore high ratios of dependency. The figures marking the extremes are of some interest: Belgium has the lowest ratio of dependency of children at 32·2, while Greece has the highest, 50·6. The range is large, and confirms the view that the countries of western Europe do not form a uniform demographic unit.

The ratios of dependency of children calculated for 1961 include the following extremes:

minima		*maxima*	
1. Fed. Germ. Rep.	31·4	1. Ireland	51·3
2. Austria	32·3	2. Netherlands	49·9
3. Sweden	34·9	3. Portugal	46·5
4. United Kingdom	35·9	4–5. Norway	43·4
5. Belgium	37·0	4–5. France	43·4

Compared with 1951, we see fairly important changes. The Federal German Republic and Austria now come to the fore as countries with the least dependency of children. On the other hand, in those countries where in 1951 the dependency of children was least, that is, Belgium, the United Kingdom and France, this dependency is likely to grow. France, which hitherto was among the minima, is now among the maxima. Sweden, however, now enters the list of countries with the smallest dependency of children.

Greece and Denmark drop out of the list of countries with the greatest dependency of children, but Norway and, as already mentioned above, France, enter this group. Ireland's leading place in this group is due to the mass emigration of adults; the ratios calculated in relation to the reduced ranks of the population of productive age are unnaturally high.

The following table shows the extreme values predicted for ratios of dependency of children in western Europe in 1971:

minima		maxima	
1. Sweden	30·9	1. Ireland	47·9
2. United Kingdom	31·6	2. Portugal	46·6
3. Austria	32·4	3. Netherlands.	42·3
4–5. Switzerland	33·1	4. France	41·3
4–5. Fed. Germ. Rep.	33·1	5. Norway	39·9

Thus in 1971 Sweden will hold the record for the lowest dependency of children. The United Kingdom returns to second place, and Austria comes third. A new element here is Switzerland's entry into the group of countries with the smallest dependency of children Switzerland has ousted Belgium, which up to now was always found among the countries with the smallest dependency of children.

Among those countries with the greatest dependency of children, the same countries occur as before, with Ireland in the lead. We shall pass over the changes occurring within this group, as a matter of lesser importance.

We should like to draw attention, however, to the fact that during these twenty years the average dependency of children in western Europe shows a steady decrease. This is seen in the following figures

1951	38·2
1961	38·0
1971	35·3

Perhaps even more characteristic is the fact that the *lowest* ratio of dependency of children are becoming still lower, as can be seen in the following figures:

1951	32·2 (Belgium)
1961	31·4 (Fed. Germ. Rep.)
1971	30·9 (Sweden)

In general, then, it can be said that the West is reducing its dependency of children, for such is the general conclusion which can be reduced from an analysis of the above ratios of dependency of children

Let us now proceed to examine the dependency of people in the post-productive age, in the light of figures also provided by O.E.C.E.

By population in the post-productive age, O.E.C.E. means men aged 65 and over, and women aged 60 and over, and that the post productive population is compared with the productive population comprising men aged 15–64 and women 15–59. We quote from the same O.E.C.E. source as before the ratios of dependency given in the following table.

PREDICTED EVOLUTION OF THE RATIOS OF DEPENDENCY OF PERSONS IN THE POST-PRODUCTIVE AGE IN FIFTEEN COUNTRIES OF WESTERN EUROPE, 1951–71

Country	Ratio of dependency, per 100 persons of productive age		
	1951	1961	1971
1 Austria	21·1	24·4	29·2
2 Belgium	21·0	24·8	28·5
3 Denmark	18·1	20·7	23·4
4 Fed. Germ. Rep.	18·4	21·8	28·3
5 France	22·4	24·0	25·3
6 Greece	14·2	15·9	19·3
7 Italy	16·2	17·7	20·3
8 Ireland	21·8	21·9	24·0
9 Luxembourg	17·6	. . .	28·1
10 Norway	18·5	22·7	26·1
11 Netherlands	15·9	18·2	19·8
12 Portugal	14·6	15·3	17·1
13 Sweden	19·9	22·5	26·2
14 Switzerland	18·6	21·9	26·6
15 United Kingdom	21·2	24·2	28·1
15 countries	19·1	21·4	24·9

Source: *L'Évolution Démographique en Europe Occidentale 1951–71*, Paris, 1956, p. 37.

The figures contained in the above table are based on "biological" predictions. Ireland is the only exception, for in her case our figures are based on "total" prediction, that is, by taking into account migration figures as well. This was necessary in view of the exceptionally large role played by migratory processes in Ireland.

The table shows that in 1951 the maximum values of the ratios of dependency of people in the post-productive age were as follows:

> minimum . . . . . . 14·2 (Greece)
> maximum . . . . . . 22·4 (France)

The highest ratio is 50 per cent greater than the lowest. In other words, in France the dependency of old people is half as great again as in Greece.

Apart from Greece, other countries belonging to the group with the lowest dependency of old people are Portugal (14·6), the Netherlands (15·9) and Italy (16·2). These may be contrasted with those countries which have the greatest dependencies of aged persons. These, apart from France, are: Ireland (21·8), the United Kingdom (21·2), Austria (21·1) and Belgium (21·0).

Here we have a clear division of Europe into two groups depending on how far the process of aging of the population has gone. On the one hand we have a group of countries with a relatively low dependency of old people, comprising countries not yet demographically old, and on the other hand we have a group of countries with a large dependency of old people, that is, countries already demographically old.

For 1961 the extreme values of the ratio of dependency of old people are as follows:

minimum . . . . . . 15·3 (Portugal)
maximum . . . . . . 24·8 (Belgium)

Whereas, before, the range between the lowest and the highest values amounted to 50 per cent of the lowest figure, this time the range has widened to 60 per cent. For although the minimum has risen, the maximum has risen much more.

The countries representing the maximum and minimum have also changed. Greece's place as the country with the smallest dependency of old people has now been taken by Portugal, while France's place as the country with the greatest dependency of old people has been taken by Belgium.

What has not changed is that Belgium (24·8), Austria (24·4), the United Kingdom (24·2), and France (24·0) have all remained in the lead as countries with large dependencies of old people, while at the other end of the scale Portugal (15·3), Italy (17·7), and the Netherlands (18·2) have all remained as the countries with the smallest dependencies in this respect.

In 1971 the marginal values are expected to be as follows:

minimum . . . . . . 17·1 (Portugal)
maximum . . . . . . 29·2 (Austria)

The range between the minimum and maximum values here reaches an unprecedented size: 70 per cent. This has come about despite a fairly large increase in the level of the lowest value. This is because the ratios of dependency of old people have risen everywhere, but incomparably more so in countries demographically old than in countries where the aging of the population is less pronounced.

In the first rank of countries with a large dependency of old people we find Austria (29·2), Belgium (28·5), the Federal German Republic (28·3), and the United Kingdom (28·1). Two facts are obvious—France has disappeared from this group, and the Federal German Republic has now come into it.

The countries with the smallest dependency of old people are, as before, Portugal (17·1), Greece (19·3), the Netherlands (19·8), and Italy (20·3).

5. RATIOS OF DEPENDENCY FOR A CROSS-SECTION OF THE WORLD

A survey of the European countries leaves us very far from obtaining a true picture of the very complicated and differentiated position as regards dependency of children and old people in the world as a whole. In order to see the whole mosaic of these elements in proper perspective, we shall have to leave the European countries aside for the moment, and, as far as the available statistics permit, review the less developed countries and even the most primitive peoples.

The United Nations demographic statistics, greatly developed over recent years, enable us to do so. On the basis of these statistics we have been able to calculate the ratios of dependency for seventy countries. Before we begin to examine these, it should be pointed out that the validity of these ratios varies. It is fairly safe to say that the statistics concerning the developed countries are reliable enough. But it would be difficult to say the same of the less advanced countries, and still less of the underdeveloped ones. We have pointed out elsewhere what large gaps occur in the statistics for countries of this type.

(a) Dependency of Children

Statistics on the dependency of children in these countries (the number of persons aged 0–14 per 100 persons aged 15–64) are given in the table on page 322.

Since lack of space prevents us from remarking on all the ratios given there, we shall confine ourselves to those at the extremes. The following marginal values occur:

minimum 31
maximum 91

THE DEPENDENCY OF CHILDREN (AGED 0–14) PER 100 ADULTS (AGED 15–64) IN DIFFERENT COUNTRIES OF THE WORLD, 1946–58

Country and year	%	Country and year	%
New Zealand (Maoris) 1953 . . .	91	Japan 1954	56
American Samoa 1950	90	Canada 1957	55
San Domingo 1950	85	Poland 1958	54
Paraguay 1950	83	Israel (Jewish pop.) 1955	53
Peru 1956.	83	Bermuda 1950	53
Puerto Rico 1950	82	Union of South Africa (Europeans)	
		1950.	50
Fiji Islands 1955	81	Iceland 1950	50
Nicaragua 1950	80	U.S.A. 1956	49
Costa Rica 1950	79	Finland 1956	49
Ecuador 1950	79	Yugoslavia 1956	48
Taiwan 1955	79	Netherlands 1955	48
Algeria (Moslems) 1953	79	Hawaii 1950	48
British Guiana 1953	76	New Zealand (Europeans) 1953 .	48
Venezuela 1950	76	Ireland (Republic) 1951	48
Mexico 1950	76	Australia 1956	47
Brazil 1950	75	Argentina 1947	47
Panama 1950	75	Portugal 1952	46
El Salvador 1950	74	Northern Ireland 1955	46
Trinidad and Tobago 1953	73	Denmark 1953	42
Honduras 1950	73	Bulgaria 1958	40
Mauritius 1952	71	Greece 1958	40
Martinique 1954	68	Algeria (white pop.) 1953	40
Turkey 1950	66	Italy 1951	40
Haiti 1950	65	Norway 1954	40
Egypt 1947	65	Spain 1950	39
India 1951	64	Hungary 1955	39
Chile 1952	63	Scotland 1955	38
Bechuanaland 1946	63	France 1955	38
Burma 1954	62	Switzerland 1954	37
Maldive Islands 1946	62	Czechoslovakia 1947	36
South Korea 1953	62	Sweden 1955	36
Portuguese Guinea 1950	60	England and Wales 1958	35
Jamaica 1951	60	Belgium 1957	34
China 1953	60	Austria 1957	33
Gold Coast 1952	59	Fed. Germ. Rep. 1957	31
Cyprus 1951	58	Germ. Dem. Rep. 1958	31

Source: Calculated by the author from data in U.N. Demographic Yearbooks.

The difference between these values is enormous. The Maoris, the indigenous population of New Zealand, have three times as many children as the people of either of the German republics, which have the least dependency of children in the world.[10]

Since the variation of this ratio of dependency of children amounts to 60 points (the difference between the maximum and minimum values), we can easily divide these values into three groups of equal range (20 points in each group). By means of such a convention we may supplement our qualitative evaluation of the separate groups, by designating the values occurring in these various groups as high, medium and low.

Thus we are able to classify the ratios of dependency of children in the following groups:

> group   I: over 70 (high dependency)
> group II: from 51–70 (medium dependency)
> group III: 50 and less (low dependency)

If we segregate the different countries into these groups according to the values of their coefficients, the composition of the groups is as follows:

Group I: the Maoris of New Zealand, American Samoa, San Domingo, Paraguay, Peru, Puerto Rico, the Fiji Islands, Nicaragua, Costa Rica, Ecuador, Taiwan, the Moslem population of Algeria, British Guiana, Venezuela, Mexico, Brazil, Panama, El Salvador, Trinidad and Tobago and Honduras—altogether 20 populations.

Group II: Mauritius, Martinique, Turkey, Haiti, Egypt, India, Chile, Bechuanaland, Burma, the Maldive Islands, South Korea, Portuguese Guinea, Jamaica, China, the Gold Coast, Cyprus, Japan, Bermuda, Canada, Israel (Jewish population) and the only European country in this group—Poland.

Group III: all other European countries given in the table, and, outside Europe, the European population of the Union South Africa, the United States, Hawaii, the European population of New Zealand, Argentina, Australia and the white population of Algeria.

Certain conclusions may be drawn from a review of these groups, namely:

(a) the ratios of dependency which we have termed high are typical of countries or populations that are economically under-privileged or demographically retarded;

(b) no such uniformity is to be found in the middle group, where the countries are on different economic levels;

(c) those countries which have a European culture have low ratios of dependency of children; those countries or communities outside Europe which have been augmented by European immigrants and assimilated by them also have low coefficients.

21*

The United Nations Population Division reached results similar to ours, except that they calculated the ratio of the number of children aged 0–14 to the number of adults aged 15–59. They found that:

(1) the underdeveloped regions of Asia, Africa and Latin America have an average of 70 children to every 100 adults;

(2) in the more economically advanced countries of Europe, North America and the Pacific the corresponding ratio is usually about 40 to 45.[11]

(b) Dependency of Old People

As in the case of children, we now give the ratios of dependency we have calculated for old people.

In this case, too, let us have a look at the extreme values.

The number of persons aged 65 and over for every 100 persons of productive age (15–64) is as follows:

minimum . . . . 2·4
maximum . . . . 20·3

In our table the Gold Coast has the lowest ratio of dependency of old people. This one-time British possession with the beautiful name is now the independent republic of Ghana, which is indeed a country without old people.[12]

At the other end of the scale comes the German Democratic Republic, which has the biggest ratio of old people to productive population in the world.[13]

Since the ratios of dependency of old people range from 2 to 20, then, as in the case of children, we propose to divide our entire material into three groups of 6 points each, classifying the ratios in these groups as low, medium and high.

We thus obtain the following groups:

Group   I: from 2 to 8 (low)
Group II: from 8 to 14 (medium)
Group III: from 14 to 20 (high)

Let us see which countries come into these different groups.

Group I contains 42 out of a total of 78 countries, that is, more than half the population surveyed. It is significant that in such a large number of countries, not one is a European country. In this group the Gold Coast comes first, and Israel last. The group comprises countries or populations that are economically underdeveloped.[14]

THE DEPENDENCY OF OLD PEOPLE (65+) PER 100 ADULTS (AGED 15–64), ACCORDING TO THE LATEST DATA

Country and year	%	Country and year	%
Gold Coast 1952	2·4	People's Rep. of China 1953	7·4
Maldive Islands 1946	3·1	Puerto Rico 1950	7·4
Ceylon 1955	3·3	Israel 1958	7·8
Kuwait 1957	3·6	Japan 1954	8·5
Greenland 1951	3·6	Martinique 1954	8·9
Singapore 1957	3·9	Bechuanaland 1946	9·1
Brazil 1950	4·3	Poland 1958	9·2
Cambodia 1959	4·3	Yugoslavia 1956	9·6
Taiwan 1958	4·7	Romania 1956	9·6
American Samoa 1950	4·7	Cyprus 1951	10·7
Burma 1954	4·7	South Africa (Europeans) 1956	10·8
Venezuela 1950	4·7	Spain 1950	10·8
Nepal 1954	4·9	Bulgaria 1958	10·9
El Salvador 1950	5·2	Czechoslovakia 1947	11·2
Egypt 1947	5·3	Finland 1958	11·3
Costa Rica 1957	5·4	Algeria (white pop.) 1953	11·3
Nicaragua 1950	5·4	Portugal 1958	11·7
Philippines 1959	5·4	Italy 1951	12·3
San Domingo 1950	5·5	Canada 1959	12·8
South Korea 1953	5·5	Hungary 1958	13·2
Peru 1956	5·6	Iceland 1957	13·3
Mauritius 1952	5·6	Australia 1958	13·6
Algeria Moslems 1953	5·7	Netherlands 1958	14·3
Panama 1950	5·8	U.S.A. 1959	14·4
Turkey 1955	6·0	Luxembourg 1958	14·7
Guinea 1955	6·1	Denmark 1953	14·9
India 1951	6·1	Switzerland 1958	15·2
Fiji Islands 1958	6·1	Norway 1954	15·5
Hawaii 1950	6·2	New Zealand (European) 1953	15·6
Mexico 1950	6·2	Scotland 1955	15·7
Argentina 1947	6·3	Northern Ireland 1958	15·9
British Guiana 1958	6·3	Austria 1957	17·1
Ecuador 1950	6·5	Sweden 1957	17·2
Jamaica 1951	6·5	Ireland (Republic) 1951	17·7
Chile 1952	6·8	Belgium 1957	17·8
Haiti 1950	6·9	England and Wales 1958	17·9
Trinidad and Tobago 1953	7·0	Fed. Germ. Rep. 1958	18·4
Paraguay 1950	7·0	France 1958	18·5
Honduras 1950	7·0	Germ. Dem. Rep. 1958	20·3

Source: Calculated by the author from material in United Nations Demographic Yearbooks.

Group II, which represents those with a medium dependency of old people, comprises 17 countries (11 European and 6 non-European as well as 2 communities of European origin resident in non-European countries). This, then, from every point of view, is a very mixed group, in which, however, European influences predominate. The European countries in this group are:

Poland	9·2	Czechoslovakia	11·2
Yugoslavia	9·6	Finland	11·3
Romania	9·6	Portugal	11·7
Spain	10·8	Italy	12·3
Bulgaria	10·9	Hungary	13·2
		Iceland	13·3

As the above table shows, Poland has the smallest dependency of old people of all the countries of Europe. It is clear that, taking the world as a whole, Poland comes about in the middle as regards dependency of old people, whereas among European countries Poland has a very small—in this part of the world an unprecedentedly small—dependency of old people.

Group III, comprising those countries with a large dependency of old people, contains 17 countries, 15 of them in Europe. The other two countries outside Europe are New Zealand (white population) and the United States.

In Europe the countries that have the greatest dependency of old people (aged 65 and over) per 100 adults are:

Germ. Dem. Rep.	20·3
France	18·5
Fed. Germ. Rep.	18·4

The cause of the greatly increased dependency of old people in the countries just mentioned is to be found principally in the decimation of adults by war, and in the drop in the birth-rate over a number of years.

(c) Total Ratios of Dependency

Let us now look at the total ratios of dependency. These are given for different countries of the world in the table on page 327.

In this table we are struck at once by the maximum and minimum values which are as follows:

minimum	46
maximum	96

DEPENDENCY OF CHILDREN AND OLD PEOPLE PER 100 ADULTS
(AGED 15–64) IN VARIOUS COUNTRIES OF THE WORLD 1946–58

Country and year	%	Country and year	%
New Zealand (Maoris) 1953 . . .	96	Poland 1957	65
American Samoa 1950	95	Ireland (Republic) 1951	65
Paraguay 1950	90	Japan 1954	64
San Domingo 1950	90	New Zealand (European) 1953 . .	64
Fiji Islands 1955	89	Bermuda 1950	63
Peru 1956	89	U.S.A. 1956	63
Puerto Rico 1950	89	Iceland 1950	62
Nicaragua 1950	86	Netherlands 1955	62
Ecuador 1950	85	Northern Ireland 1955	62
Costa Rica 1950	84	Gold Coast 1952	61
Algeria (Moslems) 1953	84	Australia 1955	60
British Guiana 1953	83	Israel (Jewish pop.) 1955	60
Taiwan 1955	83	Union of South Africa (Europeans)	
Mexico 1950	82	1950.	60
Panama 1950	81	Finland 1956	60
Venezuela 1950	81	Portugal 1952	57
Honduras 1950	80	Yugoslavia 1956	57
Brazil 1950.	80	Denmark 1953	56
Trinidad and Tobago 1953 . . .	80	France 1956	55
El Salvador 1950	79	Norway 1954	55
Martinique 1954	77	Hawaii 1950	54
Mauritius 1952.	77	Scotland 1955	54
Bechuanaland 1946	72	Argentina 1947	53
Haiti 1950	72	Sweden 1955	53
Turkey 1950	71	Switzerland 1954	52
India 1951	70	Italy 1951	52
Chile 1952	70	Greece 1953	52
Egypt 1947	70	Hungary 1955	51
Cyprus 1951	69	Bulgaria 1946	51
Canada 1957	68	Algeria (white pop.) 1953	51
South Korea 1953	67	England and Wales 1955	51
Burma 1954	67	Spain 1955	50
China 1953	67	Austria 1957	50
Jamaica 1951	66	Germ. Dem. Rep. 1957	50
Portuguese Guinea 1950	65	Belgium 1955	50
Maldive Islands 1946	65	Czechoslovakia 1947	47
		Fed. Germ. Rep. 1957	46

Source: Calculated by the author from data in United Nations Demographic Yearbooks.

There is a very large gap between the maximum and minimum total ratios of dependency of children and old people. This coefficient is more than twice as high for the Maoris of New Zealand as for the Federal German Republic. In other words, a hundred adult Maoris must feed and maintain twice as many children and old people as a hundred adults in West Germany.

Those societies which are in a position to care for more dependents—the economically advanced and wealthy countries of Europe—have reduced them to a minimum. These burdens are immeasurably greater, on the other hand, in the economically underdeveloped countries which really cannot afford them.

As a matter of fact, the present author is not the first to draw attention to this demographic paradox.

6. CONCLUDING REMARKS

This is all I have to say in general on the subject of the dependency of non-productive elements. Before laying down my pen, however, I should like to say something about, if not all, then at any rate the most extreme, cases.

As far as the upper extreme is concerned, it is obvious that it is connected with a number of very harmful phenomena. The principal harm deriving from an excessive dependency of non-productive elements on the population is the necessity of employing large numbers of children who are not yet capable of adult work, and of people no longer capable of work.

As stated in a paper prepared by the United Nations Population Division[15] and delivered at the World Population Congress in Rome, it is general practice in the rural areas of the under-developed countries to employ children aged 10–12, if not younger. In Turkey, for example, the population census taken in 1945 showed that 49 per cent of boys aged 10–14 were gainfully employed, whereas in Sweden in 1940 the corresponding proportion was no more than 2 per cent. It should be added that in Turkey the total ratio of dependency is 71, as compared with only 53 in Sweden.

The Brazilian demographer Giorgio Mortara tells us that in Brazil approximately 3,300,000 children aged less than 15 and 600,000 persons over 60 can be found working in agriculture (estimates for 1950). To these can be added a by no means small number of children and old people employed in other occupations. Moreover, these figures concern only those working outside their own homes. Therefore, concludes Mortara, it should surprise no one that in Brazil 56·3 per cent of the children are illiterate.[16] It should also be added that the total ratio of dependency of children and old people in Brazil is 80 per 100.

The American demographer and sociologist J. O. Hertzler, who is a fairly typical representative of post-Malthusian thinking, sees in children the source of the burden that weighs down the thin layer of productive population in the underdeveloped countries.[17] Hence he reaches a conclusion that on closer examination does not hold water, namely that by denying themselves a large number of children people can ensure the well-being of themselves and their offspring. Those who support this view should read a small but interesting dissertation by the Czechoslovak demographer Vladimír Srb,[18] in which he points out how mistaken in their calculations are those parents who limit the number of their children in order to give them a better life, since these children when they grow up will have to bear on their shoulders a disproportionate burden through having to maintain a large number of old people—a disproportionate burden in that it is spread over a relatively thin layer of adult population.

If it is clearly a disadvantage to be burdened with too many non-productive elements, this does not mean that the other extreme, that is, the lowest possible dependency of non-productive elements, is advantageous. In one of the United Nations demographic yearbooks we find the information that in Spanish Guinea children below the age of 15 constitute 18 per cent of the total population, persons of productive age (15–64) 81·1 per cent of the total population, and old people (65+) 0·9 per cent of the total (1950 data). According to these figures, then, for every 100 persons of productive age there are 22 children and one old person. Who would be willing to say that this is the ideal state of affairs from the demographic point of view? Surely it is clear that figures such as these reflect a demographic monstrosity.

History has never been on the side of the extremes—in the long run nothing good has come of them. This was the considered opinion of Toulemon, a historian of the doctrine of populations, who on the basis of his historical studies formulated the postulate of a moderate demographic policy.[19] Although, to tell the truth, we do not share Toulemon's hazy, impractical conception of an optimum population, we nevertheless believe that at the present day the necessity for a sensible demographic policy is obvious.

Demographers generally hold the view that low ratios of dependency are advantageous. The same view was expressed by such an authoritative institution as the Population Division of the United Nations (c.f. *The Determinants and Consequences of Population Trends: A Summary of the Findings of Studies on the Relationships between Population Changes and Economic and Social Conditions*, 1953). This opinion is based on economic premises, the most important of which is: "A relatively young population, whether it is growing rapidly or not, will spend a larger share of its income on food than an older population with the same per capita income" (*op. cit.*, p. 213).

It would be foolish to underestimate all the troubles and discomforts that dependency on the productive population of non-productive elements brings with it. But it would also be foolish to determine the number of progeny solely from the narrow point of view of temporary economic advantage. Considering the question in a wider context, economic interests that recognize the need for economic growth need not necessarily be opposed to large families, even if great sacrifices are demanded of the productive population to feed, clothe and educate them.

Let us not forget that children represent the nation's future.

REFERENCES

1. The Paris periodical *Regards* (No. 409, August 1956) informs us that 45 per cent of the old (65 yr and over) in France die as a result of insufficient food ("en raison d'insuffisance alimentaire").
2. E. ROSSET, "Proporcja ludności nieprodukcyjnej jako problem ekonomiczny i społeczny", *Zeszyty Naukowe Uniwersytetu Łódzkiego*, series I, No. 18, 1960.
3. E. METCHNIKOFF, *Études sur la Nature Humaine. Essai de Philosophie Optimiste*, Masson, Paris, 1905, pp. 170–1.
4. F. BURGDÖRFER, *Volk ohne Jugend*, 3rd edition, 1935, pp. 304–305.
5. A. SAUVY, *Théorie Générale de la Population*, Vol. 2, Biologie Sociale, Presses Universitaires de France, Paris, 1954, p. 63.
6. W. J. THORNE, *Your Future Is Now*, Eyre and Spottiswoode, London, 1950, p. 21.
7. M. CROZE, "Chronique de démographie," *J. Soc. Stat.* Paris, June 1956, p. 57.
8. "La population active dans le monde. Aspects démographiques", *Rev. Int. Travail*, Geneva, 1956, p. 186.
9. P. H. LANDIS, *Population Problems, A Cultural Interpretation*, second edition prepared by Paul K. Hatt, American Book Company, New York, 1954, p. 100.
10. In the former German Reich, similarly calculated ratios of dependency of children had the following values: 1910—56; 1925—37; 1930—33. (E. Kahn, *Der Internationale Geburtenstreik*, p. 167.)

11. Population Growth and the Standard of Living in Under-Developed Countries, United Nations Population Division, *Proceedings of the World Population Conference, 1954*, United Nations, New York, 1955, Vol. 5, p. 1108.

12. According to a census taken on 1st February, 1948, the Gold Coast population was 3,735,682. New estimates published by the Statistical Office of the United Nations refer to a population of over 4 million (*Demographic] Yearbook 1956*, p. 137).

13. It should be remembered that in the former German Reich, similarly calculated ratios of dependency of old people had the following values: 1910—8, 1925—8, 1930—9 (E. KAHN, *Der Internationale Geburtenstreik*, p. 167).

14. The presence of Israel in this group is an exception which has no influence on the general composition of the group. It is not difficult to see that the reason for this exception lies in the very marked wave of immigration to Israel after the Second World War, thus causing a large increase in the number of people in the prime of life.

15. A paper "Population Growth and the Standard of Living in Under–Developed Countries" presented at the World Population Congress in Rome, 1954.

16. G. MORTARA, "The Development and Structure of Brazil's Population", part of a joint work *Demographic Analysis, Selected Readings*, edited by Joseph J. Spengler and Otis Dudley Duncan, The Free Press, Glencoe, Illinois, 1956, p. 657.

17. J. O. HERTZLER, *The Crisis in World Population, A Sociological Examination with Special Reference to the Under-developed Areas*, Lincoln, University of Nebraska Press, 1956, p. 137.

18. V. SRB, Biologická situace v českych zemich (The Biological Situation in Czechoslovakia), *Knižnice Sociální Revue*, Prague, 1947, pp. 20–22.

19. A. TOULEMON, *Histoire des Doctrines de la Population*, Éditions Berger–Levrault, Paris, 1956, p. 11.

Part IV

FACTORS IN THE AGING OF SOCIETIES

Introduction

IN ORDER to find the factors which determine the age structure of populations, it is necessary to analyse the changes occurring in this structure over an extended period of time. Such an analysis can be either retrospective or prospective. A retrospective approach is important in obtaining empirical data, while a prospective approach is useful for conclusions of a hypothetical nature. One should not speak of one type of analysis as superior to the other since both provide valuable material concerning the various factors affecting the age structure of populations. However, it is much more difficult to draw conclusions from empirical than from hypothetical data.

The weakness of retrospective analyses is the fact that very often they do not give a very exact indication of the effects of specific factors on changes occurring in the age structure. Where one succeeds in obtaining these data, the results, of course, are of the utmost value.

What is the source of these difficulties, so frequently encountered in making retrospective analyses of the changes in the age structure of populations?

The difficulties arise from the simultaneous action of the particular factors, each of which may be variable and, what is most important, from the fact that each operates in a different direction. Since we are confronted with a phenomenon affected by various factors operating simultaneously in different directions and with different forces, we can only discover the effect of a particular factor if its operating power far outweighs that of the other factors. However, this is seldom the case.

Prospective analyses are altogether different. Since they are always based on definite assumptions as to the future trends of birth and death rates and sometimes also of migratory movements, one factor only is variable while all the rest remain constant. Such analyses enable us to draw conclusions as to the direction and force of particular factors which shape the age structure of populations. It may be concluded that demographic forecasts often allow us to draw indirect if not direct conclusions.

Decisive factors affecting the age structure are:

(1) changes in fertility rates;

(2) a progressive decline in mortality;

(3) migratory movements;

(4) war destruction.

Generally these factors are operative in all situations (though with varying strength and sometimes in different directions). Until now it has not been possible to eliminate war as a permanent factor shaping the age structure of populations. To obtain an age pyramid without considering the war factor, there would have to be a period of no less than one hundred years between wars and very few countries have as yet enjoyed such a long period free of war.[1]

In this fourth part of our study dealing with factors which shape (and sometimes mis-shape) the age pyramid of populations, we shall try to show the direction and—where possible—the force of these factors, always keeping in mind the main purpose of the study: to reveal the influence of specific factors on the aging of populations.

CHAPTER 13

The Evolution of the Number of Births and Its Effect on the Aging of Populations

1. GENERAL REMARKS

Our analysis of the effect of fertility on the age structure of populations has been based partly on empirical data and partly on data taken from hypothetical computations.

It must be kept in mind that conclusions based on empirical data are more conjectural than those deduced, because of the above-mentioned fact that the factors which affect the age structure of populations act simultaneously, and it is not possible to isolate one factor sufficiently to be able to observe its exclusive action. Where different factors operate simultaneously, it is not only possible but certain that the fertility rates are either reinforced or weakened as a result of the action of other factors (mortality or migratory movements); in some cases it may be entirely neutralized by the other factors. This is why empirical data are not adequate as a source of information about the factors in population aging.

Data unobtainable from empirical sources can be relatively easily obtained through the use of hypothetical computations; given the proper assumptions, they help to discern the effects of specific factors affecting the population age structure. It is assumed that one factor is variable while the others remain constant. Therefore, hypothetical computations play the main role in our considerations.

2. THE EFFECTS OF A DECLINE IN BIRTHS ON THE AGING PROCESS OF POPULATIONS IN THE LIGHT OF HYPOTHETICAL DEMOGRAPHIC COMPUTATIONS

Those who are not familiar with our problems will find it surprising to learn that the aging of populations has come about chiefly as a result of the decline in births and not of the prolongation of life.[2] This concept, it should be noted, is not a hypothesis to be proved but a concept already confirmed by experience.

As we already know, hypothetical computations are in this case the best means for examining the age structure of the population, assuming fertility as a variable factor while all other factors remain constant.

It is worth while to learn these conditions as well as the hypothetical picture of the developing age structure of populations depending only on one factor, namely on the decrease in births. The United Nations' publication *The Aging of Populations and Its Economic and Social Implications*, printed in 1956, contains numerous computations of this kind which we shall examine later.

(a) Great Britain

General conclusions about the effect of fertility on the age structure of populations can be drawn from the British demographic forecast for the years 1947–2047 which, as we mentioned earlier, was made in 16 variants. This abundance of variants and, therefore, of different assumptions permits a number of interesting conclusions.

Following in general the thoughts of the U. N. demographer, we shall use only 3 out of the 16 variants of the British forecast: Nos. 10, 8 and 11. They all assume a constant decline in mortality, whereas they differ with respect to the future development of fertility, assuming in the first case low fertility; in the second case medium; and in the third case high fertility.

Assumptions of the three variants:

(a) *variant No. 10*: decreasing mortality, low (decreasing) fertility, no migratory movements;

(b) *variant No. 8*: decreasing mortality, medium fertility (5 per cent above the 1935–8 level), no migratory movements;

(c) *variant No. 11*: decreasing mortality, high (increasing) fertility, no migratory movements.

On the basis of the extended period of 100 yr (1947–2047) covered by the forecast, it is possible to examine the results of a long action of various trends shaping the population's natural increase.

As we see, the median group representing the productive age varies the least; its number depends only to a small extent on fertility rates.

Fertility, however, has a decisive effect on the number of children and old people; the lower the fertility rate, the smaller the number of children and the greater the proportion of old people. With a high fertility rate the percentage of children from 0–14 yr would be 21·1 per cent in 2047, with a low rate, only 15 per cent; the proportion of old

PROJECTED AGE STRUCTURE OF GREAT BRITAIN'S POPULATION IN THE YEAR 2047

Variant	Total	Age groups (yr)		
		0–14	15–59	60+
No. 10	100·0	15·0	56·5	28·5
No. 8	100·0	19·1	57·8	23·1
No. 11	100·0	21·1	58·5	20·4

Source: *The Aging of Populations*, p. 36.

people (60 and over) would, at the same time, be 20·4 per cent with a high fertility rate and 28·5 per cent with a low rate. In the last case the proportion of old people would be twice that of children and with a high fertility rate the number of children and old people would reach a state of equilibrium.

It is clear that the above differences are exclusively the result of the varying fertility rates since the other factors remain constant.

The U. N. publication provides data on the evolving proportions of children, adults and old people throughout the entire prospective period. We are only making use of part of these data, concerning the number of old people. It should be noted that in this new compilation old age starts at 65 and not at 60. Since we are dealing with the effect of fertility on the aging process of populations, we shall use only variants No. 10, 8 and 11 (see the following table).

PROJECTED EVOLUTION OF THE PROPORTION OF OLD PEOPLE (65 AND OVER) IN GREAT BRITAIN IN THE YEARS 1947–2047

Year	Variant		
	No. 10	No. 8	No. 11
	percentage of people aged 65+		
1947	10·4	10·4	10·4
1967	13·8	13·6	13·3
1987	18·3	17·0	15·8
2007	18·5	15·7	13·7
2027	21·9	17·1	14·2
2047	21·5	17·1	14·9

Source: *The Aging of Populations*, p. 85.

Comparing the figures of variant No. 8, which assumes medium fertility, with those of the two other variants, we notice the following:

(1) in variant No. 10, which assumes decreasing fertility, the proportion of the aged grows *faster* than in variant No. 8;

(2) on the other hand, in variant No. 11, which assumes increasing fertility, the proportion of the aged grows at a *slower* rate than in variant No. 8.

Hence it is clear that decreasing fertility accelerates the aging process of the population, while increasing fertility acts in the opposite way.

(b) France

The previously mentioned French demographic forecast (1946–2001) by P. Depoid contains similar premises and conclusions.

The forecast was elaborated in 6 variants differing only with regard to the fertility levels, while the mortality levels were kept constant. Hence, the differences in the projected population age structure depend solely on the various assumed fertility levels.

Let us designate the particular variations $W_1, W_2 \ldots W_6$. They are arranged according to their fertility level, proceeding from the lowest to the highest. The following table shows the population age structure in the year 2001:

PROJECTED AGE STRUCTURE OF THE POPULATION OF FRANCE IN 2001

Variant	Total	Age groups (yr)		
		0–14	15–59	60+
W_1	100·0	15·7	59·9	24·4
W_2	100·0	18·3	60·5	21·2
W_3	100·0	20·8	60·7	18·5
W_4	100·0	23·1	60·6	16·3
W_5	100·0	25·2	60·3	14·5
W_6	100·0	27·2	59·9	12·9

Source: *The Aging of Populations*, p. 38.

The differences between the particular variants are as follows:

(1) the higher the fertility, the higher the percentage of children. The proportions of children vary considerably between 15·7 per cent and 27·2 per cent;

(2) the middle-age group shows insignificant differences; the lowest proportion being 59·9 per cent and the highest 60·7 per cent;

(3) very great differences are observed among the aged (60 and over). As fertility increases, the proportion of old people decreases. In the variant with the highest fertility rate (W_6), the proportion of old people is 12·9 per cent and in the variant with the lowest fertility (W_1), the proportion of the aged is 24·4 per cent;

(4) under conditions of highest fertility, the number of children would be more than twice that of old people, while, under conditions of lowest fertility, the number of old people would be 50 per cent higher than that of children.

These differences are of great importance and, as we mentioned before, they are all caused by the differing levels of fertility.

In the light of the above data, fertility is a very important factor influencing the age structure of the population. These data prove in particular the role of fertility in the aging process of populations.

(c) The United States of America

Vasilios G. Valaoras (*Patterns of Aging of Human Populations*) made a demographic forecast for the United States for the year 1960 using assumptions not realistic from the practical point of view but interesting from the theoretical point of view.

We shall examine only two of his variants:

(a) the variant based on the assumption of a constant fertility rate and a decreasing mortality rate;

(b) the variant based on the assumption of a constant mortality rate and a decreasing fertility rate.

PROJECTED AGE STRUCTURE OF THE POPULATION OF THE U.S.A. IN THE YEAR 1960

Variant	Total	Age groups (years)		
		0–14	15–59	60+
a	100·0	31·8	57·7	10·5
b	100·0	20·6	64·5	14·9

Source: *The Aging of Populations*, p. 42.

The first variant (a), assuming constant fertility, makes the population's age structure dependent solely on the decrease in mortality, while the second variant (b), assuming constant mortality, makes the population's age structure dependent solely on the decrease in fertility.

What are the effects of each of the isolated factors?

The proportion of old people, which is of interest to us as an indication of the aging process, is 50 per cent higher under conditions of declining fertility than under conditions of declining mortality.

Here, too, it is proved that the main factor in the aging process of population is declining fertility and not declining mortality.

(d) Central America (including Mexico)

We already know the prospective computations made by the United Nations demographers for Central America (including Mexico). They comprise several variants indicating the development of the population's age structure for the period 1950–80: they all assume identical mortality rates while the fertility rates differ. This forecast may be used, therefore, as a source of information about the effects of fertility on the aging process.

PROJECTED EVOLUTION OF THE PROPORTION OF OLD PEOPLE (65+), IN CENTRAL AMERICA, INCLUDING MEXICO, IN THE YEARS 1950–80

Year	Variants		
	(a)	(b)	(c)
1950	2·89	2·89	2·89
1960	2·92	2·99	3·07
1970	3·27	3·52	3·77
1980	3·33	3·87	4·44

Source: The Aging of Populations, p. 87.

The projected proportions of old people (65 and over) are based on the following assumptions concerning the future trend of fertility:

(a) high fertility—the fertility coefficients remain on a given high level;

(b) medium fertility—gradually declining coefficients of fertility;

(c) low fertility—rapidly declining coefficients of fertility.

Central America (including Mexico) has a fairly low proportion of old people and no important changes are anticipated in this respect in the prospective period. However, it is quite apparent that the tempo of aging is dependent on the fertility level. Therefore:

(a) should fertility maintain its hitherto high level, the percentage of old people will amount to 3·33 per cent in 1980;

(b) with a gradual decrease in fertility, the proportion of old people will increase to 3·87 per cent;

(c) a rapid decrease in fertility will result in an increase in the percentage of old people to 4·44 per cent.

Thus, the lower the fertility level, the faster the aging tempo of the population.

It should not be forgotten that retrospective computations have three unknowns, and the third unknown—migratory movements—

may either strengthen or weaken, or even neutralize, the effects of the factor which has been examined.

There is, however, an important objection to the method of prospective computations. They are hypothetical only to a certain degree; although the future trends of births and deaths are based on definite hypotheses, prospective computations are greatly influenced by previous empirical relations between fertility and mortality.

The shorter the period covered by the demographic forecast, the smaller are the effects of a hypothesis. In forecasts covering a period of 65 or 60 yr, the assumed decrease or increase in fertility levels has no influence whatsoever on the proportion of the old people because no person born during the time covered by the forecast will attain old age within such a period of time. Therefore, in forecasts which cover 65 or 60 yr the number of old people depends mainly (though not exclusively) on former fertility rates and not on fertility rates assumed for the given forecast.

Computations made for stable populations, being fully hypothetical, are more useful for our consideration. At the Session of the International Statistical Institute in Stockholm (1957), Jean Bourgeois-Pichat presented the results of his calculations made, not for real populations, but for models of stable populations. The numerous variants compiled by the French demographer differ with regard to their gross reproduction coefficient (different fertility levels) or with regard to the average expected length of life at birth (different mortality levels). They allow us to estimate the effects of fertility and mortality on the age structure of populations.

Out of the numerous computations made by the French demographer, one compilation suffices for our purposes:

AGE STRUCTURE OF A STABLE POPULATION MODEL ASSUMING DIFFERENT FERTILITIES AND CONSTANT MORTALITY

Gross reproduction rate	Average expected length of life at birth (yr)	Percentage of people		
		0–14	15–59	60+
4	50	51·5	45·8	2·7
3	50	44·6	50·9	4·5
2	50	34·2	57·2	8·6
1	50	17·8	60·7	21·5

Source: JEAN BOURGEOIS-PICHAT: *Utilisation de la notion de population stable pour mesurer la mortalité et la fécondité des populations des pays sous-développés*, p. 4.

The gross reproduction rate and the fertility level are interdependent; the higher the fertility the higher the gross reproduction rate, and vice versa.

What do we learn from the above table?

We note a great difference in the age structure, depending on the rate of fertility.

The biggest differences is seen in the group of children (0–14) where the span is threefold and in the post-productive group (60+) where the span is eightfold.

These differences, as we mentioned earlier, depend solely on the fertility levels.

Moreover:

(1) the proportion of children (0–14) decreases with a decrease on fertility;

(2) the proportion of people in the post-productive age (60+) increases with the decline in fertility.

All this proves that fertility is the main factor in the aging of populations.

The data examined fully reveal the factors which affect change, in the age structure of the population and particularly changes in the proportion of the aged in relation to the fertility levels. Hence the United Nations demographer was entirely right in stating that fertility movements have played a fundamental part in the development of the population age structure.[3]

He likewise confirmed the earlier conclusion of another U. N. demographer quoted previously: "Birth rates, and not death rates, are the major determining factor of population structure."

Due to the essential and prevalent role of fertility movements in the contemporary aging process of population, it would be advisable to observe more closely the evolution of fertility in various countries.

3. THE "DEMOGRAPHIC REVOLUTION"

In the 19th century there was a decisive turn in demographic relation, in a number of European countries. Fertility rates which had been increasing till then began to decline and the way was cleared for the systematic and widespread use of birth control. This ushered in a new era in modern demography. Adolphe Landry, the French demographer, called this process "the demographic revolution", a term which was later adopted in demographic literature.

It should be noted that when Landry wrote of the demographic revolution, he was not referring to the violent changes in demographic relations in Europe. He believed that the revolutionary character of the process lay not in its tempo but in its profundity. A new pattern of human reproduction was replacing the old and the change did not come about rapidly but over a longer period of time. According to Landry, it is possible to indicate approximately when the demographic revolution began in the various countries but it is difficult to determine its end, because the new pattern of human reproduction refers to movement and not to equilibrium.[4]

The existing statistical data regarding the natural movements of populations allow us to state that during the first half of the nineteenth century birth rates were increasing in a number of European countries.

A. Boyarsky, the Soviet demographer, points out that while the birth rate in Great Britain was between 31 and 32 per thousand about the year 1840, it had grown to 35 per thousand at the beginning of the seventh decade of that century. In Germany the birth rate amounted to 35 per thousand in the middle of the last century (1850) and at the end of the seventh decade it amounted to about 40 per thousand.

Professor Boyarsky maintains that "the increase in fertility at the beginning and in the middle of the 19th century was a certainty in many countries".[5]

In France the twilight of the high fertility era occurred much earlier; this fact will be considered at length further on.

The "demographic revolution" did not take place in all European countries and did not occur simultaneously.

MAXIMUM BIRTH RATES IN SOME EUROPEAN COUNTRIES IN THE 19TH CENTURY

Country	Years
France	1816–20
Belgium	1836–40
Sweden	1856–60
England and Wales	1871–5
Germany	1876–80
Netherlands	1876–80
Italy	1881–5

Source: BOYARSKY and SHUSHERIN, Demograficheskaya statistika, Moscow, 1951, p. 130.

Many demographers and statisticians have attempted to establish the turning point in various countries, but this has not been easy to do. Boyarsky and Shusherin made a compilation showing the periods of the highest birth rates of eight European countries, which we reproduce in a much condensed form (table on page 344).

According to Boyarsky and Shusherin, France was the first country to limit the number of children. But while the Soviet demographers indicate the years 1816–20 as the date of this event, Whipple and Novoselsky indicate the first decade of the last century. To prove their contention they use the French birth rates of the 19th century:

EVOLUTION OF BIRTH COEFFICIENTS IN FRANCE DURING THE 19TH CENTURY

Period	Number of births per thousand	Index of dynamics
1801–10.	32·9	100
1811–20.	31·8	97
1821–30.	31·0	94
1831–40.	29·0	88
1841–50.	27·4	83
1851–60.	26·3	80
1861–70.	26·3	80
1871–80.	25·4	77
1881–90.	23·9	73
1891–1900.	22·2	67

Sources: (1) WHIPPLE and NOVOSELSKY, *Osnovy demograficheskoy i sanitarnoy statistiki*, p. 486; (2) PAUL MOMBERT, *Bevölkerungslehre*, p. 307.

Landry, in his study, proves that in Paris the number of births per couple decreased from 5·0 in the years 1671–5 to 3·8 in the years 1786–8. We may conclude from these data that in the French capital birth control began very early and there was a noticeable decrease in the birth rates. In addition, Moheau in his study mentions that birth control had already begun to penetrate into rural areas in his time (Moheau, *Recherches et considérations sur la population de la France*, 1778 Edition).[6]

The French demographer, Louis Henry, asserts that France was the first country in which birth control was used in marriages and he mentions the decline in fertility in France as beginning at the end of the 18th century.[7]

346 AGING PROCESS OF POPULATION

The above data enable us to establish the beginning of the demographic revolution in time and place: it began in France at the turn of the 19th century.

From France, the demographic revolution gradually spread to other European countries. It gained a foothold in Belgium, then in Sweden and England.

According to the data of Boyarsky and Shusherin, the turning point in demographic relations in Germany occurred in the seventh decade of the last century. The authors point to the year 1876 as the twilight of the old and the dawn of the new demographic era. Although their thesis agrees with the statistics of births for particular years, nevertheless objections were made to their standpoint years ago by the distinguished German statistician, Johannes Müller. In his opinion, the years 1881–91 marked the change in the birth relations in the German Reich.[8]

In the years preceding the outbreak of the First World War, Germany was ahead of France with respect to the number of births. The arrogant Prussian militarists spoke contemptuously of the French who, they said, were daily losing the battle with Germany. They did not perceive the fact that, with the evolving birth rate in Germany, the birth levels in the two countries would soon be equal.

The German economist, Adolf Wagner, praised the positive aspects of neo-Malthusianism, which was thriving in Germany, and pointed to the advantages of birth control for the family and especially for women. The difficulty lay in the fact that neo-Malthusianism was in conflict with the Church. He wrote the following comment: "Der Gott, der dem Menschen Vernunft gegeben und Fähigkeit, nach dieser zu handeln, der auch dies als Pflicht und Gebot ihm aufgestellt hat, hat ihm doch wahrlich nicht vorgeschrieben, blindlings seinen Trieben zu folgen und die physiologisch mögliche Vermehrbarkeit zu verwirklichen, wohl gar, als ob damit etwas Gott Wohlgefälliges, von ihm Angeordnetes und Befohlenes geschähe" (*Agrar- und Industriestaat*).

The entire argument is opportunistic and has nothing to do with science. More progressive German investigators criticized Wagner's point of view, calling it "neo-Malthusianism in the name of God".[9] It should be remembered, however, that statesmen are not society's only educators. Scientists fulfil this mission too. We cannot disregard, therefore, the approach taken by the chief economist towards the neo-Malthusian doctrines which were spreading over the country. Later on we shall examine the influence of similar dicta on the demographic revolution.

The demographic revolution grew out of economic conditions and it is not fortuitous that it appeared at a time of profound economic changes in Europe, as Professor B. Smulewicz pointed out long ago.[10] The American demographer, Dudley Kirk, believed that the demographic revolution was another link in the chain of economic revolutions in Europe: "Following in the wake of the agricultural and industrial revolutions in Europe there has been a revolution in vital phenomena."[11] For him, the demographic revolution was important, not only from the economic but also from the moral point of view: it created respect for human life, which had been cheap.[12] The demographic revolution had many consequences and among others opened the door to the development of the aging process of European populations.

4. THE DEMOGRAPHIC DEPRESSION

In all countries affected by the demographic revolution there was a long and steadily increasing demographic depression expressed by a systematic decrease in births.

It would be very instructive to examine this phenomenon, not on the basis of materials from countries which had the highest birth rates (these relations are generally well known), but from countries which had average birth rates. For this purpose we have selected countries of southern Europe: Spain and Italy, as representing the mean level of demographic development.

(a) The Demographic Depression in Spain

Demographers are generally little acquainted with modern Spain. In the past they studied the demographic causes and consequences of the decline of the political and economic power of this country. Although Spain's past history overshadows the modern demographic statistics of this country, one must also keep in mind its present events.

The following compilation contains data on the birth rates in Spain for a period of 80 yr (from 1861–1940) from which we can obtain knowledge about Spain at the time when Europe was in the midst of the demographic revolution.

Scales of birth rates elaborated by statisticians are a good means of analysing and estimating them. We may attempt an estimate of the above figures for Spain using a scale prepared by Filippo Vergilii which, though outmoded now, was adequate for its time.[13]

EVOLUTION OF BIRTH RATES IN SPAIN (1861–1940)

Years	Annual birth rate in thousands	Index of dynamics
1861–70.	37·9	100
1881–90.	36·2	95
1891–1900.	34·8	92
1901–10.	34·5	91
1911–20.	29·8	79
1921–30.	29·2	77
1931–5	27·0	71
1936–40.	21·6	57

Source: JEAN DARIC, "Évolution démographique en Espagne", *Population*, Paris, 1956, No. 1, p. 96.

Filippo Vergilii divided birth rates into three groups:
(a) over 40 per thousand—high natality,
(b) from 30 to 40 per thousand—average natality,
(c) under 30 per thousand—low natality.

According to this scale, before the First World War Spain belonged to the countries of average natality which Vergilii termed normal. After the First World War, Spain dropped into the category of states of low natality.

It is surprising that Spain, an agricultural country, reacted so strongly to the demographic revolution. Over a period of 70 yr, the birth rate in Spain decreased from 37·9 per thousand for 1861–70 to 21·6 per thousand. This means a decrease of 43 per cent.

The example of Spain shows that the demographic revolution had an influence on economically underdeveloped countries, too.

(b) The Demographic Depression in Italy

The birth rate decreased in Italy as well, though not to such an extent as in Spain.

The consistent reduction in natality from the beginning to the end of the period tested led to a noticeable decrease. According to the indices of dynamics, the birth rate in Italy decreased by 39 per cent in the course of half a century.

The years 1881–5, the beginning of the period covered by the above table, were considered by Boyarsky as the apex of natality in

EVOLUTION OF BIRTH RATES IN ITALY IN THE YEARS 1881–1939

Years	Per thousand inhabitants	Index of dynamics
1881– 5.	38·0	100
1911–14.	32·0	84
1920–24.	30·1	79
1926.	27·2	72
1928.	26·1	69
1929.	25·1	66
1930–34.	24·5	64
1935– 9.	23·2	61

Source: Demographic Yearbook, 1953, etc.

Italy. The following table certainly corroborates them as the period of the highest birth rates in Italy:[14]

1872–5	. . . .	36·8
1876–80	. . . .	36·9
1881–5	. . . .	38·0
1886–90	. . . .	37·5
1891–5	. . . .	36·0

It should be noted, however, that by examining fertility coefficients and not birth rates, we obtain an altogether different picture and another turning point marking the wake of the demographic revolution in Italy.

We therefore include the extremely interesting table on page 350 prepared by an Italian demographer, Pierpaolo Luzzatto-Fegiz, which indicates three kinds of marital fertility rates: (1) average; (2) maximum; (3) minimum.

In the light of these data, the fertility of Italian women decreased earlier than is indicated in the compilation of birth rates: the period of highest fertility falls within the years 1866–75 or even earlier. It is quite possible that in this respect there was some similarity between the Italian and Spanish relations.

When Italy was under fascist rule, a widespread birth campaign was launched in the country. As Sauvy said, "dictators desire large populations".[15] Despite the great efforts of the government, this campaign failed.

Dr Ernst Kahn, a German journalist of the pre-Hitler era, explained the matter in the following way. The first symptoms of a fertility decline and particularly of the spread of "birth control" in big towns

FERTILITY OF ITALIAN WOMEN IN THE YEARS 1866–1930
(number of live births in marriages per 1000 married women from 15 to 45 yr old)

Years	Annual average	Fertility			
		Maximum		Minimum	
		rate	province	rate	province
1866–75. . . .	290	314	Puglie	264	Lazio
1876–85. . . .	284	308	Puglie	241	Lazio
1886–95. . . .	277	306	Puglie	230	Lazio
1896–1905. . .	271	313	Venezia Euganea	223	Lazio
1906–15. . . .	263	314	Venezia Euganea	209	Liguria
1921–5	248	311	Campania	160	Liguria
1930. . . .	212	293	Sardenia	131	Liguria

Source: PIERPAOLO LUZZATTO-FEGIZ, *Statistica demografica ed economica*, Turin, 1940, p. 66.

forced Mussolini, at the beginning of his rule, to fight back with all his might against a movement which could one day render absurd his imperialistic aims. Mussolini and his fascist state needed soldiers, just as German emperors had needed them in the past. How could he demand an enlargement of his frontiers without the argument of Italy's overpopulation "a country without land". Consequently, Mussolini gave orders to use all means to control the movement: to impede the flight from the country, primarily by prohibiting the concentration of industry in large towns, to levy special taxes on bachelors and award prizes to large families.

"Es scheint nun, als ob die Macht des italienischen Diktators vor dem Schlafzimmer ein Ende findet," concluded Kahn.[16] Hence in this duel between Malthus and Mussolini, the latter's statistics showed one failure after another. Kahn's clever comment was that the threshold of the conjugal bedroom marked the end of the Italian dictator's power.

Seriously speaking, we know that the real causes of this failure were indeed the strong and lasting effects of the demographic revolution in Italy.

(c) The Bottom of the Demographic Depression

In many European countries and in some countries outside Europe (the United States, Australia, New Zealand) the decline in births was quite apparent: birth rates dropped below 20 and even 15 per thousand.

Here are some record low birth rates taken from the Demographic Yearbook of the United Nations for 1954:

(a) during the quinquennial period 1925-9:

1. Sweden . . . . 16·3
2. England and Wales. . . . . 17·1
3. Switzerland . . . . 17·8
4. Denmark . . . . 17·9
5. Austria . . . . 18·4

(b) during the quinquennial period 1930-34:

1. Sweden . . . . 14·4
2. Austria . . . . 15·1
3. England and Wales. . . . . 15·3
4. Norway . . . . 15·7
5. Germany . . . . 16·3

(c) during the quinquennial period 1935-9:

1. Sweden . . . . 14·5
2. Austria . . . . 14·7
3. England and Wales. . . . . 14·9
4. Norway . . . . 15·0
5. France . . . . 15·1

The above rates express the bottom of the demographic depression which for some decades governed the population policy of northern and western Europe.

During the last three five-year interwar periods, Sweden was repeatedly distinguished by its lowest birth rates. Her nearest competitor was Austria, then England and Wales. If we add Switzerland, Denmark, Norway, Germany and France, we have all the countries with the greatest decline in birth rates.

According to the above compilation, Sweden had the lowest birth rates within the years 1930–1934, namely 14·4 per thousand.[17]

An identical level of birth rates was noted in England—14·4 per thousand in 1933. The English author, Eva M. Hubback, calls it a record low level. She also writes that, in 1931, with 4,918,000 married women under 45, the number of newborn children was 25 per cent lower than in 1871 when the number of married women under 45 was only 2,500,000.[18] Mrs Hubback wrote reasonably: "One of the most important effects of any fall in the birth rate is the change in the age distribution of the population" (Hubback, *op. cit.* p. 25–26).

Moreover, this is the main source of the population's aging process.

5. ZONES OF HIGH FERTILITY

Speaking of the demographic revolution, one should remember its limited geographical extent and the fact that in many countries, outside Europe as a rule, birth rates remained high and even very high for a long time. Due to the stabilization of births in some countries and its systematic decline in others, on the demographic map of the world there appeared spots of high and low reproduction. They were called zones of high and low fertility.[19]

We shall now examine countries not affected or not much affected by the demographic revolution, namely zones of high fertility.

(a) Zones of High Fertility in Europe

As we have already mentioned, the scale of birth rates prepared half a century ago by the Italian demographer, Filippo Vergilii, is inadequate for measuring and estimating the radically different modern conditions of human reproduction. However for old and irretrievable reproduction conditions it is better to use old measures. At present we shall use the Vergilii scale, according to which high birth rates are those over 40 per thousand.

Before the First World War three countries in Europe had such high birth rates: Russia, Romania and Bulgaria.

THE HIGHEST BIRTH RATES IN EUROPE BEFORE THE FIRST WORLD WAR

Country	Years	Per thousands
Russia	1906–1909	45·6
Romania	1912–13	43·1
Bulgaria	1910–11	41·0

Source: W. Woytinsky, Die Welt in Zahlen, Vol. I, Berlin, 1925, p. 60.

Since at that time Russia had the highest birth rate, it would be instructive to learn about Russian demographic relations.

In 1906–1909 the birth rate in Russia was 45·6 per thousand. This was the mean coefficient for all the provinces of this vast country. In some large Russian provinces, then called "gubernias", the birth rates exceeded the average.

In the years 1896–7 the following Russian provinces had the highest birth rates:

Samara   — 61·4⁰/₀₀
Voronezh — 60·8⁰/₀₀
Orenburg — 59·6⁰/₀₀
Perm   — 56·5⁰/₀₀
Symbirsk — 55·4⁰/₀₀

Stefan Szulc added the following comment to the above figures: "Very high birth rates in the European part of Russia and in some provinces... were only partly due to high fertility; even more significant was the fact of almost universal and very early marriages."[20]

We shall now examine the highest birth rates in Russia (by provinces) during the period before the outbreak of the First World War.

MAXIMUM BIRTH RATES IN RUSSIA IN THE YEARS 1909–1911

Year	Maximum birth rate	Province of
1909	59·9	Orenburg
1910	59·6	Orenburg
1911	57·5	Orenburg

Source: *Allg. Stat. Arch.*, Vol. 10, 1916/1917, p. 728.

During these three years the province of Orenburg consistently had the highest birth rate; the province of Perm had 59·3 per thousand in 1910 and the province of Samara 57·2 per thousand in 1911.

Hence, according to provincial statistics, up to the outbreak of the First World War the maximum birth rates in Russia remained on a very high level (about 60 per thousand).

After the First World War the picture changed. Romania and Bulgaria, which formerly had high birth rates, passed to the next group of medium rates. Only in the U.S.S.R.—and only for some time—did the birth rates remain high (over 40 per thousand).

According to the compilation below, Soviet statistics registered the following figures in the second decade of this century.

BIRTH RATES IN THE U.S.S.R. AND IN THE R.S.F.S.R. (1924–7)

Territory	Years	Birth rates (per thousand)
Ukrainian S.S.R.	1927	43·7
Russian S.F.S.R.	1924–7	41·7

Sources: (1) BENOY KUMAR SARKAR, *op. cit.*, p. 543 and (2) S. FOGELSON, *Ruch naturalny ludności w Polsce* (*The Natural Movement of the Population of Poland*), Warsaw, 1936, p. 85.

It appears that these were the last years of high rates; according to the U.S.S.R. Population Census of January 17, 1939, there was a decline in births. We quote the interesting analysis of this census made by Knud Stowman, the demographer of the World Health Organization: the 1939 Census shows the following age distribution of the population:

up to 7 yr — 18·9%
8-11 — 9·7%
12-14 — 7·9%

Within the age groups it was possible to find, on the basis of these figures, the absolute figures for each year:

within the first 8 yr 3,926,000
  ,,   the next 4 yr 4,102,000
  ,,   the next 3 yr 4,445,000

Thus the absolute figures change in the opposite direction from the one that might be expected; the younger the age group the smaller its number. According to Stowman, this is the result of the decline in births going on there for years.[21] In his opinion, the birth rate in the U.S.S.R. shortly before the outbreak of the Second World War was 26–27 per thousand.

It is worth while observing the recently published Soviet birth rates of recent years.

BIRTH RATES IN THE U.S.S.R. IN THE YEARS 1950–55

Year	Live births per 1000 inhabitants
1950.	26·5
1954.	26·5
1955.	26·6

Source: *Narodnoye Khozyaystvo S.S.S.R.*, C.U.S. Moscow, 1956.

The above rates seem to prove Stowman's assertion; by extrapolation of this row one obtains less than 30 per thousand.

Hence, beginning with the thirties, Vergilii's high rates disappeared from European statistics.[22]

There remained, of course, certain places in Europe where fertility was still high according to Vergilii—today we would call it very high. However, examples of these high rates could be found only in regional statistics but not in nation-wide statistics.

Even nowadays one could probably find cases of demographic primitivism.

(b) The World's Highest Birth Rates

Let us open one of the volumes of the *Demographic Yearbook* of the United Nations (1953) and mark the highest birth rates of the interwar periods: 1925–9, 1930–34 and 1935–9. It is understood from our previous remarks that European countries do not appear among these, nor do any economically developed societies.

THE WORLD'S HIGHEST BIRTH RATES IN THE YEARS 1925–1939 ACCORDING TO U.N. STATISTICAL DATA

Territory	Number of births annually per 1000 inhabitants		
	1925–9	1930–34	1935–9
Guatemala	58·1	51·1	47·2
Palestine (Moslem pop.)	53·0	50·4	49·7
Ecuador	–	–	48·0
Mauritius, Rodrigues	–	43·5	45·1
Costa Rica	46·2	44·6	44·5
Taiwan (Formosa)	42·7	44·7	44·0
N. Zealand (Maoris)	–	–	43·9
Mexico	33·3	44·5	43·5
El Salvador	44·7	43·3	42·7
Greenland	43·6	45.9	42·7
Egypt	43·9	43·7	42·8

Source: Demographic Yearbook, 1953, U.N., pp. 132–141.

From the above data it follows that Guatemala and the Moslem part of Palestine had the highest birth rates in the period between the world wars (50 to almost 60 per thousand).

And still it is doubtful whether these were the maximum rates for two reasons:

(1) only countries which then kept regular statistics concerning the population's natural movement are included in this compilation; one may ask whether the birth rates were not higher in those countries which did not keep regular statistics;

(2) there are quite important gaps in the statistical materials which served as a basis for the above calculations; in this case the reproduction level shown would be less than the true situation.

To find the underestimated numbers and consequently the underestimated birth rates it will be helpful to use the information concerning birth registrations in India and in Algeria.

**OFFICIAL AND ESTIMATED BIRTH RATES IN INDIA
IN THE YEARS 1891–1951**

Years	Birth rate	
	official	estimated
1891–1901.	34	46
1901–1911.	37	48
1911–1921.	37	49
1921–1931.	33	46
1931–1941.	34	45
1941–1951.	27	40–43

Source: Population, Paris, 1957, No. 4, p. 662.

The above compilation not only weakens but also annuls the official birth statistics of India. What good are statistical data which, according to the scale, show average birth rates and even low rates in India for the last 60 yr, while in reality, according to the estimated data, the birth rates in India were high all the time?[23]

Smaller than for India but nevertheless substantial underestimations of births are shown by the statistical data of Algeria. In the light of the data published in the *Demographic Yearbook* of the United Nations for 1954, the birth calculated for the Moslem population of Algeria amounted to:

$$1950 . . . . 39 \cdot 5^0/_{00}$$
$$1951 . . . . 40 \cdot 9^0/_{00}$$
$$1952 . . . . 41 \cdot 9^0/_{00}$$

Thus the official birth rate in Algeria amounted to about 40 per thousand. Meanwhile we learn from the article written by Léon Tabah on the population of Algeria that in reality the birth rate was about 46 per thousand ("corrigé, pour tenir compte du sous-enregistrement").[24] Hence, the real rate was 15 per cent higher than the official rate.

There is no reason to suppose that the above events were exceptional, it is more likely that things like that happened, if not in all then in most economically and culturally underdeveloped countries (sometimes with regard to one part of the population).[25] One may conclude, therefore, that the figures published in the *Demographic Yearbook* of the United Nations may also require more or less correction.

In the next table we cite from the data published by the United Nations some record high birth rates of recent years.

WORLD MAXIMUM BIRTH RATES (ABOUT 1950)

Country	Year	Births per thousand
Brit. Borneo, Brunei	1951	58·7
Costa Rica	1952	54·8
Guatemala	1951	52·4
Taiwan (Formosa)	1951	49·9
Mauritius	1950	49·7
El Salvador	1951	48·8
Singapore	1952	47·5
Réunion	1952	46·9
Ecuador	1947	46·7
Mexico	1947	46·1
Western Samoa	1951	45·9
Algeria (Moslem pop.)	1947	45·0

Source: Demographic Yearbook, 1953, United Nations, pp. 132–141.

Such high birth rates reveal the complete lack (or insufficient use) of means of contraception. In other words, we are dealing here with the phenomenon of natural fertility.[26]

According to the above table the highest birth rate was 60 per thousand; the same was shown by examination of the Russian rates. And yet they were not the highest birth rates, for the Soviet hygienist, Professor Batkis, mentioned a record high birth rate in the Tchkalov region of the U.S.S.R., where in 1935 the birth rate was 62·8 per thousand.[27]

In Mackenroth's textbook on demography we find data concerning the Arab peninsula where the birth rate amounts to over 60 per thousand.[28]

Moreover, the French investigator, Henri Bunle, mentions the birth rate of 69·2 per thousand in 1929 on the Togo territory among the native population of Kanton Lama-Kara.[29] So far as the present author knows, it is the highest birth rate ever encountered.

Very interesting are the computations prepared at the end of the last century by the German demographer, von Fircks. According to his calculations the birth rate could, in principle, reach the level of 60–70 per thousand. "Dieser Betrag wird nirgends erreicht"—concludes the author who, throughout his life, never encountered birth rates exceeding 55 per thousand.[30] Today we are much better off, having at our disposal a great deal of factual material. On the basis of this material we are in a position to prove the correctness of the computation prepared then by the German demographer.

(c) The Increase in Births in Underdeveloped Countries and Industrialization

The assertion that industrialization is a factor increasing the birth level is not a new one. Demographers turn again to this idea, since some countries in the process of becoming industrialized, experience increased birth rates.

We may cite Mexico where in 1938–9 there were 44·1 births per 1000 inhabitants annually and, in 1954, 45·8 per thousand. The same thing happened in the Malay Federation, the Belgian Congo, South Africa and South-Western Africa, in Honduras and in Nicaragua where, after the war, in 1947–9, the birth rate increased by 7 per cent, as compared with the period before the war 1934–5, according to Hertzler.[31]

This whole question—as we have mentioned above—is not entirely clear; we do not know whether there was a real increase in births or whether the registration of births was more effective. Of course, both factors may have been felt simultaneously.

Hertzler, who is very much interested in the demographic relations of underdeveloped countries, accepts this increase in births as authentic. In his opinion, the increase in births and decrease in deaths are the results of the industrialization of underdeveloped countries in recent years.[32]

This may be true. But even in this case, it cannot last for very long. Historical experience shows an opposite process: economic modernization, industrialization, urbanization, etc., are factors acting in favour of a decline in births in the long run; they likewise act in favour of the population's aging process.

6. A NEW TREND IN HUMAN REPRODUCTION. THE PROCESS OF INCREASING BIRTHS

At the end of the third decade of this century a new turn appeared in the general birth trend in many countries: the diminishing trend was replaced by a rising one.

This turn took place at the least expected moment. Let us recall the rapidly decreasing birth rates in many European countries during the First World War. The lean war years did not foretell any improvement in this respect.

The French demographer, M. Huber, maintained as early as 1939 that in twenty, twenty-five and thirty years after the First World War those born during the war years would decide the number of marriages and births: in the future there would be a new decline in births as a result of the decrease in births during the war.[33]

But this forecast did not conform to the facts; it was already untrue at the time it was said. Just when the smaller group of women born during the war began to reach the age of fertility—20 yr and over—and a noticeable decrease in births was expected, an opposite trend appeared: in some countries the birth rates began to increase instead of decreasing.

The new general trend in births manifested itself in countries of low fertility; the number of births increased in countries which formerly had low birth rates.

We shall best illustrate this turn with the table prepared by Professor Wilhelm Bickel on page 360.

In the year 1936, which opens the period examined above, the birth rates in the 15 countries lay between 14·2 per thousand (Sweden) and 22·4 per thousand (Italy).

In 1937 the values were higher: between 14·4 per thousand in Sweden and 22·9 per thousand in Italy. It should be noted that these changes apply to the same countries.

In 1938 the range was between 14·6 per thousand in France and 23·7 per thousand in Italy; this time France, not Sweden, had the lowest birth rate. With a birth rate of 14·9 per thousand Sweden ceased to be the country of lowest birth rate.

In 1939 the spread between the extreme values showed no noticeable changes: the minimum birth rate was again 14·6 per thousand in France and the maximum birth rate decreased to 23·5 per thousand in Italy. Sweden was no longer second but fourth from the end, leaving behind France, England and Wales, and Switzerland.

Finally in 1942 the lowest birth rate was only 13·1 per thousand in Belgium and the highest was 23·4 per thousand in Canada. It is understandable that a country which suffered from the war and Nazi occupation had the lowest birth rate and the one which was far away from war action had the highest. Here we notice the role of war as a factor affecting demographic phenomena.

360   AGING PROCESS OF POPULATION

BIRTH RATES IN COUNTRIES OF LOW FERTILITY IN THE YEARS
1936–9 AND 1942

Country	Year				
	1936	1937	1938	1939	1942
(a) Births per 1000 inhabitants yearly					
England and Wales	14·8	14·9	15·1	14·8	15·6
Belgium	15·2	15·3	15·8	15·3	13·1
Denmark	17·8	18·0	18·1	17·8	20·4
Finland	19·1	19·9	20·9	21·1	16·5
France	15·0	14·7	14·6	14·6	14·5
Netherlands	20·2	19·8	20·5	20·6	21·0
Germany	19·0	18·8	19·6	20·4	14·9
Norway	14·6	15·1	15·6	15·9	. . .
Switzerland	15·6	14·9	15·2	15·2	18·4
Sweden	14·2	14·4	14·9	15·4	17·7
Italy	22·4	22·9	23·7	23·5	20·2
Australia	17·1	17·4	17·5	17·7	19·1
Canada	20·0	19·8	20·5	20·3	23·4
New Zealand	18·1	18·9	19·3	20·2	23·1
U.S.A.	16·7	17·1	17·6	17·3	20·9
(b) Increase (+) or decrease (−) compared to 1936					
England and Wales	.	+0·1	+0·3	—	+0·8
Belgium	.	+0·1	+0·6	+0·1	−2·1
Denmark	.	+0·2	+0·3	—	+2·6
Finland	.	+0·8	+1·8	+2·0	−2·6
France	.	−0·3	−0·4	−0·4	−0·5
Netherlands	.	−0·4	+0·3	+0·4	+0·8
Germany	.	−0·2	+0·6	+1·4	−4·1
Norway	.	+0·5	+1·0	+1·3	. . .
Switzerland	.	−0·7	−0·4	−0·4	+2·8
Sweden	.	+0·2	+0·7	+1·2	+3·5
Italy	.	+0·5	+1·3	+1·1	−2·2
Australia	.	+0·3	+0·4	+0·6	+2·0
Canada	.	−0·2	+0·5	+0·3	+3·4
New Zealand	.	+0·8	+1·2	+2·1	+5·0
U.S.A.	.	+0·4	+0·9	+0·6	+4·2

Sources: (a) WILHELM BICKEL, *Bevölkerungsgeschichte und Bevölkerungspolitik der Schweiz seit dem Ausgang des Mittelalters*, Büchergilde Gutenberg, Zürich, 1947, p. 228; (b) the author's calculations.

The above review of minimum and maximum birth rates leaves no doubt as to the symptoms of demographic revival in countries belonging to the zones of low fertility in the years 1936–9.

This new phase of development in birth relations in the given group of countries can also be proved by studying the second part of the above compilation, figures illustrating the increase or decrease in the birth rates as compared to the year 1936.

In 1937, 10 out of the 15 countries represented in the above compilation showed an increase in the level of births in comparison with the previous year. The level decreased in the remaining five countries, including France and Germany. They are the European countries which had a special interest in demographic problems. It might seem that the change in the general trend of births, i.e., the increase of births, would have been noticed earlier in countries interested in demographic investigations, but it happened otherwise.

In the year 1938 the number of countries with a growing birth rate, compared to 1936, increased to thirteen. Thus only in two countries contained in our compilation did the new demographic trend fail to appear, namely, in France and Switzerland. The French demographers had no reason to point to a turn in birth relations since the experience of their own country did not prove it.

In 1939 the situation remained the same; two countries out of the fifteen continued to have a decreased birth level in comparison with the year 1936: again France and Switzerland. Moreover, in England and Wales and in Denmark—after a temporary increase in the years 1937 and 1938—the birth rates decreased again to the 1936 level.

As we see, some circumstances showed a turn in birth relations in countries of low fertility; others showed the opposite tendency.

We are not considering the year 1942, for birth rates during this year were to a great extent shaped by the war. The figures quoted by us clearly indicate the decrease in birth rates below the 1936 level in countries which suffered from the war. As examples we may quote Germany, Belgium, Finland and Italy. Where the war did not influence everyday life, birth rates increased beyond the 1936 level, in some cases even quite obviously: in Sweden, Canada, New Zealand and the U.S.A.

Under normal conditions, i.e., in peace time, in countries of low fertility, the evolution of births was about the same (though in some countries the turn in demographic relations took place earlier and in some later). However, during the Second World War this uniform birth development disappeared: in some countries there was a considerable decline in births and in others a considerable increase.

What factors caused an increase in birth rates in some countries and a decrease in other countries? Our reply is as follows:

(1) the decrease in births in some countries during the Second World War was due to the destructive influence of the war;

(2) the increase in births at that time in some countries was a consequence of a new reproduction trend called by the French: "la reprise des naissances."

In other words, in some countries the reproduction trend was shaped by war conditions, while in other countries the generally increasing trend, i.e. the desire to have large families, remained. One can explain it this way: the new increasing birth trend, which began in the middle of the third decade, continued in countries which did not suffer from the cataclysm of war (of course, all countries were somewhat influenced by the war, even neutral countries); on the other hand, in countries which suffered more from the war the increasing reproduction trend was overcome by the strong effects of the decreasing trend caused by the war which diminished the desire to bring up children.

The French demographer, Louis Chevalier, used a different method than Bickel. He also compared the birth rates of the war years with similar rates in the pre-war period. But primarily he considered only countries where the birth rates increased, and secondly, he compared the results of 1944 with those of 1939. These differences disclosed something new which merits our attention.

We cite this compilation with some changes:

INCREASE IN THE NUMBER OF BIRTHS DURING THE SECOND WORLD WAR

Country	Births in thousands		Increase (%)
	1939	1944	
Sweden	97	133	37
Switzerland	64	86	34
Denmark	68	90	32
Canada	229	284	24
Australia	123	153	24
U.S.A.	2265	2794	23
Norway	47	57	21
England	731	872	19
New Zealand	29	34	17
Czechoslovakia	303	347	14
France	614	636	4

Source: LOUIS CHEVALIER, Démographie Générale, Dalloz, Paris, 1951, p. 205.

The above figures are of great importance. In some countries—in spite of the war—the number of births in 1944 exceded that of 1939. This best proves the changes which occurred in the birth relations.

Although this interpretation seems to be right, it should be noted that this compilation lacks some of the countries where an increase in the number of births should also have been expected. Such countries as Germany and Belgium and others of low fertility are missing. This fact proves that in spite of the turn which occurred in the general birth trend, here and there the war cataclysm most strongly affected it.

Thus we come to the same conclusions we drew previously from Bickel's compilation.

We have noticed the apparent division between countries of low and of high fertility. It would be interesting, therefore, to mention the assertion of the demographer of the World Health Organization, Knud Stowman, already quoted. According to him, a levelling process is now operating between the zones of low and high fertility; the number of births is increasing in the zones of low fertility and decreasing in the zones of high fertility.

7. EVOLUTION OF BIRTHS ON POLISH TERRITORIES

At the end of the 18th century the Polish State ceased to exist and Polish territories were absorbed by three invaders. Data concerning the reproduction of the Polish population, after annexation and up to the revival of the Polish State in 1918, may be found in the statistics of Russia, Germany and Austria-Hungary.

The German demographer, von Fircks, provides information about the birth level of the Polish population in the 19th century. It concerns only the territories annexed by Prussia and Austria.

(1) It was observed that in Prussia in the years 1862 to 1874 the Polish population had the highest birth rates: in the province Wielkopolska (Great Poland) the birth rate was 40–51 per thousand, in Mazury 48–50 per thousand, and in Silesia to 46–47 per thousand;

(2) also in Austria the highest birth rates were noticed in the areas inhabited by Poles; in Galicia, within the years 1861–90, the mean birth rate was 44·4 per thousand.

As we see, out of 16 regions Galicia had the highest birth rate (over 40 per thousand).

The investigations made by A. Krzyżanowski and K. Kumaniecki,[34] prove that for seven decades, from 1831–1900, the birth rate in Galicia

BIRTHS IN GALICIA IN THE YEARS 1881–90
(Compared with those of the other territories then part of Austria)

Province	Thousands	Province	Thousands
Galicia	44·2	Lower Austria	34·9
Dalmatia	38·4	Carinthia	32·0
Moravia	37·7	Upper Austria	30·8
Austrian Silesia	37·6	Styria	30·4
Bohemia	37·1	Salzburg	29·7
Kraine	36·0	Tyrol	29·0

Source: ARTHUR VON FIRCKS, Bevölkerungslehre und Bevölkerungspolitik, Leipzig, 1898, p. 151.

was almost stable: it remained within the limits of 43 to 46 per thousand.

Less accurate are the data concerning territories occupied by Russia; we have therefore had to resort to estimates. According to these estimates, the birth level in the Kingdom of Poland was then almost the same as in Galicia: from 43 to 46 or 47 per thousand.

In the last years of the 19th century (1896–1900), according to Stefan Szulc, the birth rates in the Polish territories were:

in the territory annexed by Prussia 44·4$^0/_{00}$
in the territory annexed by Austria 44·2$^0/_{00}$
in the territory annexed by Russia 43·0$^0/_{00}$
in general 43·5$^0/_{00}$

It should be noticed that at the turn of the century the birth rates of the three annexed Polish territories were very high and did not deviate much from the level which demographers used to call "natural fertility", a phenomenon belonging to the old and vanishing demographic era.

At the beginning of the 20th century a new picture of demographic relations appeared in these areas: the former very high reproduction level became a phenomenon of the irretrievable past.

During the First World War there was a rapid decrease in births in these territories. In order not to repeat ourselves, we shall recall only the following:

(1) in the territory annexed by Prussia the number of births, which declined from year to year, decreased during the last year of the war by 47 per cent;

(2) in the territory annexed by Russia the highest birth decline was noticed in 1917 when the number of births decreased by 37 per cent.

After the war, the limitation of births became more general, due to the reminiscence of the war horrors and to the experience of the post-war period. Destroyed by the war and by the occupant's economic degradation, Poland was confronted with inflation, speculation, high prices and unemployment in towns and villages.

The propaganda for planned parenthood also helped. Professor Adam Krzyżanowski, the economist of the city of Cracow, who for a long time had investigated demographic problems, favoured reasonable birth control. He condemned immoderate reproduction and considered it a national weakness.

Professor Krzyżanowski warned that without sensible limitation of births, a lasting improvement would be impossible. He formulated his credo as follows: "In my opinion, reasonable limitation of births would be salutary from the economic point of view, and also for moral, political and military reasons. I do not know why in this case alone lack of moderation should be considered a virtue."[35]

In the third decade of this century the birth rate in Poland decreased to below 30 per thousand and on the eve of the Second World War it was already less than 25 per thousand:

$$1936 . . . . 26 \cdot 4^0/_{00}$$
$$1937 . . . . 25 \cdot 0^0/_{00}$$
$$1938 . . . . 24 \cdot 6^0/_{00}$$

Hence, at the time when the zones of low fertility faced a general upturn in births, in Poland the birth rate continued to decline. A general upturn in births in our country was then out of the question.

Later came years of horrible anguish and misery caused by the war and criminal Nazi occupation. We have no birth statistics for this period (1939–44). However, in all probability under the occupation the birth rate decreased to 15–16 per thousand.

After the war, under new social conditions, there was a considerable revival of births in the liberated country. This is best illustrated by the table on page 366.

According to the above compilation:

(1) the annual number of births in Poland was between 666,000 and 793,000;

(2) until recently the birth rate in Poland was very high; of the European countries only Yugoslavia could compete with Poland in this respect (Yugoslav birth rates: 1950: 30·3 per thousand; 1951: 27·1 per thousand; 1952: 29·8 per thousand; 1953: 28·3 per thousand);[36]

NUMBER OF BIRTHS IN POLAND IN THE YEARS 1950-1960

Year	Number of births in thousands	Birth rate per thousand
1950.	763·1	30·7
1951.	783·6	31·0
1952.	779·0	30·2
1953.	779·0	29·7
1954.	778·1	29·1
1955.	793·8	29·1
1956.	779·8	28·1
1957.	782·3	27·6
1958.	755·5	26·3
1959.	722·9	24·7
1960.	665·8	22·4

Sources: Rocznik Statystyczny, 1961 (Statistical Yearbook, 1961), Warsaw, 1961, p. 30.

(3) the peak of the post-war revival of births in Poland was in 1951 when the birth rate amounted to 31 per thousand;

(4) from that time on the birth rate in Poland has declined systematically; everything indicates the revival of the pre-war decreasing birth trend.

Although the evolution of reproduction relations followed the same direction as in western Europe (both here and there, a lasting decrease), there are nevertheless some quite important differences, namely:

(a) in the western countries the demographic revolution began earlier than in Poland;

(b) before the demographic revolution, the maximum number of births in the western countries was lower than in Poland.

These are facts of great importance when comparing Poland with the western countries with regard to the evolution of births; these facts have determined the advance of the population aging process.

REFERENCES

1. *A Study of War* made at the University of Chicago and published under the editorship of Professor QUINCEY WRIGHT (University of Chicago Press, 1942) contains a list of 132 wars within the years 1750–1941. From 1850–1941, Great Britain was in thirteen wars, France nine and the United States six (ELGIN F. HUNT, *Social Science. An Introduction to the Study of Society,* Macmillan, New York, 1957, p. 695).

2. A U.N. demographer wrote a few years ago: "It is a common misconception that the ageing of populations is, or has been chiefly, if not entirely, the result of declines in mortality. ... this view is false. ... Birth rates, and not death rates, are the major determining factor of population structure" ("The Cause of the Ageing of Populations: Declining Mortality or Declining Fertility?" *Population Bulletin of the United Nations*, No. 4, December, 1954, New York, p. 30).

3. "The coincidence of declining fertility and aging and the stability of age structure in countries with high fertility suggest that fertility movements have played a fundamental part in the development of this aging. Changes in mortality appear to have played only a secondary part" (*The Aging of Populations and Its Economic and Social Implications*, United Nations, New York, 1956, p. 1).

4. "Tout changement de régime, dans le domaine démographique comme ailleurs, peut être regardé comme constituant une révolution. La soudaineté du changement n'est pas nécessaire. La révolution qui nous occupe a commencé, pour les différents pays déjà affectés par elle, non pas sans doute tel ou tel jour, mais cependant à des époques que l'ont peut indiquer, au vu des statistiques, avec une précision très suffisante. Pour ce qui est de dire, par rapport à chaque pays, quand elle s'est trouvée, ou quand elle se trouvera accomplie, c'est une question qui ne comporte que des réponses arbitraires, parce que le régime nouveau se définit comme un régime non d'équilibre, mais de mouvement" (A. LANDRY, *La Révolution Démographique, Études et Essais sur les Problèmes de la Population*, Paris, 1934, p. 54–5).

5. A. BOYARSKY, *Kurs demographicheskoy statistiki*, Gosplanizdat, Moscow, 1945, p. 35.

6. A. LANDRY, *La Révolution Démographique*, p. 33.

7. L. HENRY, *Population*, Paris, 1954, No. 2, p. 198.

8. J. MÜLLER, "Grundriss der deutschen Statistik", III. Teil, *Deutsche Bevölkerungsstatistik*, Jena 1926, p. 146–7.

9. P. MOMBERT, *Bevölkerungslehre*, Jena 1929, p. 326.

10. B. SMULEWICZ, "Nekotorye voprosy vosproyzvodstva naselenia w zarubeshnych stranach," *Mirovoe khoziaystvo i mirovaya politika*, 1947, No. 3, p. 54.

11. D. KIRK, *Europe's Population in the Interwar Years*, League of Nations, 1946, p. 36.

12. "Europe entered the modern era with what might be called the primitive phase of population development. Life was cheap. Death rates were fantastically high by modern standards. The scourges symbolized by the Four Horsemen of the Apocalypse—famine, pestilence, want and war—were accepted as the inevitable destroyers of human life. On the other hand, life was as carelessly created as it was destroyed. Birth rates, like death rates, were high.... By modern standards human reproduction... was inefficient, wasteful and inhumane" (D. KIRK, *op. cit.*, p. 36).

13. F. VERGILII, *Statistica*, 11th edition, Milan, 1921, p. 182.

14. L. LIVI, *Nozioni di Statistica e Politica Demografica*, Padua, 1938, p. 74.

15. "Quant aux dictatures fasciste, hitlérienne, japonaise, elles ont cherché naturellement, une forte population, car le concept de puissance a primé le concept économique" (A. SAUVY, *Théorie générale de la Population*, Vol. I, *Économie et Population*, 2-ème Édition Revue, Presses Universitaires de France, Paris, 1956, p. 177).

16. E. KAHN, *Der internationale Geburtenstreik*, Frankfurt am Main, 1930, pp. 49–50.

17. In 1936 the birth rate decreased to 14·2 per thousand.

18. E. M. HUBBACK, *The Population of Britain*, Pelican Books, London and Aylesbury, 1947, p. 21.

19. The picture of the world's demographic relations would be clearer, if besides countries representing high and low fertility, we also examined countries representing average fertility.

20. S. Szulc, *Ruch naturalny ludności w Polsce w latach 1895–1935* (*The Natural Movement of the Population in Poland in 1895–1935*), GUS, Warsaw, 1936, p. 58.

21. K. Stowman, "Tendances récentes de la natalité", *Rapport Épidémiologique et Démographique*, Organisation Mondiale de la Santé, Geneva, 1947, No. 3, p. 38.

22. In Europe in the thirties it was not easy to find a mean birth rate. In 1935–9 only Romania and Albania represented the mean birth level. Moreover, the Romanian rate (30·2 per thousand) was on the border of low birth rates and the Albanian was somewhat higher (32·4 per thousand in 1936–9).

23. "Les résultats de l'état civil ne présentent qu'un intérêt limité, car une partie des décès et des naissances n'est pas enregistrée. D'autre part, dans l'Inde britannique les états princiers, liés à la couronne par traité, disposaient d'une vaste autonomie administrative et ne possédaient pas tous un service de l'état-civil, comme les provinces administrées par les Anglais. Ces lacunes obligent à recourir à des estimations" (E. Gilbert, "La population de l'Inde, perspectives démographiques et alimentaires,") *Population*, Paris, 1957, No. 4, p. 662.

24. L. Tabah, "La population algérienne", *Population*, Paris, 1956, No. 3, p. 432.

25. In 1957, at the Session of the International Statistical Institute in Stockholm, J. Bourgeois-Pichat estimated the gaps in birth registration in recent times (1939–51) in Columbia as 30 per cent and death registrations as even higher: 38·6 per cent.

26. "Le taux de 45 per thousand semble correspondre à peu près à la fécondité naturelle, sans restrictions volontaires" (A. Sauvy, *La Population, ses Lois, ses Équilibres*, Presses Universitaires de France, Paris, 1948, p. 74).

27. G. Batkis, *Socyalnaya gygena*, pp. 72–73.

28. G. Mackenroth, *Bevölkerungslehre, Theorie, Soziologie und Statistik der Bevölkerung*, 1953, p. 201.

29. H. Bunle, "Note sur la démographie de la population indigène au Togo", *Actes du Congrès International des Études sur la Population*, Vol. 6, Rome, 1934, p. 253.

30. A. von Fircks, *Bevölkerungslehre und Bevölkerungspolitik*, Leipzig, 1898, p. 151.

31. J. O. Hertzler, *The Crisis in World Population. A Sociological Examination with Special Reference to the Under-developed Areas*, University of Nebraska Press, Lincoln, 1956, pp. 46–7.

32. "The effects of modernization on the birth rate come about slowly, causing changes in the birth rate to lag behind those of the death rate. The first tendency of the birth rate is often slightly upward. ...This is probably due to some easing of the food supply, some improvement in general living conditions, and a somewhat improved vitality making for greater likelihood of conception and live births" (J. O. Hertzler, *op. cit.* pp. 46–7).

33. M. Huber, *Cours de démographie et de statistique sanitaire*, 6 fasc., Publication de l'Institut de Statistique de l'Université de Paris, Hermann et Cie., Paris, 1939.

34. A. Krzyżanowski and K. Kumaniecki, *Statystyka Polski* (*Statistics of Poland*), Cracow, 1915, p. 76.

35. A. Krzyżanowski, *Pauperyzacja Polski współczesnej* (*The Pauperizing of Modern Poland*), 3rd edition, Cracow, 1926. It is characteristic that this book had many editions within a short period of time.

36. *Demographic Yearbook 1954*, United Nations, New York, 1954, pp. 260–61.

CHAPTER 14

Mortality and the Aging of Populations

1. PRELIMINARY REMARKS

Up to now, in examining the demographic revolution, we have stressed only one element, namely the decrease in births. However, the demographic revolution was affected not only by the decline in births but also by the decrease in mortality. Landry, the author of the term "demographic revolution", understood it this way, and it would be wrong to limit this problem to one of its elements alone. As a matter of fact, the transition to modern demographic relations was paved by the simultaneous decline in births and mortality.

The question arises: does the decline in mortality affect the population age structure and the aging process? The reply is positive.

It would be much more difficult to decide how the decline in mortality affects the age structure of the population, whether it rejuvenates or ages. This important problem we shall now consider.

We shall now use both hypothetical computations and empirical data, as we did while studying the effects of births on the age structure of the population. As to empirical data, they are not always sufficiently accurate.

India provides an example of countries having many gaps in the registration of deaths, as illustrated in the following table:

OFFICIAL AND ESTIMATED MORTALITY RATES IN INDIA IN THE YEARS 1911–51

Years	Mortality rate	
	official	estimated
1911–21.	34·3	48·6
1921–31.	25·3	36·3
1931–41.	23·0	31·2
1941–51.	19·4	27–31

Source: Population, Paris 1957, No. 4, p. 662.

369

As we see, the official mortality rate in India is always lower than the real one. During the forty years examined above (1911–51), the difference between the official and the estimated rates was about 30 per cent. It should be added that the estimates of the natural movement of the population were made by the distinguished investigators Kingsley Davis (*Population of India and Pakistan,* Princeton, 1951) and Coale and Hoover.

The above example is not an isolated one; in general, one must admit that the registration of deaths as well as births is not complete, particularly in underdeveloped countries.

[2. THE ROLE OF MORTALITY IN THE AGING PROCESS

In relation to births, there is no doubt that every child not born (in the case of a decline in births) helps cause the aging of the population. But in relation to human lives saved (in case of a decline in mortality), the same cannot be stated in general, as some help rejuvenation and others the aging of the population. Obviously, it all depends on the age of the person saved.

For example, consider the loss of children. If the deaths among infants decrease, then the number of children increases to the same extent.

But, on the other hand, a decline in mortality among old people increases their number and that causes the aging of the population.

As the decline in mortality appears simultaneously in different age groups—young and old—the resulting changes in mortality levels vary according to the number of people in different age groups, i.e., whether more people were saved in the younger or in the older age groups.

From a theoretical point of view, there are three possible results of a decrease in mortality:

(1) a decline in mortality due to a preponderance of lives saved in the younger age groups, which in the end results in the rejuvenation of the population;

(2) a decline in mortality due to a preponderance of human lives saved in the older age groups, which in the end results in the aging of the population;

(3) an equal decline in mortality in both younger and older age groups which does not affect the structure of the population by age.

Thus the matter appears in theory; in this connection the results of experience are important.

French demographers have advanced the revealing concept that in the development of the aging process up to now neither the second nor the third theoretical possibility mentioned above ever appeared in reality. All experience so far supports the thesis that a decrease in mortality had a rejuvenating effect. The progress in the process of the aging of populations does not contradict this concept; this process would have been even more apparent if not for the rejuvenating effect of the decline in mortality.

In order to prove this concept, its proponent, J. Bourgeois-Pichat elaborated a number of hypothetical computations with the aim of presenting the changes in the population age structure, depending only on the decline in mortality. One of those retrospective computations shows what would be the changes in the population age structure of France, and what the present structure would be, if there had been no decrease in births.

As his starting point, the French demographer chose the structure of the population in 1776, i.e., the beginning of the period of decline in mortality in France. Its assumptions were very simple:

(1) fertility remains constant;
(2) mortality decreases as it actually did.

The table below shows the results of these calculations.

HYPOTHETICAL DEVELOPMENT OF FRANCE'S POPULATION AGE STRUCTURE IN THE YEARS 1776–1951 ASSUMING CONSTANT FERTILITY

Year	Total	Age groups		
		0–9	10–64	65+
1776	100·0	23·5	72·2	4·3
1806	100·0	25·6	69·4	5·0
1836	100·0	26·1	69·2	4·7
1866	100·0	27·1	68·6	4·3
1896	100·0	27·5	68·0	4·5
1926	100·0	28·1	67·8	4·1
1951	100·0	29·4	66·8	3·8

Source: J. BOURGEOIS-PICHAT, Évolution de la population française depuis le XVIIIe siècle, Population, Paris, 1951, No. 6.

The table shows that under conditions of constant fertility, the age structure of France's population today would be unusually young. The proportion of children (0–9 yr of age) would be higher today than in 1776, and the proportion of aged people (65 and over) would be lower than in those days. The changes would, of course, result from the decrease in mortality, since fertility remained constant.

Alfred Sauvy made similar remarks about the above table. He asserted that the effect of the decline in mortality is unimportant and tends to cause a rejuvenation of the population. In his opinion, the experience the table presents is fully convincing: only the decline in fertility affected the aging of France's population.[1]

As we know from previous considerations, a positive and fruitful tool of analysis for disclosing the role of individual factors of the aging of populations is the method of computing a stable population model. This method, which previously enabled us to reveal the effects of fertility on the age structure of the population, will help us now to determine the analogous effects of mortality.

To this end we present the next table which is only part of a larger compilation elaborated by J. Bourgeois-Pichat.[2]

MODEL POPULATION STRUCTURE STABILIZED BY AGE, ASSUMING CHANGING MORTALITY AND CONSTANT FERTILITY

Gross reproduction coefficient	Expectation of life at birth	Percentage of population by age groups		
		0–14	15–59	60+
3	30	41·3	54·5	4·1
3	40	43·1	52·5	4·4
3	50	44·6	50·9	4·5
3	60·4	46·0	49·6	4·4
3	70·2	47·3	48·4	4·3

Source: J. BOURGEOIS-PICHAT, *Utilisation de la notion de population stable pour mesurer la mortalité et la fécondité des pays sous-développés,* Uppsala, 1957, p. 4.

There are five different patterns of stable population models whose reproduction varies only by the average length of life, i.e., by mortality rates.

It is evident that these differences have an insignificant effect on the population age structure. The decline in mortality causes only a small increase in the proportion of children and a small decline in the proportion of people in their productive age, while there are almost no changes in the proportion of people in their post-productive age.[3]

By examining the changes occurring in the age structure of a model stable population as a result of changes in the fertility level, an altogether different picture was obtained. Then the changes were quite important and the increase in the number of old people was immense. This time we do not notice these changes.

Therefore, one may assume on this basis that fertility very much affects the population age structure, while the role of mortality in this respect is slight.

Moreover, it follows from the above data that mortality may become the source of rejuvenation; this is indicated by the increase in the proportion of children, as already defined, while the proportion of aged people remains in general unchanged.

We remember the opinion of a United Nations demographer concerning the role of fertility and mortality as factors of the changes in population age structure: "Birth rates, and not death rates, are the major determining factor of population structure." The results of our considerations have proved the correctness of this assumption.

Of course, all these comments apply to the complete process of population aging. Thus its chief cause is the decrease in fertility, not in mortality. The decrease in mortality has so far resulted chiefly in a reduction and not an intensification of the process of population aging.

One should notice, however, the conditional and probably transitory character of a situation where the decline in mortality in the final analysis causes rejuvenation of the population.

Historical experience allows the assumption that the overcoming of primitive demographic conditions starts above all with the decline in the mortality of children and young people; mortality trends in older age-groups meet greater obstacles.

In more developed societies the mortality rate of infants and children is already low and it tends gradually to the minimum level. It may be anticipated that in the course of time it will be possible to eliminate the remaining infant and child mortality. When that occurs and when death among young people becomes a memory of the evil past, then the decline in mortality—if it has to proceed further—will appear only among older people where a certain resistance to a reduction in mortality has been noticeable.[4]

It is easy to understand that a decline in mortality in this situation will not cause rejuvenation but, on the contrary, the aging of society. Thus the aging process will then result from the decline in mortality.

Hence, societies more advanced with regard to demography (i.e., societies of low mortality rates) cannot expect a slower aging tempo as a result of a decline in mortality. On the contrary, with the course of time decline in mortality will accelerate the tempo of the aging of populations.

Moreover, underdeveloped countries will probably follow the path of the more advanced.

3. THE DECLINE IN MORTALITY — ITS BEGINNING AND CAUSES

The decline in mortality, which marks the beginning of the "demographic revolution", began earlier in some countries than in others. It is not easy, therefore, to establish its starting point. The investigator has two alternatives: (1) to determine the earliest date of the turn in demographic relations or (2) to determine the date when the decline in mortality became a general phenomenon.

As to the first alternative, the decline in mortality appeared first in Sweden.

The following table illustrates the evolution of mortality in Sweden for a period of 150 yr:

EVOLUTION OF MORTALITY IN SWEDEN 1801–1955

Period	Mortality (per thousand)	Period	Mortality (per thousand)
1801–10	27·9	1901–1910	14·9
1811–20	25·8	1925	11·7
1821–30	23·6	1937	11·5
1831–40	22·8	1945	10·7
1841–50	20·6	1950	10·0
1851–60	21·7	1954	9·6
1861–70	20·2	1955	9·3

Source: Various statistical publications.

This compilation shows a continuous decline in mortality which started at the beginning of the last century. On this basis one can state that the decline in mortality has lasted 150 yr in Sweden.

Is it possible this process began earlier? Was there no decline in mortality in Sweden in the 18th century?

The above table cannot provide an answer to this question since its earliest data concern the 19th century. The German demographer, Gerhard Mackenroth, quotes data regarding the average duration of life in Sweden, on the basis of life tables available since the middle of the 18th century.

EVOLUTION OF LIFE EXPECTANCY AT BIRTH IN SWEDEN 1755–1940

Years	Life expectancy (years)	
	males	females
1755–75	33·2	35·7
1841–45	41·9	46·6
1871–80	45·3	48·6
1901–10	54·5	57·0
1936–40	64·3	66·9

Source: G. MACKENROTH, *Bevölkerungslehre*, 1953, p. 84.

On the basis of these data Mackenroth advances the process of the decline in mortality in Europe to the middle of the 18th century. Nevertheless, his conclusions are uncertain since he has no proof of the decline in mortality in Sweden in the second half of the 18th century: it could have remained on the same level during that period.

Since Mackenroth's thesis is uncertain the beginning of the 19th century undoubtedly remains valid for Sweden. It is worth while to mention the view of the American sociologist, Hertzler, that the decline in mortality in the Western societies started at the beginning of the last century.[5]

Another method of demographic investigation is based on mass and not sporadic phenomena.

About 150 yr ago the decline in mortality in Europe was not as yet a mass phenomenon; that began only in the middle of the 19th century. Hence, the American demographer, Mortimer Spiegelman, was right in saying: "It is little more than a century since a few countries of western Europe began to record the first appreciable reductions in death rates."

The above mentioned views seem to explain completely the problem: the modern process of the decline in mortality began about 150 yr ago in Sweden and in western Europe it became a general phenomenon about 50 yr later—or about 100 yr ago.

What was the cause of this change in mortality relations?

Hertzler spoke about the improvement in economic and social conditions as a basis for the decline in mortality in Europe. Dr Ernst Höijer put the question similarly when speaking of the reasons for the decline in mortality in Sweden. The turn in mortality relations in that country reflects its higher cultural and the accompanying improvement in public welfare in Sweden.[6]

We agree as to the role of the factors mentioned by the Swedish demographer. There is no doubt that both the economic and cultural conditions played the main role in the modern decline in mortality— and not only in Sweden. However, there is no doubt that without the great medical discoveries and the progress of sanitation technique the change would be impossible.

It appears to us that the concurrence of two dates has more than symbolic significance: the data of the discovery of the vaccination against smallpox by Jenner (1796) and the date of the origin of the modern decline in mortality (beginning of the 19th century). Jenner's discovery made possible resistance to the threatening social calamity which smallpox previously constituted. It indicated, besides, the principle of disease prevention instead of the exclusive principle of cure which dominated in those days. To put it differently, Jenner's vaccination applied the idea of prophylactics to medicine.

In the opinion of several demographers, it was precisely the progress in the sphere of sanitation which cleared the road for the decline in mortality.

As an illustration may be cited here the consideration of H. W. Methorst, for years the excellent general secretary of the International Statistical Institute, who spoke about the evolution of mortality in his native Netherlands,[7] at the World Conference on Population at Geneva in 1927.

If follows from his report that the mortality rate underwent a strong fluctuation in the Netherlands during 1840–70 as a result of various epidemics, including cholera. The picture changed after 1870. From then on the Netherlands experienced a systematic decline in mortality, with the single exception of 1918, when the terrible flu epidemic (called Spanish Influenza) took such a large number of victims. According to Methorst, the introduction of measures for the prevention of infectious diseases determined the decline in mortality rates.

The cause of the decline in mortality on the territory of the present Federal German Republic during the last seventy-five years is similarly interpreted by West German statisticians.

Discussing the decline in mortality among the productive-age population (15–65) the official F. G. R. statistician declares that the mortality decline in Germany has been caused by the decided progress in hygiene and the achievements in the struggle against contagious diseases.[8]

A third group of commentators on the question are those who relate the decline in mortality to economic factors and progress in sanitation.

Attempts at such an interpretation as underlying the decline in the death rate were made at the World Population Conference at Geneva in 1927 by the Italian statistician A. Niceforo, then professor of demography at the University of Naples. He connected the reduction of the mortality rate with the totality of the changes which appeared in the 19th century. In his opinion, it is not possible to ascribe the decline in mortality exclusively to the progress of medicine and hygiene.[9] At the same time he stressed the role of purely economic factors ("...the increase of food supplies, the greater ease of distribution, the spread of economic activities, take an important place, and lead to a rise in the standard of living, both material and mental"). He called attention to the fact that the 19th and the first years of the new century brought greater changes in living standards than all the preceding centuries. "There is a greater difference," he maintained, "between the living standards of our time and at the beginning of the 19th century than during the thousand years which separate Louis XV from Justinian."

Mortality declined rapidly in Italy over the forty years preceding the First World War. Commenting on this phenomenon, the Italian statistician and demographer Livio Livi showed that the decline in mortality was the result of two factors: improvement in economic conditions and progress in hygiene and sanitation.[10]

The equivalence of the roles of economic and sanitary conditions as determining the decline in mortality is also stressed by the French scholar Marcel Reinhard who was interested in the development of the world population over the 18th, 19th, and the first half of the 20th centuries. Considering the question of the decline in mortality in France in the period from 1870–1914, he mentions as the two main sources of that process of improvement the economic situation and the progress in sanitary conditions. The decline in mortality and the substantial prolongation of human life were effected not by either of these factors taken separately, but by the merging of the two.[11]

Alfred Sauvy's investigations throw new light on the decline in mortality. Without negating the role of the economic factor, this author strongly stresses the significance of medical progress. "Le progrès médical," writes Sauvy, "prend actuellement le dessus." Hence, progress in health protection now takes precedence over other factors.

This is confirmed by the conspicuous decline in mortality in under-developed countries. We cite below the data presented by the author:

DECLINE IN MORTALITY RATES OF SELECTED UNDERDEVELOPED COUNTRIES 1937/38–1954

Country	Mortality rates	
	1937/38	1954
Ceylon	21·4	10·4
India	22·8	13·2
Mexico	23·7	12·9
Puerto Rico	19·7	7·6

Source: ALFRED SAUVY, *Théorie Générale de la Population*, Vol. I, 1956, p. 244.

Hence, the decline in mortality is substantial in these countries: but it cannot be maintained that their economic developments have been equal. We also know that in Ceylon, for example, the application of DDT had a determining effect on the decline in mortality. The conclusion that the improvement of sanitary conditions was decisive to the decline in mortality is therefore correct.[12]

The French demographer also mentions Spain as a country with an appreciable decline in mortality despite the misery tormenting the working people ("où cependant la misère des travailleurs est grande"). Thus, from 17·3 per thousand in 1930, the mortality rate declined in Spain to 9·7 per thousand in 1954, i.e., to the pre-war level of the opulent Netherlands.

It would be incorrect and purposeless not to recognize or to fail to evaluate all these facts. They undoubtedly attest to the existence of situations where the factor of sanitation attains a decided precedence over the economic factor. But such situations are by no means exclusive. It is possible to show—and without much difficulty—converse situations in which the decisive role falls to economic and not medical factors.

Let us consider the comparative mortality rates among the white and coloured populations of the United States or the Union of South Africa contained in the table below.

AVERAGE LIFE EXPECTANCY OF WHITES AND COLOURED
IN THE U.S.A. AND UNION OF SOUTH AFRICA

Population	U.S.A. 1939–1941		Union S. Africa 1935–1937	
	male	female	male	female
White	62·8	67·3	59·0	63·1
Coloured	52·3	55·6	40·2	40·9

Source: T. LYNN SMITH, *Population Analysis*, 1948, pp. 252–254.

They show that the average life-span of a Negro is 10·5 yr shorter in the United States than that of a white inhabitant and that among women the colour differential is as high as 11·7 yr.

There is an even greater difference in the Union of South Africa, where "coloured" males live on the average 18·8 yr less than white males, and coloured women—22·2 yr less than white women.

Of course, the cause of such a tremendous and highly lamentable difference is not the colour of the skin; its source is the material and moral degradation of the coloured people. The economic factor operates here in full.

On the other hand, attempts at a purely economic interpretation of differences in mortality levels must be regarded as doubtful. It is similar with the tendency to correlate mortality levels with the *per capita* national income.

Alfred Sauvy, who does not share the thesis of the existence of a strict correspondence between mortality rates and the national income *per capita*, occupied himself closely with this problem in his book, *Théorie Générale de la Population*. The French demographer made a critical evaluation of this thesis in a table, in which the succession of countries according to their *per capita* national incomes is merged with a grouping of these countries according to their life spans (e_0^o).

We present that chart on page 380 with a changed composition—as the starting point we take their succession according to the life expectancy. This change appeared to us desirable for didactic reasons.

As can easily be seen from the table, the order of succession of countries according to mortality level (with the average life-span as the measure and a precise one at that) does not agree with their order according to *per capita* national income.

If national income alone determined peoples' longevity, then Norway should have figured not in the first place but in the ninth in the first

AVERAGE LIFE EXPECTANCY (e_0^0) AND PER CAPITA NATIONAL INCOME IN SELECTED COUNTRIES ABOUT 1949

Country	Life expectancy		National income	
	place	years	place	per capita in dollars
Norway	1	72·3	9	590
Sweden	2	72·0	4	820
Netherlands	3	70·5	11	500
New Zealand	4	70·3	6	750
Denmark.	5	69·5	8	690
Australia	6	69·1	7	700
Canada	7	69·0	2	900
Switzerland	8	68·5	3	850
United Kingdom	9	68·3	5	775
Fed. German Republ. .	10	68·1	13	320
USA	11	68·0	1	1440
France	12	65·5	12	480
Belgium	13	65·0	10	580
Italy.	14	64·0	14	230

Source: ALFRED SAUVY, *Théorie Générale de la Population*, Vol. 2, *Biologie Sociale*, Paris, 1954, p. 92 (author's arrangement).

column of the table. Apart from France and Italy, all other countries would have been higher in the table.

While certain facts testify for the dependence of the mortality level on the *per capita* national income, (for example, Belgium, the Netherlands, France or Italy, where higher national incomes correspond to greater longevity), other facts contradict this thesis (the primacy of Norway and the Netherlands in the table). The French demographer asserts in conclusion that the role of the economic factor is negligible beyond a certain limit.[13]

With this we conclude our consideration of the interpreting of differences in mortality levels. The results of these considerations are clear enough: the "biological" interpretation (as defined by Niceforo) does not give satisfactory results, while the exclusively economic interpretation is also fallacious. Only a composite interpretation which considers all the different sides of the problem and the various influences—including the cultural—to which little attention is usually devoted, can properly clarify the changes in the mortality level.

It is consequently necessary to assert that the low mortality rates registered by modern statistics are not the fruits of any one change, but of the totality of changes in economic, social, cultural and sanitary conditions.

4. THE LOWEST MORTALITY RATES IN THE WORLD

In the course of our studies up to now we have more than once touched on the case of a very considerable reduction in the mortality rate. In Sweden, for example—as we have seen—the mortality rate declined during the last 150 yr to one-third of its level in the first decade of the 19th century. But the Swedish figures, although undoubtedly exciting, do not by any means indicate the maximum reduction in mortality over that period. This is so for two reasons: first, because the mortality level at the beginning of the 19th century was not particularly high in Sweden, and secondly, its present rate is not the lowest in the world.

We refrain from seeking the highest figures of the past, and give instead the lowest current figures. The following countries are identified by very low mortality rates.

MORTALITY RATES OF SELECTED COUNTRIES IN RECENT YEARS

Country	Year	Deaths per 1000 of population
Israel	1953	6·7
Netherlands	1959	7·1
U.S.S.R.	1958	7·2
Greece.	1959	7·3
Japan	1959	7·4
Bulgaria	1958	7·9
Canada	1958	7·9

Source: Statistical Yearbook, 1960, Warsaw, 1960, p. 476.

We have mentioned seven countries with mortality rates lower than 8 per 1000, and the above table is far from being complete since it does not consider a number of other countries with equally low mortality levels. But it must not be forgotten that we are dealing here with raw mortality rates, which in great measure depend on the population structure according to age. In many countries the composition of the population structure according to age is propitious for an exceptionally low general mortality rate.

5. MORTALITY IN RELATION TO AGE

It is sometimes said that *mortality is a function of age.* This saying is true to the extent that there is a different probability of death for each rung of the age ladder.

The probability of death is very high in the first year of life (infancy), after which it declines from year to year and reaches the lowest level at about 12 yr. Then the probability of death rises. At first slow, this increase changes with the approach to old age, becoming more rapid with the advance of old age. The probability of death retraces its direction with time, then exceeds the high mortality level of infancy.

The great differences involved here are disclosed by the table below containing the probability of death in Italy, multiplied by 1000, calculated: (1) for infants, (2) for the ages in which mortality is the lowest and (3) for the ages in which it is the highest. From the data presented by the Italian demographers Gini and Galvani at the nineteenth session of the International Statistical Institute in Tokyo (1930) we have selected by probabilities for 1901, since—besides the wide margin between the minimum and maximum death probabilities—they show the high mortality level at the beginning of this century.

PROBABILITIES OF DEATH IN ITALY IN 1901
(VALUES MULTIPLIED BY 1000)

Probability	Age (yr)	Sex	
		male	female
For infants	0	177·77	160·90
Lowest	12	2·84	3·29
Highest	100	540·46	492·59

Source: C. GINI and L. GALVANI, Uniformità nelle tavole di mortalità, Hague, 1930.

It can be seen from the table how insecure was the first year of life for children. This is an indication to us of the need to devote closer attention to the problem of infant mortality.

Compared with the great infant mortality the probability of death at 12 yr seems like an ideal state. But we will soon see that even this probability was relatively very high at the beginning of the century.

What are today's mortality rates in individual age groups? We will find the answer in the exceedingly interesting table on page 383. M. Pascua, who made the table, noted that the statistics of countries with the lowest mortality rates also have the lowest death rates in individual age groups. The data illustrate the lowest mortality levels in 1950.

It shows that the countries with the lowest mortality, those in which at least one group of the population possesses record low coefficients

THE LOWEST DEATH RATES AMONG MALES AND FEMALES
OF INDIVIDUAL AGE GROUPS   PER 1000 OF EACH GROUP IN 1950*

Age	Males		Females	
	Country	Per thou-sand	Country	Per thou-sand
0–1	Sweden	26·2	New Zealand	18·8
1–4	England and Wales	1·4	Denmark	1·1
	New Zealand		U.S.A.	
5–9	Denmark	0·5	Denmark	
			Sweden	0·4
			New Zealand	
10–14	Netherlands	0·5	Netherlands	0·3
15–19	Netherlands	0·9	Netherlands	
	Denmark		Denmark	0·5
			Sweden	
20–24	Denmark	1·1	Denmark	
			Netherlands	0·7
25–29	Netherlands	1·3	Netherlands	
			Denmark	0·9
			Norway	
30–34	Netherlands	1·3	Netherlands	1·1
35–39	Netherlands	1·7	Norway	1·5
40–44	Netherlands	2·6	Norway	2·0
45–49	Netherlands	4·1	Norway	3·4
50–54	Norway	6·9	Norway	4·8
55–59	Norway	10·7	Norway	7·3
	Netherlands			
60–64	Netherlands	16·4	Norway	12·6
65–69	Norway	26·6	Norway	21·0
70–74	Norway	42·4	Norway	35·8
75 and over	Canada	107·6	Canada	101·3
			U.S.A.	
General	Netherlands	7·7	Netherlands	7·2

* Swedish data of 1949, New Zealand of 1951.

Source: M. PASCUA, Recent Mortality Trends in Areas of Lower Death Rates, *Proceedings of the World Population Conference*, 1954, United Nations, New York, 1955, p. 266.

of deaths, are the Netherlands, Norway, Sweden, New Zealand, England and Wales, Denmark, the U.S.A. and Canada.

The data further indicate that in countries of the lowest mortality, the death rates are reduced to levels undreamed of at the beginning of our century. This would be the result of a comparison of the lowest mortality rates of 1950 with the Italian coefficients of 1901.

The question arises, to what extent the mortality level has declined in various age groups. This is a basic problem for us, since—as we know—a drop in mortality among the younger age groups reacts in favour of rejuvenation of the population, while a decline in mortality among the older age groups, on the contrary, hastens the aging of the population.

To clarify these questions let us consider Polish statistics which are very instructive because of the tremendous drop in mortality in People's Poland as compared with its level between the two world wars.

MORTALITY RATES IN POLAND FOR 1931/32 AND IN 1958 BY AGE AND SEX

Age groups	Mortality rates				Indices	
	1931/32		1958		1931/32 = 100	
	male	female	male	female	male	female
0–4	49·9	41·7	19·0	15·1	38	36
5–9	3·5	3·5	0·8	0·5	23	14
10–14	2·5	2·8	0·7	0·4	28	14
15–19	4·0	3·9	1·3	0·7	32	18
20–24	5·6	5·2	2·0	1·0	36	19
25–34	5·6	6·1	2·4	1·4	43	23
35–44	7·4	7·3	3·5	2·3	47	31
45–54	14·0	10·2	8·1	4·8	58	47
55–64	29 1	21·9	20·2	11·9	69	54

Source: Statistical Yearbook, 1960, Central Statistical Office (GUS), Warsaw, 1960, p. 33 (indices calculated by the author).

While reading the above table one should remember that the greater the magnitude of the mortality decline, the lower is the index.

In all age groups the indices are lower for women than for men, which means that mortality among women declined to a greater degree than among men. Moreover, the differences by sex are great.

Let us return to the problem which most concerns us at present, i.e., to the decline in mortality in relation to age. For males we find the lowest indices among children from 5–9. The decline in mortality was thus the greatest in this group. The index here is 23, showing a 77 per cent drop in mortality. Next in order are the age groups: 10–14 (a decline of 72 per cent), 15–19 (68 per cent decline), 20–24 (64 per cent decline), 0–4 (62 per cent decline), 25–34 (57 per cent decline), and 35–44 (53 per cent decline).

We have enumerated the age groups in which the mortality decreases were the greatest. All age groups included in the first 45 y. of life are to be found in our list.

The picture is different for the older age groups. True, there ha been a mortality decline here also, but it has not been as significant as among the young people. It can also be observed that the resistance to a greater decline in mortality increases with age.

The results for women are basically similar. First place in mortality decline is occupied by the age groups 5–9 and 10–14; mortality dropped by 86 per cent in these groups. Similar magnitudes are shown by the age groups 15–19 (82 per cent decline), 20–24 (81 per cent decline), and 25–34 (77 per cent decline). From the age of 45 yr the mortality decline is clearly less and it further diminishes with increasing age.

Hence we have the most explicit information as to which age groups have benefited most from the progressive reduction in mortality—clearly, the younger age groups.

Dr M. Pascua made some interesting calculations which throw light on the lack of uniformity in the mortality decline among different age groups. He based his calculations on the mortality data of thirteen European countries, jointly constituting almost 40 per cent of the total population of Europe. He considered the following countries: Belgium, Denmark, England and Wales, Finland, France, Ireland (Northern Ireland excluded), Italy, Norway, Scotland, Spain, Sweden, and Switzerland.

With the mortality rates of 1900 as a basis, Pascua estimated the hypothetical number of deaths for 1947 for each of the thirteen countries corresponding to the mortality levels at the beginning of the century. Comparing these estimated numbers with the actual number of deaths in 1947, the author established the number of human lives saved by the decline in mortality.

The results of the calculation—which we present here in the form of a table—are as follows:

APPROXIMATE ESTIMATE OF HUMAN LIVES SAVED IN 13 SELECTED EUROPEAN COUNTRIES IN 1947 IN COMPARISON WITH THE MORTALITY LEVELS OF 1900

Age (yr)	Number of deaths in 1947		Lives saved	
	hypothetical	actual	number	percentage
0–1	692,000	274,000	418,000	60
1–5	417,000	74,000	343,000	82
5 and over	3,078,000	2,087,000	991,000	32
Total	4,187,000	2,435,000	1,752,000	42

Source: Calculation by Dr M. Pascua in *Epidemiological and Vital Statistics Report*, 1950, Vol. 3, No. 2–3, p. 62.

The above table demonstrates the fruits of the struggle against mortality. The balance sheet of the thirteen countries involved was 1,752,000 fewer deaths in 1947 than was to be expected on the basis of the 1900 mortality level. Of principal significance for us, however, is the division of the lives saved according to age, since to snatch children from death is one thing, and to prolong the lives of the aged is something else.

The greatest benefits from medical progress accrued to the youngest age groups: infants and children from 1–5 yr, with the latter profiting far more than the infants from the percentage of deaths avoided. If we combine the children of both these age groups, then we obtain 761,000 deaths saved, which is 69 per cent of the hypothetical number of deaths from birth to 5 yr. In other words, 100 deaths theoretically assumed, only 31 were experienced.

The situation is not so favourable for the rest of the population— each 100 theoretically assumed deaths reduce in practice to 68.

Pascua's estimate also enables us to single out the aged over 75. The actual number of deaths among them amounts to 82 per cent of the hypothetical number, which shows that at that age it was possible to avoid only 18 per cent of the deaths.

Since the data discussed by us possess a purely theoretical character, Dr Pascua correctly detects in them "a rough indication of the great progress made during the first half of the twentieth century in reducing mortality in western and south-western European countries".[14] This type of calculation is also a contribution towards recognizing the factors which either hasten or counteract the process of aging of European societies.

The diversity in the mortality decline of different age groups impels us to look into the relations within individual age groups. Let us turn first to infant mortality.

6. INFANT MORTALITY IN A CROSS-SECTION OF THE WORLD

It would be difficult to proceed with a consideration of infant mortality without defining the special importance of the problem. And this may be done in various ways, for example:

(a) by showing that a high infant mortality level is a misfortune for nations, for it weakens its vitality at the very foundation. It also indicates the useless squandering of important material outlays, as Professor Dietrich, leader of the movement for child care in Germany, pointed out;

(b) by stressing that infant mortality is one of the most sensitive barometers of a nation's social conditions, and at the same time of the value of the health service activity and of social legislation, as is properly asserted by the American demographer Dudley Kirk;[15]

(c) by raising the question of the relation between infant mortality and the process of population aging, which we have to work out.

Let us now look into this problem.

Two elements are essential for investigating the course and perspectives of the population aging process. One is the actual level of infant mortality, and the other is the direction of its development. Let us begin with the second element.

Theoretically considered, infant mortality may follow two directions: falling or rising. We mention this in order to elucidate the counteracting influences of each of these tendencies on the population aging process. Thus, a decrease in infant mortality results in the multiplication of the number of children and consequently, like a rise in the birth rate, tends to rejuvenate the population. On the other hand, an increase in infant mortality means an aging effect on the population structure according to age. Fortunately, today's reality shows only one direction of development of infant mortality—the declining direction. As far as the present infant mortality level is concerned, it is the factor which decides about the future.

Though it may sound paradoxical, it is nevertheless a fact that the changes for the future lie, not with the low, but with the high, infant mortality levels. Countries already close to the complete elimination of infant mortality cannot count on the struggle against infant deaths being for them, as heretofore, a factor retarding the tempo of population aging. If there should be a complete elimination of infant mortality, this would naturally mean the final extinction of that factor to which more than one country would in the future be indebted for a certain slowing down of the tempo of population aging.

Countries in which infant mortality is still appreciable are in a different position. Successes in the struggle against infant mortality, which advanced countries already have behind them, offer promises for the more distant, rather than the near future for countries of retarded development. In time they, too, will undoubtedly control the high infant mortality. It is then that the factor that reduces the tempo of population aging already forgotten elsewhere will operate in the retarded countries.

25*

This is why investigation of the aging of societies cannot end with infant mortality even when it has been stabilized in some countries.

Investigation of the dynamics of infant mortality enables us to deal with the role played by that factor in the transformation of population structure according to age. Since infant mortality—with only few exceptions—has changed in a constantly declining direction, this factor has had the effect of checking the process of population aging.

Infant mortality is measured by coefficients which indicate the number of deaths during the first year of life per 100 live births. Theoretically these coefficients may lie within the limits of 0 (the complete absence of infant deaths) and 100 (the death of all infants). In practice, they vary greatly, from almost 100 per cent to an almost completely non-existent infant mortality.

Examples of unusually high infant mortality are found, as might be expected, in primitive societies where birth control and proper infant care are equally unknown.

Naturally, one should not exaggerate. Concern for children also exists in primitive societies, but it is not based on knowledge of the proper methods. As for the lack of birth control, this is not an absolute rule. On the contrary: the eminent English investigator F.A.E. Crew spoke at the World Demographical Conference at Geneva (1927) about birth control today in primitive agrarian communities, and in historical societies.[16]

Yet there still are many primitive societies in which childbearing is governed by the natural law of fertility. Children are born in large numbers, but they also die in large numbers. Infant mortality often assumes alarming proportions in these societies.

At the International Congress of Population Research, in Rome (1931), Umberto Gabbi, the Italian analyst, gave some alarming data on infant mortality among the native African populations. The results of these investigations are presented in the table on page 389.

Rarely can one find data as terrible as those contained in this table. For it follows from the data that at the beginning of this century 40–70 per cent of the children brought into the world perished among the African peoples in the first year of life.

What was the cause of this tremendous harvest of deaths?

Investigations showed that some of the children died because of syphilis, some of malaria and the rest of other diseases. There is no doubt that not all these diseases resulted from poverty and ignorance. In many cases the cause of death was lack of medical care, of proper

INFANT MORTALITY AMONG NATIVE AFRICANS AT THE BEGINNING OF THE 20TH CENTURY
(per 1000 births)

Territory	Mortality (%)	Notes
Anglo-Egyptian Sudan, Nile region .	50	syphilis, malaria among causes
Anglo-Egyptian Sudan, Wadi-Halfa region	to 93·8	
Central Africa, Alberta	80	
West Africa	30–80	
East Africa, Uganda	33	according to hospital statistics (1891–1920)
Portuguese South Africa.	40–50	
South Africa, Natal	40–50	
General	40–70	

Source: UMBERTO GABBI'S report at the International Congress to Investigate Population Problems, Rome, 1931.

nursing, of cleanliness and proper nourishment; the lack of everything included in "puericulture", or the proper upbringing of children.

Umberto Gabbi's work was continued by Arne Barkhuus who spoke at the last Demographic Congress in Rome (1954) about general and infant mortality among the African people living south of the Sahara.[17]

He cited a number of interesting statistics collected by different investigators. One of these, D.B. Jelliffe, advanced the supposition that the most frequent infant death rates in Africa lie between 30 and 50 per cent. It is interesting that the above infant mortality ceiling is not exceeded by any of the sources cited.

Barkhuus himself advanced the supposition that Africa is characterized today by a decline in both general and infant mortality. A comparison of the figures selected by Barkhuus with those once given by Gabbi confirms this supposition. But these are only conjectures and not proofs.

Let us turn to civilized societies. It is known in advance that the progress of the civilization of a people must affect the mortality, and particularly infant mortality. There must be fewer such deaths in civilized societies than among primitive peoples.

But two facts must be considered:

(1) the common appelation "civilized societies" covers an exceedingly large range of economic and cultural variations; among them

are differences in the sphere of "puericulture" practised by these
societies;

(2) civilization is by no means monolithic. There are also primitive
social formations within contemporary societies—so sociologists maintain.[18]

These facts do not justify the expectation of uniform infant mortality
in civilized societies. Quite the contrary; we must be prepared for
very great disparities particularly for the earlier—we were tempted
to say agrarian—stages in the march of civilization.

In Czarist Russia, a very backward agrarian country, infant mortality
was exceedingly high. We present figures below which indicate the
level of that mortality in several provinces. These figures also document
the hunger of the population and their low level of living.

**THE HIGHEST INFANT DEATH RATES IN THE STATISTICS
OF CZARIST RUSSIA FOR DIFFERENT PERIODS**

Period	Territory	Percentage
1867–81	Perm Province	43·8
1867–81	Kostroma Prov.	40·6
1888–97	Don region	43·9
1888–97	Bessarabia Prov.	41·7
1909	Perm Prov.	39·6
1910	Viatsk Prov.	36·6
1911	Kursk Prov.	36·0

Sources: (1) Rossiya (Russia), Vol. 14, *Novorossiya i Krym* (*New Russia
and the Crimea*) edited by Semionov-Tian-Shanski, Petersburg, 1910,
Devrien edition, p. 176. (2) PAUL GEORGIEVSKY, "Säuglingssterblichkeit im
Europäischen Russland in den Jahren 1909, 1910 u. 1911", *Allg. Stat. Arch.*
8, 1914, pp. 47–8.

As the table shows, 40 per cent and more of the new-born did not
even reach the first year of life in a number of provinces. "Czarist
Russia," states Batkis, "from the viewpoint of infant mortality occupied
the inglorious first place among the countries of the world." Infant
mortality reached from 30–40 per cent and even to 50 per cent in some
provinces.[19] Hence we find the same high infant mortality as among
the negroes in Portuguese South Africa or in Natal.

Several German states had very high infant mortality in the 19th
century. Bavaria had the highest, maintaining a level of 30 per cent
or more up to 1877, and exceeding 35 per cent in 1858–65. After

1877 mortality began to decline and approximate those of other German provinces. Following are the figures:

Year	Death-rates (%)
1881	28·4
1891	27·4
1903	25·0
1910	20·2
1912	17·7

Between 1864 and 1912, i.e., within less than half a century, infant mortality was cut in half in Bavaria.

Not only Bavaria was at that time the scene of a reduction in infant mortality. All of Europe, all of the cultured world, began the struggle against excessive infant mortality, which came to be recognized as a national misfortune.

It was thus defined by Professor Dietrich who, as we saw earlier, was one of the leading proponents of modern child care. "High infant mortality," he wrote, "is an economic and national misfortune, since it means, first, the purposeless creation and premature destruction of numerous economic values, and second, because the causes of high child mortality also lower the resistance of the infants remaining alive, and in that manner lower the nation's vitality" *(Wörterhandbuch der Staatswissenschaften)*. The struggle was crowned with complete success, and the extent of the infant mortality reduction in many countries merits attention.

So that the scale of the first achievements of the struggle against infant mortality may be appreciated, we reiterate on page 392 data culled from our own work over more than 30 yr.

The reduction of infant mortality was therefore a general European phenomenon. It took place in countries of high infant mortality as well as in those of medium and low levels.

While we dealt previously with the decline of infant mortality levels below 30 per cent and then below 20 per cent, we can now speak of rates below 10 per cent. A record low in infant mortality before the First World War was achieved by Sweden (7·3 per cent).

Infant mortality was very low in Norway, perhaps even lower than Sweden. This is indicated by the following Norwegian rates:

1876–1885 . . . . 10·0
1886–1895 . . . . 9·7
1896–1905 . . . . 8·8

REDUCTION OF INFANT MORTALITY IN SEVERAL EUROPEAN COUNTRIES FROM THE PERIOD 1884–1893 TO 1914

Country or region	Death-rates (⁰/₀₀)		Drop in infant mortality (%)
	1884–93	1914	
Sweden	10·7	7·3	by 32
England	14·6	10·5	by 28
Switzerland	16·4	9·3	by 43
France	16·7	10·9	by 35
Netherlands	17·5	9·5	by 46
Italy.	19·0	13·0	by 32
Prussia	20·8	16·4	by 20
Austria	24·9	18·4	by 26
Wurtemberg	26·1	14·5	by 45
Bavaria	27·9	19·3	by 30
Saxony	28·3	17·1	by 40

Source: EDWARD ROSSET, *Zagadnienia gospodarki samorządowej miasta Łodzi* (*Economic Problems of the Lodz City Government*), Chap. 3, Infant Care, Lodz, 1926, p. 36.

When the infant mortality rate fell below 10 per cent, and when it appeared that it would continue to decline, demographers began to consider the future end to this trend.

The well-known Danish statistician and demographer, Harald Westergaard, stated the view that with the *then existing state of hygiene* the practical minimum for infant mortality would be about 7 per cent. It must be added that this statement was made at the beginning of the present century.[20]

Among biologists the problem of the end to the decline in infant mortality assumed different, very dangerous forms. It concerned the limit to the reduction of infant mortality, the limit beyond which it could not go.

The idea of deliberately refraining from avoiding deaths of weak individuals, lacking in vitality, is not new. It was voiced in its time by the evolutionists, led by the famous Herbert Spencer (1820–1903). Spencer believed that by preserving weak, sick individuals not well adapted to the struggle for existence, medicine and hygiene impair natural selection, thus weakening society.

In agreement with this theory, the German statistician Franz Žižek expressed the opinion that a certain part of infant deaths is a necessity imposed by nature in order to eliminate naturally weak children ("zur Eliminierung der von Natur aus zu schwachen Kinder").[20]

Other critics of the reduction of mortality claimed that a decline in infant mortality would raise the mortality on all other rungs of the age ladder. The gains in prolonging human life would thus be small, while society would lose much by the average decline in economic and biological efficiency.

Wilhelm Lexis was pessimistic about the chances for, and gains from, a struggle against infant mortality. He asserted that even under the most advantageous conditions infant mortality remains large, and if better nursing and better feeding reduce the number of infant deaths, this only postpones death for many children for several years.[22]

Karl Ballod (*Sterblichkeit und Lebensdauer in Preussen*) also believed that modern medicine and hygiene had only succeeded in postponing some of the deaths from infancy to adulthood.

The thesis that completely to eliminate infant mortality would be pointless if not harmful was revived in the inter-war period by the Viennese doctor, E. Stransky (*Sozialhygiene im Säuglings- und Klein-kinderalter, Vienna, 1929*). He anticipated that the progressive decline in infant mortality would reduce its level to 3 per cent. This, he thought, was the proper minimum of infant mortality and hence an end to the struggle against mortality since it would be impossible to go further. If infant mortality should fall below this minimum, Stransky thought, it would be damaging to society, since it would lower the quality of human material and would cause an increase in mortality for older children.

As we see it, the theory of the Viennese hygienist, although arrayed in the garments of concern for human welfare, is essentially anti-humanitarian.

At the time of the outbreak of the Second World War (1939) five European countries and two outside of Europe (the Netherlands, Norway, Iceland, Sweden, Switzerland, New Zealand (without the Maoris) and Australia) were close to the level of infant mortality which Stransky considered optimal. In many countries the war checked the decline in infant mortality, but with the end of the war that tendency was fully revived.

In the light of the latest data infant mortality has fallen on page 394 3 per cent in a number of countries.

We have mentioned ten countries in which the infant mortality level dropped below 3 per cent. Of these, seven are in Europe and three in other parts of the world.

Sweden has long held the world record. It is also the first country in which the infant mortality rate fell below 2 per cent. The Netherlands follows close behind.

COUNTRIES WITH THE LOWEST INFANT MORTALITY LEVELS ABOUT 1958

Country	Year	Percentage
1. Sweden	1958	1·58
2. Netherlands	1958	1·72
3. New Zealand (European pop.) .	1953	2·00
4. Norway	1958	2·05
5. Australia	1958	2·14
6. Switzerland	1958	2·22
7. Great Britain	1958	2·33
8. Denmark	1958	2·34
9. Iceland	1951	2·60
10. U.S.A.	1958	2·69

Source: Concise Statistical Yearbook, 1961, Warsaw, 1961, p. 211.

The rates of the advanced countries provide a picture of the maximum attainments of the struggle against infant mortality.

The situation is different at the other pole of social and demographic relations. Infant mortality is high in underdeveloped countries, while it often reaches dizzy heights in primitive societies. Besides, it is a rule that the worse the relations, the more uncertain are the statistics, and for countries with the worst conditions no statistical data are, in the main, available.

That is why it is so difficult to say anything definite about the worst conditions. In any case, it is to be expected that the highest infant mortality rates found in an international review will be far from the worst cases in fact, of which we can learn only occasionally by special probes and inquiries.

THE HIGHEST INFANT MORTALITY RATES NOTED IN 1951–3

Country	Year	Percentage
Burma	1953	23·0
Egypt	1951	12·9
India	1952	11·6
Chile	1953	11·4
Peru	1953	11·4

Source: Statistical publications of the U.N. and others.

A number of points are to be noted from this table:

(1) the highest infant mortality rate noted is 23 per cent; in countries not providing statistics a much higher infant mortality level certainly exists;

(2) among states providing regular population statistics the Burmese coefficient (23 per cent) is a rarity. None equal to it, or even approximating it, are to be found in any country collecting demographic statistics;

(3) the magnitudes next in order are of an entirely different nature. Outside of Egypt, where close to 13 per cent of the newborn die in the first year of life, three other countries mentioned by us—India, Chile and Peru—have infant mortality rates near 11·5 per cent; thus they are only half the Burmese value.

Yugoslavia has the highest level of infant mortality among European countries—8·62 per cent, according to available data.

Let us now investigate the situation in Poland.

At the turn of the century the infant mortality rate was 21–22 per cent on Polish territories. In the first years of the 20th century there was a certain, though inconsiderable, decline. Infant mortality continued to be excessively high—every fifth Polish child died in the first year of life.

The figures for Poland were double, or even almost triple those of certain western European countries. This gives us some idea of the number of unnecessary deaths in Poland in those days.

Poland's infant mortality rates published by the Central Statistical Office in the inter-war years were based only partly on trustworthy material, such as the material from the western and northern voivodships. The rest were not worth much. This applies to the then central, and even more to the eastern, voivodships.

If we limit ourselves to reliable rates we obtain the following table of the evolution of infant mortality in the western and northern voivodships:

Year	Percentages	
	western	northern
1896–1900.	21·6	21·9
1926–1930.	16·6	16·8
1931–1935.	14·8	15·7
1936–1938.	14·4	15·2

The situation is clear—infant mortality did decline in Poland, but the process was quite slow, incomparably slower than in countries advanced in *puericulture.*

It is not out of place to recall that at the time when our lowest infant mortality rate was 14–15 per cent, world statistics recorded coefficients one-fifth as high.

In recent years our statistics registered the following infant mortality rates:

INFANT MORTALITY IN POLAND IN 1950–60 IN PERCENTAGES

Year	Total	Urban	Rural
1950	11·1	10·2	11·6
1951	11·8	10·6	12·5
1952	9·6	8·7	10·2
1953	8·8	8·0	9·4
1954	8·3	7·6	8·9
1955	8·2	7·3	8·9
1956	7·1	6·5	7·5
1957	7·7	7·0	8·3
1958	7·2	6·4	7·8
1959	7·1	6·4	7·7
1960	5·6	5·0	5·9

Source: Rocznik Statystyczny, 1961 (Statistical Yearbook, 1961), Warsaw, 1961, p. 30.

Thus, important progress is to be noted in the struggle against infant mortality—in the decade 1950–60 it was reduced to half.

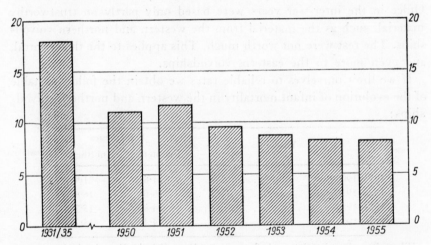

Fig. 6. Comparative infant mortality in Poland before the war (1931–5) and after the war (1950–55) (deaths in the first year of life per 100 live births).

We know from previous considerations that the struggle against infant mortality is essentially a struggle for the rejuvenation of society. A declining infant mortality rate checks the tempo of population aging. This means of counteracting population aging does not have any great significance for societies where infant mortality has been reduced to a minimum. For other countries the struggle against infant mortality may become an efficacious means of slowing up the population aging, particularly when fertility is declining.

7. ADULT MORTALITY

The usual division of populations into three main age groups, with the adult middle group by far the most numerous, is not very suitable for an analysis of the changes in the mortality levels of those populations.

Its unfitness results primarily from the fact that the changes in mortality operate within the middle-aged group of persons from 40–50 yr with a strength different from others. The decline in mortality is usually much lower among the older groups than among the younger.

The French demographer Bourgeois-Pichat considers it necessary to divide the adult population groups also because different causes induce mortality reductions among the younger and older age groups. This demographer holds that a mortality decline among those below 30 serves to rejuvenate the population, whereas a mortality decline among older age groups favours population aging.

The fact stressed by West German statisticians assumes special significance in the light of the French demographer's thesis. Thus, there has been a mortality decline among all adult age groups (15–65 yr) within the last 75 yr on the territory of the Federal German Republic. But, characteristically, among the youngest, the 15–25 age group, the reduction was lower than among the 25–35 age group.

West German statisticians see the cause of this phenomenon in the fact that a large number of unfortunate accidents occur among the 15–25 age group.[23]

The loss of young people in unfortunate accidents is one element in population aging.

French demographers have called attention to the excessively high mortality of adults in their country, particularly of males. In this respect France has the sad privilege of towering over the other civilized countries which are comparable to her.[24]

What is the cause of this "sad privilege"? French investigators believe the chief source of the excessive male adult mortality in France to be widespread alcoholism.

These same investigators call attention to the economic consequences of the excessive mortality of males in the productive age. In a study entitled "La mortalité des adultes en France" (*Population*, Paris, 1946, No. 4) S. Ledermann estimates that the reduction of male adult mortality to the level of England would bring an economic gain to France of over 100,000 additional work-years annually. Jean Daric, who made this calculation, adds: "De tels chiffres soulignent l'importance de la lutte à mener en France contre la surmortalité, pour accroître le nombre des producteurs."[25]

Naturally, the excessive mortality of adults also has its demographic consequences. It suffices to recall the thesis of Bourgeois-Pichat regarding the significance of deaths in age groups under 30 in order to understand the aging effect of an excessive number of deaths at that age.

It would follow from this thesis that excessive deaths in the above-mentioned age limit hampered the process of population aging in France. We do not know the net effect of these two interacting forces— aging and rejuvenation. However, the importance of the problem is clear.

Let us now review some international data.

At the World Population Conference in Rome (1954), the American demographer Mortimer Spiegelman, already known to us as the co-author of the demographic study *Length of Life*, presented the results of his investigation of the evolution of mortality rates in the older ages.[26] The author compared the general mortality rates and those for four age groups (to 25, 25–44, 45–64, 65 and over) for 1930 and 1950, using data from western European countries as well as all English-speaking countries.

We note the data of greatest interest to us from Spiegelman's report. We are interested primarily in the 45–64 age group, which we regard as the eve of old age.

The lowest, average and highest mortality rates of males in that age group (calculated per 1000 persons aged between 45 and 64) are as follows:

about 1930		*in 1950*	
Denmark	11·7	Norway	8·9
Norway	12·0	Netherlands	9·1
Netherlands	12·6	Sweden	10·0
average	16·0	*average*	13·6
Switzerland	19·1	Union of S. Africa	16·6
France	20·4	Scotland	16·9
Finland	23·3	Finland	19·5

Within the twenty-year interval covered by these data there was a decided drop in the mortality of males of 45–64. This is indicated by all the values characterizing mortality: the decline in the lowest, average and highest values. It is to be observed that the average, calculated for nineteen countries, was reduced by 15 per cent during the twenty years.

The 1950 minima are very favourable. In Norway, the Netherlands or Sweden, out of every thousand males aged 45–64 between nine and ten die yearly, while twenty die in Finland. How many lives could be preserved in Finland if they managed to reduce adult mortality to the level of Sweden or Norway!

Following are the mortality rates per thousand for women aged 45–64:

about 1930		*in 1950*	
Norway	9·9	Norway	6·5
Australia	10·1	Netherlands	7·2
New Zealand	10·5	Sweden	7·8
average	12·4	*average*	8·7
U.S.A.–whites	13·9	Union of S. Africa	9·9
Scotland	13·9	Scotland	10·2
Ireland	17·9	Ireland	10·8

The achievements of the struggle against mortality are greater among women than among men. The average mortality of women aged 45–64 declined in the course of the twenty years involved by 30 per cent. The reduction is therefore twice as great as among men. The lowest female rate (Norway) declined by 34 per cent in that period, and the highest (Ireland) by 40 per cent.

Minima appeared which could not have been dreamed of in the past. We have in mind the Norwegian minimum of 6·5 per thousand. Amazing, too, is the fact that the *worst* female rates of 1950 are on the level of the *best* of 1930.

We have dealt hitherto with the second half of the productive age (45–64), which we called the eve of old age. The consequence of this manner of discussing age groups is that the preservation of human beings in this range supports the old age groups. The more people we save from death in the later productive years the more old people there will be with time. It is thus that the *reduction of mortality in the second half of the productive age is grist for the mills of the population aging process.*

8. MORTALITY OF THE AGED

The least susceptible to reduction is the mortality of the aged. Nevertheless, many countries have achieved some results in reducing the mortality rate in this age group as well.

In the first half of the 20th century the following decline of the mortality rate among the aged was registered in the Netherlands.

MORTALITY OF THE AGED IN THE NETHERLANDS
IN 1899–1900 AND 1946–7

Sex and age	Death rates per 1000		Index
	1899–1900	1946–7	(1899–1900 = 100)
Males			
60–64.	31·4	17·8	57
65–69.	48·6	28·9	60
70–74.	77·9	47·8	61
75 and over . . .	150·2	119·9	75
Females			
60–64.	27·3	15·8	58
65–69.	43·7	26·7	61
70–74.	69·6	45·6	66
75 and over . . .	143·3	103·8	72

Source: *Epidemiological and Vital Statistics Report*, 1950, Vol. 3, No. 2–3.

Mortality thus declined in all old age groups. At the threshold of old age, in the 60–64 group, a mortality reduction of 42–43 per cent was achieved.

The two succeeding age groups registered somewhat smaller results: in the 65–69 group the decline amounted to 39–40 per cent, and in the 70–74 group, to 34–39 per cent. The lowest mortality decline is to be seen among the Netherlands' oldest inhabitants (75 and over): 25–28 per cent.

We now summarize the mortality rates of persons 65 yr and over. As above, we give the lowest, average and highest mortality rates. The figures for males are:

about 1930		*in 1950*	
Norway	64·6	Norway	59·4
Canada	70·9	Netherlands	61·8
New Zealand	71·3	Canada	63·8
average	79·7	*average*	73·2
England and Wales . . .	90·1	England and Wales . . .	81·1
Scotland	93·7	Scotland	81·7
France	97·0	Finland	87·0

A reduction of the mortality rates over the two decades 1930–50 is confirmed here, too, although it is not as large in percentage as among adults. The average for nineteen countries contained in the statistics of an American demographer dropped by 8 per cent.

It is worth noting that the 1930 maximum no longer appears after the twenty years. The new maximum—except for the very unfavourable Finnish rates—approximates the average level of twenty years before.

Norway continues to register the lowest mortality rates for the aged. Canada is its competitor in this respect while it has recently been outdistanced by the Netherlands.

Following are the figures for women:

about 1930		*in 1950*	
Norway	58·3	Norway	51·7
Australia	59·7	Canada	53·4
New Zealand	62·3	U.S.A. (whites)	54·0
average	69·6	*average*	59·6
Scotland	76·2	Ireland	65·8
Switzerland	76·7	Scotland	66·6
France	79·2	Finland	68·8

Here is a repetition of what we saw above. The results for women are also better than for men among the aged. While the average calculated for nineteen countries dropped by 8 per cent for men, for women the decline was 14 per cent.

The improvement in the mortality relations of women 65 yr old and over is expressed by the following:

(1) the 1930 maximum is not repeated;

(2) the new maxima are lower than the average mortality levels of 1930;

(3) the new average (of 1950) corresponds to the lowest rates of twenty years before.

Again the lowest mortality is to be found in Norway. It is perhaps possible to assume on this basis that the most favourable conditions for old age exist at present in Norway.

A decline in the mortality of the aged is of course a factor in population aging.

Whereas the mortality decline among the younger age groups hastens the rejuvenation of populations, among the aged it accelerates population aging. And since, as has been demonstrated, the mortality decline in young age groups was immeasurably stronger than among the older, it is not difficult to conclude that in the general accounting the reduction of mortality has, as hitherto, reacted either in favour of population aging, or against it. The decline in mortality undoubtedly slowed down the tempo of that process.

9. CAUSES OF DEATH

An analysis of the problems of mortality with respect to its relation to the process of population aging requires consideration of the causes of death among people of different ages and of the mortality tendencies from various diseases.

The American Metropolitan Life Insurance Company estimated that mortality in 1942–6 among the white people aged from 45–74 insured with that company, who were employed in industry and lived in cities, compared as follows with that of 1911–5 (an interval of 31 yr):

CHANGES IN MORTALITY AMONG PERSONS INSURED WITH THE METROPOLITAN LIFE INSURANCE CO. (U.S.A.) ACCORDING TO DATA FOR 1911–15 AND 1942–6

Causes of death	Decrease (−) or increase (+) in mortality rates from the given causes of death (%)	
	males	females
Typhoid fever	−98·0	−96·6
Pneumonia, influenza	−73·7	−83·7
Tuberculosis	−71·3	−83·0
Syphilis	−57·2	−70·5
Cancer—all forms	+29·1	−10·1
Diabetes	+ 9·7	+44·2
Heart diseases	−19·9	−34·5
Diarrhoea and intestinal catarrh	−89·8	−93·6
Appendicitis	−13·7	−33·3
Suicide	−62·3	− 3·8
Murder	−48·7	−46·7
Accidents	−48·8	−48·9
General	−37·1	−43·9

Source: Statistical Bulletin, Metropolitan Life Insurance Company, 1947, No. 4, p. 9.

Although the above statistics pertain only to the white, urban population and are further restricted as to occupation, they are of wide significance. For they provide some conception of the achievements of modern medicine and hygiene in the struggle against disease and deaths in the advanced ages (45–74).

In the light of the Metropolitan Life Insurance Company statistics, the causes of death which formerly cost many human lives seen to be in full retreat, if this term may be used in this connection. The statistics show a tremendous decline is such causes of death as typhoid, diarrhoea and intestinal catarrh, pneumonia and tuberculosis. However, there are diseases which are expanding their sway. These are primarily cancer (together with other malignant tumours) and diabetes. Deaths from cancer have risen among men by 29 per cent and dropped among women by 10 per cent. Diabetes has increased among men and women and its growth is furthermore almost five times as great among women as among men.

As to the general result, it shows an important decrease in mortality among the 45–74-year-olds, with a drop of 37 per cent, in the male mortality during the period investigated, and of 44 per cent for women.

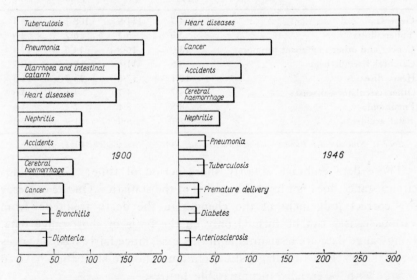

FIG. 7. The principal causes of death in the U.S.A. at the beginning and in the middle of the 20th century (number of deaths per 100,000 people)

Do the above facts have any influence on the population aging process? Undoubtedly. The reduction of mortality in the advanced ages is a factor favouring population aging.

Of another character are the West German statistics cited below. They pertain, not to chosen groups but to the population as a whole. The classification of the causes of death are different here from the statistics of the Metropolitan Life Insurance Company. The difference is that while the American data showed percentage differences in the mortality levels, the West German statistics give mortality rates calculated per 10,000 population, by sex.

Such diversity of conceptions naturally does not favour the comparison of data. On the other hand, it cannot be questioned that nonuniform, varying conceptions stimulate a broader outlook on the problems investigated. So it is in this case.

Let us now examine the West German data.

THE MOST IMPORTANT CAUSES OF DEATH IN THE FEDERAL GERMAN REPUBLIC IN 1933 AND 1950 ACCORDING TO SEX

(per 10,000 population)

Cause of death	Males		Females	
	1933	1950	1933	1950
General.	114·7	111·9	108·7	96·1
Tuberculosis	7·9	5·2	6·7	2·9
Cancer and other malignant tumours . .	13·0	16·8	14·6	17·1
Cerebral haemorrhage	8·8	11·6	9·2	12·7
Heart diseases	12·1	17·5	13·7	16·3
Other circulatory diseases	4·7	4·7	4·1	4·8
Pneumonia	8·5	5·1	7·4	4·4
Fatal accidents	5·1	6·9	1·9	2·3

Source: Statistik der Bundesrepublik Deutschland, Vol. 75, Wiesbaden, 1953, p. 19.

These data embrace a fairly short period of time: 17 yr. This circumstance does not lessen the value of the statistics. On the contrary —a correct judgement of the changes in the death frequency from various causes can be formed only on the basis of short-range data. Long-range data are less suitable in this case, since fairly basic changes may take place in the diagnostic technique and we shall then have to reckon with essentially incomparable figures.

The general mortality rate declined in West Germany over a seventeen-year period. Male mortality was reduced from 11·5 per thousand to 11·2 per thousand, and female mortality from 10·9 per thousand to 9·6 per thousand.

In these general coefficients the specific individual situations are obliterated, and they are essential for recognizing the mortality trends at the present time. The problem is that, of the indicated seven causes of death, some betray a tendency to decline, while others tend to rise.

Two causes of death show a declining tendency: (1) tuberculosis (2) pneumonia. The number of annual deaths from tuberculosis per 10,000 persons declined to 5·2 for men and to 2·9 for women. As compared to 1933 the male coefficient indicates a drop of one third, and the female of more than half. Death from tuberculosis had already been appreciably reduced.

The same may be said of pneumonia. From 8·5 in 1933 the coefficient of male deaths from that disease fell to 5·1 in 1950, i.e., the mortality level declined by 40 per cent. Equally high was the decline of mortality from pneumonia among women.

However, there are, causes of death which consume increasing numbers of victims. Four such appear in the table: (1) cancer and other malignant tumours, (2) cerebral haemorrhages, (3) heart diseases and (4) fatal accidents.

Deaths from cancer have catastrophically multiplied. Whereas the mortality rate from that disease amounted to 13 per 10,000 among males in 1933, it rose to 16·8 by 1950. This means close to 30 per cent increase in the mortality rate. Among women the rise in the mortality rate from cancer amounted to 17 per cent in the same period. There is no escaping the conclusion that cancer tends to assume first place among the causes of death. For women this is already an established fact.

A competitor of cancer, from the viewpoint of the frequency of deaths, is heart disease, which is the second source of mass mortality. Within the seventeen years considered, the mortality rate for heart diseases rose among men by 45 per cent and among women by 19 per cent. It is obvious that both of these worst causes of death show a considerably greater increase among men than among women.

There was an increase, too, in the number of deaths brought about by fatal accidents, the frequency of which in the seventeen-year period rose by 35 per cent among men and by 21 per cent among women.

The mortality trends demonstrated in the above breakdown into various causes of death are undoubtedly connected with population aging. Some of them are the effects and others the causes of this process.

If there has been an increase in mortality from cancer, cerebral haemorrhage and heart diseases, then the assumption is justified that this, too, is occasioned by changes in the age structure of the population, that is by an increase in the proportion of the aged. If there has been a reduction in the number of deaths from tuberculosis, then a certain portion of the preserved human lives—old people—is an element favouring population aging.

It may be hoped that the terrible plague of our times, malignant tumours, will be conquered in time. The direct effect of a victory over cancer will be the extension of human life. The population aging process will then have another source of development.

Contemporary French demographers project a division of mortality into endogenic and exogenic. *Endogenic* refers to the results of biological factors, while *exogenic* mortality is the result of environmental influences. A classic example of the first is the recently mentioned tumours as well as circulatory disease. An example of the second is tuberculosis.

At the International Population Conference in Rome (1954) the French demographers Tabah and Sutter presented the results of their investigations, from which it follows that in recent times in Western Europe endogenic mortality has exhibited a clear predominance. Of every 100 deaths, those in this category amount to:

Sweden 79
United Kingdom 72
Italy 65
France 56

J. Beaujeu-Garnier says of these data that they provide a forecast of the new demographic epoch in which deaths from non-biological causes will be rare exceptions.[27]

The further stage in the struggle against premature death will involve the conquering of several types of endogenic mortality. And since endogenic mortality flourishes with age, its reduction results in increasing the number of the aged.

Perhaps not everything that brings progress carries with it the aging of society, but many things do.

REFERENCES

1. "La baisse de la natalité est l'unique responsable du vieillissement" (A. SAUVY' "Le vieillissement des populations et l'allongement de la vie", *Population*, Paris, 1954, No. 4, p. 679).
2. Out of numerous patterns quoted by the French demographer, we have chosen those which have the gross reproduction rate equal to 3. It is one of the highest rates encountered in practice, representing the reproduction relations in under-developed countries, where birth control has been adopted only to a small extent.

Where the limitation on births has been applied to a greater degree, the gross reproduction rate is 1–1·5, while in countries of natural fertility it is 3–4.

3. J. BOURGEOIS-PICHAT writes: "L'effet de la baisse de la mortalité considéré sur la composition par âge n'est pas très important. Cette baisse produit un rajeunissement par la base de la pyramide des âges et peu de changement au sommet" (*Utilisation de la notion de population stable pour mesurer la mortalité et la fécondité des populations des pays sous-développés*, Uppsala, 1957, p. 2).

4. A U.N. demographer hopes that the mortality of older people will decrease in the future: "There are, moreover, grounds for optimism with regard to future mortality trends among older persons." (*The Aging of Populations and Its Economic and Social Implications*, New York, 1956, p. 83). This is our conclusion, too.

5. "It may be pointed out that until about 150 years ago in the Western world, fluctuations in over-all economic and social well-being were reflected in oscillations of the death rate, the birth rate remaining constantly high." (J. O. HERTZLER, *The Crisis in World Population*, 1956, p. 30).

6. "Mit der kulturellen Aufwärtsentwicklung und dem dadurch bedingten grösseren Wohlstand begann die Kurve der Todesfälle etwas zu sinken." (E. HÖIJER, *Die Bevölkerungsentwicklung in Schweden im Vergleich mit der Deutschlands*, Verlag Gustav Fischer, Jena, 1943, p. 3).

7. H. W. METHORST, "Results of the differential birth rate in the Netherlands," *Proceedings of the World Population Conference*, London, 1927, p. 170.

8. "Auch hier wirkt sich als Folge der zunehmenden Hygiene und der Erfolge der ärztlichen Therapie in erster Linie das Zurückdringen der Sterbefälle an Infektionskrankheiten aus, insbesondere der Tuberkulosesterblichkeit, die gegenüber der Zeit vor dem ersten Weltkrieg bis heute auf weniger als ein Viertel ihrer damaligen Häufigkeit zurückgegangen ist." (*Statistik der Bundesrepublik Deutschland*, Band 75, Wiesbaden 1953, p. 19).

9. "It is not due wholly to advances in medicine and hygiene, but is a fact that must be examined both from the biological and the sociological points of view." (A. NICEFORO, "The development of the population in Italy," *Proceedings of the World Population Conference*, London 1927, p. 64).

10. "... una forte flessione della mortalità, dovuta al miglioramento economico, ed al progresso igienico e sanitario." (L. LIVI, *Nozioni di Statistica e Politica Demografica*, Padua, 1938, p. 73).

11. M. R. REINHARD, *Histoire de la Population Mondiale de 1700 à 1948*, p. 235.

12. "La forte baisse de la mortalité constatée depuis quinze ans est-elle d'origine économique ou médicale et sanitaire? La réponse n'est pas douteuse, dans la majorité des cas: alors que les conditions économiques ont souvent été médiocres, au cours de cette période, le développement sanitaire a connu, au contraire, un certain essor: diffusion de la pénicilline et des sulfamides, lutte contre les insectes (D.D.T.), vaccinations diverses" (A. SAUVY, *Théorie Générale de la Population*, seconde édition, 1956, Vol. 1, p. 244).

13. "Le seul fait que les Pays-Bas, la Norvège aient pu parvenir à une mortalité très basse suffirait à montrer qu'au-dessus d'un certain seuil, le pouvoir économique proprement dit ne joue pas qu'un rôle négligeable" (A. SAUVY, *Théorie Générale de la Population*, Vol. 2, p. 93).

14. M. PASCUA, "Evolution of mortality in Europe during the twentieth century", *Epidemiological and Vital Statistics Report*, 1950, Vol. 3, No. 2–3, p. 62.

15. "Infant mortality is one of the most sensitive barometers of social conditions. The infant is extremely vulnerable to most causes of death. Consequently the number of infant deaths is very closely correlated to the quality of health protection the community affords its members. The evaluation placed on the individual human life, the knowledge and education of parents, the quality of the physical environment enjoyed by the population, the effectiveness of public health and social legislation—these are collectively and sensitively measured by the level of infant mortality." (D. KIRK, *Europe's Population in the Interwar Years*, League of Nations 1946, p. 174).

16. F. A. E. CREW, "Concerning fertility and sterility in relation to population", *Proceedings of the World Population Conference, London, 1927*, p. 221.

17. A. BARKHUUS, "Non-European general and infant mortality in the non-self-governing territories in Africa south of the Sahara" *Proceedings of the World Population Conference, 1954*, U.N., New York, p. 351 ff.

18. "Lorsqu'on analyse les éléments composant une société, ceux-ci ne se révèlent jamais homogènes. Une nation est composée de groupes et d'individus dont les mentalités diffèrent et sont quelquefois extrêmement éloignées les unes des autres. Comme l'avait dit Gustave Le Bon, il y a parmi nous des représentants vivants de presque toutes les mentalités historiques: il y a des hommes du moyen âge et d'autres qui ont une mentalité paléolitique" (G. BOUTHOUL, *La Surpopulation dans le Monde*, Payot, Paris, 1958, p. 60).

19. G. BATKIS, *Socyalnaya gygena*, Medgiz, 1940, p. 79.

20. H. WESTERGAARD, *Die Lehre von der Mortalität und Morbilität*, Jena, 1901, p. 403.

21. F. ŽIŽEK, *Grundriss der Statistik*, second ed., Munich-Leipzig, 1923, p. 255.

22. W. LEXIS, *Abhandlungen zur Theorie der Bevölkerungs- und Mortalitätsstatistik*, p. 87 ff.

23. *Statistik der Bundesrepublik Deutschland*, Vol. 75, Allgemeine Sterbetafel 1949/51, Wiesbaden, 1953, p. 19.

24. "La France a, en effet, le triste privilège de compter un taux de mortalité adulte masculine extrêmement élevé. Elle se place, à cet égard, au tout dernier rang des pays du monde de civilisation comparable à la sienne" (Daric).

25. J. DARIC, *Vieillissement de la Population et Prolongation de la Vie active*, p. 46.

26. M. SPIEGELMAN, "An international comparison of mortality rates at the older ages." *Proceedings of the World Population Conference, 1954*, United Nations, New York, pp. 289–310.

27. "On est en somme sur le chemin d'une population ne mourant plus que pour cause d'usure ou de vice de fabrication" (J. BEAUJEU-GARNIER, *Géographie de la Population*, Vol. I, Paris, 1956 p. 180).

CHAPTER 15

Migration as a Factor in the Aging of Populations

1. GENERAL REMARKS

WITH births and deaths, migration is among the principal factors which influence the age structure of the population.

We differentiate between two types of migrations: migration outside of a country (emigration, immigration) and internal migration (moves from place to place within a country). Naturally, only migrations outside of a country influence the population structure of the country as a whole. Internal moves are without influence in this respect, since they cancel one another out.

All migrations exert an influence on the local age pyramid (province, county, municipality), although it is clear that the influence of various types of migration is not uniform. Here, as a rule, internal migration is of greatest importance, since it is much more frequent than emigration. The attention of demographers has been occupied particularly by the problem of the "flight from the rural areas" and its effect upon the age structure of the urban population, on the one hand, and of the rural population on the other.

The situation with regard to migrations is similar to that of deaths. The fact of migration does not in itself indicate the consequences for the age structure of the population. Here, the age of the migrants is of decisive significance. If young people leave the family hearth, this process tends to age the population of the given region. The immigration of young people has the reverse effect—this process makes the population structure younger.

Hence, it is as necessary to divide migrants according to age as it is to divide deaths. However, this principle is not always realized.

Switzerland, as Dr A. Koller states, does not provide age statistics of migrants. And we would not be able to say much about the age structure of the Swiss population, if it were not for the statistics of foreigners living in Switzerland. For the classifying of foreigners according to age clearly shows that foreign immigration primarily changes the structure of the population of productive age.[1]

Do the statistics of foreigners, referred to by Koller, provide an investigator with material enabling an integral evaluation of the effect of migration on the age structure of the population? In our opinion the statistics of foreigners do not properly fulfil this function. True, the more recent immigration is completely covered by the statistics, but part of the older immigration will not be found in the statistics of foreigners since many of them have been naturalized. Thus statistics of foreigners cannot provide a proper picture of the age structure of the population.

Now let us consider French statistics.

According to census figures the number of foreigners in France amounted to:

1931	2,900,000
1936	2,500,000
1946	1,700,000

Between 1931 and 1936 the number of foreigners decreased in France by 400,000. What caused this decline? Primarily naturalization. "Si, entre 1931 et 1936, un recul s'est manifesté, c'est surtout en raison du grand nombre de naturalisations" (Daric).

The fact that the statistics regarding foreigners show the complete, inconsequential, new migration, but only part of the old, distorts the effect of immigration upon the age structure of the country's population.

Moreover, the lack of information on the age of migrants is not the only deficiency of migration statistics. Such statistics do not use the material accurately and often cause estimates to be more or less approximate.[2]

2. EXTERNAL MIGRATIONS

We have emphasized the importance of the structure of migrants according to age for estimating the essence and effects of migration movements. This applies equally much to external and internal migrations. This is why we begin the detailed consideration of the problems of external migration with the question of the age of the emigrants.

It is known from statistics that young people, in the first half of the productive age, predominate among those leaving the family hearth. This is due to a number of factors, the principal one probably being that young people have little to lose and much to gain, and that they are not frightened by the hardships and troubles of wandering over the world and settling in foreign lands. This is also influenced by immigration policy, which has so often excluded older immigrants (over 40, for example).

But let us look at the figures.

Sauvy cites interesting data on the ages of immigrants. We reproduce them here as important evidence.

IMMIGRATION STRUCTURE ACCORDING TO AGE IN RELATION TO THE POPULATION STRUCTURES OF THE U.S.A. AND SWEDEN IN 1950

Specification	Total	Age groups			
		0–19	20–39	40–59	60+
Immigrants . .	100	28·2	49·5	18·5	3·8
U.S.A.	100	34·3	30·6	22·9	12·2
Sweden . . .	100	29·1	30·3	25·9	14·7

Source: A. SAUVY, *Théorie Générale de la Population*, Vol. 2, Paris, 1954, p. 260.

It is necessary to point out that the term "immigrants" covers 600,000 persons who in 1950 flowed into the U.S.A., Canada, Argentina, Australia and South Africa.

It would be very instructive to compare the age structures of the above body of immigrants with that of the two countries included in the table. One of them, the United States, is a great immigration receptacle, while the other (Sweden) represents an age structure which is free from the distorting influence of two world wars.

The table shows that:

(1) half of the total number of immigrants falls into the age group 20–39, while the share of this age group in the total populations of the United States and Sweden is not even a third;

(2) in the second half of the productive age (40–59) the relation is reversed—the percentage of immigrants is smaller than the populations of that age;

(3) there is a glaring disproportion in the age group of 60 and over—the percentage of immigrants is one-third or one-fourth of the populations of this age.

It is obvious that this difference does not fail to have an effect on the age structures of the countries of immigration as well as on those of emigration. This will soon be made clear by an analysis of concrete statistical material, of which we present selected data illustrating the relations in classical countries of immigration (U.S.A.) and emigration (Ireland).

(a) The United States

In the 19th century, particularly in its second half, the United States of America absorbed a tremendous wave of immigrants from different parts of the world, mainly from Europe.

The following table, derived from the interesting work of Dr J. Isaac, shows immigration into the U.S.A. according to the last country inhabited by the newcomers.

IMMIGRATION TO THE U.S.A. IN 1821-1924 ACCORDING TO THE IMMIGRANTS' LAST PLACE OF RESIDENCE

	Absolute figures	Countries of last residence (%)				
		Western & northern Europe	Eastern & southern Europe	British North America	Mexico	Other countries
1821–40 . .	743,000	78·8	1·2	2·2	1·5	16·3
1841–90 . .	14,685,000	81·2	8·2	7·0	0·1	3·5
1891–1915 .	16,943,000	25·6	66·8	3·2	0·8	3·6
1921–4. . .	2,345,000	25·2	41·3	18·6	8·7	6·2

Source: J. ISAAC, Economics of Migration, London, 1947, p. 62.

As we know, migration statistics are far from being entirely accurate. Hence, the above statistics cannot be considered as fully accurate. One figure must be regarded with especial reservation: the percentage of immigrants from eastern and southern Europe in 1920 was actually higher than shown in the table above. This inaccuracy has its source in the desire to by-pass the restrictions applied by the U.S. government against immigration from those parts of Europe.[3]

What were the ages of the immigrants when they settled in the United States? The answer is given by the table (page 413), which, despite irregularities caused by the non-uniform distribution by age groups, provides a clear picture of the age structure of the immigration.

It follows from this table that immigration into the United States had a fairly well defined character from the viewpoint of the immigrants' ages. Thus:

(1) the percentage of children among the immigrants was relatively insignificant;

(2) the percentage of those aged 45 and over was even smaller (there were years when it amounted to not more than 5–6 per cent);

(3) the basic mass of immigrants (two-thirds, and often three-quarters) were between 15 and 44

Hence, there mainly flowed into the U.S. young people burdened with few children and fewer old persons.

STRUCTURE OF IMMIGRATION TO THE U.S.A. IN 1880–1939 ACCORDING TO AGE

Years	Total	Age groups		
		0–14	15–44	45+
1880–1884. . .	100	22·4	67·4	10·2
1890–1894. . .	100	15·1	77·0	7·9
		0–13	14–44	
1899–1904. . .	100	12·5	82·0	5·5
1905–1909. . .	100	11·9	83·4	4·7
1910–1914. . .	100	12·7	81·7	5·6
		0–15	16–44	
1920–1924. . .	100	18·6	72·2	9·2
1925–1929. . .	100	16·3	74·7	9·0
1930–1931. . .	100	17·1	72·1	10·8
1931–1939. . .	100	17·1	66·7	16·2

Source: J. ISAAC, Economics of Migration, p. 183.

In his comments on the above table, Dr Isaac explains the causes of the increase in the number of older immigrants (45 yr and over) noted after the First World War. Two factors operated here, namely: the immigration policy limiting the flow of unqualified persons and thus directed against young people, and the flow of older people from the Nazi Third Reich due to the persecution raging there.[4]

This immigration structure according to the age of the immigrants becomes clearer when compared with the analogous structure of the U.S. population in general. This data is contained in the next table.

POPULATION STRUCTURE OF THE U.S.A. ACCORDING TO AGE IN 1880–1940

Years	Total	Age groups		
		0–14	15–44	45 and over
1880	100	38·1	45·8	16·0
1920	100	31·8	47·3	20·8
1940	100	25·0	48·3	26·7

Source: J. ISAAC, Ibid., p. 183.

It can now be seen how little the age structure of the immigrants resembles the age structure of the U.S. population. The difference appears in all three age groups. Moreover, as was to be expected, the share of children (0–14) and older people (45 and over) remains lower among the immigrants, while persons belonging to the middle age groups (15–44) are continually greater in number than is the case among the general population of the United States.

Let us now turn to the age structure of the U.S. population according to the classification schemes established by us previously, i.e., by separating out the age group of interest to us: older people of 65 and over.

Since we have dealt with the age-profile of the U.S. population in earlier sections of this work, we limit ourselves here to a very brief presentation of the relations interesting us over a fifty-year interval.

THE U.S. POPULATION STRUCTURE ACCORDING TO AGE IN 1850, 1900 AND 1950 (IN PERCENTAGE)

Year	Total	Age groups		
		0–19	20–64	65+
1850	100	52·5	44·9	2·6
1900	100	44·4	51·5	4·1
1950	100	33·9	58·0	8·1

Source: (1) Dublin, Lotka and Spiegelman, *Length of Life*, p. 256; (2) *Demographic Yearbook*, United Nations, 1954, p. 125.

It is not difficult to gather from the above table that the United States was a country of children and young people, in the fullest sense of the term, during the first half of the last century. We base this assertion on the fact that children and young people below twenty then constituted the majority of American society. There were practically no old people—they hardly numbered 2·6 per 100 inhabitants. Such an age profile is characteristic for a society which was shaped to a great degree by the influx of immigration. It is necessary to add that the unusually high percentage of children was a product, not only of the fertility which was high for that time, but also of the fact that the age group having the highest fertility was best established in American society by strong immigration.

The picture was altogether different at the beginning of the present century, and more so in the second half. Now we see fewer and fewer children and more old people. Time has its effect. Young people who flocked to the "Land of Promise" and acquired children and dollars grew old with time. The number of grandfathers but not of grand-children began to increase, for the offspring of the immigrants adop-ted the cult of the dollar and gave up the cult of children.

It would perhaps be appropriate to compare our conclusions with the opinions of an investigator who has more to say than we on the demography of American society. We refer to the American sociologist and demographer, Paul H. Landis. He says the following on the effects of immigration and immigration policy on the population structure of the United States:

(1) changes in immigration policy as well as in birth rates have a decided effect upon the age composition;

(2) our nation in previous generations accepted thousands, even a million in some years, of immigrants from foreign nations;

(3) the majority were young;

(4) the cutting off of this large supply of youth was not without effect on the age structure of the population of the United States;

(5) their admission in large numbers from 1890–1914 explains in considerable part the high ratio of those in late middle age and old age in the population in the 1940s.[5]

Such are the conclusions of a commentator who looks at demo-graphic phenomena with the eyes of a sociologist.

We feel justified in stating that there is no diversion between our estimate of the effects of immigration (and the changes flowing from it) on the population structure according to age and that of Landis. In the comments of the American sociologist we find partly a con-firmation and partly a supplementation of our assertions. Particularly essential for us is the statement regarding the role of immigration as a factor checking the process of population aging. This effect was strong as long as immigration was large, and while the ranks of the immigrants were composed of a high percentage of young people. After immigration was checked and its proportion of youth limited, the reverse consequences of immigration became manifest. Nor is there anything strange in this—a decrease in the immigration of young people could only cause the age structure of the population to grow older.

(b) Ireland

Let us now see the situation in a classical country of emigration. Ireland is known to be such a country. With Scotland, Ireland provided the majority of emigrants from the British isles to the New World as early as in the 18th century. The causes of the migratory movement were economic and religious. Both factors operated in Ireland.[6]

But the migratory movement from Ireland in the 18th century was a minor event in comparison with the mass migrations which that country experienced in the 19th century. This time economic factors played the decisive role. It was the spectre of poverty and hunger facing the Irish in connection with the deterioration of the national economy which occurred about the middle of the last century.

Ireland is the only country in Europe where over a long period emigration was appreciably greater than the natural increase so that the population decreased following emigration. It lost more than half its population within several scores of years, and the cause of this great depopulation was emigration.

The figures below illustrate the depopulation of Ireland:

1841	6,529,000
1871	4,053,000
1901	3,222,000
1911	3,140,000
1926	2,972,000
1936	2,968,000

Ireland's great demographic drama was enacted between 1841 and 1901. In the course of these sixty years Ireland lost more than half its population. Within the following thirty-five years the country's population decreased by 10 per cent.

And what effect did the mass migrations from Ireland have upon the age structure of that country's population?

The age structure of the Irish population has interested investigators for a long time. Johann Edward Wappäus, the already forgotten German statistician and demographer of the 19th century, in his demographic statistical manual published close on 100 years ago, pointed to the particularly low proportion of 30 to 40-year-old persons in Ireland. Let us recall the figures he presented:

France	14·7%
Netherlands	13·4%
Great Britain	13·1%
Ireland	11·7%

Some time later M. Haushofer referred to the figures of Ireland as a shocking example of (as he called it) "how powerfully need affects the composition of the youngest age group."[7]

Let us recall the primary fact from our investigation that Ireland is one of the countries with the highest proportion of old people. The small number of people in Ireland of virile age and the large proportion of aged is the consequence of emigration.

(c) Conclusions

We now formulate the facts we have established:

(a) one of the lowest proportions of the aged, possessed by the United States, is the result of the great wave of immigration,

(b) one of the highest proportions of the aged, possessed by Ireland, results from the great wave of emigration.

These facts excellently illustrate the effects of immigration and emigration.

The following truths may be formulated by generalizing the experiences of various countries:

(1) emigration, by reducing the ranks of the youth in a country, hastens the aging process of the population;

(2) immigration, by increasing the youth in a country, hastens the rejuvenation of the population.

In agreement with the latter assertion, French demographers have emphasized that if it were not for the inflow of foreigners recruited in their vast majority among the young, the process of population aging in France would have reached a much higher degree than it actually did. Jean Daric estimates that within the last 150 yr the surplus of immigration over emigration increased the population of France by about 4 million. The crop of immigrants would be a million higher if we considered their offspring. Without immigration the French population would have been smaller by 5 million today, and the proportion of the aged would have been higher still. Hence the conclusion that under French conditions immigration played an important role as a factor in rejuvenating the population.[8]

3. INTERNAL MIGRATIONS

There is a vast diversity of forms and types of internal migration. And the composition of internal migrants is no less varied; they differ as to sex, age, education, trades, etc. To this is related the diverse paths of migration, which are often unintentional when the wanderer's staff leads into the unknown.

Changes in places of residence remain, as hitherto, subjects of police rather than scientific interest. Besides the Germans, who can boast of an appreciable literature on internal migration, no great interest is to be found in this problem among sociologists, demographers and statisticians. And this poverty is all the worse for the lack of any statistical material in this field.

We wish to deal with only one problem in this work: the exchange of populations between urban and rural areas. We wish to establish how that exchange reacts upon the age pyramid of the population in these areas.

Socialist theoreticians announce the future abolition of all differences between city and country. It would therefore be all the more desirable to fix the nature of the differences still existing. City and country represent today two entirely different organisms, not only from an economic, cultural and sociological viewpoint, but also from the demographic. We will attempt to elucidate whether there is also a difference in the process of population aging, and if so, to what extent it is conditioned by the population exchange between the rural and urban areas.

(a) The Urbanization Process

We would like to introduce the question by calling attention to the unusual fluidity characterizing modern industrial societies.

Dealing with the situation in the U.S.A. Józef Chałasiński stresses that "fluidity is among the most characteristic traits of the American population. There is an internal migration in the United States on a scale not to be found in other countries. This, of course, pertains to local populations, some of which expand at the expense of others."[9]

Statistical data on the proportions of urban and rural populations in the U.S.A. show a more rapid growth in the urban than in the rural areas.

URBAN AND RURAL POPULATIONS OF THE U.S.A. IN 1880–1940

Year	Total population	Divided	
		urban	rural
1880.	100	28·6	71·4
1890.	100	35·4	64·6
1900.	100	40·0	60·0
1910.	100	45·8	54·2
1920.	100	51·4	48·6
1940.	100	56·5	43·5

Source: (1) E. B. REUTER, Population Problems, pp. 36–37; (2) S. CHANDRASEKHAR, India's Population, p. 30.

During the sixty years 1880–1940, the percentage of the city population doubled in the U.S.A. Until 1910 the rural population towered numerically over that of the cities, while the census of 1920 disclosed a predominance of the urban population. And this predominance increased from census to census.

The urbanization process is unusually rapid in the Soviet Union. This is shown by the following figures, which present the average annual growth of the city population in different periods:

1897–1914	500,000
1920–23	700,000
1923–6	1,000,000
1926–39	2,400,000

Professor Gozulov states that this rapid growth of the urban population in the U.S.S.R. is the result of the industrialization of the country and of the collectivization of agriculture. The transition to large-scale collectivized agriculture and the mechanization of agricultural labour enabled the freeing of a large number of workers from agricultural production who were directed to the cities where industrial construction and production expanded.

The effects of the population shifts referred to above are reflected in the following figures:

URBAN AND RURAL POPULATIONS IN THE U.S.S.R.
IN 1897–1939

Year	Total population	Divided	
		city	rural
1897.	100	11·5	88·5
1914.	100	15·0	85·0
1920.	100	15·6	84·4
1923.	100	15·5	84·5
1926.	100	17·9	82·1
1939.	100	32·8	67·2

Source: A. GOZULOV, *Statystyka ekonomiczna*, Translated from the Russian, Warsaw, 1956, PWN, p. 52.

The progress of urbanization between 1926 and 1939 is very striking. We learn from the *Soviet Manual of Statistical Theory* that the urban population amounted to 26 million in 1926, to 61 million in 1940, and according to the latest manual (published in 1953) to about 80 million. Often great new cities arose on wastelands, while old cities and industrial centres expanded tremendously. Thus, the socialist industrialization of the country induced a great increase in urban population.[10]

The ratio between the urban and rural populations is also changing in Poland.

URBAN AND RURAL POPULATION OF POLAND IN 1900—1960

Year	Total population	Divided	
		urban	rural
1900.	100	17·7	82·3
1921.	100	24·6	75·4
1931.	100	27·4	72·6
1946.	100	31·8	68·2
1950.	100	39·0	61·0
1955.	100	43·0	57·0
1960.	100	48·1	51·9

Source: Statistical Yearbooks, 1939, 1956, 1961.

Until recently Poland was a country with a decided predominance of rural population. In the 1920's, for example, the rural population was three times as numerous as the urban. The rural population is larger even today, but its excess over the urban population is now insignificant.

It follows from the above figures that the question of migration is a large-scale problem.

(b) Age of Migrants

There is reason to stress that internal migration statistics remain poor. We know little regarding the migrants from whom the demographic profile of the modern city is shaped. Usually we do not know their age, sex or occupation.

This is undoubtedly an important gap in our knowledge of the demography of urban and rural areas.

In the opinion of Schubnell,[11] migration statistics face a task with a range and importance we are still unable to define. The author proposes a migration analysis of the distribution of migrants according to sex, age and vocation. It would be difficult not to support proposals which I myself have carried out successfully on the statistics of a large city.[12]

Migration statistics which do not differentiate migrants according to sex, age and vocation are largely fallacious. The very investigation of problems which we regard as belonging to a large-scale category is fallacious.

It is clear that not only the volume of migration, but also the composition of the migrants is important, particularly according to age.

A large proportion of those who leave the rural areas and move to the cities are young people. They move to the cities with the hope of finding employment. According to Tulippe, the search for work is the mainspring of internal migration.[13]

Investigations conducted in Poland in 1952 and 1953 show that the most numerous groups among migrants who refreshed the city populations were of the following ages: 15–19, 20–24 and 25–29. The combined share of these three age groups in the total number of emigrants from the rural areas amounted to from 60–70 per cent. Hence, the rural areas lost to the cities mainly young people between 15 and 30 yr.

There is no need at this time to go into the question of how many of them move to the cities to study and how many to work. What is important is the fact that under the impact of migration the strongest age groups are being depleted in the rural areas, while the cities benefit from them most.

4. POPULATION STRUCTURE OF URBAN AND RURAL AREAS ACCORDING TO AGE

We know that population shifts are not the only factor determining the age structures of urban and rural populations. Birth and death rates also exert an influence on the age profile of urban and rural populations, among whom the birth and death rates are vastly different. It would appear that under these conditions it is impossible to draw conclusions regarding the importance of one or another factor on the basis of the differences appearing in the age structures of the population of urban and rural areas.

Actually, however, the situation is different. As is known, fertility is higher in the rural areas than in the cities. Also, death rates are higher in rural than in urban areas. Both these factors encourage the rejuvenation of the countryside. But since not the rural areas but the cities possess a younger age structure, it is clear that the third factor, population shifts, acts in the opposite direction, causing rural areas to age and cities to rejuvenate. The impact of this factor is so strong that it overshadows the first two: births and deaths.

(a) France

We begin our detailed analysis with France, which particularly attracts our attention because of the advanced population aging in that country.

French statistics, as we know, reckon old age from the age of 60. It is hence with this conception that we primarily establish the ratio of the aged to the population of departments with different degrees of urbanization.

The table below shows how the share of older people in the total populations appeared in departments which are: (a) mainly agricultural; (b) industrial; (c) mixed:

THE PROPORTION OF AGED (60 AND OVER) IN FRANCE
IN 1876 AND 1936 AS DISTRIBUTED IN AGRICULTURAL,
INDUSTRIAL AND MIXED DEPARTMENTS

Departments	1876	1936
Agricultural	11·9	16·5
Industrial	10·9	12·5
Mixed	12·9	16·8
France	11·8	14·7

Source: J. Daric, *Vieillissement de la population et prolongation de la vie active*, p. 26.

The above figures do not establish the certainty that the process of population aging is more advanced in agricultural than in industrial departments. What is more, if the preponderance of agricultural over industrial departments was relatively small in 1876, then it became greater sixty years later. Hence, agricultural departments not only outdistance industrial departments from the viewpoint of population aging, but the tempo of the further development of this process is more rapid in agricultural departments.

These facts may be seen directly from the table. But the table does not tell us anything regarding the causes which produced these facts. This involves the knowledge and experience of the interpreter of the phenomena.

Jean Daric showed that the phenomenon of population aging in France's agricultural departments was the result of the *flight from the rural areas*.[14] Dealing with this question in one of his later works, the French demographer reiterated his previous position with only the slight correction that besides the flight from the countryside, a source of the more advanced aging process in agricultural departments is the attractive power of large cities and industrial centres for the youth.[15]

It is to be seen from this that the French demographer was aware of the decisive role of population shifts as a source of the difference in the pyramid of population aging between city and country. Without denying the correctness of this standpoint we wish only to call attention to one fault in this interpretation: its failure to explain the reasons for the highest coefficients of aging in the mixed departments.

We next present data regarding the share of the aged in the total number of people in rural and urban communities in France after the Second World War (1946), this time, based on another age classification which reckons old age from the age of 65.

This data is presented in the table below:

PERCENTAGE OF PERSONS OF 65 AND OVER IN THE FRENCH POPULATION AS DISTRIBUTED BETWEEN RURAL AND URBAN AREAS IN 1946

Type of community	Total	Sex	
		male	female
Rural and urban communities			
Rural	12·8	11·5	14·1
Urban	9·3	7·4	10·9
Urban communities			
Less than 5000	10·7	9·1	12·2
5000–10,000	9·8	8·1	11·2
10,000–50,000	9·4	7·5	11·1
50,000 and higher	8·6	6·6	10·4

Source: *The Aging of Populations and Its Economic and Social Implications,* United Nations, New York, 1956, p. 19.

It is opportune to ascertain once again that the process of population aging is more advanced in the rural than in the urban areas: while 9·3 per cent of the urban population are aged, 12·8 per cent of the rural population are aged. The proportion of old people in rural areas is close to 40 per cent higher than the corresponding proportion in the cities.

The above table also provides information regarding the differentiation of the proportion of aged depending upon the size of city communities. It seems that the larger the city the lower is the proportion of aged. The older age group is relatively most numerous in the smallest cities, i.e. in those which differ least—mainly from a demographic viewpoint—from rural communities.

Everything points to the fact that the differences have their main source in the migratory movement. It is possible that not only the flight from the village operates here; perhaps an aggravating factor is the flight from the smaller to the larger cities, and from the larger to the largest. Nothing else but the predominance of youth in these migrations can either hasten or check the population-aging process.

(b) Germany

Let us now turn to old German statistics.

These statistics distinguish the following types of communities:
(a) rural localities ("Landorte")—up to 2000 inhabitants,
(b) rural towns ("Landstädte")—from 2000 to 5000 inhabitants,
(c) small cities ("Kleinstädte")—5000 to 20,000 inhabitants,
(d) medium sized cities ("Mittelstädte")—20 to 100,000 inhabitants,
(e) large cities ("Grossstädte")—over 100,000 inhabitants.

Müller gives the following data for Bavaria in a somewhat more compact form (with the second and third groups combined):

POPULATION STRUCTURE OF BAVARIA IN 1919 ACCORDING TO AGE AND COMMUNITY SIZE

Type of community	Total	Age groups		
		0–19	20–59	60+
Rural communities . . .	100	43·4	47·1	9·5
Small cities	100	40·1	51·1	8·8
Medium cities.	100	38·1	54·4	7·5
Large cities	100	32·0	60·4	7·6

Source: JOHANNES MÜLLER, Grundriss der deutschen Statistik, Part III, pp. 33–34.

The dependence of the population age structure upon the type of community appears here in all its consequences. Thus:

(1) the number of children and young people decreases with an increase in the size of the settlement; children and young people are most numerous in the rural areas and fewest in the large cities;

(2) the proportion of the adult population shows a contrary trend—it increases with the size of the community. Thus there are fewest adults in rural areas and most in large cities;

(3) the share of the older people decreases fairly regularly as the community size increases. The largest percentage of the aged is to be found in rural areas and the smallest in medium-sized cities.

To Müller, as to Daric, it is clear that the causes of these differences must be sought in internal migration, which denudes the rural areas of the middle-aged and increases their numbers in the cities.[16]

On the basis of a further, very detailed, study he points to the great differences in the distribution of the 25–29 age-group—it composes 6·7 per cent of the population in rural localities, and 9·2 per cent in large cities.

The fact that the higher age groups show a contrary relationship is ascribed by Müller to the reversal of the migration wave. Many older persons return to the rural areas; and the very unhealthy mode of life of the city people results to a great extent—in the author's opinion—in the thinning out of the ranks of the aged.

Undoubtedly, part of the migrants from the rural areas remain in the cities only as long as they retain employment. But this is perhaps not the only category of persons who in their old age move to the country. There are also natives of the city who want to spend the last years of their lives in country retirement.[17] Both these factors speed the process of aging of the rural population.

(c) Spain

Let us turn to Spain. We consider Spain because, unlike Germany, it is less advanced in the process of population aging.

The following figures characterize the aging level of three Spanish areas divided according to their degree of urbanization, i.e. city, country and mixed areas:

PERCENTAGE OF PERSONS 65 AND OVER IN SPAIN IN 1950

Specification	Percentage
City areas	6·7
Mixed	7·2
Rural	7·7

Source: J. DARIC, "Évolution démographique en Espagne", *Population*, Paris, 1956, No. 1, p. 89.

Here, too, population aging is greater in the rural than in the urban areas. In his comment, the author of the above table, Jean Daric, stresses that this phenomenon is the consequence of emigration from rural to urban areas.

5. FINAL REMARKS AND CONCLUSIONS

The foregoing analysis enables us to establish that migration plays no small role in shaping the age structure of the population and that the advancing process of population aging is to a great measure dependent on it.

We have established in detail that:

(1) young people predominate among emigrants who leave the countries of their birth in search of better conditions of existence;

(2) the preponderance of youth among migrants ensures changes in the age structure of the countries of emigration at the expense of the middle-aged groups. On the other hand, the effects of the migration movement are the reverse for the countries of immigration, where the middle-aged groups gain in strength;

(3) the thinning out of the population in the productive age induces a relative rise in the proportion of older people, thus speeding the process of population aging in countries of emigration;

(4) immigration has a reverse effect. It causes a weakening of the process of population aging in the countries accepting migrants;

(5) internal migrations react similarly; in the areas of outflow of young people in the productive age, there is a decline of the middle-aged groups and a simultaneous relative rise in the proportion of the aged. The situation is reversed in the areas absorbing large numbers of migrants in the productive age;

(6) the *flight from the country*[18] is the source of essential differences in the age structure of the populations of urban and rural areas. The process of population aging is more advanced in the rural than in the urban areas;[19]

(7) another factor hastening the process of aging of rural populations is the frequent phenomenon of old people returning to, or moving to the country with the desire to spend their last years in rural retirement;

(8) the process of population aging is further fed in the rural areas by the greater exodus from the country than from the cities;

(9) the influence of migration, particularly external, on the age structure of the population in city and country is so great that as a rule it overshadows the other factors, such as birth and death rates.[20]

REFERENCES

1. A. KOLLER, "Umschichtungen in der schweizerischen Bevölkerung," *Schweiz. Z. Volkswirtsch. u. Stat.*, 1956, 92, No. 3, p. 285.

2. "They are therefore subject to a considerable margin of error and cannot claim to do more than convey a rough idea of the trends of international migration during the past century". (J. ISAAC, *Economics of Migration*, International Library of Sociology and Social Reconstruction, (Ed. Dr K. MANNHEIM), London, 1947, p. 59).

3. "The share of the Eastern and Southern European countries after 1920 is somewhat higher than is indicated in this table. In order to evade the restrictions a substantial number immigrated clandestinely or took up temporary residence in other American countries" (J. ISAAC, *Economics of Migration*, London, 1947, p. 62).

4. "A marked increase of the older age-groups at the expense of the middle group is noticeable after 1924, mainly as a consequence of the restrictive measures. These discriminated in practice against young people of working age by giving preference to relatives of earlier immigrants and by excluding other applicants without means or special qualifications. Since 1933 U.S.A. immigration has been largely recruited from refugees and from nationals of some of the neighbour states. Among the refugees were many elderly people who would not have emigrated but for persecution, and who were admitted to the U.S.A. on the strength of their special qualifications or their independent means" (J. ISAAC, *op. cit.*, pp. 183–4).

5. P. H. LANDIS, *Population Problems, A Cultural Interpretation*, Second edition prepared by Paul H. Hatt, American Book Co., New York, 1954, p. 99.

6. "The number of emigrants who left the British Isles in order to become settlers in the New World increased considerably in the course of the eighteenth century. The new settlers came mainly from Ireland and Scotland. Scottish emigration was largely due to changes in the agricultural structure of the country in connection with the break-up of the clan system. In the case of the Irish settlers the motive was economic distress or religious prejudice at home" (J. ISAAC, *op. cit.*, p. 18).

7. M. HAUSHOFER, *Wykład Statystyki*, (*A Lecture on Statistics*), Polish edition, p. 183.

8. "Le vieillissement de la population française eût été plus accentué encore sans l'immigration, qui est intervenue comme un important élément de rajeunissement." (J. DARIC, *Le Vieillissement de la Population en France et ses Conséquences Économiques et Sociales*, p. 97).

9. J. CHAŁASIŃSKI, *Społeczeństwo i wychowanie* (*Society and Upbringing*), Warsaw, 1948, pp. 206–207.

10. *Teoriya Statistiki*, (joint work), Moscow, 1953, p. 251.

11. H. SCHUBNELL, "Der Beitrag der Bevölkerungsstatistik zur Untersuchung der Zusammenhänge zwischen Bevölkerung und Wirtschaft", *Allg. Stat. Arch.*, 1955, 39, No. 4, p. 288.

12. Professor Rosset, author of this work, was for many years chief of city statistics in Lodz. (Editor's note).

13. O. TULIPPE, *Le vieillissement de la population belge*, Brussels, 1952, p. 44.

14. "Cela met bien en évidence l'influence de l'exode rural sur le vieillissement des départements agricoles" (J. DARIC, *Vieillissement de la Population et Prolongation de la Vie active*, 1948, p. 26).

15. J. DARIC, *Le Vieillissement de la Population en France et ses Conséquences économi-ques et sociales*, 1955, p. 96.

16. J. MÜLLER, *Grundriss der deutschen Statistik*, Part III, Jena 1926, p. 33.

17. The American sociologist D. F. ALLEGER provided some interesting information in *Rural Sociology* (of June, 1955), on this special category of migrants. According to this information, of the 400,000 persons who yearly reach the retirement age, an appreciable part move to the country, planning to derive some additional income from various agricultural pursuits. On the basis of an inquiry conducted in Florida, Alleger states that these casual farmers adapt themselves well to the conditions of life new to the majority of them. (*Population*, Paris, 1956, No. 1, p. 183).

18. This phrase, so universally used today, is to be found in French statistics of the 17th century of the famous Marshal Vauban (E. ROSSET, *Historia Statystyki*, (*History of Statistics*), Lodz, 1950, p. 34).

19. Our conclusions apply to the total city population and to the total rural population. If we consider particular cities and particular rural areas, then the results of the investigation may, naturally, be different. In some cases the situation may be quite the opposite of that which we have defined as typical. For we also know of cases of flight from the cities which may be less sporadic than at first appears.

20. In individual cases the role of birth and death rates may be greater than that of population migrations. In his interesting study of population aging in Belgium, Professor Tulippe showed that in a whole number of districts (*arrondissements*) the age structure of the population was shaped under the powerful influence of the birth rate while in other districts infant mortality played a similar role.

CHAPTER 16

War as a Population Aging Factor

1. PRELIMINARY REMARKS

What are the repercussions of the cataclysm of war on demographic relations? Does it exert any influence on the age structure of the population? Does it have any reaction on the process of population aging?

The above questions concern very essential problems which cannot remain unanswered in this work.

Statisticians and demographers have long been interested in the demographic effects of war. In 1872, at the conclusion of the Franco-Prussian war of 1870–71, the German statistician, Dr Ernst Engel, published a series of excellent contributions ("Beiträge zur Statistik des Krieges von 1870/71") in *Zeitschrift des Preussischen Statistischen Bureaus*, containing a statistical analysis of war deaths according to the cause and place.

The First World War evoked an extensive literature on the demographic effects of that war. This literature was initiated by the noted demographer, Liebman Hersch, who wrote on the question in Swiss journals while the war was still in progress. The estimate of war losses made by various authors (Döring, Woytinsky, etc.) became famous.

The demographic problems ensuing from the war also occupied the author of this book. The fruit of my labours was the thesis regarding the existence of a demographic law of war. On the invitation of Professor Corrado Gini I read my thesis at the International Congress of Population Research in 1931 at Rome.[1] Two years later I published a more extensive study on these problems.[2]

On the basis of statistical materials from the countries which participated in the First World War (1914–18), it was possible to assert in this work that war is the source of a deep and unavoidable transformation, not only in political and economic relations, but also in demographic phenomena. Population processes—the natural population movement as well as migration—experience a variety of disturbances under the influence of war, and all these perturbations last longer than the war. They also appear after the war in what is called the compensatory period closing the demographic war cycle. The state of the people as well as their constitutions undergo important changes as a result of war. These involve mainly a regrouping in the sex structure in favour of women and in the age structure to the benefit of the adults.

In relation to the theme of this work, let us consider the last-named problem: the regrouping in the age structure of combatants after the First World War, in favour of the middle age groups.

2. THE DEMOGRAPHIC EFFECTS OF THE FIRST WORLD WAR (1914–18)

After the terrible slaughter which took millions of lives of people in the prime of life during the First World War, the percentage of adult population, so severely reduced by war, was greater than before the war. How did this happen? Did the war affect other age groups still more? It seems that it did. In fact, the war caused the greatest devastation among children.

This phenomenon is well illustrated by the figures below which are based on statistics of the German Reich and culled by us from the collection *Die Welt in Zahlen*,[3] popular in its time.

(a) Germany

As a result of the war the number of births decreased in Germany. If we take as the point of departure the number of births in 1914 (when the population level was still normal) then we get the following deficit in births in the five years following:

1915	−548,000
1916	−812,000
1917	−934,000
1918	−918,000
1919	−575,000

The yearly deficit in births thus fluctuated between half a million and a million. In total it grew during the five years (1915–19) to the tremendous number of 3,787,000 unborn. This birth deficit was the direct consequence of the war.

In a similar manner the losses induced by the increased number of deaths was calculated. Taking as a basis the estimated number of deaths in 1913 (the 1914 figure could not be regarded as normal this

time), the increase in deaths in successive war years was calculated
thus:

1914	+286,000
1915	+432,000
1916	+270,000
1917	+312,000
1918	+575,000

As can be seen, the increase in the number of deaths is incomparably
lower than the deficit of births; they range from a low of 270,000 to
a high of 575,000. The highest annual increase in deaths corresponds
to the lowest annual deficit of births. The total increase in deaths in
the five war years (1914–18) amounted to 1,875,000, which is equal
to half of the deficit in births. To avoid misunderstanding it is necessary
to state clearly that mortality statistics embrace both those killed in
the battlefields and those who died as a result of wounds. Woytinsky
fixed their number at 1,523,000.

Adding the two types of war losses, we have:

unborn children	3,787,000
war deaths	1,875,000
total	5,662,000

Thus, according to Woytinsky's estimate, German population losses
from the deficit of births and increase in deaths total 5,662,000, of
which one-third were deaths from war and two-thirds unborn children.

Estimates of German population losses made by other statisticians
show a higher number of war deaths. Burgdörfer maintained that
there were approximately one million more deaths in the German
Reich during the war of 1914–18 than could normally be expected,
while the number of soldiers killed or who died of wounds numbered
two million.[4] According to C. Döring's calculation, cited by Žižek,
German population losses totalled 6,300,000.[5]

The highest estimate of supernumerary deaths is to be found in
Burgdörfer. The increased number of deaths among the civilian population ("eine zivile Mehrsterblichkeit") and soldiers' deaths numbered
about three million supernumerary deaths. But even this high estimate of war deaths falls short of the births unrealized because of the
war. Hence the thesis is valid that the greatest losses in connection
with the First World War were born in Germany, not by the middle-
aged but by the youngest age groups.

(b) France

In contrast with Germany, France was among the countries of the lowest fertility. There is nothing strange therefore in the fact that the war births deficit was lower in France than in Germany. We base ourselves again on the uncomplicated but not too accurate estimates of Woytinsky.

As compared with the number of births in 1914, the French deficit in births during 1915–19 amounted to:

1915	−260,000
1916	−350,000
1917	−320,000
1918	−260,000
1919	−206,000

The annual deficit in births thus fluctuated in France between 200,000 and 350,000. In the five years 1915–19 the total number of missing births amounted to 1,396,000.

At the same time the following high number of supernumerary deaths was noted (in relation to the number of deaths in 1913):

1914	+388,000
1915	+328,000
1916	+228,000
1917	+118,000
1918	+368,000

As can be seen, the war brought about a high number of human sacrifices in France too. The least painful year (1917) showed 118,000 war fatalities. The number was twice as high in 1916 and three times as high in 1914, 1915 and 1918. In total, five years of war took 1,430,000 human lives.

It would have to be acknowledged on the basis of these data that the surplus of deaths more or less equalled the deficit in births. This assertion would, however, be risky in view of the different results to be found in other sources.

The French author Mme Beaujeu-Garnier claims that French war losses in the first world war amounted to 1,500,000 without counting the deficit in births, which she fixes as 1,780,000.[6] In the light of these figures, which are correctly calculated and certainly closer to the truth, in France as in Germany, the loss of births was the chief item in the demographic casualities borne by them.

(c) Polish Territory

The paucity of available statistical material—we possess only the data contained in *The Demographic Laws of War*—allows us to present a more or less complete account of population losses only for the Prussian-annexed part of Poland and for the Christian population of the Polish Kingdom when annexed by Russia. Our estimate runs to 1918 as the last year of the division of Poland.

In the Prussian-annexed territories the deficit in births during the four years 1915–18 amounted to 364,000, and to 391,000 in the Polish Kingdom. We thus counted 755,000 lost births, not in five but only four years, without counting Galicia and the western territories, which were part of the Polish State during the twenty years between the two world wars. For the entire territory of Poland, and for a period of five years (if we include 1919, which is not considered in the above estimate) the deficit in births would easily exceed a million.

The above calculation fixes the deficit in births in relation to the number of births in 1914. But the assumption is justified that if the First World War had not broken out, then the number of births in 1915–19 would have been greater than in 1914. Hence the conclusion that we are underestimating the deficit in births.

Let us now deal with the second kind of war losses in the field of demography, namely with the excess of deaths above the usual norm. This time we take 1913 as the norm.

The war years were disastrous for the population of the Polish lands. In the five war years (1914–18) 48,000 supernumerary deaths were recorded in the part annexed by Prussia, and 212,000 among the Christian population of the Kingdom.

If there were small differences above between the part annexed by Prussia and the Kingdom, here the differences are striking. There were four times as many supernumerary deaths in the Kingdom as in the part annexed by Prussia. How can this disproportionately high surplus of deaths in the Kingdom be interpreted?

In a historical essay devoted to the health conditions in the Kingdom under German occupation (1914–18) Dr Henryk Trenkner wrote that "the lack of clothes, fuel and the wanderings of the people for the purpose of obtaining supplies, which took place under the worst possible hygienic conditions, resulted in the spread of contagious diseases among the population. Hunger diminished the resistance of the organism, created favourable conditions for the spread of disease and increased mortality."[7] The author enumerated the following epidemics which the Kingdom experienced: typhoid fever, typhus, dysentery. There were even cases of cholera.

It is necessary to add to this the tremendous mortality from tuberculosis in the cities and towns of the Kingdom. In Lodz the coefficient of deaths from tuberculosis in 1917 was 92·5 per 10,000 inhabitants.[8] In Warsaw it was still higher, reaching 113·5 that same year. Tuberculosis simply mowed down the people.

Hence the surplus of deaths was far behind the deficit in births. Thus, in the Polish territories, as in Germany, the war victims were primarily children, whose numbers were not adequately replaced for many years.

(d) Infant Mortality During the First World War

It is necessary to remember that the ranks of the children were thinned out during the First World War, not only because of the lack of a new crop. They were also decimated as a result of increased mortality. Part of the supernumerary deaths, referred to above, were of children.

Let us cite several characteristic facts from the period of the First World War:

(1) the infant mortality rate in France, which was below 11 per cent before the war, reached 12·8 per cent in 1914–19;

(2) in Belgium, during the concluding phase of the war (1917–18), the child mortality rate exceeded the 1914 level. Thus it was

1914	13·0
1917	14·0
1918	14·6

The facts leave no doubt that the increase in child mortality had no small share in the increased death rate during the war.

However, we must not ignore the opposite situation—the *decline* in child mortality in some places during the war. This took place in the *first years of the war* in Belgium, for instance. How can one explain a decrease in infant mortality during universal impoverishment of the people, brought about by war?

Basically this is not a new phenomenon. Let us remember the fact established by Karl Marx in the first volume of *Capital*. Thus at a time of general unemployment and want during the crisis brought about by the curtailment of cotton shipments as a result of the American Civil War, doctors observed a recession of infant mortality in England. Marx explained that the industrial stagnation returned their mothers to the children—at least for a time.

We have a somewhat similar situation here. The war brought numerous troubles and the lack of means of subsistence to large numbers of people, but at the same time—perhaps because of the very hardships—improved the concern for children. Of these two antagonistic factors (one acting against the children and the other in their favour) the second factor dominated for a time. Thus may be explained the decline in infant mortality noted in certain European countries in the first period of the war. But when in the later war years the peoples' living conditions noticeably worsened, the effects of this factor swamped the parents' efforts to keep their children alive, and a rise in infant mortality followed.

Thus we see that during the First World War two factors militated against the children:

(1) the tremendous decrease in births (the deficit in births was greater than the surplus of deaths among the adult and aged population);

(2) the increase in the number of deaths among children, primarily among infants.

(e) Traces of the Cataclysm of War in the Post-war Age Pyramids

When censuses were renewed after the First World War, they showed that the combatant countries had suffered a devastation of the youth and people in the prime of life who perished on the battlefields; but they indicated an even greater holocaust—which is not surprising—among the children.

Let us consider the changes (presented in the table on page 436) effected by the war in the age structures of the population of four countries: Germany, France, Belgium and Czechoslovakia.

The structure indices used here decrease only in the children's group (0–14 yr). The proportion of adults increased after the war. The percentage of old people also increased. As we know, this is considered the measure of population aging.

Thus in Germany, France, Belgium and Czechoslovakia the process of population aging, begun during the First World War, progressed further. And the situation did not differ in many other countries where the number of births decreased and where the adult population was reduced by the vast losses on the battlefields, so that the proportion of the aged could not but increase.

A COMPARISON OF THE AGE STRUCTURE OF THE POPULATIONS OF GERMANY, FRANCE, BELGIUM AND CZECHOSLOVAKIA BEFORE AND AFTER THE FIRST WORLD WAR

Country and year	Total	Age groups		
		0–14	15–59	60 and over
Germany				
1910.	100	34·0	58·1	7·9
1919.	100	28·5	62·5	9·0
France				
1911.	100	25·5	61·5	12·5
1919.	100	22·7	63·6	13·7
Belgium				
1910.	100	30·5	60·1	9·4
1920.	100	24·9	64·8	10·3
Czechoslovakia				
1910.	100	33·9	57·2	8·9
1921.	100	27·8	62·5	9·7

Sources: (1) E. Rosset, *Prawa demograficzne wojny*, p. 55 ff.; (2) V. Srb, *Biologická situace v českých zemich*, 1947, p. 37.

3. THE DEMOGRAPHIC EFFECTS OF THE SECOND WORLD WAR (1939–1945)

The Second World War greatly outdid the First with respect to the colossal losses of human lives. Barbarism under the sign of the swastika, ruling for several years over a large part of Europe, organized the planned destruction of entire peoples. With incredible cruelty the Jewish populations of Germany and of the occupied countries were murdered. Poles were ruthlessly destroyed. According to the famous book by Lord Russell of Liverpool, entitled *The Scourge of the Swastika*, (London, 1954), a total of 12 million people perished at the hands of the Nazis horde. Shawcross, chief prosecutor for Great Britain, cited the same figure at the Nuremberg trials (July 26, 1946). Involved here are exclusively the civilian victims of the "Brown Plague", who perished in Nazi death-camps, in ghettoes, in places of mass execution, in Gestapo torture chambers, jails, etc., etc.

(a) The Demographic Balance of the War in the Third Reich

How did the natural population movement shape itself during the Second World War?

Statistics of the natural population movement of countries which were in the German sphere of influence, primarily in Germany itself, do not provide a true picture of the reality. Everything which the Nazi ringleaders did not wish to disclose was deliberately eliminated from the mortality statistics. They thus hid the extermination of anti-Nazi elements and of the Jewish people, the deaths in concentration camps and of those transported to Germany from other lands as slave labourers.

Despite this camouflage, German statistics have not succeeded in hiding the fact that all the typical demographic expressions of war made themselves felt in the very first years of the war. This refers to such facts as:

(1) the decrease in the number of births below the level of 1939 or below the pre-war level;

(2) the increase in the number of deaths among civilians over the level of 1938, or above the pre-war level;

(3) the increase in infant mortality.

As we know, German statistics remained silent about the deaths on the battlefields and under the ruins of bombed houses. But the increasing numbers of death notices in the German press, ornamented with the picture of an Iron Cross and the huge number of ruined houses in German cities attacked from the air by the Allies, leave no doubt as to the importance of these war losses.

Let us look at the rather fragmentary data in our possession.

The number of births on the territory of the German Reich before the Nazi annexations (the "Altes Reichsgebiet") amounted to:

1939	1,413,230
1940	1,402,255
1941	1,308,232
1942	1,055,915

We do not know the number of births in the years following, but those cited give a clear picture of the evolution of births in Germany during the Second World War. This was, of course, an evolutionary decline.

If the figures of the three war years (1940, 1941, 1942) are compared with the numbers for 1939 taken as the norm, then the deficits of births in the first three war years were as follows:

1940	− 10,975
1941	−104,998
1942	−357,315

The sum total of the birth deficits in the above three years (1940–42) amounted to 473,288. And we learn from the same source—the official German statistical organ—that during the first four war years (1940–43) the birth deficit in Germany amounted to 892,000.[9]

Within the range of these figures it is not difficult to conclude that by adding the two additional war years (1944 and 1945) the German birth deficit would increase to two million. The *German balance sheet of population during the Second World War* drawn by West German statisticians refers to a birth deficit exceeding two millions.[10]

Below are the numbers of civilian deaths, which—as we have said—do not include the victims of aerial attacks:

1938	949,284
1939	1,009,333
1940	1,045,708
1941	995,573
1942	990,383

We now take 1938 as the norm. As compared with the figure for that year there was a fairly appreciable increase in civilian deaths during the war years.

In the first years of the war the excess of deaths among civilians over the 1938 norm amounted to:

1939	60,049
1940	96,424
1941	46,291
1942	41,099

We are now able to underscore the incompleteness of the German war mortality statistics. Even so, the increase in deaths in the first war years amounted to between 40,000 and 100,000 annually, among the civilian population alone, not including the victims of aerial bombardment. It can be imagined how that number rose in the later war period, particularly when the war moved to the territory of the German Reich.

What is the general balance sheet of the demographic losses borne by the German nation in connection with the Second World War instigated by Germany?

Immediately after the end of the war many statisticians in different countries undertook an accounting for the purpose of establishing the demographic losses brought about by the Second World War. In these accounts the Germans naturally constituted one of the highest figures.

German statisticians made two such accounts for their country. One was published under the title "Attempts at a German balance sheet of the Second World War" in *Wirtschaft und Statistik* of September, 1949 (as the name indicates, this was a provisional balance sheet). The second, as we stated, was published seven years later in the same journal, and that balance sheet may be considered as definitive.

Not only the provisional but also the definitive balance sheet operates with approximate values and cannot pretend to complete accuracy.

Let us note that both cases involve estimates based, not on the registration of individual cases but, out of necessity, on the *balance method*. "Statistics documenting German war losses based on the

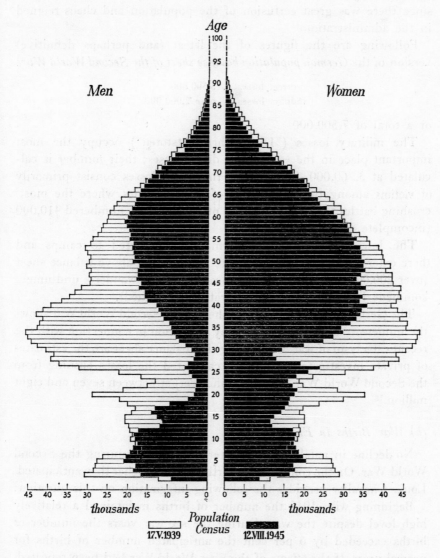

FIG. 8. Berlin's age structure of the population before (1939) and after (1945) the war

registration of individual cases will never be possible", asserted the West German statistical administration. "The only way," it states further, "to obtain a picture of at least the volume of losses is to make a balance of the population."

Dr K. Horstmann explains that the normal registration of deaths, like mortality statistics, could not be obtained by the end of the war since there was great cerfusion of the population and chaos reigned in the administration.[11]

Following are the figures of the latest (and perhaps definitive) version of the *German population balance sheet of the Second World War*:

> direct losses... 5,500,000
> indirect losses... over 2,000,000

or a total of 7,500,000.

The military losses ("Die Wehrmachtstoten") occupy the most important place in the estimate of direct losses; their number is calculated at 3,760,000. The rest of the direct losses consist primarily of victims among the populations of the territories where the most crushing battles took place. Victims of aerial attacks numbered 410,000 (incomplete estimate).

The Jewish population of Germany, transported to camps and there exterminated in gas chambers, figure in the above balance sheet (over 200,000 persons) under the heading "Ausgewanderte und umgekommene Juden" (Jews who emigrated or perished).

The German population balance sheet of the Second World War shows the immensity of the losses borne by the nation in connection with the recent cataclysm of war. Confirming that balance sheet are the estimates of private investigators who have calculated the losses ensuing from the Second World War (direct and indirect) at between seven and eight million.[12]

(b) War Births in France

No decline in natality was registered in France during the Second World War. On the contrary, the birth rate was higher than anticipated. Louis Chevalier provides the following information on this question:

Beginning with 1940 the number of births maintained a relatively high level despite the war. During the six war years the number of births exceeded by 6 per cent the anticipated number of births for normal years. If the effects of the First World War had been repeated, the annual number of births would have amounted to about 410,000, whereas the yearly average during the Second World War amounted to 590,000, or 180,000 more births. This enabled France to avoid an additional population loss of at least one million. This was the result of the appreciable increase in fertility of unseparated couples.[13]

The increase in births during the war is itself undoubtedly a very real phenomenon, particularly when compared with the catastrophic decline in births during [the First World War. We cannot however, ignore the fact that the 6 per cent increase in births referred to by the French demographer is estimated by assuming the pre-war exceptionally low fertility in France. Whether this assumption was correct for the 1940's, or whether a higher number of births should have been assumed, is a matter for discussion.

Today, *ex post facto*, in the light of the experiences of countries belonging to the low fertility zone, it seems certain that demographic prognoses made for these countries before the war were not very realistic, for they did not take into consideration the transformations in the process of development of the birth rate at the end of the 1930s. This transformation was not perceived at first by statisticians.

As far as we are concerned, we are not convinced of the correctness of Chevalier's estimates. The 6 per cent increase in births of which the French demographer speaks seems to conceal a much less favourable reality. If it had not been for the war, if it had not been for the operation of the demographic law of war, the number of births would have been higher in France during 1940–45 than that actually recorded. If that is so, it is necessary to speak of a war deficit in births, and not of a 6 per cent increase.

(c) The Operation of the Demographic Law of War during the Second World War

We complete the picture of the war demography of Germany and France with the scant information provided in his time by B. Smulewicz, which throws light on the demographic perturbations experienced by the southern and south-eastern European countries during the Second World War. Following is a group of comparable data:

(1) in Italy during 1939–43 the birth rate declined by 13·5 per cent and mortality increased simultaneously;

(2) in Rumania the birth rate was 25 per cent lower in 1943 than the level of 1938, while mortality increased by 9 per cent in the same period;

(3) in 30 of the largest Greek cities, in 1942, the birth rate was practically half of the pre-war level, while the mortality rate almost trebled;

(4) Yugoslavia lost 13 per cent of its pre-war population during the Second World War.

Hence we see that the demography of a whole series of European countries drawn into the whirlpool of the Second World War is characterized by manifestations known to us from the preceding war. These manifestations in their time provided the impulse for formulating the *demographic laws of war*.

There were countries, however, and it would be a mistake not to recognize this, in which the case was different despite the war raging in Europe and in the world. The war did not prevent an increase of the birth rate in more than one country. Such was the case, for example, in Denmark, the Netherlands and in a number of other countries of the *low fertility* zone, particularly in the later years of the war.[14]

Does it follow that the "demographic laws of war" did not operate during the most cruel and bloodiest of all wars—the Second World War?

In our opinion, the nomenclature "demographic laws of war" conceals a certain singular tendency, or more precisely, a certain combination of particular tendencies which condition the impact of the war upon demographic relationships. The operation of each of these tendencies may coincide with, or, on the contrary, may oppose the operation of general tendencies which are independent of the war.

During the First World War (1914–18) the decline in births, which we reckon as one of the principal demographic laws of war, was accompanied by a general decrease in fertility.

The case was different during the Second World War (1939–45). Shortly before the outbreak of the war there was a turn in the general birth tendency. The declining tendency gave way to a rising tendency.

This new general birth tendency expressed itself so strongly here and there that even the outbreak of the war and its destructive effects could not cancel out the rising birth movement. The particular tendency was replaced by the immeasurably stronger opposing general tendency.

In our opinion the demographic laws of war have always operated, although their operation is not always visible.

(d) Wartime Infant Mortality

Let us now turn to the problem of infant mortality during the Second World War. We begin with the situation in Germany.

For lack of data regarding the range of wartime infant mortality in the German Reich (the U.N. demographic yearbooks do not include this data) we limit ourselves to Berlin figures.

INFANT MORTALITY IN BERLIN IN 1935-43

Year	Percentage	Year	Percentage
1935–39	6·0	1944	12·3
1940.	5·9	1945	35·9
1941.	5·7	1946	12·3
1942.	6·7	1947	8·5
1943.	6·6	1948	7·5

Source: Demographic Yearbook, 1953, United Nations, New York, 1953, pp. 222–223.

We learn from the above table that by 1942 infant mortality in the German capital exceeded its level of the five preceding pre-war years (1935–9). And when the war action began to intensify for the Berlin population (the tremendous aerial attacks of 1944) infant mortality was more than double the pre-war norm (from 6–12·3 per cent) and by 1945, when Berlin was on the front lines, it reached the monstrously high level of 35·9 per cent.

War activity ended in the first days of May, 1945 but for several years the infant mortality rate in Berlin remained on a higher level than before the war.

Can the Berlin figures be extended to the situation in Germany as a whole? It would seem so. For it can be imagined that everywhere bombing disorganized life, especially where the front lines approached, which means over the whole territory of Germany in certain periods. As in the capital, an increase in infant mortality had to follow.

Figures for Budapest are similar. There, before the war, infant mortality stood at 8–9 per cent. In 1945, during the siege of the city, which lasted 6 weeks (from the beginning of the year to February 12) and for several months following infant mortality reached 30–40 per cent in the Hungarian capital.

Following are the infant mortality rates for the months when they reached the highest levels:

1945 February	35·5%
1945 March	32·1%
1945 June	39·8%
1945 July	37·7%
1945 November	29·3%

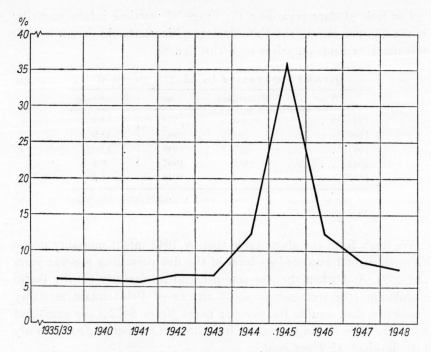

FIG. 9. Infant mortality in Berlin during the Second World War (1939–45). Deaths in the first year of life per 100 live births.

The yearly balance of infant mortality in Budapest in 1945 equalled 27·5 per cent. Thus, the pre-war level was exceeded more than 3 times over.

These Berlin and Budapest figures leave no doubt as to the destructive effects of war on the mortality among the youngest citizens. But if we wish to obtain a more complete and definitive picture of this condition, we must go beyond the necessarily limited city statistics and turn to nation-wide data concerning the natural population movements.

During the Second World War the infant mortality curve was, in general, similar to that observed during the First World War. Thus in a number of European countries, owing to the improved care for children, a temporary decline in infant mortality was reached during the war.

But this decline did not take place everywhere. In France, the Netherlands, and Italy, not even a temporary decline in mortality was noted.

A particularly large increase in infant mortality could be observed in the Netherlands and Austria. In both countries the maximum infant mortality rate (for 1945) was double the level of the last five years before the war (1935–9).

(e) War Deaths of the Aged

The increase of civilian mortality during the war is, of course, not limited to children. No section of the population can be free from the heavy and painful sacrifices connected with war. Particularly great is the toll in death among the adult population, including the aged.

The problem of the increase in the mortality of the aged during war has not as yet been closely investigated, although this is by no means a small problem. It is not out of place to observe that it is difficult to evaluate the correctness of many demographic balance sheets, including the figures of the life tables of the early post-war years, due to the inaccurate knowledge of the process of the hastened mortality of the aged during war.

We know that, at the end of the war, population censuses show an increase over the pre-war period in the proportion of the aged. Is it possible to assert on this basis that the aged are immune from the destructive effects of war? Such a conclusion would certainly be wrong.

For the proportion of the aged to increase it is not necessary for their actual numbers to increase. It is not even necessary that the number of the aged be maintained. An increase in the proportion of the aged can also appear when there is an actual decrease in their numbers. This can occur when the other age groups are reduced to a greater degree.

Such situations were not rare after the First World War. Let us recall in this connection our conclusions as to the role of children unborn as a result of the war, in the shaping of post-war demographic relationships. Such unborn children were without doubt one of the factors in the increase in the proportions of aged observed after the war.

What do the absolute figures say in this case?

Let us return to the highly instructive war statistics of Budapest. In the capital of Hungary the number of deaths at the age of 60 and over, or deaths of the aged, amounted to the following: under normal conditions (in 1938) to 6500, and under abnormal conditions (1945) to 19,000.

Hence we can assert that there was a tremendous increase in the number of deaths among the aged of Budapest. The cause of this rise was the unprecedentedly difficult conditions of existence, caused by the cataclysm of war.

(f) Changes in the Post-war Age Structure of the Population (using Poland as an Example)

The changes in the age structures of European populations resulting from the Second World War were not as uniform as those of the First World War (1914–18). Several of the post-war age pyramids again show a thinning out of the proportion of children and an increase in the proportion of the aged. But besides these more or less classical shifts, we notice other changes in the age structure. In certain countries there was a simultaneous increase in the proportion of the aged and in that of children.

A combination of different factors determined that the age pyramid shaped itself one way in some countries and differently in others. It is certainly not without significance whether countries of the low fertility zone are involved (during the Second World War a general tendency to increased birth rates was operative in this zone), or countries belonging to the high fertility zone, to whom this tendency was foreign. Nor is it a matter of indifference to what extent the war permeated the life of a given country, and to what degree it weakened the material and moral bases of existence of its people.

It is not necessary to seek far for an example of a country which suffered most heavily from the last war—such a country is Poland.[15]

Let us see how the age structure of the population looked in Poland before the outbreak of the war (January 1,1939) and several years after it ended (1949).

AGE STRUCTURE OF THE POPULATION IN POLAND ACCORDING TO AGE BEFORE THE OUTBREAK OF AND AT THE END OF THE SECOND WORLD WAR

Year	Total	Age groups		
		0–14	15–64	65+
1939	100	32·5	62·5	5·0
1949	100	28·3	66·6	5·1

Source: Publications of the Central Statistical Office.

We have here the following characteristic facts closely related to the cataclysm of war:

(1) there was a sharp decline in the proportion of children as a con-

sequence of the tremendous drop in the number of births during the Second World War;

(2) the proportion of adults increased despite the tremendous losses borne by precisely this sector of the population, which is explained by the fact that the other age groups suffered even greater losses;

(3) the proportion of the aged increased extremely little, which justifies the supposition that a large number of older people perished in Poland during the extended occupation.

In the final account the process of population aging gauged by the percentage of old people does not show any great improvement. From 5 per cent before the war, the proportion of the aged rose after the war to 5·1 per cent. However, if we calculated the aging index by the method of the French demographers, then we would have to state that the process of population aging experienced not such a small acceleration in Poland as a result of the Second World War.

In the light of the experience of both world wars the cataclysm of war in the final result accelerates the aging of combatant societies.

4. CONCLUSIONS

We should now like to summarize briefly the results of our investigations on the aging of societies.

The following may be taken as our conclusions:

(1) births, deaths and population migrations exert a simultaneous influence upon the process of aging as compared to the rejuvenation of populations;

(2) on a national scale the effect of the birth rate is decisive; as heretofore a decline in fertility has been the principal factor in the progressive aging of societies;

(3) the effect of mortality is not uniform; the death of children reacts differently on the process of population aging than does the death of the aged. Hence, an analysis of the effects of that factor requires a differentiated analysis;

(4) the population aging process has been checked in many countries by the progressive decline in infant and young children's mortality. But where the mortality of infants and young children is reduced to insignificant proportions, the role of that factor loses its former significance by the very nature of things;

(5) external migrations have been and still are of great significance, although the epoch of great migrations has basically passed. If not

for immigration the process of population aging would have been much more accentuated in many countries;

(6) in the relations within a country, population migrations have a decisive influence primarily on the shaping of the age structure of urban and rural populations. Since the bulk of migrants consist of people of the virile age, emigration from the countryside is a factor in the aging of rural populations. Immigration to the cities has the reverse effect: it checks the aging process of the urban populations;

(7) the population aging process was greatly encouraged by both world wars. War accelerates population aging because it thins out the ranks of youth who perish on the battlefields and of the children who do not come into the world as a result of war.

REFERENCES

1. E. ROSSET, *Les Lois démographiques de la Guerre*, Comitato Italiano per lo Studio dei Problemi della Popolazione, Rome, 1932.
2. E. ROSSET, "Prawa demograficzne wojny", Lodz, 1933 (Doctoral Dissertation).
3. W. WOYTINSKY, *Die Welt in Zahlen*, Book I, Rudolf Mosse Buchverlag, Berlin, 1925, pp. 107–108.
4. F. BURGDÖRFER, "Eugenik und Krieg", *Actes du Congrès International des Études sur la Population*, Vol. 2, Rome 1934, p. 389.
5. F. ŽIŽEK, *Grundriss der Statistik*, 2nd edition, Munich-Leipzig, 1923, p. 256. For Europe as a whole Döring estimated the population losses caused by the First World War at 35 million.
6. J. BEAUJEU-GARNIER, *Géographie de la Population*, Vol. 1, 1956, p. 100.
7. H. TRENKNER, "Sprawy zdrowia pod okupacją niemiecką," (The Health Situation under German Occupation), *Zdrowie*, (*Health*), Warsaw, No. 17–18, 15 Nov. 1933.
8. E. ROSSET, *Zagadnienia gospodarki samorządowej miasta Łodzi*, (*Problems of the Self-administered Economy of the City of Lodz*), Chapter 4: "Gruźlica", Tuberculosis, Lodz, 1926, p. 44.
9. *Wirtschaft und Statistik*, 1943, pp. 287–289.
10. "Deutsche Bevölkerungsbilanz des 2. Weltkrieges", *Wirtschaft und Statistik*, 1956, No. 10. Here we read: "Mittelbar hat der Krieg... einen Geburtenausfall von über 2 Millionen verursacht" (p. 493). In comparison with the First World War the German birth deficit declined, but nevertheless occupied an important place in the balance sheet of total losses sustained by the German people during the Second World War.
11. "Die normale Registrierung der Sterbefälle bei den Standesämtern und eine darauf gegründete Statistik liessen sich gegen Kriegsende nicht mehr durchführen, weil die Bevölkerung allzusehr in Bewegung und die Verwaltungsorganisation in Unordnung geraten war". (K. Horstmann, Deutsche Bevölkerungsbilanz des 2. Weltkrieges. Einführung und Zusammenfassung, *Wirtschaft und Statistik*, Vol. 10, Oct. 1956, pp. 493–4).

12. The estimate of German losses by Professor Waszak is particularly accurate. He estimated the direct war losses at 5,500,000 and the total losses at 7,000,000, while stipulating that these figures were probably low. (Stanisław Waszak: *L'Aspect démographique de l'Allemagne après la IIe Guerre*, Poznań, 1948, pp. 36–37).

13. L. CHEVALIER, *Démographie générale*, Paris, 1951, p. 195.

14. BOYARSKY and SHUSHERIN, (*Demographicheskaya statistika*, p. 154) believed that the increase in the fertility rates noted in certain European countries during the Second World War, is illusory. We do not share that opinion.

15. Six million inhabitants of Poland, or 17 per cent of the total population of the country, died at the hands of the barbaric Nazis. Losses resulting from the decline in births are not included.

Conclusions

As a brief summary of the results of our considerations, we may state the following facts.

1. Investigations concerning the aging of populations are still in an early stage of development. In this respect, the science of demography shares the fate of biology which has not made much progress with regard to the problems of old age; from the biological and demographic points of view, old age still remains *terra incognita*.

2. The aging of populations is, in principle, a phenomenon as old as the world: it was known in ancient and prehistoric times, as is testified by archeological findings; in those far-off times the progress of civilization and the subsequent decline in mortality favoured the aging of the population; new economic and consequently moral aspects were important in impelling societies to renounce the practice of exterminating the aged.

3. The modern process of population aging has another aspect: it results mainly from the decrease in births and not—as in olden times or as it may be in the future—from a decrease in mortality; thus the nature of the aging process was historically determined.

4. The history of the modern aging process started in the 19th century, the age of "demographic revolution", and its cradle was in France—the first country to increase the number of grandparents at expense of the number of grandchildren.

5. Other European countries followed this example, mainly Great Britain, Germany, the Scandinavian countries (led by Sweden), Belgium, Austria etc.—the zones of the most advanced population aging process.

6. Although the progressive decline in fertility has been the cardinal factor in the aging of societies, other factors, such as migration, have had an important influence on the population structure by age.

7. Until now, in spite of all appearances, the decline in mortality has been reducing the tempo of population aging. This is because the decline in mortality has been highest among infants and children and therefore tended to increase the number of children and young

450

people; it has been a sort of counterbalance to the aging process resulting from the decrease in the number of births.

8. The two world wars contributed greatly to the aging process in European countries by decreasing births (particularly during the First World War), as well as by a rapid loss of young people and those in the productive age.

9. Under the circumstances, a sharp division into "young" and "old" societies appeared (from the demographic standpoint). We have questioned the above terminology as unsubstantiated and unsuitable; very often a primitive approach to demographic problems is concealed behind the mask of "youth".

10. This sharp division permits us to suppose that we are approaching a definite demographic phase consisting of a rapid acceleration of the aging process in some societies, while in other societies this problem will be completely unknown. It would logically follow that the next demographic phase will, in general, be a levelling out of these differences on an international scale.

11. In the near future we may expect some stabilization and even recession in the old age level of the countries most advanced in the population aging process, while simultaneously it will advance in countries which are now in the high fertility zones.

12. The aging of people in the productive age advances parallel with the general aging process; factory employees grow older, and they constitute the part of society which carries the full load of productive activity.

13. Distaste and even hostility towards old people, which characterize primitive people, are losing their significance in contemporary society whose existence is more and more based on the work and experience of older people. "Gerontophobia" reflects unfortunate relics of past eras of civilization.

14. The aging of populations creates a whole range of consequences in economic, social and political relations, which has so far been investigated only to some degree and requires further and more profound study.

But in concluding this work, we consider it desirable to stress the need for further investigation of the problem which has so greatly affected the life of many contemporary societies and which will, in the future, determine the economic and social conditions in many societies today considered "young".

In our opinion, this problem will undoubtedly attract the attention of many more research workers in the future. Of necessity, the demographers of those countries which will face the new situation caused by the population aging process will be forced to take an interest in it.

However, it would be wrong to impose the aging process of population on one branch of science only—demography. Though the voice of the demographer is very important here, it seems necessary that sociologists, economists and ecologists should join in the research on the aging of societies. This would permit a better acquaintance with the problem which the prematurely deceased French demographer, Jean Daric, considered a decisive factor concerning the fate of contemporary societies.

Selected Bibliography

1. DEMOGRAPHY

DE ARRUDA GOMES, O. L., "Quelques considérations sur la précision des recensements démographiques du Brésil", *Proceedings of the World Demographic Congress*, Rome, 1954.

BALLOD, C., *Die mittlere Lebensdauer in Stadt und Land*, Duncker und Humblot, Leipzig, 1899.

BARCLAY, G. W., *Techniques of Population Analysis*, New York and London, 1958.

BARKHUUS, A., "Non-European general and infant mortality in the non-self-governing territories in Africa south of the Sahara," *Proceedings of the World Population Conference, 1954*, United Nations, New York, 1955.

BEAUJEU-GARNIER, J., *Géographie de la population*, Édition Génin, Librairie de Médicis Paris, 1956.

BELSHAW, H., *Population Growth and Levels of Consumption*, George Allen and Unwin, London, 1956.

BÉNARD, J., *Vues sur l'Économie et la Population de la France jusqu'en 1970*. Presses Universitaires de France, Paris, 1953.

BENJAMIN, B., "Recent fertility trends in England and Wales", *International Population Conference, Vienna, 1959*.

BERNERT, E. H., *America's Children*, New York–London, 1958.

BERNHARD, W., "Effects of the changes in the structure of the German population". *Proceedings of the International Statistical Conference, India. December 1951*; *Bulletin of the ISI*, Vol. XXXIII, Part IV.

BICKEL, W., *Bevölkerungsgeschichte und Bevölkerungspolitik der Schweiz seit dem Ausgang des Mittelalters*. Büchergilde Gutenberg, Zürich, 1957.

BICKEL, W., "Bevölkerungsdynamik und Gesellschaftsstruktur", *Schweiz. Z. Volkswirtsch. u. Stat.*, No. 3, 1956.

BILLETER, E. P., "Eine Messzahl zur Beurteilung der Altersverteilung einer Bevölkerung", *Schweiz. Z. Volkswirtsch u. Stat.*, No. 4, 1954.

BOGUE, D. J. (editor), *The Population Situation in the U.S. in 1975*, Scripps Foundation, 1957.

BOYARSKY, A., *Kurs demographicheskoy statistiki (Gosplanizdat)*, Moscow, 1945.

BOYARSKY, A., and SHUSHERIN P., *Demographicheskaya statistika*, Moscow, 1951.

BOURGEOIS-PICHAT, J., *Utilisation de la notion de population stable pour mesurer la mortalité et la fécondité des populations des pays sous-développés*, Uppsala, 1957.

BOUTHOUL, G., *La Surpopulation dans le Monde*, Payot, Paris, 1958.

BOVEN, I., *Population*, London–Cambridge, 1955.

BRAND, W., "The world population problem", *International Population Conference, Vienna, 1959*.

BUNLE, H., "Note sur la démographie de la population indigène au Togo". *Actes du Congrès International des Études sur la Population* (édités par le Prof. Corrado Gini), vol. 6, Rome, 1934.

BUQUET, L., *L'Optimum de la Population*, Presses Universitaires de France, Paris, 1956.

BURGDÖRFER, F., *Volk ohne Jugend*. Geburtenschwund und Überalterung des deutschen Volkskörpers, ein Problem der Volkswirtschaft, der Sozialpolitik, der deutschen Zukunft. 3rd ed., Heidelberg-Berlin, 1935.

BURGDÖRFER, F., *Sterben die weissen Völker?* Die Zukunft der weissen und der farbigen Völker im Lichte der biologischen Statistik (George D. W. Callwey Verlag) Munich, 1934.

BURGDÖRFER, F., "Eugenik und Krieg" (*Actes du Congrès International des Études sur la Population*, Vol. 2) Rome, 1934.

BURGDÖRFER, F., *Geburtenschwund—die Kulturkrankheit Europas* (Kurt Vowinckel Verlag), Heidelberg-Berlin-Magdeburg, 1942.

CALITSUNAKIS, D., "Évolution de la population de la Grèce et reconstruction Hellénique", *Bulletin of the ISI*, Vol. 33, Part IV, Demography and Labour Statistics.

CARR-SAUNDERS, A. M., *The Population Problem: a Study in Human Evolution* (Clarendon Press) London, 1922.

CHANDRASEKHAR, S., *India's Population, Fact and Policy* (John Day) New York, 1946.

CHARLES, E., "The effect of present trends in fertility and mortality upon the future population of Great Britain and upon its age composition" (L. HOGBEN, editor), London, 1938. A symposium of population studies in a joint work: *Political Arithmetic*.

CHEVALIER, L., *Démographie Générale* (Dalloz) Paris, 1951.

COONTZ, S. H., *Population Theories and their Economic Interpretation* (Routledge and Kegan Ltd.) London, 1957.

COX, P. R., *Demography* (Cambridge University Press) Cambridge, 1950.

CREW, F. A. E., Concerning fertility and sterility in relation to population (*Proceedings of the World Population Conference*) London, 1927.

CROZE, M., "Chronique de démographie," *J. Soc. Stat.*, Paris, June 1956.

DARIC, J., "Evolution démographique en Espagne", *Population*, No. 1, Paris, 1956.

DASZYŃSKA-GOLIŃSKA, Z., *Zagadnienia polityki populacyjnej* (*Problem of Population Policy*), Warsaw, 1927.

DELAPORTE, P. J., "Changements de l'évolution de la mortalité en Europe pendant et après la seconde guerre mondiale", (*Proceedings of the World Population Conference, 1954*, United Nations) New York, 1955.

DORN, H. F., "Mortality" (Joint work: *The Study of Populations, an Inventory and Appraisal*, edited by P. M. HAUSER and O. D. DUNCAN, The University of Chicago Press, 1959).

DUBLIN, LOTKA and SPIEGELMAN, *Length of Life* (The Ronald Press Company, revised edition) New York, 1949.

FAJFR, JUREČEK and ULLMANN: *Sčitani lidu, domu a bytu*, Prague, 1960.

FARR, W., *Vital Statistics* (Edward Stanford) London, 1885.

VON FIRCKS, A., *Bevölkerungslehre und Bevölkerungspolitik*, Leipzig, 1898.

FOGELSON, S., *Ruch naturalny ludności na Polesiu*, Warsaw, 1936.

FOURASTIÉ, J., "La croissance des classes jeunes et le problème de l'emploi", *Population*, No. 1, Paris, 1956.

FREUDENBERG, K., "Die Sterblichkeit in hohen Lebensaltern", *Schweiz. Z. Volkswirtsch. u. Stat.*, No. 4, 1955.

FREUDENBERG, K., "Grundzüge der Sterblichkeitsentwicklung nach dem Alter während eines Zeitraums von 80 Jahren für Deutschland" (*Proceedings of the World Population Conference, 1954*, United Nations) New York, 1955.

GABRIEL, J., "Évolution et tendances actuelles de la mortalité en Belgique" (*Proceedings of the World Population Conference*, 1954, United Nations), New York, 1955.

GEORGIEVSKY, P., "Saüglingssterblichkeit im Europäischen Russland in den Jahren 1909, 1910 und 1911", *Allg. Stat. Arch.*, 8, 1914.

GINI and GALVANI, *Uniformità nelle tavole di mortalità*, The Hague, 1930.

GLASS, D. V. and Grebenik, E., *The Trend and Pattern of Fertility in Great Britain* (H. M. S. O., 2 vols.), London, 1954.

GREBENIK, E., "Development and Demography in Great Britain" (Joint work: *The Study of Population*, edited by P. M. HAUSER and O. D. DUNCAN, The University of Chicago Press), Chicago, 1959.

GONZALES, L. Ma., Post Censal Population of the Philippines: 1949–1956 (*Proceedings of the International Statistical Institute*, 30 Session, Stockholm, 1957).

HEBETTE, F., L'évolution démographique de la Belgique, *Population*, No. 1, Paris, 1954.

HERTZLER, J. O., *The Crisis in World Population. A Sociological Examination with Special Reference to the Under-developed Areas.* (University of Nebraska Press), Lincoln, 1956.

HORSTMANN, K., Deutsche Bevölkerungsbilanz des zweiten Weltkrieges. Einführung und Zusammenfassung. *Wirts. u. Stat.*, No. 10, 1956.

HÖIJER, E., Die Bevölkerungsentwicklung in Schweden im Vergleich mit der Deutschlands (Kieler Vorträge gehalten im Institut für Weltwirtschaft an der Universität Kiel), Jena, 1943.

HUBBACK, E. M., *The Population of Britain* (Pelican Books) London, 1947.

HUTCHINS, G., *Women Who Work* (International Publishers) New York, 1934.

ISAAC, J., *Economics and Migration* (With an introduction by Sir A. CARR-SAUNDERS, International Library of Sociology and Social Reconstruction, Editor: Dr. K. MANNHEIM) London, 1947.

JAIN, S. P., "Mortality trends in India" (*Proceedings of the World Population Conference, 1954*, Vol. 1, United Nations) New York, 1955.

KAHN, E., *Der internationale Geburtenstreik*, Frankfurt a. M., 1930.

KIRK, D., *Europe's Population in the Interwar Years* (League of Nations, 1946).

KOLLER, A., "Umschichtungen in der schweizerischen Bevölkerung", *Schweiz. Z. Volkswirtsch. u. Stat.*, No. 3, 1956.

KROTEVICH, S., "Vsekilayskaya perepis neseleniya," *Vestnyk Statistiki*, No. 5, Moscow, 1955.

KUCZYNSKI, R., *A Demographic Survey of the British Colonial Empire*, Vol. 3, (Oxford University Press), London, 1948–1953.

KULA, W., "Stan i potrzeby badań nad demografią historyczną dawnej Polski", (The State and Requirements for Studies of the Historical Demographic of Early Poland), *Roczniki Dziejów Społecznych i Gospodarczych*, Vol. 13, Poznań, 1951.

LANDIS, P. H., "*Population Problems. A Cultural Interpretation*", 2nd edition prepared by P. K. HATT (American Book Company), New York, 1954.

LANDRY, A., *Traité de Démographie* (Payot) Paris, 1945.

LEIBENSTEIN, H., *A Theory of Economic-Demographic Development.* (Princeton University Press) Princeton, New Jersey, 1954. Foreword by F. NOTESTEIN.

LESTER, R. A., *Economics of Labour*, (The Macmillan Company) New York, 1948.

LEXIS, W., *Abhandlungen zur Theorie der Bevölkerungs- und Mortalitätsstatistik*, 1903.

LINDER, F. E., "World demographic data" (Joint work: *The Study of Population an Inventory and Appraisal*, edited by P. M. HAUSER and O. D. DUNCAN, The University of Chicago Press) Chicago, 1959.

LIVI, L., *Nozioni di statistica e politica demografica*, Padua, 1938.

LORIMER, F., *The Population of the Soviet Union, History and Prospects*, (League of Nations) Geneva, 1946.

LORIMER, F., "The development of demography" (Joint work: *The Study of Population, an Inventory and Appraisal*, edited by P. M. HAUSER and O. D. DUNCAN, The University of Chicago Press) Chicago, 1959.

LUZZATTO-FEGIZ, P., *Statistica demografica ed economica*, (Unione Tipografico-Editrice Torinese) Turin, 1940.

MACKENROTH, G., *Bevölkerungslehre. Theorie, Soziologie und Statistik der Bevölkerung* (Springer Verlag), Berlin, 1953.

MACURA, M., "La population de Yougoslavie et ses conditions de développement", *Population* No. 2, Paris, 1955.

MALTHUS, T. R., *Prawo ludności* (Polish edition, Cracow, 1925).

MCCLEARY, G. F., *Population: Today's Question*, London, 1938.

METHORST, H. W., "Results of differential birth rate in the Netherlands" (*Proceedings of the World Population Conference*), London, 1927.

MOMBERT, P., *Bevölkerungslehre* (Verlag Gustav Fischer) Jena, 1929.

MORTARA, G., "The development and structure of Brazil's population", *Population Studies*, No. 2, London, 1954.

MORTARA, G., "Quelques données sur la fécondité de la femme au Brésil," *Congrès International de la Population, Vienna, 1959*.

NICEFORO, A., "The development of the population in Italy", (*Proceedings of the World Population Conference*), London, 1927.

NOTESTEIN, F. W., and others, *The Future Population of Europe and the Soviet Union*, Population Projections, Geneva, 1944.

NOVOSELSKI, S., *O smertnosti i prodolzhitielnosti zhizni w Rosyi*, Petrograd, 1916.

PASCUA, M., "Evolution of mortality in Europe during the Twentieth Century", *Epidemiological and Vital Statistics Report*, No. 2–3, Vol. III, 1950.

PASCUA, M., "Recent mortality trends in areas of lower death rates" (*Proceedings of the World Population Conference, 1954*, United Nations), New York, 1955.

PEARL, R., *Introduction to Medical Biometry and Statistics*, 3rd ed., Philadelphia-London, 1941.

PHILIPPOT, R., *Initiation à une Démographie Sociale*, Louvain–Paris, 1957.

PTUCHA, M., *Ocherky po statistike naseleniya*, Moscow, 1960.

RAHTS, J., Sterbetafeln (Joint work: *Die Statistik in Deutschland*, Vol. 1, 1911).

REINHARD, M. R., *Histoire de la Population Mondiale de 1700 à 1948*, (Éditions Domat-Montchrestien), Paris, 1949.

REUTER, E. B., *Population Problems*, Philadelphia, 1923.

ROBBINS, L., Notes on Some Probable Consequences of the Advent of a Stationary Population in Great Britain, *Economica*, April, 1929.

da ROCHA, M. V., La mortalité au Brésil (*Proceedings of the World Population Conference, 1954*, United Nations), New York, 1955.

ROMERO and MEDINA, "La América latina como laboratorio demográfico", (*Proceedings of the World Population Conference, 1954*, United Nations), New York, 1955.

ROSSET, E., *Prawa demograficzne wojny (Demographic Laws of War)*, Łódź, 1933.

ROSSET, E., "Les lois démographiques de la guerre" (*Actes du Congrès International des Études sur la Population*, édités par le Prof. C. GINI, Vol. 8) Rome, 1934.

ROSSET, E., "Zapomniana funkcja biometryczna" (Forgotten Biometric Function), *Zeszyty Naukowe Wyższej Szkoły Ekonomicznej w Łodzi*, No. 3, 1957.

ROSSET, E., "Prognozy demograficzne" (Demographic Forecasts), *Zeszyty Naukowe Wyższej Szkoły Ekonomicznej w Łodzi*, No. 5, 1958.

ROSSET, E., "Tablica wymieralności jako barometr postępu społecznego" (Life Tables as a Barometer of Social Progress), *Ekonomista*, No. 1, 1960.

ROSSET, E., "Ludność produkcyjna w Polsce, jej liczebność i dynamika rozwojowa" (The Productive Population of Poland, its Number and Dynamics of Growth), *Zeszyty Naukowe Wyższej Szkoły Ekonomicznej w Łodzi*, No. 10, 1960.

ROSSET, E., "Proporcja ludności nieprodukcyjnej jako problem ekonomiczny i społeczny" (The Proportion of the Unproductive Population as an Economic and Social Problem), *Zeszyty Naukowe Uniwersytetu Łódzkiego*, series I, No. 18, 1960.

ROSSET, E., "Sytuacja demograficzna świata" (The World Demographic Situation) *Zeszyty Naukowe KUL*, IV, 1961, No. 4 (16).

ROSSET, E., Płodność kobiet miejskich i wiejskich w Polsce (Fertility of Urban and Rural Women in Poland), *Zeszyty Naukowe Wyższej Szkoły Ekonomicznej w Łodzi*, No. 15, 1961.

RUSSELL, J., *British Medieval Population* (University of New Mexico Press) Albuquerque, 1948.

SAITO, H., Sur la table de mortalité des Japonais, (No. 4, *XIX-e Session de l'Institut International de Statistique*), Tokio, 1930.

SARKAR, B. K., I quozienti di natalità, di mortalità e di aumento naturale nell'India attuale nel quadro della demografia comparata, (*Actes du Congrès International des Études sur la Population*, édités par le Prof. C. GINI, Vol. 6) Rome, 1934.

SAUVY, A., *Richesse et Population* (Payot), Paris, 1943.

SAUVY, A., *L'Europe et sa Population* (Éditions Internationales) Paris (no date of publication given).

SAUVY, A., *La Population, ses Lois, ses Équilibres.* (Presses Universitaires de France) Paris, 1948.

SAUVY, A., *Théorie Générale de la Population* (Vol. 1: *Économie et Population*, Vol. 2: *Biologie Sociale*, 2-me édition revue). (Presses Universitaires de France) Paris, 1956.

SAUVY, A., Vue générale et mise au point sur l'économie et la population française, *Population*, No. 2, Paris, 1955.

SAUVY, A., Les tendances de la population active en France, *Population*, No. 3, Paris, 1955.

SAUVY, A., *De Malthus à Mao Tsé-Toung, le Problème de la Population dans le Monde*, (Édition Denoel) Paris, 1958.

SCHUBNELL, H., Der Beitrag der Bevölkerungsstatistik zur Untersuchung der Zusammenhänge zwischen Bevölkerung und Wirtschaft. *Allg. Stat. Arch.*, No. 4, Vol. 39, 1955.

SCHWIDETZKY, J., *Das Problem des Völkertodes. Eine Studie zur historischen Bevölkerungsbiologie* (Ferd. Enke Verlag) Stuttgart, 1954.

SILBERMAN, L., "Essential concepts and methods in demography" (Addendum to the second edition of *Population Problems* by P. H. LANDIS).

SMITH, T. L., *Population Analysis*, first edition, New York–Toronto–London, 1948.

SMULEWICZ, B., Nekotorye voprosy vosproizvodstva naseleniya w zarubezhnych stranach. *Mirovoye Khozyaystvo i Mirovaya Politika*, No. 3, 1947.

SMULEWICZ, B., *Kritika burzhuaznych teoriy i politiki narodonasyelenya*, Moscow, 1959.

SPENGLER, J., The social and economic consequences of cessation in population growth (*Actes du Congrès International des Études sur la Population*, édités par le Prof. C. GINI, Vol., Rome, 1934).

SPENGLER, J., *Population Theory*, Illinois, 1952.

SPIEGELMAN, M., An International Comparison of Mortality Rates at the Older Ages. (*Proceedings of the World Population Conference, 1954*, United Nations) New York, 1955.

SRB, V., *Biologicka situace v českych zemich*, Prague, 1947.

STOWMAN, K., "Tendances récentes de la natalité". *Rapport Épidémiologique et Démographique* (Organisation Mondiale de la Santé), No. 3, Geneva, 1947.

STRUMILIN, S. G., *Problemy ekonomiki truda*, Moscow, 1957.

SZULC, S., *Ruch naturalny ludności w Polsce w latach 1895–1935 (The Natural Movement of the Population in Poland in 1895-1935)*, (GUS—Central Statistical Office), Warsaw, 1936.

SZULC, S., "Dawne tablice wymieralności Królestwa Polskiego" (Early Life Tables in the Kingdom of Poland), *Kwartalnik Statystyczny* (Statistical Quarterly) (GUS—Central Statistical Office,) No. 2, Vol. V, Warsaw, 1928.

SZULC, S., "Polskie tablice wymieralności 1927 roku" (Polish Life Tables for 1927) *Kwartalnik Statystyczny (Statistical Quarterly)*, No. 1, Vol. 8, Warsaw, 1931.

TA CHEN, New China's Population Census of 1953 and its Relation to National Reconstruction and Demographic Research. (The International Statistical Institute, Session 30) Stockholm, 1957.

TABAH, L., "La population algérienne", *Population*, No. 3, Paris, 1956.

TEICHMANN, U., *Bevölkerungs- und Wirtschaftswachstum*, Cologne-Deutz, 1957.

THOMAS, D. S., *Social and Economic Aspects of Swedish Population Movements, 1750–1933*, New York, 1941.

THOMPSON, W. S., *Population Problems*, third edition (McGraw-Hill Book Company, Inc.) New York–London, 1942.

TOULEMON, A., *Histoire des Doctrines de la Population* (Éditions Berger-Levrault) Paris, 1956.

TROGER, E., La situation démographique de l'Autriche. *Population*, No. 3, Paris, 1955.

VON UNGERN-STERNBERG, R., *Bevölkerungsverhältnisse in Schweden, Norwegen und Dänemark*, Berlin, 1937.

URLANIS, B., *Woyny e narodonaselenye Evropy*, Moscow, 1960.

URLANIS, B., *Rost naselenya v Evrope* (Ogis-Gospolitizdat), 1941.

VIELROSE, E., "Ludność Polski w okresie powojennym z punktu widzenia demografii potencjalnej" (The Population of Poland after the War from the Point of View of Potential Demography), *Przegląd Statystyczny (Statistical Review)*, No. 2, Warsaw, 1955.

VIELROSE, E., "Polskie tablice wymieralności 1948 roku" (Polish Life Tables for 1948), *Studia i Prace Statystyczne (Statistical Studies and Papers)*, No. 2–3, second year.

WANDER, H., "Die Bedeutung der Auswanderung für die Lösung europäischer Flüchtlings- und Bevölkerungsprobleme" (Kieler Studien, *Forschungsberichte des Instituts für Weltwirtschaft an der Universität Kiel*, herausgegeben von Prof. F. BAADE) Kiel, 1951.

WASZAK, S., *Perspektywy demograficzne powojennych Niemiec*, Poznań, 1947.

WASZAK, S., *L'Aspect Démographique de l'Allemagne après la Deuxième Guerre*, Poznań, 1948.

WATSON, C., "A survey of recent Belgian population policy", *Population Studies*, No. 2, London, 1954.

WEGMÜLLER, W., "Die statistischen Grundlagen der Bevölkerungsprognose," *Schweiz. Z. Volkswirtsch. u. Stat.*, No. 3, 1956.

WESTERGAARD, H., *Die Lehre von der Mortalität und Morbilität*, Jena, 1901.

WHELPTON, P. K., "A calculation of future development of population". (*Actes du Congrès International des Études sur la Population*, édités par le Prof. C. GINI, Vol. 7) Rome, 1934.

WHELPTON, P. K., *Forecasts of the Population of the United States, 1945–1975*. (Bureau of the Census) Washington, 1947.

WHIPPLE and NOVOSELSKI, *Osnovy demographicheskoy i sanitarnoy statistiki*, Moscow, 1929.

WILLCOX, W. F., *Studies in American Demography* (Cornell University Press) Ithaca, 1940.

WINKLER, W., *Typenlehre der Demographie*. Reine Bevölkerungstypen, Vienna, 1952.

World Population and Resources, a report by PEP (Political and Economical Planning) London, 1956.

2. AGING OF POPULATION

BOVERAT, F., *Le vieillissement de la population* (Éditions Sociales Françaises) Paris, 1946.

DARIC, J., *Vieillissement de la Population et Prolongation de la Vie Active*. (Presses Universitaires de France) Paris, 1948.

DARIC, J., "Le vieillissement de la population dans l'Europe de l'Ouest et son effet sur la population active", *J. Gerontol.*, Vol. 6, supplement to No. 3.

DARIC, J., "Le vieillissement de la population en France et ses conséquences économiques et sociales" (Joint work: *Précis de Gérontologie*, Masson, et Cie., Paris, 1955).

KERN, E., "Die Frage der Überalterung," *Allgem. Stat. Arch.* No. 1, Vol. 41, 1957.

MAIER, W., "Studie über die Entwicklung der Bevölkerungsstruktur. Alterndes und sterbendes Volk?" *Allgem. Stat. Arch.* No. 1, Vol. 39, 1955.

"Old age in the Modern World" (*Proceedings of the Third Congress of the International Association of Gerontology, London, 1954*).

ROSSET, E., *Proces starzenia się ludności (Aging Process of Population)* (PWE—Polish Economic Publications) Warsaw, 1959.

ROSSET, E., "Starzenie się ludności produkcyjnej w Polsce i w świecie" (Aging of the Productive Population in Poland and the World), *Kultura i Społeczeństwo (Culture and Society)*, No. 1, Warsaw, 1961.

SAUVY, A., "Le vieillissement des populations et l'allongement de la vie", *Population* No. 4, Paris, 1954.

SHENFIELD, B. E., *Social Policies for Old Age*. A review of social provision for old age in Great Britain. (Routledge and Kegan Paul) London, 1957.

SLEESWIJK, J. G., "The social consequences of aging in the Netherlands", *J. Gerontol.*, Vol. 6, Supplement to No. 3.

SZULC, S., "Zagadnienie przedłużenia życia ludzkiego w świetle demografii" (The Problem of Extending Human Life in the Light of Demography), *Przegląd Statystyczny* (*Statistical Review*) No. 2, Warsaw, 1955.

SZULC, S., "Starzenie się społeczeństw ludzkich" (Aging of the Human Society), *Przegląd Statystyczny* (*Statistical Review*), No. 3, Warsaw, 1955.

"Triangle" Vieillissement des populations. *J. Sandoz Sci. Méd.*, 4 décembre 1955.

TULIPPE, O., "Le vieillissement de la Population Belge". Étude régionale. *Les Cahiers d'Urbanisme*, No. 10, Brussels, 1952.

3. GERONTOLOGY, HYGIENE, EUGENICS, ETC.

BATKIS, G., *Socyalnaya gygena*. (Varkomzdrav U.S.S.R.) Medgiz, 1940.

BINET and BOURLIÈRE, "Problèmes biologiques généraux posés par la sénescence de l'organisme" (Joint work: *Précis de Gérontologie*) Paris, 1955.

BOCHENEK, A., *Anatomia człowieka*, (*Human Anatomy*), Vol. 1, 5th edition. Revised and completed by Michał Reicher, Warsaw, 1952.

BOGOMOLEC, A., *Prodleniye zhizni*, Kiev, 1938.

BURGDÖRFER, F., Eugenik und Krieg (*Actes du Congrès International des Études sur la Population*, édités par le Prof. C. GINI, Vol. 2), Rome, 1934.

FRENKIEL, Z., *Udlinyeniye zhizni i aktivnaya starosth*, Leningrad, 1945.

GRANT–SCHNEIDER, M., *More Security for Old Age*. A report and a program, New York, 1937.

HERRE, P., *Schöpferisches Alter*, 2nd edition, Leipzig, 1943.

KAPLAN, J., *Das Alter als soziales Problem* (Rascher Verlag) Zürich, 1956. Translated from English.

KAPŁUN, S., *Sanitarnaya statistika truda*, Moscow-Leningrad, 1924.

MAJER, J., "Długowieczność" (Longevity), (*Encyklopedia Powszechna S. Orgelbranda*) Warsaw, 1861.

METCHNIKOFF, E., *Études sur la Nature Humaine. Essai de Philosophie Optimiste*, Masson et Cie., Paris, 1905.

MECHNIKOFF, E., *Essais Optimistes*, A. Maloine, Paris, 1907.

NAGORNY, A., *Starenie i prodlenie zhizni*, Moscow, 1950.

VISCHER, A. L., *Das Alter als Schicksal und Erfüllung*, 3rd edition. (Bruno Schwabe und Co. Verlag) Basle, 1955.

INDEXES

Name Index

463

Geographical Index

Abyssinia, 68
Ahmadabad, 70
Aden, 68
Afghanistan, 68
Africa, 64–65, 71, 389
Albania, 200, 203, 208, 368
Alberta, 389
Algeria, 80, 199, 201, 203, 205, 207–8, 322–28, 355–57
American Samoa, 199, 203, 205, 207, 322–28
Angola, 286
Arabia, 68
Argentina, 16, 23, 63, 66–67, 127, 133, 183, 185–87, 195–96, 200, 205, 207, 212, 242–43, 322–28, 411
Australia, 21–22, 69, 127, 129, 183, 185, 192–93, 195, 198, 200, 204, 208, 211, 236–37, 322–28, 350, 360, 362, 380, 394, 399, 401, 411
Austria, 124, 131, 174–75, 179, 181, 183, 185–86, 192–96, 198, 201, 205, 209, 211, 223, 251–54, 269–71, 289–91, 293–95, 305, 316–28, 351, 363–64, 392, 445, 450
Austro-Hungary, 363

Barbados, 133, 200, 204, 208
Bavaria, 390–92, 424
Bechuanaland, 200, 204, 208, 322–28
Belgian Congo, 132–33, 358
Belgium, 21, 63, 68, 123–24, 131, 160, 173–75, 177–79, 183, 185, 188, 191– 94, 198, 201, 205, 209, 211, 226–29, 246, 268–71, 289, 316–28, 344, 346, 359– 63, 380, 434, 436, 450
Berlin, 440, 443–44
Bermuda, 200, 204, 208, 322–28
Bhutan, 68
Bohemia, 181–82, 364

Bolivia, 66–67
Brandenburg, 122
Brazil, 75, 133, 183, 192–97, 199, 204, 207, 243–45, 322–28
British Guiana, 21–23, 127, 129, 133, 199, 203, 205, 207, 322–28
Budapest, 443–46
Bulgaria, 75–76, 124, 131, 183, 185, 192–94, 201, 205, 208, 314, 322–28, 352, 381
Burma, 200, 204, 207, 322–28, 394–95

Cambodia, 199, 203, 207
Canada, 21–22, 63, 129, 131, 133, 159, 175, 178, 183, 185, 188–89, 193, 195, 197, 200, 202, 204, 208, 212, 287, 322– 28, 359–62, 380–81, 383, 400–401, 411
Central America, 277–80, 341–43
Ceylon, 21–22, 133, 183, 187, 200, 204, 207, 239–42, 378
Chiapas, 305–6
Chile, 16, 21–22, 192–93, 200, 204, 207, 322–28, 394–95
China, 68–69, 79–80, 200, 204, 208, 322–28
Columbia, 188, 193, 199, 207, 286
Connecticut, 64
Costa Rica, 16, 133, 199, 203, 207, 277– 78, 322–28, 355, 357
Cuba, 20, 181
Cyprus, 200, 204, 208, 322–28
Czechoslovakia, 124, 130–31, 201, 205, 208, 288, 314, 322–28, 362, 436

Dalmatia, 364
Damawand, 82
Denmark, 21–22, 77–78, 124, 126–27, 129–31, 159–60, 173–75, 177–79,

Subject Index

473